Revisioning
the Political

Feminist Theory and Politics

Virginia Held and Alison Jaggar
Series Editors

Revisioning the Political

Feminist Reconstructions of Traditional Concepts in Western Political Theory

edited by

Nancy J. Hirschmann and Christine Di Stefano

WestviewPress

A Division of HarperCollinsPublishers

Feminist Theory and Politics

Published in 1996 in the United States of America by Westview Press, 5500 Central Avenue, Boulder, Colorado 80301-2877, and in the United Kingdom by Westview Press, 12 Hid's Copse Road, Cumnor Hill, Oxford OX2 9JJ

Library of Congress Cataloging-in-Publication Data
Revisioning the political : feminist reconstructions of traditional
   concepts in western political theory / edited by Nancy J. Hirschmann
   and Christine Di Stefano.
        p.   cm. — (Feminist theory and politics)
   Includes bibliographical references.
   ISBN 0-8133-8639-X (hard). — ISBN 0-8133-8640-3
(pbk.).
     1. Feminist Theory. 2. Feminist theory—Political aspects.
3. Political Science. 4. Power (Social sciences). 5. Women in
politics.   I. Hirschmann, Nancy J. II. Di Stefano, Christine.
III. Series.
HQ1190.R485 1996
305.42—dc20   96-28881
                                                                                CIP

The paper used in this publication meets the requirements of the American National Standard for Permanence of Paper for Printed Library Materials Z39.48-1984.

10   9   8   7   6   5   4   3   2   1

For Our Parents

Contents

Chapter 12

All the Comforts of Home: The Genealogy of Community

Chapter 13

Reflections on Families in the Age of Murphy Brown: On Gender, Justice, and Sexuality

Preface and Acknowledgments

*F*eminist political theory as it has developed over the past twenty-five years since Shulamith Firestone's *The Dialectic of Sex* has been extremely effective in critiquing the patriarchal biases of political theory. We have analyzed, picked apart, and deconstructed major figures in political theory from Plato to Rawls; we have examined the nature of women's systematic exclusion from the realm of politics, citizenship, and participation; we have explored the antifeminist limitations of supposedly sympathetic or parallel theoretical enterprises such as marxism, democratic theory, anarchism, psychoanalysis, critical race theory, critical legal studies, socialism, and poststructuralism. In all of these, feminists have finely honed the tools of critique, offering increasingly subtle and sophisticated analyses of the working of patriarchy and its double-edged construction and erasure of women.

But there has been considerable dissatisfaction about feminism's failure to suggest concrete alternatives. If feminists want to suggest that existing theories are problematic and exclusive in terms of race, gender, sexuality, and class, what kinds of structures and theories might we want to put in their place?

The essays in this volume were commissioned and selected with this question in mind. The purpose of this volume is to offer a diversified (but by no means comprehensive) selection of feminist analyses of concepts that are central to political theory: justice, freedom, autonomy, authority, democracy, privacy, obligation, power, community, equality, and care. (While most of the concepts analyzed in this volume are traditionally central to political theory, "care" stands out as a notable exception.) The essays aim to do more than offer feminist critiques of existing theories of these concepts, however; they instead provide feminist visions of how such concepts could be reconstructed. We seek to put forth feminist "blueprints" for constructing "positive" feminist theories and for shaping a feminist political world.

The essays presented here are for the most part "new" essays, commissioned by the editors from theorists explicitly working in the area of conceptual analysis and reconstruction. Many of these essays, however, though not published before in the form presented here, draw on and are adapted from the respective authors' books and other works on the relevant concepts. Some essays have drawn on and expanded themes and ideas developed in previously published work, while portions of other essays contain direct excerpts. Accordingly, we gratefully acknowledge permission to reprint from the following works:

Allen, Anita. 1988. *Uneasy Access: Privacy for Women in a Free Society*. Totowa, NJ: Rowman and Littlefield.

Eisenstein, Zillah. 1994. *The Color of Gender: Reimaging Democracy*. Berkeley: University of California Press.

Hartsock, Nancy C. M. 1987. "Foucault on Power: A Theory for Women?" In *The Gender of Power: A Symposium*. Ed. Monique Leijnaar. Leiden: Vakgroep Vrouwenstudies/Vena.

Hirschmann, Nancy J. 1992. *Rethinking Obligation: A Feminist Method for Political Theory*. Ithaca, NY: Cornell University Press.

Hirschmann, Nancy J. 1996. "Revisioning Freedom: Relationship, Context, and the Politics of Empowerment." *Political Theory* 24 (1). Thousand Oaks, CA: Sage Publications.

Jones, Kathleen B. 1993. *Compassionate Authority: Democracy and the Representation of Women*. New York: Routledge.

Phelan, Shane. 1994. *Getting Specific: Postmodern Lesbian Politics*. Minneapolis: University of Minnesota Press. Chapter 5, 76–97.

Christine Di Stefano wishes to thank Gregg Miller for his excellent research assistance and bibliographic sleuthing and the Department of Political Science at the University of Washington for its support of this project. Finally, we thank Spencer Carr at Westview Press for encouraging and supporting this endeavor at its inception.

Nancy J. Hirschmann
Christine Di Stefano

Revisioning
the Political

1

Introduction

Revision, Reconstruction, and the Challenge of the New

Nancy J. Hirschmann and Christine Di Stefano

During the 1960s and 1970s—a time of political and cultural ferment for many of the Western democracies—political theorists interested in identifying, analyzing, and contributing to politicized contests over the discursive meaning of core political values developed the notion of "essentially contested concepts" (Gallie 1955, Connolly 1974). A cynical, positivist interpretation of essentially contested concepts would claim that such concepts offer an unreliable blueprint for the analysis of political life; that their contested, polemical, and unstable nature displays the disappointing sign of their failure. For those less threatened by the inevitably ideological character of language, however, essentially contested concepts serve as important (and often, hopeful) reminders of the instability of existing political arrangements and of those sensibilities that reflect and nourish them. During this final waning decade of the twentieth century, we witness an even more thoroughgoing appreciation of the instability and potential mutability of political arrangements, sensibilities, and categories of analysis, ranging from the most concrete—to wit, the startling changes in Eastern Europe, both for good and bad—to the most abstract—poststructural, postmarxist, postmodern, posttheory.

Feminists, of course, need no introduction to the world of essentially contested concepts. They are accomplished practitioners of the art of conceptual contestation, particularly as this involves the identification and destabilization of gendered concepts. Indeed, contestation is central to the feminist enterprise, and many feminists agree with Julia Kristeva that

1

feminism's major responsibility, as well as its most effective and powerful strategy, is to engage in perpetual contestation, critique, and deconstruction: "If women have a role to play . . . it is only in assuming a *negative* function: reject everything finite, definite, structural, loaded with meaning, in the existing state of society" (Kristeva 1980a, 166). "A feminist practice can only be . . . at odds with what already exists so that we may say 'that's not it,' and 'that's still not it'" (Kristeva 1980b, 137).

Yet in this volume, we seek to go beyond this strategy of critique to engage in the process of *reconstruction*. The notion of feminist reconstruction is controversial, and many reject it outright. Indeed, whereas many consider the term "postmodern," whether applied to architecture, politics, or theory, as a shorthand expression for the heightened awareness of contingency and conceptual contestation (see Bauman 1992, Flax 1990, Harvey 1989, Hekman 1990, Jameson 1991), some feminists criticize constructivism as falling into the modern, masculinist trap of "totalization," of replacing one hegemonic theoretical world view for another. As Judith Butler suggests, "The pursuit of the 'new' is the preoccupation of high modernism; if anything, postmodernism casts doubt upon the possibility of a 'new' that is not in some way already implicated in the 'old'" (Butler 1992, 6). For feminism, of course, this "old" is patriarchy. Given that feminists have particularly demonstrated the degree to which our language, concepts, vocabulary, and epistemology are all formed and shaped by patriarchy, by the systematic oppression of women, then it would seem extremely difficult to imagine how we could even begin to think about feminist alternatives. Where would the conceptual vocabularies and concrete visions come from? How could we create anything genuinely "new" that is not shaped and determined by that very patriarchy which we seek to escape?

As a result of this concern, many feminist theorists have become extremely cautious and self-critical—if not skeptical and pessimistic—about the possibility of developing constructive theories of politics and political concepts. At a time when such deconstructive techniques of critique, questioning, destabilizing, creating uncertainty, and challenging accepted meanings are at the forefront of feminist theorizing, they might well ask, why would we seek to develop a volume that reconstructs traditional concepts in political theory?

Reconstruction and the Problem of the New

OUR ANSWER STARTS with the recognition that political theory has traditionally been about the creation of new pictures and visions of politics. From Plato and Aristotle to the early social contract theorists to John Rawls, the "great books" of political theory have offered radically "new" pictures of the state and of politics that have captured the imaginations of large numbers of people at critical junctures in history. Feminist political theorists have brought to bear on this discursive enterprise different epistemological perspectives, ontological frameworks, and sets of experiences and values that demonstrate that the problems of such "new" visions—true to Butler's charge—often stem from the very same "old" ones they claim to replace. Feminist theory over the past twenty-five years has revealed that the history of political thought has often been one of barely masked power, disingenuously representing the beliefs and values of particular subjects in particular places and times as timeless, universal, and eternally true. Such constructions have been importantly based on a vision of humanity that is historically specific and consistently exclusive in terms of class (propertied), race (white), sex (males), and gender (masculine subjects). Accordingly, feminists perform vital analytical and political work in critiquing the particular visions of politics put forth in these "malestream" theories (O'Brien 1981).

However, does this history of exclusion that feminists identify make the enterprise of political theory itself intrinsically problematic for feminists? Is the visionary dimension of political theory something that feminists must in the end avoid? Is the very term "feminist political theory" an oxymoron, and is "political theory" *per se* something feminists should avoid except from the perspective of tearing it apart? Or has this enterprise of critical deconstructive techniques, having been extremely powerful for feminist critique, occluded other feminist endeavors *vis-à-vis* political theory? In making us reluctant to take the risks of offering positive visions, has postmodernism curtailed the usefulness of feminism as a theoretical method? Have we become so afraid of the dangers and pitfalls of totalization, universalism, and absolutism that we shy away from one of the major traditional enterprises of political theory? If that enterprise is so fundamentally flawed that it needs to be changed, how will feminist theory bring such change about?

Such questions have been raised by other feminists as well. In a recent—and often contentious—debate among four prominent feminist theorists, Seyla Benhabib sounded an alarm concerning discernible trends within contemporary feminist theory:

> The retreat from utopia within feminist theory in the last decade has taken the form of debunking as essentialist any attempt to formulate a feminist ethic, a feminist politics, a feminist concept of autonomy, and even a feminist aesthetic. The fact that the views of [Carol] Gilligan or [Nancy] Chodorow or Sara Ruddick (or for that matter [Julia] Kristeva) articulate only the sensitivities of white, middle-class, affluent, first-world, heterosexual women may be true (although I have empirical doubts about this). Yet what are we to offer in their place? As a project of an ethics which should guide us in the future are we able to offer a better vision than the synthesis of autonomous justice thinking and empathetic

care? As a vision of the autonomous personality to aspire to in the future are we able to articulate a sense of self better than the model of autonomous individuality with fluid ego boundaries and not threatened by otherness? As a vision of feminist politics are we able to articulate a better model for the future than a radically democratic polity which also furthers the values of ecology, nonmilitarism, and solidarity of peoples? Postmodernism can teach us the theoretical and political traps of why utopias and foundational thinking can go wrong, but it should not lead to a retreat from utopia altogether. For we, as women, have much to lose by giving up the utopian hope in the wholly other (Benhabib 1995, 30).[1]

Benhabib raises some crucial questions that feminist theory must grapple with. How should we approach the question of feminist reconstruction? And what is the relationship between reconstruction and utopia? According to Benhabib, feminists who refuse reconstruction have effectively turned their backs on utopia, on the task of imagining, articulating, and helping to create a hospitable, pleasurable, interesting, and empowering world for women. Such a world would indeed be "wholly other." For other feminists, however, the utopian promise is best nurtured by means of critical vigilance towards that which poses as utopian, even—and especially—when in "feminist" guise. This vein of feminist theorizing urges us toward the "wholly other" through calculated gestures of disappointment and refusal, reminding us that the value of utopia lies in its high standards and elusive promise. To what extent does reconstruction betray utopia by settling for less in the name of practical, positive thinking? Or does the ultimate betrayal of utopia consist in the "holy," otherworldly, refusal to work with familiar materials that lie at hand, within relatively easy cognitive and imaginative reach?

But perhaps casting this debate in terms of "utopia" is misleading. What is the *concrete* impact on women's daily lives of the refusal to engage in reconstructive enterprises? And by this we do not only refer to feminist political theorists, who may become marginalized and devalued for this refusal (obviously not a sufficient reason not to engage in such work, for feminism is strongly opposed to such co-optation by patriarchy, but an important issue to recognize nonetheless), but to all women. For we are all affected in our day-to-day interactions with the state and public agencies, with bosses and colleagues in the workplace, with partners and children in families, by the meaning that cultures attribute to notions of "justice," "freedom," "privacy," "rights," and so forth.[2] These concepts are not simply the private domain of intellectuals who are paid to engage in esoteric debates over abstruse intellectual notions; they play a vital role in the structuring of social relations.

Through an examination of some key concepts, this volume will provide an opportunity to engage such issues. Since contemporary feminist political theory really developed as a subfield with Susan Moller Okin's

Women in Western Political Thought, a dominant segment of feminist political theory *has* been devoted to analysis and critique, specifically to analyzing and critiquing major *figures* in political theory, such as Aristotle, Locke, Marx, and Rawls.[3] Such analysis has, of course, been constitutionally limited to critique, since one cannot really " reconstruct" historical figures *per se* (although the attempt to "reconstruct" particular theorists' *arguments* is a dominant strain of political theory not at all foreign to feminists). More recently, however, feminists have been engaged in the analytic task of critiquing major *concepts*, which would seem to lend itself more readily to the "positive" enterprise of reconstruction. Nancy Hartsock's *Money, Sex, and Power* was one of the first books to undertake such a task, analyzing the concept of power (her essay for this volume is based in part on that work); she offered a powerful critique of "masculinist" theories of power as domination and then also offered a "feminist" reconstruction of power as empowerment. In the past ten years, there has been a virtual explosion of conceptual analysis, ranging from contract (Pateman 1988) to justice (Okin 1989) to rights (Minow 1990, Williams 1989). Indeed, almost all of the contributors to this volume have written or are currently in the process of writing books on their respective concepts (see Allen 1986; Eisenstein 1988, 1994; Hartsock 1984; Hirschmann 1992; Jones 1993; Mansbridge 1983; Phelan 1994; Tronto 1993; Young 1990).[4]

It is true that the enterprise of this volume is akin to what Butler refers to as "high modernism" in that it offers feminist attempts to develop "new" concepts, or "new" formulations of old concepts. And in this, the "new" concepts presented in this volume are very much indebted to the "old," in part precisely because these analyses take place within the discourse of political theory. But rather than a weakness, we view this as a strength: indeed, part of the power of these "new" conceptualizations lies in the ways in which they can turn the old, patriarchal meanings around and against themselves. In this sense, then, the volume is also "postmodern" in its explicit acknowledgment that these supposedly "new" concepts are genealogically embedded within a traditional canon, within a culture and history of engagement with political questions and issues. The mantle of the "new" is taken on in earnest, but also self-consciously and ironically. If an important feminist insight developed through our critique of "malestream" theory has been that women are excluded, and even that their exclusion is a foundation for these very theories, then bringing women back into these visions is at once reactionary—because it tries to fit women into an existing, antiwoman framework—and radical—because the fact that women generally won't fit requires a serious alteration in the framework. The feminist reshaping of political theory must needs be interactive; as feminism changes the face of patriarchy and the framework of political theory, feminism itself changes as well.

The Three Sisters of Conceptual Analysis

THE ESSAYS IN this volume offer a variety of methodological solutions to the problem of constructing feminist political theory. The theorists we have chosen all approach feminist theorizing in quite different ways, ranging from postmodernism to standpoint theory to radical liberalism. And in this, what unites the essays despite their methodological differences is the interdependence of the concepts they analyze. In conceiving the volume as a series of essays on "different" concepts, we quickly realized the self-contradiction, for a key notion of feminist conceptual theory is the realization that concepts are intertwined.[5] As a result of the various epistemological, ontological, and experiential assumptions that feminism has brought to bear on the canon of political theory, feminism offers a radical challenge to the notion of politics itself and has instigated a redefinition of politics to include things that "mainstream" theory considers completely nonpolitical, such as the body and sexuality, the family, and interpersonal relationships. The feminist questioning and rejecting of the private-public dichotomy leads directly to the questioning and rejecting of other artificial dichotomies and divisions. The traditional opposition between freedom and obligation, authority and equality, rights and duties, justice and power, all begin to seem nonsensical as the intimate interdependencies of these concepts come to light. Accordingly, Zillah Eisenstein argues that privacy is essential to equality, just as Anita Allen argues that equality is key to privacy; Nancy Hirschmann argues that equality is in turn essential to an understanding of freedom, and freedom is necessary to an understanding of obligation. Similarly, Joan Tronto, in arguing that "care" needs to be considered as a political concept, postulates it as vital to authority, just as Kathleen Jones develops a notion of "compassionate" authority that gives central importance to care. Jane Mansbridge argues that care and equality are both vital to democracy; and democracy is in turn central to Shane Phelan's complex, pluralized notion of community, a similar version of which is entailed by Iris Young's notion of justice. Nancy Hartsock's understanding of power is related to *eros* as well as community; and according to Christine Di Stefano, a refigured community of "others" is similarly important to autonomy, as Molly Shanley and Martha Ackelsberg suggest—coming full circle—that it is important to privacy. We believe this conceptual interdependency is an important key to solving the puzzle of "the new."

Feminist conceptual analysis in political theory may be broken out into three distinct but interrelated projects: (1) interrogating and contesting the apolitical postures of concepts that claim to be nonpolitical; (2) scrutinizing what may be termed, with insights provided by Jane Flax (1992), the "innocent space" of political theorizing; (3) rethinking concepts that are already understood as political. We will briefly discuss each of these projects in turn.

In challenging, changing, and broadening our notions of the political, feminist politicization of concepts such as "community," "family," "privacy," and "care" adds to the existing stock of available political terms, thus enriching the political vocabulary. But such moves do not involve merely taking these concepts as they are currently understood and simply thrusting them into politics. If community and family stand as the "other" in relation to the state, and care stands as the "other" in relation to a procedurally objective politics, then conceiving these as intrinsically connected to politics and the state is inherently radical. Indeed, such politicization of new terms inevitably forces a reconsideration of the old, officially political terms to which they are related. The politicizing of these concepts not only changes the concepts but must needs change the conceptual realm of "the political" as well.

This is particularly illustrated with regard to the concept of "privacy." Viewing this concept as political would seem to be so radical as to be inherently contradictory: if the fundamental duality of the modern age is *between* public and private, viewing privacy *as* political would seem to smash the duality altogether. It is highly significant that three essays in this collection (Allen, Shanley and Ackelsberg, and Eisenstein) engage the concept of privacy, and that these three essays are significantly different from one another. It is obvious that the concept of privacy has been used, with a great deal of success, to keep Western women out of official political arenas. It has also been used to erase the political significance of a variety of relations and experiences that have often comprised the core of women's life experiences. When *Second Wave* feminists insisted that "the personal is political," they were, in effect, declaring war on the conceptualization of the private sphere of the household as prepolitical. Yet the recognition of its politics produced a reaction against the private sphere; in the aftermath of *Second Wave* feminism, many feminists shied away from the concept of privacy altogether.

The three essays here challenge the wisdom of this move. Recognizing that privacy can be and has been used to "shield" (or, more accurately, "bar") women from social and political intervention into reproductive decisionmaking, for instance, Anita Allen seeks to use privacy according to the same logic with which it has been used previously to keep women and domestic issues out of the political arena. This should not be surprising, for "the home" captures the historical essence of privacy. Yet it is not exactly "the same," for her essay brings to light central issues of defining concepts as "political" from a feminist perspective. For instance, in noting that domestic violence *violates* women's privacy under the rubric of *protecting* (men's) privacy, Allen argues not that we need a new *definition* of privacy per se, but rather we need new *contexts* in order for old definitions of privacy to work for women. By introducing the notion of "decisional privacy," which is related to but distinct from the standard notion of "personal privacy," Allen defends the concept of privacy but critiques the way it is implemented and applied to women. In this, she addresses the issue of "feminist reconstruction" in a different way than some of the other authors, effectively advocating that we do not need to rethink the concept *per se* as much as we need to rethink *the way we think about* the concept.

Similarly, Zillah Eisenstein's essay, which identifies privacy as central to equality, approaches privacy laterally, as it were, rather than head-on. Focusing on issues of bodily integrity, particularly sexuality and reproduction, Eisenstein approaches privacy through its historical basis in individual freedom; and she defines freedom in the standard liberal terms of the noninterference of others and the state, the "right to be left alone." Yet, she calls this approach a "radical revisioning," because such freedom has never really been realized, particularly for women of color. Pushing privacy to its logical conclusion, "democratizing" our notion of privacy, does more than "extend" an existing concept to provide equality of access to historically denied groups, but radically transforms our way of thinking about privacy and the meaning it plays in our political lives. For "extending" the notion of privacy to women of color requires the recognition of difference, which in turn requires a recognition of different privacy *needs*. This, she argues, entails a revisioning of individuality as having a "collective meaning." Such a collectivity eludes the standard opposition to individual difference through the notion of "specifying" equality. Thus what starts as a standard utilization of existing notions ends up in a seriously radical "revisioning."

In their rich and detailed exploration of the politics of the public-private distinction, Martha Ackelsberg and Mary Lyndon Shanley argue against a purely analytical approach to the definition of these terms. What is ultimately at stake is not the definition but rather a political struggle over power and resources. Privacy has been used historically to reinforce power as well as to challenge it. Sex, race, class, and sexual orientation significantly influence determinations of what is to count as public and private. The history of these terms, including their contemporary deployment in such arenas as the Clarence Thomas confirmation hearings, serves as an important reminder of the contestatory contexts within which these definitions circulate and accumulate further refinements. Ackelsberg and Shanley argue against the analytic dream of coming up with the final, all-purpose definition of public and private that will work for all times and circumstances. Rather, they propose that feminist efforts to define these terms should take their cues from contextual political considerations. How will a certain understanding of public-private, applied to particular contexts, relate to decisionmaking authority and the allocation of resources? This, they argue, is the real and recurring issue at stake in any attempt to define public and private.

Feminists continue to debate the relative merits and demerits of a privacy approach to reproductive issues. What might be termed the "feminization" of privacy and of related terms such as "care" poses a series of challenges and opportunities for feminist political theorists. For these concepts simultaneously shed light on women's historical exclusion from politics, on the dynamics of gender-based oppression, and on the task of revisioning the political in the light of its constitutive exclusions. In this, the essays on care and community in this volume are especially noteworthy. Joan Tronto's essay shows not only that care is important to the political realm but that its *exclusion* from the political realm throughout history has *itself* been intensely political. Tronto shows how treating care as a political concept forces a fundamental reorientation to "politics," to our understanding of what is to count as "political," and to our orientation towards the question of "political goods" and "good political order." Sitting at the heart of the public-private split, care has a powerful potential to interrupt that dichotomy and force us to rethink what it is that we do when we theorize about politics. Taking care as a political concept affords us the ability to raise questions that we could not give voice to before because of their supposed relegation to the private sphere and makes other questions and issues normally dominant in the public sphere appear irrelevant or even nonsensical.

In her essay, Shane Phelan similarly shows that viewing community as a political concept has an extremely radicalizing power for feminist theory. Community—or the lack thereof—is often seen as the *background* for politics; not as politics per se but as the basis for politics. Moreover, theorists tend to treat community as a "thing" rather than a process; either individuals create and found community (individualism), or community is the basis for individuality (communitarianism). Rarely are they seen as mutually constitutive and emergent, or "compearing." Phelan shows how complementary forms of essentialist thinking bind together notions of "community," "identity," and "the self." Loosening or tightening any one of these will affect our thinking about the others. The project of revisioning community is especially important for feminists because the idea of community has had a powerful—as well as controversial and damaging—hold on the contemporary feminist imagination. Phelan argues that a genealogical approach to community—in contrast to identitarian and deconstructive accounts—can help us to honor the desire for mutual belonging and recognition without reifying or domesticating community. Treating community as an ongoing political negotiation about what we will have in common, as being-in-common (as opposed to being common), means that we must give up and confront the myth of community as security.

These essays thus help us "revision the political" by radically challenging what we think of *as* political. And this brings us to the second project for feminist political theorists, which involves scrutinizing the "innocent space" of political theorizing (Flax 1992). The innocent space is the foundational space of political theory; here we find concepts that "ground" particular notions of the political and are very often taken for granted as noncontestable. For example, particular models of human nature are frequently invoked by political theorists as the obvious and unproblematic starting points for elaborate ruminations on freedom, justice, and equality. Or indeed, certain concepts—such as freedom, equality, community, and autonomy—are taken as the foundational given on which other concepts—such as obligation, justice, and democracy—are based. On closer inspection, this innocent space displays far more "corruption" than was previously appreciated and accounted for. This "corruption" consists of instability in what was thought to be firm and fixed; it is revealed in the cultural and historical specificity of concepts and norms that were presumed to be universal; and it surfaces whenever a persuasive case can be made that "innocent" starting points or foundations are themselves the effects or outcomes of power.

So, for instance, in her essay on freedom, Nancy Hirschmann argues that freedom is a constituent element in the conception of human nature that founds much of Western political theory but is constructed and defined as freedom for men at the expense of freedom for women. Particularly important to state of nature theory and contemporary liberalism, the "naturally free" individual provided the ontological basis for conceptualizations of obligation, property, justice, and democracy. Yet, this founding concept generally excluded women from its scope. Women's "natural" embeddedness in both maternal relationships and monogamous heterosexual relations means that they are not fit "subjects" of liberty, for they can neither make "free" choices, nor access "right reason." But underneath this lies an even deeper assumption that freedom depends on self control; whether the self is abstractly individualistic or communal, control over the self must be absolute if freedom is to be preserved. Women's location in the concrete and everyday, of course, reveals the impossibility of such control; but that is why they must be excluded from freedom. Indeed, their responsibility for the uncontrollable aspects of human relationship is what permits the myth of control to be perpetuated. But feminism can turn this on its head, for women's history of relationship can also provide a reconstruction of freedom, both as liberation ("freedom from") and self-realization ("freedom to"). Like Allen, Hirschmann emphasizes the need for new contexts within which freedom can be realized; but she also asserts that such contexts reshape the meaning of freedom such that it borrows from the two existing dominant definitions and yet creates a "third term."

The masculinist version of freedom is closely related to the account of autonomy that Christine Di Stefano critiques in her essay. Di Stefano suggests a mutual imbrication, or enmeshment, between concepts of autonomy and concepts of the subject. "Who we are" is a foundational assumption in Western political theory, and the answer to that question will produce different notions of the criteria for autonomy. Thus the masculinist construction of the self as inherently opposed to the Other yields a concept of autonomy as separation and abstract independence, a concept that many feminists have rejected. But this is in fact no less problematic than certain feminist notions of autonomy deriving from locations of the self in a web of relationships. This feminist conception simply inverts the terms of the masculinist configuration, it does not reconfigure them. Both conceptions, Di Stefano argues, thus fail to interrogate exactly what the "self" is that is "autonomous." Julia Kristeva's theory of abjection offers a different approach, one that interrogates the divisions and connections not only between selves—or between self and others—but within selves as well. Only by such radical rethinking of the "subject" of autonomy can feminists potentially escape the duality that masculinism has established.

When we interrogate the "innocent" space of political theorizing, we both simplify things and make them more complex. In the absence of foundational assumptions, political theorists must work harder to persuade audiences of the plausibility and rigor of their visions; this is a task well known to feminists, who must constantly unearth hidden masculinist assumptions that are taken to be natural "givens" while being required to defend their own competing assumptions, which are viewed as "political agendas." But shrinking spaces of innocence within political theory also provide additional points of entry into the field, particularly for those who have felt excluded or alienated. Those of us who fail to recognize ourselves in the metanarrative of social contract theory, for example, might find an opening when we are no longer forced to begin our inquiry with property-owning males in an implausible state of nature.

Although the first two types of feminist conceptual theorizing seek to politicize nonpolitical concepts, a third endeavor for feminist conceptual analysis consists in rethinking concepts that are already understood as political; for example, power, justice, rights, authority, obligation, legitimacy. In bringing women's histories, experiences, and perspectives to bear on specific constructions of politics, the basis for calling concepts "political," as well as the definitions themselves, will change. Thus Nancy Hirschmann, in her essay on obligation, draws on women's historical location in relationships to critique obligation as exclusively founded on contract and consent. It is by virtue of the public-private split, and the illusion that women occupy a sacred realm of the completely nonpolitical, that the definition of obligation as self-assumed is made possible. Rethinking obligation from the ontological and epistemological standpoint of women's historical activities of caretaking reveals a different construction of obligation and indeed of politics. For it is in the so-called private realm that the counter-narrative of self-assumed obligation—namely, "given" obligations stemming from the character of human relationships about which we often have little choice—is articulated and its own political status revealed.

Care and connection, and the specific activities that women have historically engaged in, are also central to Kathleen Jones's reformulation of authority as "compassionate authority" and Nancy Hartsock's feminist concept of "power to." Both authority and power have, from a typically feminist perspective, negative connotations: a hierarchy of right, which often barely masks a hierarchy of coercion and force, whereby one person gains at the expense of one, several, or even many others. The notion of relationships on which they are based is one that posits conflict and the struggle for domination. But these visions are decidedly masculinist; just as Hartsock specifies the understanding of power as domination as particular and masculine, so does Jones identify the "dispassionate gaze" of authority as having a specifically masculine genealogy essential to a concept of "judgment" that requires the annihilation of "the inner life," which is seen as "feminine."

Because of this, it might seem antithetical to feminism to develop "alternative" theories of power and authority; feminists, it might seem, should want to reject these concepts altogether. But both Hartsock and Jones envision different ways of seeing these concepts that emerge out of women's historical experiences of care, connection, and relationship that posit mutuality and cooperation, nurturance, and support. In her book-length account of feminist standpoint theory, Hartsock (1984) identifies such experiences in a literal way: the caretaking work that women do in the family and culture creates a materialist consciousness that contradicts the conceptualization of power as domination, for such caretaking work takes place within an epistemological perspective of connection and mutuality. Jones takes a less literal but no less direct approach: borrowing Benhabib's notion of the "concrete other," Jones points out that the standard of judgment based on identity *with* the other excludes women from the start. She identifies women's historical recognition of "difference and plurality" as leading to the further recognition of the need for empathy and understanding in authoritative judgment. But both authors emphasize the theme of care and relationship as an epistemological framework that allows us to do what Sandra Harding called "reinventing ourselves as other" (Harding 1991, 268). In the process, both theorists uncover the affirmative dimension and potential hidden in these concepts by their historical masculinization and encourage feminists to rethink these traditionally political concepts in a powerfully reclamatory fashion.

Jane Mansbridge similarly draws on such insights in "reconstructing democracy" for feminism. Indeed, she notes that what Jones and Hartsock identified as masculinist notions of power and authority feed directly into dominant notions of democracy as "adversarial." Such a democratic politics is based in power and is linked to masculinist perspectives and experience. However, another equally vital aspect of democratic politics is persuasion. Mansbridge identifies this latter mode in the history of women's contributions to democratic theory; and although this is not its only source by any means, Mansbridge argues for a strong link between this voice of persuasion and women's historical experiences of care and connection. Furthermore, recognizing that democracy requires both power *and* persuasion, Mansbridge seeks not to invert the dominant order but rather to open it up to allow greater play to the process of persuasion—namely communication, relationship, and emotion—rather than simply the force and coercion of power.

In the final essay of this collection, Iris Marion Young re-examines the question of justice, which, as all students of political theory know, is the primary political virtue. Young's approach is informed by the ethos of care developed by other feminist theorists, but it refuses to treat care and justice as mutually exclusive virtues. According to Young, the ultimate ideal for justice should be liberation rather than fairness. In analyzing issues of gender and sexuality as issues of justice that cannot be adequately addressed by the distributive paradigm, Young expands the potential uses of justice for feminists. A crucial move in this effort to revision justice is Young's deconstruction of The Family. She proposes that we substitute an enlarged form of domestic partnership for the heterosexual nuclear family unit, thus expanding the granting of privileges that are currently withheld from "illegitimate" family forms, including, but not limited to, homosexual couples and households. In effect, redefining justice means redefining The Family. Anything short of this will not simply *limit* the reach of justice; it will *perpetuate injustice* by failing to contest the arbitrary line between "legitimate" and "illegitimate" relationships that are sanctioned by the privileging of the marriage relation. Young's essay serves as an important reminder to feminist theorists of the political pitfalls of simple-minded theoretical reformism (creating more justice for The Family) as well as of the possibilities for radically reforming traditional concepts (extending justice to a plurality of family forms).

Feminist Nostalgia and the Challenge of the New

THESE INVESTIGATIONS OF concepts that are traditionally seen to lie at the heart of modern politics thus heighten our awareness that the meanings of these terms have in fact a quite provisional status. Furthermore, these investigations underscore the complementary and constitutive relations among these terms and between these terms and the political culture within which we live. Thus the third project of revisioning commonplace "political" concepts is intimately bound up in the second project of scrutinizing the foundations for these political concepts; and this in turn involves the utilization of freshly politicized concepts from the first project. In effect, this invites and requires us to "revision the political" as a whole, to redefine what we mean not only by "political concepts," but by "politics" as well.

But does such redefinition obviate Butler's warning: that is, of working within the old to create the new; using language and concepts of the old when that is precisely the barrier to be overcome? This is important to ask, because a particular hazard for feminist conceptual analysis is what we might call "homesickness" or nostalgia for the feminine; the urge to domesticate nasty masculine politics and to substitute in its place a friendly feminine politics. For instance, a number of essays in this collection draw at least implicitly on the work of Carol Gilligan, which is highly vulnerable to such charges of "nostalgia." In arguing that the dominant rights- and justice-based moral reasoning is masculinist, or even male-associated, Gilligan seems to suggest (despite her claims to the contrary) that "women's" moral voice of care, connection, concern, and responsibility is a voice missing from moral debate; and even that it is actually a *better* voice; hence its absence is to the detriment of us all (Gilligan 1982, 1988). Other feminists have pointed out the problems with this: not only its possible race and class bias, but the fact that this voice has emerged *because of* women's oppression under patriarchy. According to such critics, the "voice of care" will perpetuate women's oppression; and at the least, it is just as historically located and context-specific as the mainstream theories it seeks to displace.

Given such criticisms, the recurring themes of care and connection found in so many of the essays might make some readers uneasy about the hidden message this volume may seem to be communicating about women's "nature," substituting its own set of universalist foundations for the masculinist ones we seek to reject. That is not our intent, and we believe that such a representation of our enterprise here would be seriously mistaken. Many of the essays give intellectual attention to these notions not because women are "essentially" caring, nurturant, and giving but rather because women's *historical* location in the activities of care, of responsibility for nurturance and relationship, provide the socio-ontological basis for an epistemological perspective of care. This perspective is thus "feminine" historically and contingently, not essentially; but it *is* excluded and devalued structurally and across time with decidedly ahistorical intent. And, because this perspective is "feminine," it is also implicated in the experience of subordination. In this respect, the cautionary note surrounding "add women and stir" approaches should be extended to unprocessed feminine ingredients as well.

While sensitive to the particularity of relationship, the plurality of differences in modes of relationship and connection, and the diversity of political issues such differences raise, the essays also recognize the ability of a connection perspective to challenge existing frameworks of political theory. Care and connection are thus used by many theorists less as a *solution* to the problem of women's exclusion than as a *tool* to point this exclusion out. If relationship, connection, and care are of central importance to women's visions of what it means to be a person, then autonomy cannot be radical independence; freedom cannot be just the absence of interference from others; obligation cannot be purely contractual; power cannot be simply domination; authority cannot be impersonal and dispassionate; equality cannot be based exclusively on sameness but must recognize particularity; justice cannot be based on the simple equal allocation of resources but must refer to specificity of need; privacy cannot be opposed to politics and publicity; democracy as a political form cannot be solely adversarial and based on power any more than community can ignore the differences and individuality of persons giving and receiving care; and indeed care itself must be seen as political.

These reformulations, we believe, transcend the possible limitations and biases of the early research that may have stimulated such theoretical insights. Clearly, feminists need to refuse the bait of feminine nostalgia; but we must do this even as we insist on making a difference. For indeed, such nostalgia will prevent us from using women's historical experiences to critical purpose, a purpose that is necessary to "making a difference." And this difference decidedly needs to be made. The essays in this volume show that women have been denied access to the political realities of mainstream political concepts: that women have been denied freedom and equality; have been subjected to power and authority and unable to exercise it in the public realm; have been sequestered in the private sphere but denied access to the ultimate in privacy, namely control over our own bodies; have experienced unjust distribution of resources through sexist property laws and wage scales as well as employment discrimination and sexual harassment; have been made socially, economically, and legally unequal; have been denied autonomous control of our life choices; have had communities built on our backs, literally through our labor as well as figuratively through our exclusion from exercising authority and negotiating the terms and conditions of community; and have been denied opportunities to consent and make contracts while having obligations and duties forced upon us as wives, mothers, domestic servants, migrant laborers, slaves, office workers, sex workers, and industrial workers.

But the essays also demonstrate that women are fundamentally excluded from these concepts such that these concepts could not have been defined in the ways they are without women's exclusion. This deep-seated conceptual exclusion suggests the need for feminists to reconceptualize. After all, if our "contingent" exclusion were all that was the matter, then why could we not just extend these concepts to women, simply, as Sandra Harding (1986) originally coined the phrase, "add women and stir"? And if we could do that, then why are women still subject to the difficulties just identified: of inequality, of denial of autonomy and privacy as well as of public access, of power and authority, and of exclusion from community? All of the theorists in this volume, to varying degrees, agree that this conceptual exclusion is a problem; but they do not wish to stop at the level of pointing this out. Rather, they seek a reformulation, a "solution," to the problem of women's exclusion.

It is important to note, however, that the point of these analyses is not to get at the "fundamental" meaning of these terms, as if feminists have cornered the "Truth" of political concepts; and this, we believe, may be our solution to the puzzle of the "new." In refusing to pass off these revisionings under the mantle of "Truth", we also recognize the need, often ignored in political theory, to take responsibility for these visions in the light of political agendas that reflect distinctively feminist priorities. One of the central insights that feminist criticism has offered is to point out that most of the universal and abstract claims that modern political theory habitually makes are, in fact, historically specific and politically motivated. (If they are not politically motivated, then they are most definitely politically effectual.) But feminism never (or at least rarely) seeks to replace such "partial and perverse" pictures with "genuinely" universal ones.[6] In this respect, the feminist revisionings of the political contained in this volume would never claim political innocence for themselves. A feminist approach to political concepts urges attention to the constitutive contexts and effects of political discourse (including feminist discourse) as well as to alternative models of political culture, to who and how we are and how we might wish to be.

The Example of Rights

THE NECESSITY OF such a dynamic approach to feminist conceptual analysis is illustrated by many of the concepts we include but perhaps should be illustrated with regard to rights, a concept missing from our book (though we had hoped that two erstwhile contributors would write on this concept). Feminists have long been suspicious of the concept of rights; as a central notion in Enlightenment discourses, talk about "natural rights" seemed to be a coded term for the disingenuous exclusion of the poor, men and women of color, and white women by propertied white males. Carol Gilligan's identification of rights as a dominantly "masculine" perspective showed the damage that a rights and rules emphasis does, particularly to women, but to men as well. Others, following Gilligan, have identified rights as the voice of power and domination, finding the voice of care to cohere with powerlessness (Hare-Mustin and Marecek 1990; Sinopoli and Hirschmann 1991). Rights, then, could be seen as instruments of oppression, inherently antagonistic to feminist egalitarian visions.

Yet in *The Alchemy of Race and Rights*, Patricia J. Williams compares her views on rental agreements with the experience of a white male colleague, and finds that rights are extremely important for those who have been historically and systematically denied them (a claim that could similarly be made about privacy, freedom, equality, autonomy, democratic citizenship, and justice). Williams suggests that the critical legal studies, postmodernist, and feminist calls to reject rights should be viewed with critical caution; if rights embody the voice of power, perhaps women should not be too quick to abandon that voice.

But this suggests that we have a paradox. On the one hand, Western rights discourse exists at women's expense, for it is premised on women's exclusion; it is not insignificant that at the time when rights dialogue emerged, women were socially constituted as among the first "rights" of men. In particular, rights to black male and female slaves, and to white women through marriage, were among the central rights that emerged from Enlightenment property rights (Pateman 1988, Eisenstein 1981). Women's subservience would thus seem to be, in some sense, foundationally necessary to rights. On the other hand and at the same time, as numerous international women's groups attest, rights are a vital and necessary discourse for women. Which of these positions is more sustainable from a feminist perspective?

Rather than choosing between them, however, perhaps both of these positions can be maintained simultaneously if we critically question and evaluate their apparent contradiction.[7] The starting point for this evaluation lies in women's multiple or intersecting identities, which feminism of color makes most apparent. For instance, Williams's account suggests that because of African American women's multiple identities (or more precisely, because the multiplicity of their identity cannot be hidden or denied, in contrast to white women who often fail to see their racial identity and focus "just" on gender), rights discourse can be interrogated, intersected, and challenged in radically new ways that allow women to use rights without denying the ways in which rights are constructed to exclude them.

Kimberle Crenshaw similarly argues that women of color's "intersectionality" provides a perspective of multiple standpoints from which to view and assess rights and that this multiplicity allows us to see both the disempowerment produced by liberal rights formulations (which are racist as well as sexist) and the ways in which rights can and must be changed to accommodate different women's experiences. For instance, Crenshaw relates the story of an Hispanic woman who was denied admittance to a battered women's shelter on the basis that her inability to speak English would inhibit her ability to partake in mandatory support group discussions. Her son was not allowed to translate for her because that would "further victimize the victim" (Crenshaw 1991, 1263).

Such experiences clearly illustrate the ways in which individualist approaches even within a feminist context are used against women of color by white women; the individualist conception of rights and autonomy as involving independence and separateness would seem to conflict with feminist values of safety and relationship. But Crenshaw also demonstrates that examining this *from the perspective of intersectionality* is what *reveals* its contradictions. Thinking about rights from the perspective of multiplicity thus opens the door to their reformulation, for instance, by combining both individualist and group-based approaches to rights: the "values" of safety and relationship lend themselves to a reconstruction of the *right to* safety, to nondamaging relationships, and to inclusion in community. Similarly, Vickers et al. note that in Canada, First Nations women utilize a collective rather than individualist notion of rights to make claims against the state as well as within dominantly white feminist organizations (Vickers et al. 1993). Thus Crenshaw notes that "the social power in delineating difference need not be the power of domination; it can instead be the source of social empowerment and reconstruction" (Crenshaw 1991, 1242).

In this, the fact that it is women of color and international feminists who are holding on to and advocating the notion of rights, whereas the feminists who tend to reject rights are white Westerners, may reveal a deeper problem with rights than white Western feminism allows us to see: that is, perhaps it is not that rights operate against "women" per se, but against the *multiplicity* of women's identity. After all, it is not just women of color who experience such multiplicity; we all do, but middle-class whites are more easily able to sustain a myth of unified identity because the dominant culture reflects their experience more closely. As a result, as long as rights discourse locates women "as women," and *only* "as women," the failure of rights to protect women is ensured, precisely because women are *never* "only" women. That does not mean that the discourse of rights inevitably fails, but it does suggest the need to rethink "women's rights" in the modern world, to reflect difference and specificity.

From this perspective, rights discourse is a problem for women insofar as it always places women in a single identity box; if we think of "women's rights" in the white racist West, we see how limiting they have always been for women of all races and classes, particularly in constructing a dichotomous choice between difference and equality. But if women can recognize that and reconstruct rights to accommodate our multiplicity, perhaps we can adapt rights discourse to the ends of gender equality and justice.[8]

This is also true for men, of course; men are alleged to have rights to choose the direction of their lives, but as social contract theory reveals, these rights protect them in reality only if they make very particular choices and only if they have the specific characteristics that make them "individuals," namely property, whiteness, and egocentric strategic reasoning capacities. "Rights" discourse thus works against multiplicity in all its forms, not just "women's" multiplicities. Nevertheless, within this limiting framework, rights for men *have* historically covered a relatively vast array of choices, while for women they have often been limited to making their prescribed roles more tolerable; think of how "women's rights" as a separate category from "human rights" has operated historically to link women with marriage and childcare. This has in part been historically necessary, since it is precisely women's location within the family that has shaped our oppression; but it nevertheless contributes to the establishment of the dilemma.

Thus this "reconstruction" is once again limited by its old terms and yet is able to get beyond them. It is "reconstructive" but not *ex nihilo*, or "from scratch." We are—contra Audre Lorde (1984)—forced to use the master's tools to dismantle the master's house, but even further, to use the master's materials to build a new house, to perform the reconstruction. As a result, many of the old issues, meanings, and problems may persist. But in the process, we do not *just* recycle the old. Rather, new tools and new materials are made: a metal hammer can be used to nail two boards together, but it can also be used to smash the boards apart, just as it can be used to nudge other boards into place; and it can even be melted down to create hinges and nails. It is in the effort to transcend the old *through* the old and with assistance from the new that the new can emerge; but there is—can be—no one right way to do this. It must be somewhat spontaneous and *ad hoc*, improvising as we go.

(In)Conclusion

IT IS THIS dynamic that accounts for the considerable methodological and substantive differences within feminist theory illustrated by the essays in this volume. One of the most egregiously false characterizations of feminism is that it is a political and intellectual monoculture. As we observed at the beginning of this essay, feminists even dispute the desirability of reconstruction as a theoretical enterprise. And as the essays attest, differences persist even among feminists committed to the task of reconstruction. Some, like Eisenstein and Allen, insist that "rethinking" primarily requires just that: to think more deeply and consistently about the definitions mainstream theory has offered so that their foundations are more truly realized for women's circumstances. Others, such as Mansbridge, Jones, and Young, suggest a more fundamental restructuring. These differences are instructive, for they offer us renewed opportunities to rethink comfortable assumptions and entrenched commitments, not only within political theory, but within feminism as well. They are vital to the ongoing work of revisioning feminism itself, and they display the vitality of contemporary feminist theorizing. But they all result in a call for serious, fundamental change to the face of politics, political theory and political life.

And indeed, it is perhaps this feature more than any other that unites these essays under the banner of "feminism." Tania Modleski argues that the significance of feminist theorizing exceeds particular feminist efforts "to redefine traditional models ... of authority, power, and hierarchy." Rather, "every time a feminist critic speaks and writes as a woman in a world that has always conspired to silence and negate women she brings into being a new order and enacts the scandal of the speaking body in a far more profound way than those people already authorized to speak by virtue of their gender" (Modleski 1991, 53). Modleski discerns two simultaneous functions or dimensions in feminist writing: the performative and the utopian. The "utopian" function would apply to specific efforts to reconstruct political concepts in the light of women's emancipatory aspirations. The substantive outcomes of feminist conceptual theory—various feminists' visions of how freedom, or equality, or justice should be realized, their particular visions of the political—will of course be the subject of engaged and committed disagreement, as well as occasional and partial agreement, among feminists. The utopian function is thus what distinguishes these essays from one another; it is a force that drives not only this volume, but feminist theory, apart, threatening, from the sheer power of the diversity of views contained within it, to fragment into political and intellectual disarray. The performative dimension, however, is what links these essays together; it represents a larger commitment to the process of theorizing about and on behalf of "women," regardless of the differences of our particular visions.[9] Each essay, in its own way, enacts a seizure of power from men on behalf of women—"perhaps the most difficult act of all for women to perform" (Modleski 1991, 54)—in its effort to revision the political. In this respect, we suggest that feminist efforts to revision the political constitute seizures of power the significance of which should not be underestimated.

To make this politicized claim on behalf of the particular reconstructions of political concepts contained in this volume, however, is not to claim that power has been successfully or finally seized by and on behalf of all (or even any) women with the publication of this or any other volume of academic writing. It is not to claim that such power is, ultimately, seizable. We are also well aware that feminism in the academy and in the world at large continues to underrepresent the needs and aspirations of many women. We are painfully aware of the fact that the contributors to this volume do not represent an accurate or full sampling of the varieties of women's emancipatory aspirations; and indeed, this may ironically be due to our own personal location in the disciplinary norms of political theory, our struggles to resist them notwithstanding.[10] We also believe that any bid for power is partial, temporary, and—perhaps inevitably—seduced by its own claims to innocence.

Does that bring us to the conclusion that in fact our project is doomed from the start? Hardly. Indeed, such partiality and incompletion is one of the most important theoretical and political contributions that feminism has made to conceptual analysis. The artificial closure that political theory has often brought to its analysis of politics is responsible for the worst excesses of its intellectual power. Its assertion of universality in the obvious face of its particularity, of timelessness in the face of historical and cultural specificity, has been the driving force behind the exclusivity of political concepts in the modern era. The refusal to bring such closure—even at the expense of no closure at all but only an open-ended and unanswered set of questions dangling at the end—has been one of feminism's strengths. The courage of this conviction has not come without a price, of course—all of the contributors to this volume have been witnesses to, if not victims of, the too frequent dismissals of feminist theory as "not theoretical enough" even today, in 1996—but it is a price that has been worth its cost. For in holding to the refusal to bring closure lies the hope that political theory as a discipline can be itself transformed, rethought, revisioned.

It is in such a hope that we engage in this enterprise, laying claim to the "authorship" of the constituent foundations of contemporary political theory, its "essentially contested concepts." Feminism must, we believe, take the risk of going beyond declarations of what is not, to the affirmation of what might be. And it *is* a risk: affirming the (inevitably imperfect) positive while at the same time refusing closure is a particularly treacherous balancing act, constantly subject to the high winds of academic hot air. But it is necessary to the future of the discipline. The essays in this collection maintain that balance skillfully, and we trust they will stimulate colleagues and students alike (for the task is decidedly multigenerational) to their own "revisionings."

Notes

1. It is perhaps significant that Benhabib raises such questions, since her co-edited volume *Feminism as Critique* was one of the earliest to undertake explicitly the "feminist project of a theoretical construction" (Benhabib and Cornell 1987, 1). This construction took as its focus "different strands of twentieth-century Marxism" rather than Western political concepts, but many of our concerns for the constructive potential of feminism are shared. Harding and Hintikka (1983) is also cited as an early "constructive" effort, though its focus on issues of epistemology and philosophy of science make it considerably different in scope and intent than the present volume, as well as different in what it considers "reconstruction."

2. In saying "we," we do not mean to flatten out the great variety of experiences and needs of women according to differences of class, race, historical epoch, culture and ethnicity, sexuality, age, and physical ability, but rather to show solidarity with "other" women and to avoid the objectification inevitably involved in talking about "them."

3. For feminist critiques of the Western political theory canon, see the following: Brown (1988), Clarke and Lange (1981), Coole (1993), Di Stefano (1991), Eisenstein (1982), Elshtain (1981), O'Brien (1981), Okin (1979), Pateman (1988), Pitkin (1984), Saxonhouse (1985), Shanley and Pateman (1991), Zerilli (1994), and the new *Rereading the Canon* series, edited by Nancy Tuana and published by Pennsylvania State University Press.

4. This is another way in which the essays reflect the tension between "new" and "old," in that most of these essays draw on or are adapted from these other, previously published works and yet were specifically constructed and rewritten for this volume.

5. Feminists, of course, do not hold exclusive rights to this insight. Other political theorists, perhaps most notably Marx, were acutely aware of the interdependencies among concepts. The "systematic" nature of their political visions and theories displays the effort to map these interdependencies into a unified vision of political life. But most modern Western theorists postulate a strict dichotomy between freedom and obligation, rights and duties, equality and authority, justice and power. That critical analysis of these theories reveals that the dichotomies cannot truly be sustained, and that the theories in fact *end up* with conceptual interdependence, does not alter the significance that they explicitly *argue for* the distinctness of core concepts.

6. Whether it ends up doing so in spite of itself is another matter, as feminists of color have argued against white Western feminism. See hooks (1984), Hull, Scott, and Smith (1982), James and Busia (1993), Mohanty, Russo, and Torres (1991), Moraga and Anzaldúa (1983).

7. The ideas for this discussion of rights were stimulated by a response to an earlier draft paper by Stanlie James, "Towards a Theoretical Articulation of Human Rights with Women's Rights," considered for this volume. Although James (unfortunately for us) decided that her other commitments would not permit her to contribute to our volume, our response to her very stimulating paper is reflected in many of the ideas contained in the present discussion. See James (1995).

8. Rights discourse has been deployed politically and strategically, with some notable successes, on behalf of women in the workforce. For a recent study of the role of rights discourse in several comparable worth campaigns, see Michael McCann (1994).

9. Benhabib's definition of feminist theory as "the theoretical articulation of the emancipatory aspirations of women" offers a useful orientation (Benhabib 1995, 29). Her definition delimits the enterprise to manageable proportions without predeciding particular outcomes. The key terms in this definition are "emancipatory" and "women." Feminists may disagree about the emancipatory aspirations of women; they may even disagree about how to define the term "women"; but agreeing to disagree about these terms, *because they have been judged to be of political and intellectual significance and priority*, brings them together as feminists.

10. We consciously decided to include specifically feminist *political theorists* in this volume. There is one philosopher (Young—who is in regular attendance at American Political Science Association meetings) and one legal theorist (Allen). The rest are political theorists, employed in departments of political science. We thought this was an important move to communicate with our discipline that it is in fact changing, and our colleagues must change with it. At the same time, such a

decision is inherently conservative: the vast majority of political theorists (including feminist political theorists) are white, for instance, and those who are women of color are overburdened by demands placed on them to provide representations of other-than-white voices. Unwilling to populate our volume with reprints, and seeking to collect papers by the authors of recent and forthcoming books that focus on conceptual analysis, we decided to risk the charge of homogeneity in the belief that the essays themselves would speak to, and invite further contributions to, issues of diversity, difference, and representation within feminism.

References

Allen, Anita. 1988. *Uneasy Access: Privacy for Women in a Free Society.* Totowa, N.J.: Rowman and Littlefield.

Bauman, Zygmunt. 1992. *Intimations of Postmodernity.* London: Routledge.

Benhabib, Seyla. 1995. "Feminism and Postmodernism." In *Feminist Contentions: A Philosophical Exchange.* New York: Routledge.

Benhabib, Seyla and Drucilla Cornell, eds. 1987. *Feminism as Critique.* Minneapolis: University of Minnesota Press.

Brown, Wendy. 1988. *Manhood and Politics: A Feminist Reading in Political Theory.* Totowa, N.J.: Rowman and Littlefield.

Butler, Judith. 1992. "Contingent Foundations: Feminism and the Question of 'Postmodernism.'" In *Feminists Theorize the Political.* Ed. Judith Butler and Joan Scott. New York: Routledge.

Clarke, Lorenne and Lynda Lange, eds. 1979. *The Sexism of Social and Political Thought.* Toronto: University of Toronto Press.

Connolly, William. 1974. *The Terms of Political Discourse.* Lexington, Mass.: D. C. Heath.

Coole, Diana. 1993. *Women in Political Theory: From Ancient Misogyny to Contemporary Feminism.* Boulder, Colo.: Lynne Rienner.

Crenshaw, Kimberle. 1991. "Mapping the Margins: Intersectionality, Identity Politics, and Violence Against Women of Color." *Stanford Law Review* 43:1241–1299.

Di Stefano, Christine. 1991. *Configurations of Masculinity: A Feminist Perspective on Modern Political Theory.* Ithaca, N.Y.: Cornell University Press.

Eisenstein, Zillah R. 1982. *The Radical Future of Liberal Feminism.* New York: Longman's.

Eisenstein, Zillah R. 1988. *The Female Body and the Law.* Berkeley: University of California Press.

Eisenstein, Zillah R. 1994. *The Color of Gender: Reimaging Democracy.* Berkeley: University of California Press.

Elshtain, Jean Bethke. 1981. *Public Man, Private Woman: Women in Social and Political Thought.* Princeton, N.J.: Princeton University Press.

Flax, Jane. 1990. *Thinking Fragments: Psychoanalysis, Feminism, and Postmodernism in the Contemporary West.* Berkeley: University of California Press.

Flax, Jane. 1992. "The End of Innocence." In *Feminists Theorize the Political*. Ed. Judith Butler and Joan Scott. New York: Routledge.

Gallie, Bernard. 1955. "Essentially Contested Concepts." *Proceedings of the Aristotelian Society* 56:167–198.

Gilligan, Carol. 1982. *In a Different Voice: Psychological Theory and Women's Development*. Cambridge, Mass.: Harvard University Press.

Gilligan, Carol et al., eds. 1988. *Mapping the Moral Domain*. Cambridge, Mass.: Harvard University Press.

Harding, Sandra. 1986. *The Science Question in Feminism*. Ithaca, N.Y.: Cornell University Press.

Harding, Sandra. 1991. *Whose Science? Whose Knowledge? Thinking from Women's Lives*. Ithaca, N.Y.: Cornell University Press.

Harding, Sandra and Merrill B. Hintikka, eds. 1983. *Discovering Reality: Feminist Perspectives on Epistemology, Metaphysics, Methodology, and Philosophy of Science*. Dordrecht, The Netherlands: D. Reidel.

Hare-Mustin, Rachel T. and Jeanne Maracek. 1990. *Making a Difference: Psychology and the Construction of Gender*. New Haven, Conn.: Yale University Press.

Hartsock, Nancy C. M. 1984. *Money, Sex and Power: Toward a Feminist Historical Materialism*. Boston: Northeastern University Press.

Harvey, David. 1989. *The Condition of Postmodernity: An Enquiry Into the Origins of Cultural Change*. Oxford: Basil Blackwell.

Hekman, Susan. 1990. *Gender and Knowledge: Elements of a Postmodern Feminism*. Cambridge: Polity Press; Boston: Northeastern University Press.

Hirschmann, Nancy J. 1992. *Rethinking Obligation: A Feminist Method for Political Theory*. Ithaca, N.Y.: Cornell University Press.

hooks, bell. 1984. *Feminist Theory: From Margin to Center*. Boston: South End Press.

Hull, Gloria T., Patricia Bell Scott and Barbara Smith, eds. 1982. *All the Women Are White, All the Blacks Are Men, But Some of Us Are Brave: Black Women's Studies*. Old Westbury, N.Y.: The Feminist Press.

James, Stanlie. 1995. "U.N. Treatment of Multiple Oppressions: A Black Feminist Perspective." *Journal of African Policy Studies* 1 (1): 53–69.

James, Stanlie. N.d. "Towards a Theoretical Articulation of Human Rights with Women's Rights." Unpublished manuscript.

James, Stanlie M. and Abena P.A. Busia, eds. 1993. *Theorizing Black Feminisms: The Visionary Pragmatism of Black Women*. New York: Routledge.

Jameson, Fredric. 1991. *Postmodernism, or, The Cultural Logic of Late Capitalism*. Durham, N.C.: Duke University Press.

Jones, Kathleen. 1993. *Compassionate Authority: Democracy and the Representation of Women*. New York: Routledge.

Kristeva, Julia. 1980a. "Oscillation Between Power and Denial." In *New French Feminisms*. Ed. Elaine Marks and Isabelle deCourtivron. Amherst: University of Massachusetts Press.

Kristeva, Julia. 1980b. "Women Can Never Be Defined." In *New French Feminisms*. Ed. Elaine Marks and Isabelle deCourtivron. Amherst: University of Massachusetts Press.

Lorde, Audre. 1984. *Sister Outsider.* Trumansburg, N.Y.: Crossing Press.

Mansbridge, Jane. 1983. *Beyond Adversary Democracy.* Chicago: University of Chicago Press.

McCann, Michael W. 1994. *Rights at Work: Pay Equity Reform and the Politics of Legal Mobilization.* Chicago: University of Chicago Press.

Minow, Martha. 1990. *Making All the Difference: Inclusion, Exclusion, and American Law.* Cambridge, Mass.: Harvard University Press.

Modleski, Tania. 1991. *Feminism Without Women.* New York: Routledge.

Mohanty, Chandra Talpade, Ann Russo and Lourdes Torres, eds. 1991. *Third World Women and the Politics of Feminism.* Bloomington: Indiana University Press.

Moraga, Cherríe and Gloria Anzaldúa, eds. 1983. *This Bridge Called My Back: Writings By Radical Women of Color.* Watertown, Mass.: Persephone Press.

O'Brien, Mary. 1981. *The Politics of Reproduction.* Boston: Routledge and Kegan Paul.

Okin, Susan Moller. 1979. *Women in Western Political Thought.* Princeton, N.J.: Princeton University Press.

Okin, Susan Moller. 1989. *Justice, Gender, and the Family.* New York: Basic Books.

Pateman, Carole. 1988. *The Sexual Contract.* Palo Alto, Calif.: Stanford University Press.

Phelan, Shane. 1994. *Getting Specific: Postmodern Lesbian Politics.* Minneapolis: University of Minnesota Press.

Pitkin, Hanna. 1984. *Fortune Is a Woman: Gender and Politics in the Thought of Niccoló Machiavelli.* Berkeley: University of California Press.

Saxonhouse, Arlene. 1985. *Women in the History of Political Thought: Ancient Greece to Machiavelli.* New York: Praeger.

Shanley, Mary Lyndon and Carole Pateman, eds. 1991. *Feminist Interpretations and Political Theory.* University Park: Pennsylvania State University Press.

Sinopoli, Richard and Nancy J. Hirschmann. 1991. "Feminism and Liberal Theory." *The American Political Science Review* 85 (1):221–233.

Tronto, Joan. 1993. *Moral Boundaries: A Political Argument for an Ethic of Care.* New York: Routledge.

Vickers, Jill et al. 1993. *Politics As If Women Mattered: A Political Analysis of the National Action Committee on the Status of Women.* Toronto: University of Toronto Press.

Williams, Patricia J. 1989. *The Alchemy of Race and Rights: Diary of a Law Professor.* Cambridge, Mass.: Harvard University Press.

Young, Iris Marion. 1990. *Justice and the Politics of Difference.* Princeton, N.J.: Princeton University Press.

Zerilli, Linda M. G. 1994. *Signifying Woman: Culture and Chaos in Rousseau, Burke, and Mill.* Ithaca, N.Y.: Cornell University Press.

2

Community/
Sexuality/Gender

Rethinking Power

Nancy C.M. Hartsock

*I*n recent decades, many of us have learned a great deal about the extent to which our society is structured by relations of domination and submission, relations constructed most importantly out of differences of race, gender, and class. Yet we need more theoretical clarity about *how* these relations of domination are constructed, how they operate, how they interact with and mutually structure one another, and how social theories have both justified and obscured them. My interest in this essay centers on (1) how relations of domination along gender lines are constructed and maintained, and (2) whether social understandings of domination itself have been distorted by men's domination of women. How can we develop theories that can provide a more complete understanding both of the variety of relations of domination and of the transformations necessary to create a more egalitarian society? I want to argue that an essential part of such a theory and practice is a critique of power relations—of the ways the exercise of power of some over others is constructed, legitimated, and reproduced.

Our opposition to relations of domination makes it essential for feminists to examine the exercise of power more directly. Is the exercise of power best understood as the ability to compel obedience? To what extent should power be understood as energy or ability? And if we look more closely at the exercise of power over others can it really be connected with masculinity? If so, are there ways of exercising power that can be characterized as feminine or feminist?

Gender and Power: Masculinity, Violence, and Domination

As I BEGAN to think about power, I came to believe that theories of power are implicitly theories of community. To examine theories of power is to involve oneself in questions of how communities have been constructed and how they might be structured in more liberatory ways. The fundamental question posed for theorists of power is that of the legitimate bases on which a community of actors can be organized and maintained. But if theories of power are always/already theories of community, they must also address issues that center on *eros*. This is both a logical point (*eros* and power both involve questions about fusion and community) and a commonplace observation (many social scientists have noted that power is linked with notions of potency, virility, and manliness).

There is more to my claim than this, however. Like power relations, relations structured by *eros* involve the establishment of social relations with others. They, like exercises of power over others, represent the creation of a sort of community. This community may be fragile and instrumental or deep-going and intrinsically valuable to its members. To the extent that either sexual relations or other power relations are structured by a dynamic of domination/submission, the community as a whole will be structured by domination.

It has become commonplace in contemporary feminist literature to claim that we should understand sexuality not as an essence or set of properties defining an individual, or as a set of drives and needs (especially genital) of an individual. Rather, we should understand sexuality as culturally and historically defined and constructed. Anything can become eroticized, and thus there can be no "abstract and universal category of 'the erotic' or 'the sexual' applicable without change to all societies" (Padgug 1979a, 11). Rather, sexuality must be understood as a series of cultural and social practices and meanings that both structure and are in turn structured by social relations more generally (Weeks 1981; Butler 1990).

If sexuality is a social and historical construction, how has contemporary Western culture shaped sexuality? There is a surprising degree of consensus that hostility and domination, as opposed to intimacy and physical pleasure, are central to sexual excitement. Robert Stoller contends that in our culture "it is hostility—the desire, overt or hidden, to harm another person—that generates and enhances sexual excitement" (Stoller 1979, 26).[1] Moreover, he contends, "the same dynamics, though in different mixes and degrees, are found in almost everyone, those labeled perverse and those not so labeled" (Stoller 1979, 6). He suggests as well that if researchers of sexual excitement look closely, they will discover that "permutations of hostility will be found far more frequently than is acknowledged today." To underline this point, we should note that he states that he chose the term hostility, rather than power or aggression, to indicate that "harm and suffering" are central to sexual excitement (Stoller 1979, 23, 6).

As Stoller outlines it, the mechanisms that construct sexual excitement rest most fundamentally on fetishization and on the dehumanization and objectification of the sexual object. And these are associated with debasement of the object and the construction of mystery, risk, illusion, and a search for revenge. The sexual object is to be stripped of its humanity; the focus is on breasts, buttocks, legs, and penises, not on faces.

Stoller is not alone in finding hostility in sexual excitement. Many theorists have commented on the relation of hostility and anger to sexual excitement. For example, Kinsey noted that "the closest parallel to the picture of sexual response is found in the known physiology of anger (Kinsey et al. 1953, 705, quoted in Dworkin 1979, 182).[2] Or consider a psychologist's note that sex can be a power weapon and that "in general it has far more intimate relationships with dominance feeling than it has with physiological drive (Maslow 1942, 291, quoted in Stember 1976, 145). And Kate Millett has commented that in some literary sources "the pleasure of humiliating the sexual object appears to be far more intoxicating than sex itself" (Millett 1970, 304, quoted in Stember 1976, 150).

References to the relation of sexual excitement and hostility are not limited to passing comments. These links are at the center of philosopher/pornographer Georges Bataille's theory and fiction. As he describes it, "Sexual activity is a form of violence." And the desire of the "potential killer in every man" to kill relates to the taboo on murder in the same way that the desire for sexual activity relates to the various prohibitions on it (Bataille 1977, 90). Killing and sexual activity share both prohibitions and religious significance.

Issues of sexuality and hostility appear as well in the context of analyses of racism. Thus one writer notes that the practice of linking apes, blacks, and Jews with mythological satyrs "reveals that there are sensitive spots in the human soul at a level where thought becomes confused and where sexual excitement is strangely linked with violence and aggressiveness" (Mannoni 1964, 111, quoted in Stember 1976, 164). Another writer, in the context of an argument about the connections between racial hostility and sexuality, makes a fairly detailed case that "the gratification in sexual conquest derives from the experience of defilement—of reducing the elevated woman to the 'dirty' sexual level, of polluting that which is seen as pure, sexualizing that which is seen as unsexual, animalizing that which is seen as 'spiritual'" (Stember 1976, 149). In the context of these statements it is not surprising to encounter a common sense view that sex is dangerous and violent (English et al. 1981, 52ff).[3]

The hostility Stoller analyzes is fueled in part by danger and the construction of risk. Childhood traumas, frustrations, and dangers are turned into risks where there is a more clearly calculable outcome, where the degree of risk can be carefully controlled. This risk, then, can be experienced as excitement, the childhood trauma re-created as adult sexual script. Stoller concludes that sadomasochism has to be seen as a central feature of *most* sexual excitement and that the desire to hurt others in revenge for having been hurt is essential for most people's sexual excitement all the time, but not all people's excitement all the time (Stoller 1979, 113).

Stoller would probably not agree with my use of this term in another context, since he wants very much to keep the term as a way to characterize deviance (Hartsock 1983b; Stoller 1975, 97). In this context he defines perversion as "the erotic form of hatred," a fantasy either acted out or restricted to a daydream of doing harm: "Murder that sexually excites, mutilation for excitement, rape, sadism with precise physical punishments such as whipping or cutting, enchaining and binding games, defecating or urinating on one's object—all are on a lessening scale of conscious rage toward one's sex object" (Stoller 1975, 56).

Yet Stoller found two puzzles in his work on perversion. He continually ran into the problem that by his definition "deviant" behavior, and a great deal, perhaps even most, of contemporary "normal" heterosexual sexual activity must be labeled perverse. Thus he himself notes that we risk finding that there is very little sexual behavior that might not have a touch of the perverse and complains that "the idea of normality crumbles" (Stoller 1975, 97, xvii). Stoller is not alone in finding this difficulty (Barry 1979; Dworkin 1979). Andrea Dworkin calls attention to a statement from *Sex Offenders: An Analysis of Types:* "If we labeled all punishable sexual behavior as a sex offense, we would find ourselves in the ridiculous situation of having all of our *male* histories consist almost wholly of sex offenders" (Gebhard et al. 1965, 6, cited in Dworkin 1979, 52; italics mine).

This quotation points toward the second puzzle Stoller found in his work but did not analyze. Why, he asks, is perversion (i.e., gross hostility or eroticized hatred) found more in males (Stoller 1975, 9)? And he raises several other important and related questions. He wonders whether "in humans (especially males) powerful sexual excitement can ever exist without brutality also being present." Given that psychoanalysis explains why women are as perverse as men, why has it not explained why they are not (Stoller 1975, 9, 88, 98)? His own analysis in *Sexual Excitement* follows this pattern; as he himself notes, he has not dealt with the issue of how women are unlike men rather than like them in the construction of sexual excitement (Stoller 1979, 220–221). In addition, Stoller wonders why women neither buy nor respond to pornography as intensely as men (he defines pornography by the presence of hostility and a victim) and begins to ask whether the question itself is wrong. Women, Stoller argues, do buy "masochistic" but "romantic" and "unsexual" stories, and thus, he suspects, the definition of pornography hinges on what is pornography for men (Stoller 1975, 89–91).[4]

These gender differences indicate that the account we have of sexual excitement works better for men than women. In addition, I take these differences to suggest that what we treat as sexuality and sexual excitement is a gendered masculine sexuality and masculine sexual excitement. The culturally produced dynamics of hostility that structure sexual excitement correspond to a masculine sexuality that depends on defiling or debasing a fetishized sexual object. Thus we are dealing with a gendered power relation based in what our culture has defined as sexuality.[5] In turn, this cultural construction of sexuality must be understood to express the experience of the ruling gender.[6] This of course is to be expected if one takes seriously, as I do, Marx's argument that the ideas of the ruling class express the dominant material relations of a historical period in the form of ideas. Thus, the ways our culture both constructs and theorizes sexuality express the dominance of men over women in the form of ideas. But just as the ideas of the capitalist class in capitalist societies are at once the ideas that express its experience and its dominance and also those that structure social relations for other classes, so too we can expect that because of masculine cultural hegemony, these sexual dynamics typify some women. (Note that the patient with/on whom Stoller worked out much of his theory of sexual excitement was a woman.) This does not change the fact that these dynamics are more typical of men than women and correspond more to men's rather than women's experience.[7]

What is the theoretical significance of the association of sexuality and power for a more liberatory understanding of power? If the sexual dimension of power implies a masculinity structured by violence and domination, how could feminists *both* understand *and* practice power differently? Should feminists conclude that sexuality is inseparable from violence, that in some sense sex *is* violence? If hostility is so omnipresent—for men, and given our culture, women, too—is there any escape?

Alternative Theories

Women on Power: An Alternative Tradition

THE GENDER CARRIED by power in the modern world, as in the ancient, leads to the domination of others, domination of external nature, and domination of one's own nature. Or perhaps more precisely, the repression/denial of *eros* in a masculinist society underlies the definition of both sexuality and power as domination. Yet this is only half the story. Communities structured by forms of *eros* that express women's experiences might take quite different form. This suggestion is supported in an interesting way by the fact that although few women have theorized about power, their theories bear striking similarities both to one another and to theories of power that have been characterized as feminist understandings of power. My several cases, Hannah Arendt, Dorothy Emmet, Hanna Pitkin, and Berenice Carroll, clearly constitute only suggestive evidence for my argument. Yet I believe it is significant that I was unable to discover any woman writing about power who did not stress those aspects of power related to energy, capacity, and potential.

Arendt uses ancient Greek sources as the foundation for her theorization of power and violence, yet she incorporates them in ways that systematically reduce the conflictual nature of the oppositions between necessity and freedom, intellect and body, and social and natural worlds. As a result, she is able to put forward a vision of power and community surprisingly akin to Marx's suggestions about the kinds of social relations possible in communist society.[8] Several aspects of Arendt's theorization deserve comment, among them her explicit rejection of an understanding of power that sees power as power over others or as domination, her differentiation of power from violence, and her redefinition of power as action in concert. Each of these aspects of her argument about power are part of her understanding of the possibilities for action in a more humane community. Power is at once the "glue" that holds the community together, the means by which the community is constituted, and even the means by which immortality is attained and death overcome. Power, then, is importantly connected to Arendt's understanding of action and its meaning in public life.

The key words in Arendt's account of power seem to be "ability," "potentiality," and "empowerment." The community as a whole is central to her understanding: against widespread definitions of power as related to domination, Arendt argues that power "corresponds to the human ability not just to act but to act in concert. Power is never the property of an individual; it belongs to a group and remains in existence only so long as the group keeps together. The moment the group, from which the power originated to begin with disappears ... [the ruler's] power also vanishes" (Arendt 1969, 44).[9] If power were more than the potentiality of being together and did not depend on the inherently temporary agreement of many wills and intentions, omnipotence might be a possibility. Power shares with action the quality of having no physical limitation in human nature or in bodily existence (Arendt 1958, 201). "Power springs up whenever people get together and act in concert, but it derives its legitimacy from the initial getting together rather than from any action that then may follow" (Arendt 1969, 52). Arendt adds one more qualification for an attribution of power. Power is "actualized" (but, like other potentials, can never be "materialized") where "word and deed have not parted company, where words are not empty and deeds not brutal, where words are not used to veil intentions but to disclose realities, and deeds are not used to violate and destroy but to establish relations and create new realities" (Arendt 1958, 200). Power, then, is benign and operates for the good of the community.

Arendt distinguishes power from strength, which she defines as the property of an individual, and from force, which she holds should be reserved for reference to the forces of nature or the force of circumstances [i.e., "the energy released by physical or social movements" (Arendt 1969, 44–45)]. She also distinguishes power from authority, which she sees as an unquestioning recognition by the one who must obey. Perhaps most important in this context, she distinguishes power from violence, which she argues is close to strength, but is distinguished by its instrumental character. Exercises of power, like action, need no justification because power is an end in itself, whereas violence, because of its instrumental character, does need justification, and "even if justified can never be legitimate" (Arendt 1969, 51–52).

Arendt makes several important claims about the relations of power and violence: (1) violence can destroy power; (2) violence and power are opposites; (3) violence and power are most commonly found together. Violence is always capable of destroying power, and this destruction can end in the use of what she terms "terror" to maintain domination—that is, a form of government that, having destroyed all power, all the ability of citizens to come together to act as a group, atomizes the populace and isolates them from each other. Thus, tyrannies are characterized by the powerlessness of subjects who have lost the human capacity to speak and act together (Arendt 1958, 203). Tyrannies are political systems that have destroyed community. Despite the fact that violence can destroy power, the most common forms of government rest only to some extent on violence and depend as well on the power behind the violence.[10] Indeed this is one of the reasons for the confusion of power with violence; a special case, the power of government, a monopolizer of (legitimate) violence, has been mistaken for the general (Arendt 1969, 47).

Second, violence and power are opposites, and where the one rules, the other does not appear. Violence occurs when power is in jeopardy (Arendt 1969, 56).[11] Implicit in her claims about the opposition of violence and power are several other oppositions or dualities, among them the fact that power is an end in itself, whereas violence is not; that power is only possible in a community and that violence destroys community; that power is a potential, and can only be actualized in word and deed (perhaps even for the common good), whereas violence can be stored up and unleashed without regard to community and can be the action of a single individual. As Arendt has so tellingly stated, "Real political action comes out as a group act" (Arendt 1979, 310).

Third, despite their deep opposition, power and violence are often found together. This argument undermines Arendt's case that the two are in fact opposites: nothing is less common, she holds, than to find power and violence in their pure forms (Arendt 1969, 47). Despite her claim that the distinction between the two is not "watertight," her general effort to distinguish the two is undermined by this admission (Arendt 1979, 325). The significance of her effort to distinguish power from violence emerges in her discussion of the close connection between power and community. Because violence is a denial of community, it represents for her a denial of the possibility of political action. As such, it must be understood as fundamentally opposed to power.

With this move, her account of power leads us once again back to questions of community—a community in which power functions as a kind of glue. Power springs up whenever people come together and act, and its legitimacy comes from the act of creating a community (Arendt 1969, 52). Since power comes into being with, and represents, in a sense, the end or purpose of the community, power is what holds the community together. It is what keeps the public realm in existence since without being talked about by men, the world would no longer contain the possibilities of immortality and community and would degenerate into a "heap of unrelated things" (Arendt 1958, 200 and 204). Without power, the space of appearances constructed by action and speech would fade away as quickly as the speech itself (Arendt 1958, 200, 204). Finally, power, like the constitution of the *polis* or public space, enables the individual to overcome his individual death and to in a sense live on as a part of the community (Arendt 1969, 27).

These modifications of the agonal model of politics and power share some important features with the ideas of several other theorists of power. Dorothy Emmet argues that power as a key concept of social science should be distinguished from domination, since the production of intended effects need not be the achievement of intended effects through coercing other people (Emmet 1953–1954, 4). She criticizes Bertrand Russell, among others, because although he attempts to define power as a generic form of energy, he discusses only what Emmet terms domination (Emmet 1953–1954, 5). Emmet points in particular to the "dislogistic associations of power with domination," which are "carried over into discussions of other aspects of power" (Emmet 1953–1954, 8). She, relying in turn on Mary Parker Follett's distinction between "power over" and "power with," or "coercive" and "coactive" power, discusses the advantages of freeing the latter from its association with domination (Emmet 1953–1954, 9). This in turn allows her to suggest that it might be more helpful in understanding power to notice the variety of meanings of the word. She suggests a rough typology of power as (1) causal efficacy, (2) creative energy, (3) personal influence, (4) ritual power, and (5) legal power. In contrast to giving attention to the varieties of power she has pointed to, Emmet argues that most theorists have devoted attention only to what she characterizes as a subtype of group 1, type 1b—power as psychological pressure, manipulation, and domination by means other than naked force (Emmet 1953–1954, 13, 26). Emmet carries her case further with an argument that those who have theorized about power are usually so concerned with type 1b that "they hardly notice that there is a distinction between the power some people have of stimulating activity in others and raising their morale and the power which consists in moulding the opinions and practices of others through various forms of psychological pressure" (Emmet 1953–1954, 13–14). Although she recognizes that the two may shade into each other, she holds that they are recognizably different.

She shares with Arendt the sense that political power goes beyond the power of coercion, although she does not go so far as Arendt in her refusal to define power as domination. She does share the conviction that "the power of coercion is only effective when it reinforces the prestige of a general respect for authority" and that if a population is determined to make the power of a government ineffective, it has a good chance of succeeding despite superior forms of coercion available to the state (Emmet 1953–1954, 15–16).

In addition, Emmet's discussion of power shares with Arendt's an emphasis on the relation of power and community. Power, she too believes, is not a thing but a capacity or relation between people (Emmet 1953–1954, 19). She is also concerned to discuss the way the exercise of ritual power can make for the coherence of a community. She cites the example of the coronation of Queen Elizabeth as a ritual that "gathered up a number of the aspects of the non-coercive kinds of power" (Emmet 1953–1954, 18). She has hopes for a redefinition of power as a way of referring to "any kind of effectiveness in performance" but also wants to include the aspect of psychological or psychic energy or *mana* (Emmet 1953–1954, 22, 24–26).

What is important for my purposes is the emphasis her analysis, like Arendt's, gives to the relation of power to community, to the argument that power is not something possessed or stored up, and to the rejection of power as domination (or, rather, her stress on aspects of power other than domination). Her theorization of power both as creative energy and her stress in more operational terms on the ways it can be manifested— through production of ideas or art, through stimulating productive effort in others, and through a heightening of vitality—coupled with her effort to find terms with which to refer to power as "effectiveness" move her theory beyond Arendt's and lead her to a central focus on effectiveness rather than potential or capacity. Thus, one can, on the basis of Emmet's theory, find a number of interesting common threads of concern in her theory and in Arendt's. Still, Emmet does not downplay effective action or replace it with the capacity to act in concert.

Hanna Pitkin, in her discussion of the contributions a "Wittgensteinian perspective and Austinian tools of analysis" could make to political science, briefly examines the concept of power (Pitkin 1972, 275). It is interesting that she explicitly relies on Dorothy Emmet's suggestion that power is better thought of as a "capacity" word rather than a "thing" word, and shows the linguistic support for the suggestion that "power over" may differ significantly from the concept of "power to." Specifically, she points to the fact that "power over" is inherently relational. This differentiates it from the power to act, since one may have the power to do something alone (Pitkin 1972, 276–277). Thus, Pitkin too can be said to recognize explicitly the close connection of power to community, and call our attention to an aspect of power other than domination, power as capacity to act. In addition, her use of Emmet's argument and Emmet's use of Follett's earlier argument suggests the existence of a common historical thread linking the few women who have theorized about power.

The commonality of these three writers around questions of power has been echoed by more explicitly feminist theorists: One finds an understanding of power as energy and competence rather than dominance in a number of works by feminist theorists (Carroll 1972; Hartsock 1974; Janeway 1980; Rothschild 1976). Thus, for example, Berenice Carroll argues, in a style very similar to that adopted by Emmet, that it is time to say farewell to the understanding of power as dominance (Carroll 1972, 605). Again, with Emmet, she argues that "to be without the power of dominance is perceived as being very nearly without the power to act at all, or at least as being without the power to act effectively" (Carroll 1972, 607). Carroll's case is more extreme than Emmet's, but, like Emmet, she puts forward an inventory of the "powers of the allegedly powerless." These include (1) disintegrative power; (2) inertial power; (3) innovative power, norm-creating power; (4) legitimizing, integrative power, or socializing power; (5) expressive power; (6) explosive power; (7) power of resistance; (8) collective power, cooperative power; (9) migratory power, population power (Carroll 1972, 608–609). Carroll's discussion of the powers of the powerless is offered as "a beginning toward reinterpreting the idea of power in terms of competence instead of dominance" (Carroll 1972, 614), and she concludes by citing Arendt's argument that the conception of power as dominance is partial and misleading and that one must not take the question of who rules whom to be the most critical political issue (Carroll 1972, 615).

The common thread connecting the theorizations and tendencies I have discussed is the writers' concern to argue against the understanding of power simply as dominance or domination; to attempt to point to other meanings of the term more associated with ability, capacity, and competence; and to urge reconsideration of assumptions about power. In every case, what has been emphasized are understandings of power that move away from an exclusive focus on domination. These reunderstandings of power, like Arendt's reformulation, are not without difficulties. First, there is a consistent tendency to refuse to confront the problems attendant on acting on or changing the world, the problem of the possibility of doing harm to others by one's actions.[12] Second, by stressing power as energy, capacity, and effectiveness, these arguments have a tendency to direct attention away from relations of domination that must be confronted. Finally, all these theories fail to address directly the genderedness of power and its importance in structuring social relations.

Despite these difficulties, I believe it is significant that such a large proportion of the theorists who make these moves and express these concerns are women. Although very few women have addressed the issue of power, I have found none who does not give at least some attention, if not central place, to the understanding of power as energy or ability.[13] There seems to be a dialogue or at least some evidence of a series of common concerns and common inclinations among these women to shift the discussion away from analyses of domination. What is striking is that the theorists considered here would seem to have little else in common. Both their theoretical interests and their political commitments and inclinations differ profoundly.

If differing life experiences lead to differing world views, the systematic differences between the theoretical accounts of power produced by women and men can be taken to be indications of systematic and significant differences in life activity that have epistemological content and consequences.[14]

Foucault on Power: A Theory for Women?

Although those women who have theorized about power have stressed aspects of power other than domination, there are, as I noted above, problems with these accounts. There remain many open questions. If women, writing from the perspective of a dominated group, understand power in different ways than most men who write about power, perhaps resources for a more adequate theorization can be found in other literatures. For example, can the accounts of domination written out of other experiences of domination and resistances to domination make fruitful contributions to a theorization of power that can be politically useful? What might such a theory look like? What kinds of common claims can be made about white women and women of color, about women and men of color, about Western peoples and those they have colonized? In the effort to develop more adequate theories of power, useful to the dominated, one might expect helpful guidance from those who have argued against totalizing and universalistic theories that have structured the dominant theoretical discourse in Western societies.

Many radical intellectuals have been attracted to a series of diverse writings ranging from literary criticism to the social sciences, generally termed postmodern. The writers, among them figures such as Foucault,

Derrida, Rorty, and Lyotard, argue against the faith in a universal reason we have inherited from Enlightenment European philosophy. They reject stories that claim to encompass all of human history: As Lyotard puts it, "Let us wage war on totality" (Lyotard 1984, 81). In its place they propose a social criticism that is *ad hoc*, contextual, plural, and limited. A number of feminist theorists have joined in the criticism of modernity put forward by these writers. They have endorsed their claims about what can and cannot be known or said or read into/from texts. Despite their apparent congruence with the project of understanding how power relations have been structured for the purpose of resisting (and perhaps transforming these relations), I will argue these theories would hinder rather than help.

Foucault's writing on power is one example of a postmodern theorization in which many feminists see an important resource for reformulating understandings of power, but in my view, his account of power in the end subverts the project. Foucault is a complex thinker, and I propose to make just two points about his work. First, despite his obvious sympathy for those who are subjugated in various ways, he writes from the perspective of the dominator, what I call "the self-proclaimed majority." Second and related, perhaps in part because power relations are less visible to those who are in a position to dominate others, systematically unequal relations of power ultimately vanish from Foucault's account of power—a strange and ironic charge to make against someone who is attempting to illuminate power relations.[15]

Foucault's world is not my world but is a world in which things move, rather than people, a world in which active subjects become re-created as passive objects, a world in which passivity or refusal represent the only possible choices. Thus, Foucault writes, the confession "detached itself" from religion and "emigrated" toward pedagogy (Foucault 1978, 68), or he notes that "hypotheses offer themselves" (Foucault 1980, 91). Moreover, he argues that not only do subjects cease to be sovereign but also that external forces such as power are given access even to the body and thus are the forces that constitute the subject as a kind of effect (Foucault 1978, 142–143).

Edward Said has argued that one's concept of power is importantly shaped by the reason one wishes to think about power in the first place. First, he suggests, you might imagine what you could do if you had power. Second, you might speculate about what you would imagine if you had power. Third, you might want to assess what power you would need to initiate a new order. Or, fourth, you might want to postulate a range of things outside any form of power we presently understand. Foucault, he argues correctly, is attracted by the first two. Thus, Foucault's imagination of power is "with" rather than "against" power (Said 1986, 151). Said gives no "textual" evidence to support his assertions. But I believe there are a number of indications that Foucault is "with power," that is, understands the world from the perspective of the rulers. First, from the perspective of the ruling groups, other "knowledges" would appear to be illegitimate or "not allowed to function within official knowledge," as Foucault himself says of workers' knowledge (Foucault 1977, 219). They would appear to be, as Foucault has variously categorized them, "insurrectionary," "disordered," "fragmentary," lacking "autonomous life" (Foucault 1980, 81, 85–86). To simply characterize the variety of "counter-discourses" or "antisciences" as nonsystematic negates the fact that they rest on organized and indeed material bases (Said 1986, 154). Second, and related, Foucault calls only for resistance and exposure of the system of power relations. Moreover, he is often vague about what exactly this means. Thus, he argues only that one should "entertain the claims" of subjugated knowledges or bring them "into play" (Foucault 1980, 83, 85). Specifically, he argues that the task for intellectuals is less to become part of movements for fundamental change and more to struggle against the forms of power that can transform these movements into instruments of domination.

Perhaps this stress on resistance rather than transformation is due to Foucault's profound pessimism. Power appears to him as ever expanding and invading. It may even attempt to "annex" the counter-discourses that have developed (Foucault 1980, 88). The dangers of going beyond resistance to power are nowhere more clearly stated than in Foucault's response to one interviewer who asked what might replace the present system. He responded that to even imagine another system is to extend our participation in the present system (Foucault 1977, 230; 1980, 84–85). Foucault, then, despite his stated aims of producing an account of power that will enable and facilitate resistance and opposition, instead adopts the position of what he has termed official knowledge with regard to the knowledge of the dominated and reinforces the relations of domination in our society by insisting that those of us who have been marginalized in various ways remain at the margins.

The result of these positions is that power becomes evanescent, and systematic power relations ultimately vanish from his work. This may be related to my first point: domination, viewed from above, is more likely to appear as equality. Foucault has a great deal to say about what exactly he means by power. Power

> must be understood in the first instance as the multiplicity of force relations immanent in the sphere in which they operate and which constitute their own organization; as the process which, through ceaseless struggles and confrontations, transforms, strengthens, or reverses them; or on the contrary, the disjunctions and contradictions which isolate them from one another; and lastly, as the strategies in which they effect (Foucault 1978, 92–93).

(A very complicated definition.) He goes on to argue that power is "permanent, repetitious, and self reproducing. It is not a thing acquired but rather exists in its exercise. Moreover, power relations are not separate from other relations but are contained within them." At the same time (and perhaps contradictorily) power relations are both intentional and subjective, although Foucault is careful to point out that there is no head-quarters which sets the direction (Foucault 1980, 97). His account of power is perhaps unique in that he argues that wherever there is power, there is resistance.

Much of what Foucault has to say about power stresses the systematic nature of power and its presence in multiple social relations. At the same time, however, his stress on heterogeneity and the specificity of each situation leads him to lose track of social structures and instead to focus on how individuals experience and exercise power. Individuals, he argues, circulate among the threads of power. They "are always in the position of simultaneously undergoing and exercising this power" (Foucault 1980, 98). Individuals are to be seen not as an atom that power strikes, but rather the fact that certain bodies and discourses are constituted as individuals is an effect of power. Thus, power must not be seen as either a single individual dominating others or as one group or class dominating others (Foucault 1980, 98).

With this move Foucault has made it very difficult to locate domination, including domination in gender relations. He has on the one hand claimed that individuals are constituted by power relations, but he has argued against their constitution by relations such as the domination of one group by another. That is, his account makes room only for abstract individuals, unmarked individuals who historically have been male, Euroamericans of a certain class.

Foucault takes yet another step toward making power disappear when he proposes the image of a net as a way to understand power. For example, he argues that the nineteenth-century family should be understood as a "network of pleasures and powers linked together at multiple points," a formulation that fails to take account of the important power differentials within that family (Foucault 1978, 45). The image of the net ironically allows (even facilitates) his ignoring of power relations while claiming to elucidate them. Thus, he argues that power is exercised generally through a "net-like organization" and that individuals "circulate between its threads" (Foucault 1980, 98). Domination is not a part of this image; rather, the image of a network in which we all participate carries implications of equality and participation rather than the systematic domination of the many by the few. Moreover, at times Foucault seems to suggest that not only are we equals but that those of us at the bottom are in some sense responsible for our situations: power, he argues, comes from below. There is no binary opposition between rulers and ruled, but rather manifold relations of force that take shape in the machinery of production, or families, and so forth, and then become the basis for "wide ranging effects of cleavage that run through the social body as a whole" (Foucault 1978, 94). Certainly in the analysis of power, Foucault argues that rather than begin from the center or the top—sovereignty—one should con- duct an ascending analysis of power, starting from the "infinitesimal mecha- nisms," each of which have their own history. One can then see how these have been colonized and transformed into more global forms of domination. It is certainly true that dominated groups participate in their own domina- tion. But rather than stop with the fact of participation, we would learn a great deal more by focusing on the means by which this participation is exacted. Foucault's argument for an "ascending analysis" of power could lead us to engage in a version of blaming the victim.

Finally, Foucault asserts that power must be understood as "capillary," that it must be analyzed at its extremities (Foucault 1980, 95). But the image of capillary power is one that points to the conclusion that power is everywhere. After all, in physical terms, where do we not have capillaries? Indeed, Foucault frequently uses language that argues that power "per- vades the entire social body" or is "omnipresent" (Foucault 1978, 92–93). Thus, all of social life comes to be a network of power relations—relations that should be analyzed not at the level of large-scale social structures but rather at very local, individual levels. Moreover, Foucault notes important resemblances between such diverse things as schools and prisons, or the development of sexuality in the family and the institutions of "perversion." The whole thing comes to look very homogeneous. Power is everywhere, and so ultimately nowhere.

In the end, Foucault appears to endorse a one-sided wholesale rejec- tion of modernity and to do so without a conception of what is to replace it. Indeed, some have argued persuasively that because Foucault refuses both the ground of foundationalism and the "ungrounded hope" endorsed by liberals such as Richard Rorty, he stands on no ground at all and thus fails to give any reasons for resistance. Foucault suggests that if our resistance succeeded, we would simply be changing one discursive identity for another and in the process create new oppressions (Horowitz 1987, 63–64).

The "majority" and those like Foucault who adopt the perspective of the "majority" or the powerful can probably perform the greatest possible political service by resisting and by refusing the overconfidence of the past. But the message they send is either that one should abandon the project of modernity and substitute a conversation (as Rorty suggests) or that the only option is to adopt a posture of resistance. But if we are not to abandon the project of creating a new and more just society, neither of these options will work for us.

Requirements/Resources for Theorizing Power

FEMINISTS NEED TO do something other than ignore power relations (as Rorty does) or resist them as figures such as Foucault and Lyotard sug- gest. We need to transform them and to do so, we need a revised and reconstructed theory (indebted to Marx among others) with several important features.

First, rather than getting rid of subjectivity or notions of the subject, as Foucault does—we need to substitute his notion of the individual as an effect of power relations, of subjectivity as subjection; we need to engage in the historical, political, and theoretical process of constituting ourselves as subjects as well as objects of history. We need to recognize that we have the possibility to make history, as well as to exist as the objects of those who have made history. The point is to develop an account of the world that treats our perspectives not as subjugated or simply disruptive knowledges but as primary and constitutive of a different world, an account that exposes the distortions of the view from above.

It may be objected that I am calling for the construction of another totalizing and falsely universal discourse. But that is to be imprisoned by the alternatives imposed by Enlightenment thought and postmodernism: Either one must adopt the perspective of the transcendental and disembodied voice of "reason" or must abandon the goal of accurate and systematic knowledge of the world. Other possibilities must be (perhaps can only be) developed by feminists and by a number of hitherto marginalized voices. I believe that feminists can learn a great deal from other groups attempting to understand the workings of systematic relations of domination: although there are important differences in lived experience, there may be important similarities and commonalities.

Moreover, our shared history of marginalization and oppression will work against the creation of a totalizing discourse. This is not to argue that oppression creates "better" people: On the contrary, the experience of domination and marginalization leaves many scars. Rather, it is to note that marginalized groups are far less likely to mistake themselves for the universal "man." But even if we will not make the mistake of assuming our experience of the world is the experience of all, we still need to name and describe our diverse experiences. What are our commonalities? What are our differences? How can we transform our imposed otherness into self-defined specificities?

Second, we must do our work on an epistemological base that indicates that knowledge is possible—not just conversation or a discourse on how it is that power relations work. Conversation as a goal is fine; understanding how power works in oppressive societies is important. But if we are to construct a new society, we need to be assured that some systematic knowledge about our world and ourselves is possible. Those critical of modernity can call into question whether we ever really knew the world (and a good case can be made that "they" at least did not). They are in fact right that they have not known the world as it is rather than as they wished and needed it to be; they created their world not only in their own image but in the image of their fantasies. To create a world that expresses our own various and diverse images, we need to understand how it works.[16]

Third, we need a theory of power that recognizes that our practical daily activity contains an understanding of the world—subjugated perhaps, but present. Here I am reaffirming Gramsci's argument that everyone is an intellectual and that each of us has an epistemology. The point, then, for subjugated groups is to "read out" the epistemologies in our various practices. I have argued elsewhere for a "standpoint" epistemology—an account of the world with great similarities to Marx's fundamental stance (Hartsock 1983a, 1983b). Although I would modify some of what I argued there, I would still insist that we must not give up the claim that material life, embodied in our daily practices, not only structures but sets limits on the understanding of social relations, and that, in systems of domination, the vision available to the rulers will be both partial and distorted.

Despite the fact that much remains to be done, we have moved a certain distance toward a more adequate and liberatory understanding of power. Such a theory would need to give an account of how social institutions have come to be controlled by only one gender; it would locate the points at which conflicts between women and men are generated, and make clear the specific relations between individual intentional actions and structural constraints. As a theory that took account of the perspectives and experiences of a number of dominated groups it would point to commonalities and points of contact across differences. By locating the sources of women's oppression in history and material life, by encompassing the concrete and varied specificities of women's lives, it could provide the terrain on which both the commonalities of women's situations and differences of race, class, and sexuality could be understood. It would neither reduce power to domination nor ignore systematic domination to stress only energy and community.

Despite the fact that such a theorization remains to be achieved, it is possible to say something about some features of such a theory and to point to a variety of resources that could contribute to its construction. One important resource for such a theory is the recapture of the possibilities Audre Lorde has described as inherent in the mythic personage of Eros—"born of Chaos, and personifying creative power and harmony. When I speak of the erotic, then I speak of it as an assertion of the life-force of women" (Lorde 1978, 3–4). Feminist reformulations of *eros* not only can take positive forms but can take over and transform the terrain of work. Marxian theory provides some guidance as to what this might mean. Marx's stress on sensuality as well as community suggests that there may be an erotic pleasure available in work itself—in all the various senses of the term—sensual, bodily, creative, and in community with others. It is worth noting that the Marxian account of unalienated production includes the erotic joys of work itself—the making of an object that expresses one's life force, or *eros*. This account also stresses the importance of another or others with whom to share the object, and for whom it can be a means to satisfy their needs, and thus underlines the importance of community.

Audre Lorde has put forward strikingly similar arguments. She writes, "We are taught to separate the erotic demand from most vital areas of our lives other than sex." As a result, she holds, our work is robbed of its erotic value (Lorde 1978, 3). She describes the possible empowering erotic nature of work: sharing of a pursuit that can in turn lessen the other differences between the participants and an acceptance of and "underlining of [the] capacity for joy" (Lorde 1978, 5). In these suggestive statements of the erotic possibilities contained in work as well as other aspects of our lives, we can begin to see some of the outlines of an understanding of power that stresses both its dimensions of competence, ability, and creativity and does not lose sight of the importance of effective action in the world, action at least in part defined by its sensuality and its variety of connections and relations with others in the community.

A second resource for a theory of power centered on *eros* could be located in a better understanding of women's sexuality. Yet because what our culture has constructed as sexuality expresses masculine experience, we are only at the beginning of the necessary research and discussion.[17] Contemporary arguments about the nature of a "feminist sexuality" have so far produced little more than polarization.[18] Yet these arguments both raise the issue of what sexual women might look like and also illustrate how *eros*, even in negative forms, poses different problems for women than for men. Because of masculine hegemony, one would expect that women's sexual excitement too would depend on hostility and transgression, and to some extent this is true. But even among feminists whose sexual excitement has been characterized as deeply structured by masculinist patterns, there is some evidence to support the contention that women are less perverse than men, that is, that women's sexual excitement depends less than men's on victimization and revenge.[19]

Contemporary feminist efforts to understand and remake difference represent a third important area in which to find resources for a more adequate theorization of power. The collective effort to recognize and use differences has taken the form of efforts on the one hand to reject claims of commonality and universality—which in fact make invisible women of color or lesbians—and on the other to prevent differences from taking the form of radical alterity. Here, too, Audre Lorde is the source of important advice: "Advocating the mere tolerance of difference between women is . . . a total denial of the creative function of difference in our lives. For difference must be not merely tolerated, but seen as a fund of necessary polarities between which our creativity can spark like a dialectic. Only then does the necessity for interdependency become unthreatening" (Lorde 1981, 99). Discussions have recently turned to questions that go beyond issues of difference simply among women and have suggested that the fields created by intersecting axes of domination provide a rich source of information about and theorizations of the possibilities for an expanded discussion of the nature and importance of systematic social lines of fault.

Directions in which a more adequate understanding of power must move are visible, if only hazily. Our understanding of power must be rooted in and defined not simply by women's experience but by the systematic pulling together and working out of the liberatory possibilities present in that experience. Such an understanding of power would recognize that relations with another may take a variety of forms, forms not structured fundamentally by alterity but distinction. The body—its desires and needs, and its mortality—would not be denied as shameful but would be given a place of honor at the center of the theory. And creativity and generation would be incorporated in the form of directly valuing daily life activities—eroticizing work and accepting the erotic nature of nurturance. Given my contention that life activity structures understanding, however, such a theory may remain only a rudimentary vision in a world structured by systematic domination and alienation. Thus, like Marx's brief statements about his vision of the nature of unalienated production, the development of a feminist theory of power must stand as a challenge for action.

Notes

1. I should note at the outset that I have many difficulties with the positions Stoller takes and I note them here in part to indicate that the points I take from him and use are just that and not an endorsement of the system of thought he puts forward. In particular, I oppose his unquestioning acceptance of the existence of the vaginal orgasm (Stoller 1979, 88; Stoller 1975, 23); his stress on the centrality of maternal responsibility in producing "normal" heterosexuals (Stoller 1975, 138, 154, 161); and his account of how people become homosexuals (Stoller 1975, 153). Nor do I share his concerns: I do not believe that homosexuality should be considered either a perversion or a diagnosis, and I am not interested in the psychological origins of gender identity (Stoller 1975, xvi, 199ff.) At times as well, Stoller's discussion is marred by a masculinist understanding of the world, e.g., his statement that "it is hard to imagine a little girl, confronted with this task, who would not envy boys and their aggressive, penetrating, hedonistic, arrogant, unfettered, God-granted, antisocial, unsympathetic, humiliating penis" (Stoller 1979, 74). Thus he seems to accept without question the social and cultural meanings associated with the penis.

2. Andrea Dworkin (1979, 182) adds that the reference in Kinsey et al. (1953, 705) indicates that this physiology is true of both males and females. Her own style of presentation suggests that she does not believe this to be true.

3. We should not be surprised to find this violence deeply ingrained in language itself: the best known of the vulgar sexual verbs comes from the German *flicken*, meaning "to strike"; similar violent verbs are present in Latin, Celtic, Irish, Gaelic, and so forth; and consider other contemporary English terms, such as "screw" or "bang" (Lawrence 1975, 32).

4. But see for example Rubin (1981, 1989).

5. If these are the dynamics of "normal" heterosexual excitement, we can begin to understand both the existence of rape and rape fantasies and the widespread depiction of violence against women for purposes of arousing sexual excitement.

6. But see Rubin (1981).

7. I do not mean to suggest that women are simply victims in anything like the way MacKinnon (1989) does. I am instead pointing to large-scale cultural definitions that individual women must confront and that many feminists have chosen to resist.

8. I am not alone in noticing the similarity to Marx (Bakan, 1979, 49; Arendt, 1979, 325–326).

9. See also Arendt (1958, 200).

10. This is what Arendt defines as opinion (1969, 49). She holds that even the power of masters over slaves rested on a "superior organization of power—that is, on the organized solidarity of the masters" (1969, 50). She points out that Vietnam showed the helplessness of superiority in means of violence, in the fact that power is of the essence of all government (1969, 51).

11. In another context, she argues that what undermines political communities is the loss of power and the substitution of violence (Arendt 1958, 200).

12. See Kateb (1977, 174–177), for a discussion of the harmful consequences of this move.

13. A few men have put forward similar arguments (Bay 1968; Connolly 1974; Russell 1938), but they represent a minority of the men who have written on the subject. (Interestingly enough, these theorists would probably describe themselves as socialists.)

14. For a more developed articulation of the claim that gender-based differences in life experiences carry epistemological and potentially political consequences, see Hartsock (1983a, 1983b). Others have stressed particular activities such as mothering (Ruddick 1990), caretaking (Gilligan 1982, Tronto 1993), reproduction (O'Brien 1981), being daughters (Chodorow 1978).

15. Although I lack the space to make important qualifications about my understanding of Foucault I made some effort at a more balanced presentation elsewhere (Hartsock 1989).

16. My language requires that I insert qualification and clarification: I do not mean to suggest that white Western women share the material situation of the colonized peoples but rather to argue that we share similar positions in the ideology of the Enlightenment.

17. See the articles in the special issues on sexuality published by several journals: Alderfer et al. (1981); Padgug (1979b); Stimpson, Stanton, and Burstyn (1980); Stimpson and Person (1980).

18. See for example Rubin (1981), and *Off Our Backs* 12 (6) (1982).

19. Thus one finds that the lesbian proponents of sadomasochism hold that "the desire to be sexual and the desire to be combative are complexly intertwined" (Farr 1981, 183). Yet, in their fiction and autobiographical statements, one can see echoes of a different experience. In terms of *eros* one finds that in terms of fusion with another, empathy with the other partner receives far more attention than separation from the other by means of domination and submission (Califia 1980a, 1980b; Hollibaugh and Moraga 1980). Rather than treat the body as a loathsome reminder of mortality whose needs must be projected onto the body of another, the rejection of the body takes the form of a need for permission to enjoy the pleasures of the flesh without guilt or responsibility (Califia 1980b, 167; Califia 1981, 131; Rubin 1981, 215; Schmuckler 1981, 98–99; Zoftig 1981, 88, 93). In sum, it can be said that, for women, the cultural construction of sexuality shapes even the negative forms of *eros* in less dangerous ways than for men.

References

Alderfer, Hannah et al., eds. 1981. *Sex Issue.* Special issue #12, *Heresies: A Feminist Publication on Art & Politics* 3 (4).

Arendt, Hannah. 1958. *The Human Condition.* Chicago: University of Chicago Press.

Arendt, Hannah. 1969. *On Violence.* New York: Harcourt, Brace, and World.

Arendt, Hannah. 1979. "Hannah Arendt on Hannah Arendt." In *Hannah Arendt: The Recovery of the Public World.* Ed. Melvyn Hill. New York: St. Martin's Press.

Bakan, Mildred. 1979. "Hannah Arendt's Concepts of Labor and Work." In *Hannah Arendt: The Recovery of the Public World.* Ed. Melvyn Hill. New York: St. Martin's Press.

Barry, Kathleen. 1979. *Female Sexual Slavery.* New York: Avon Books.

Bataille, Georges. 1977. *Death and Sensuality.* New York: Arno Press.

Bay, Christian. 1968. *The Structures of Freedom.* New York: Atheneum.

Butler, Judith. 1990. *Gender Trouble.* New York: Routledge.

Califia, Pat. 1980a. "Feminism and Sadomasochism." *Heresies* 12: 30–34.

Califia, Pat. 1980b. *Sapphistry.* New York: Naiad Press.

Califia, Pat. 1981. "Jessie." In *Coming to Power.* Ed. Samois. Palo Alto, Calif.: Up Press

Carroll, Berenice. 1972. "Peace Research: The Cult of Power." *Journal of Conflict Resolution* 16 (4):585–616

Chodorow, Nancy. 1978. *The Reproduction of Mothering.* Berkeley: University of California Press.

Connolly, William. 1974. *The Terms of Political Discourse.* Lexington, Mass.: D. C. Heath.

Dworkin, Andrea. 1979. *Pornography: Men Possessing Women.* New York: Putnam's.

Emmet, Dorothy. 1953–1954. "The Concept of Power." *Proceedings of the Aristotelian Society* 54:1–26.

English, Deirdre, Amber Hollibaugh and Gayle Rubin. 1981. "Talking Sex: A Conversation on Sexuality and Feminism." *Socialist Review* 11 (4):43–62.

Farr, Susan. 1981. "The Art of Discipline: Creating Erotic Dramas of Play and Power." In *Coming to Power*. Ed. Samois. Palo Alto, Calif.: Up Press.

Foucault, Michel. 1977. *Language, Counter-Memory, Practice: Selected Essays and Interviews*. Ed. Donald Bouchard. Ithaca, N.Y.: Cornell University Press.

Foucault, Michel. 1978. *The History of Sexuality: An Introduction*. New York: Pantheon.

Foucault, Michel. 1980. *Power/Knowledge*. Ed. Colin Gordon. New York: Pantheon.

Gebhard, Paul et al. 1965. *Sex Offenders: An Analysis of Types*. New York: Harper and Row.

Gilligan, Carol. 1982. *In a Different Voice: Psychological Theory and Women's Development*. Cambridge, Mass.: Harvard University Press.

Hartsock, Nancy C.M. 1974. "Political Change: Two Perspectives on Power." *Quest: A Feminist Quarterly* 1 (1):10–25.

Hartsock, Nancy C.M. 1983a. *Money, Sex, and Power: Toward a Feminist Historical Materialism*. New York: Longman.

Hartsock, Nancy C.M. 1983b. "The Feminist Standpoint: Developing the Ground for a Specifically Feminist Historical Materialism." In *Discovering Reality: Feminist Perspectives on Epistemology, Metaphysics, Methology, and Philosophy of Science*. Ed. Sandra Harding and Merrill B. Hintikka. Dordrecht, The Netherlands: D. Reidel.

Hartsock, Nancy C.M. 1989. "Foucault on Power: A Theory for Women?" In *Feminism/Postmodernism*. Ed. Linda Nicholson. New York: Routledge.

Hollibaugh, Amber and Cherríe Moraga. 1980. "What We're Rollin' Around in Bed With." *Heresies* 13:58–62.

Horowitz, Gad. 1987. "The Foucaultian Impasse: No Sex, No Self, No Revolution." *Political Theory* 15:61–81.

Janeway, Elizabeth. 1980. *Powers of the Weak*. New York: Alfred A. Knopf.

Kateb, George. 1977. "Freedom and Worldliness in the Thought of Hannah Arendt." *Political Theory* 5 (2):141–182.

Kinsey, Alfred C. et al. 1953. *Sexual Behavior in the Human Female*. Philadelphia: W. B. Saunders.

Lawrence, Barbara. 1975. "Four-Letter Words Can Hurt You." In *Philosophy and Sex*. Ed. Robert Baker and Frederick Elliston. Buffalo: Prometheus Books.

Lorde, Audre. 1978. *The Uses of the Erotic*. New York: Out and Out Books.

Lorde, Audre. 1981. "The Master's Tools Will Never Dismantle the Master's House." In *This Bridge Called My Back*. Ed. Cherríe Moraga and Gloria Anzaldúa. Watertown, Mass.: Persephone Press.

Lyotard, Jean-François. 1984. *The Post-Modern Condition: A Report on Knowledge*. Minneapolis: University of Minnesota Press.

MacKinnon, Catharine. 1989. *Toward a Feminist Theory of the State*. Cambridge, Mass.: Harvard University Press.

Mannoni, O. 1964. *Prospero and Caliban.* New York: Praeger.

Maslow, A. H. 1942. "Self-Esteem (Dominance-Feeling) and Sexuality in Women." *Journal of Social Psychology* 16:259–294.

Millett, Kate. 1970. *Sexual Politics.* New York: Doubleday.

O'Brien, Mary. 1981. *The Politics of Reproduction.* Boston: Routledge and Kegan Paul.

Padgug, Robert. 1979a. "Sexual Matters: On Conceptualizing Sexuality in History." *Radical History Review* 20:3–23

Padgug, Robert A., ed. 1979b. *Sexuality in History.* Special issue of *Radical History Review* 20 (Spring-Summer)

Pitkin, Hanna. 1972. *Wittgenstein and Justice.* Berkeley: University of California.

Rothschild, Joan. 1976. "Taking Our Future Seriously." *Quest: A Feminist Quarterly* 2 (3):17–30.

Rubin, Gayle. 1981. "The Leather Menace: Comments on Politics and S/M." In *Coming to Power.* Ed. Samois. Palo Alto, Calif.: Up Press.

Rubin, Gayle. 1989. "Thinking Sex: Notes for a Radical Theory of the Politics of Sexuality." In *Pleasure and Danger.* Ed. Carole Vance. New York: Pandora.

Ruddick, Sara. 1990. *Maternal Thinking* Boston: Beacon.

Russell, Bertrand. 1938. *Power.* New York: Norton.

Said, Edward. 1986. "Foucault and the Imagination of Power." In *Foucault: A Critical Reader.* Ed. David Hoy. New York: Pantheon.

Schmuckler, Sophie. 1981. "How I Learned to Stop Worrying and Love My Dildo." In *Coming to Power.* Ed. Samois. Palo Alto, Calif.: Up Press.

Stember, George Herbert. 1976. *Sexual Racism.* New York: Harper and Row.

Stimpson, Catharine R. and Ethel Spector Person, eds. 1980. *Women—Sex and Sexuality, Part I.* Special issue of *Signs: Journal of Women in Culture and Society* 5 (4).

Stimpson, Catharine R., Donna C. Stanton, and Joan N. Burstyn, eds. 1980. *Women—Sex and Sexuality, Part II.* Special issue of *Signs: Journal of Women in Culture and Society* 6 (1).

Stoller, Robert. 1975. *Perversion.* New York: Pantheon.

Stoller, Robert. 1979. *Sexual Excitement: The Dynamics of Erotic Life.* New York: Pantheon.

Tronto, Joan. 1993. *Moral Boundaries: A Political Argument for an Ethic of Care.* New York: Routledge.

Weeks, Jeffrey. 1981. *Sex, Politics, and Society.* Essex: Longman.

Zoftig, Sarah. 1981. "Coming Out." In *Coming to Power.* Ed. Samois. Palo Alto, Calif.: Up Press.

3

Revisioning Freedom

Relationship, Context, and the Politics of Empowerment

Nancy J. Hirschmann

*T*he March 15, 1992 *New York Times* ran an article about a twenty-three-year-old unemployed single mother in West Virginia who became pregnant as a result of date rape.[1] Due to federal policy, she had trouble locating an abortion clinic but finally found one four hours away in Charleston. They told her she was seventeen weeks pregnant, and they performed abortions only until sixteen weeks, so they referred her to a clinic in Cincinnati that would perform an abortion up to nineteen and a half weeks for a cost of $850. When she went there one and a half weeks later, however, they said that she was actually twenty-one weeks pregnant so referred her to a clinic in Dayton that would perform the abortion for $1675. She refinanced her car, sold her VCR, borrowed money, and went to Dayton. They said that she was a high risk patient because of an earlier Caesarean delivery and that she would have to go to Wichita, and it would cost $2500. "I just didn't think I could manage that," she says. "Now that I know I have to have it, I'm trying to get used to the idea ... I'm not thinking about adoption, because I've never understood people having a baby just to give it away. So I've been thinking a lot about trying to love this baby the way I love my daughter." Can we say that this woman has freely chosen her role as mother?

A woman in Philadelphia is beaten by her husband and goes to a battered women's shelter. This is the second time in a year that this woman has come to the shelter. However, she refuses to press charges with the police. And after spending some time at the shelter, during which time her husband has initiated contact with her, she declares her intention to return to him. She says that he has apologized and that she forgives him, that he is basically a good person and has promised to change, that he loves her and is a good father, that she loves him, that it was partly her fault anyway. Is she free if she returns to her husband?

In the movie *Mr. and Mrs. Bridge,* Joanne Woodward plays a woman who seems to subvert herself completely to her husband. She rarely ventures a political opinion, she defers to her husband, she is extremely self-deprecating and has so effectively effaced herself that at the end of the movie, she risks freezing to death while trapped in her car because she won't yell for help. The implication is that she doesn't want to disturb anyone and simply waits passively, until her husband gets home to rescue her. She doesn't appear to be holding these views out of fear or coercion. Her husband is somewhat overbearing but not violent; he doesn't overtly seek to control her; he clearly loves her and demonstrates his consideration and respect in various ways. Is Mrs. Bridge free or not?

Charlene is a lesbian. She is also an attorney with an extremely conservative Wall Street firm that has never had a woman partner. Charlene wants very badly to make partner. Accordingly, she is not open about her sexuality. Her lover, Sally, believes this is a mistake, not only tactically, but from the perspective of personal cost as well. Though Charlene declares that the relationship is more important to her than anything, she has become so fearful about colleagues finding out about their relationship that she and Sally have virtually stopped going out of the house together; and the stress is affecting not only Charlene's health but the relationship as well. Sally is beginning to contemplate "outing" Charlene. She feels that this would liberate Charlene from her fears, her anxiety, her extra stress and save the relationship. Is she right?

Many of us probably have immediate, perhaps even gut-level, reactions to these examples; for instance, most of us would initially say that the pregnant woman is unfree and that Sally is wrong. But I want to suggest that there is really no simple answer to the question of freedom in any of them. Furthermore, I want to suggest that the dominant discourse of freedom in philosophy and political theory—which founds as well as reflects our popular, everyday conceptions—is inadequate to fully encompass these complexities and is gender-biased. I want to suggest that a feminist theory of freedom is necessary not only to understand the relationship of women's experience to existing notions of liberty but also to the construction of a new conception of liberty that can accommodate as well as contest or criticize such experiences.

A Masculinist Theory of Freedom?

IN HIS FAMOUS essay "Two Concepts of Liberty," Isaiah Berlin articulates two theoretical orientations to liberty, namely "negative" and "positive" liberty. According to Berlin, negative liberty consists in an absence of external constraints. The individual is free to the extent that she is not restrained by external forces, primarily viewed as law, physical force, and other overt coercion. "By being free in this sense I mean not being interfered with by others," Berlin says. "The wider the area of non-interference, the wider my freedom" (Berlin 1971, 123). Berlin's general notion that restraints come from outside the self, that they are "other," is an important tenet of negative liberty; other people's direct (or, in some cases, indirect) participation "in frustrating my wishes" is the relevant criterion in determining restraint. For this reason, negative liberty is sometimes called an "opportunity concept" (Taylor 1979); the significant factor in determining whether I am free is that no other person or thing is actually preventing me from doing what I want. Nothing is barring me from taking advantage of opportunities that I would otherwise pursue but for this restraint.

Furthermore, these desires that I must be able to pursue unimpeded if I am to be free are seen as coming from me and from me alone. Desires may be reactions to external stimuli, of course (I may not have a desire to eat a chocolate chip cookie until I happen to smell the ones you have just removed from the oven), but the important fact is that I can identify a desire as *mine*, regardless of *why* I have it. Negative liberty draws clear-cut lines between inner and outer, self and other, subject and object. Desires come from within, restraints from without; desires are formed by subjects, by selves, they are thwarted by objects, by others.

Positive liberty challenges this duality by focusing on what might be called "internal barriers": fears, addictions, compulsions, which are at odds with my "true" self can all inhibit my freedom. This involves qualitative evaluation about our desires: we can have desires that are higher or lower, good or bad, significant or trivial, genuine or false. Because of this, it is not enough to experience an absence of external restraints, because the immediate desires I have may frustrate my true will. For instance, let's say that I have determined to give up smoking or that I am struggling to combat a compulsive eating disorder. We can imagine stressful situations that tempt me to break my resolve by having "just one" cigarette or going on a binge "just this one time." If I really want to quit smoking or stop binging, we could argue that the immediate, short term desires violate my larger, longer term desires that I honestly feel are more important to me. So being able to smoke or binge uninhibited doesn't mean I'm free. Indeed, positive liberty says that when I sneak a cigarette in the bathroom or go on a binge, I am not just weak-willed but "unfree" because I am violating my "real" will, my true desires that I have reflected on at some length. Positive liberty is thus sometimes called an "exercise concept"; we have to exercise our full capacities if we are to be free.

Logically, then, positive liberty also requires that this "strong evaluation" can be performed by others who may know my true will as well as I— indeed, sometimes better than I, particularly when I am in the grip of these self-destructive short-term desires. This leads to the conclusion that these others can "interfere with," or "guide," my actions in order to help me realize my true will and hence to realize my freedom. As you snatch the cigarette from my lips, or lock me out of the kitchen, positive liberty says that such "interference" itself directly enhances my liberty.

Although both positive and negative conceptions inform popular understandings of liberty—after all, most of us can understand, in an everyday sense, how the cheating smoker and the compulsive binger are both free and not free—negative liberty is more common in our dominant conception. As a central element of the ideology of liberalism that characterizes Western democracy—the doctrine of individualism and rights that emerged from the Enlightenment—negative liberty plays a prominent part in the ideological and political landscape of the West. Positive liberty has developed as more of a leftist (though sometimes rightist) reaction to liberalism's individualistic tendencies. As such it might seem that positive liberty has more to offer feminism. For instance, feminists like Carol Gilligan assert that rights have a masculinist bias to them, whereas community is of greater historical importance to women, which might support such a claim (Gilligan 1982; Coole 1993).

But I think both models are gender biased. Furthermore, I maintain that this dualistic typology of positive and negative liberty is theoretically inadequate to deal with many questions raised by women's historical and material experience. Indeed, whereas these two orientations toward liberty are generally seen by political theory as opposed, even mutually exclusive, from a feminist perspective they can be seen to embody similar approaches and assumptions and demonstrate similar problems. Throughout history, theorists of both persuasions generally denied women both the "opportunities" and the "exercise" of freedom; negative liberty theorists such as Hobbes and Locke barred women from public life on the basis of their "natural" inferiority, which meant that they were incapable of forming and acting on rational choice. Women's diminished humanity disqualified them from taking advantage of the "opportunities" of liberal society and required that they be ruled by men. Indeed, women's restraint in the private sphere was one of the things that made negative liberty in the public sphere possible for men. That is, freedom could be defined as abstract choice for men only because women were bound to the aspects of life that are not necessarily chosen. Even Mill, in spite of his remarks against women's subjection, delimited women's freedom more than men by failing to challenge the structural barriers to women's choice. The notion of what counted as a barrier is in some places extended to include social custom and norms, and in other places they are considered natural and self-evident. Like Wollstonecraft, Mill suggested that women learn to be irrational by being denied education and being trained to engage in trivial pursuits; yet, he also seemed to believe that the social construction of motherhood and wifehood in his contemporary times was naturally ordained (Mill 1991, 522–523).

Positive libertarians such as Rousseau and Hegel similarly denied women's rationality, requiring them to adopt very particularized and structured roles within the family as a means of guaranteeing the stability of the state. All people could be free only by following their true will; but women were too emotional to know what their will was. Furthermore, their irrationality confused men and impeded *their* ability to know the true will. So women could "exercise" their greatest freedom only by being restrained in the private realm and allowing men to act for them in the public realm.

Even so, freedom is considered the central concept in at least modern Western political philosophy (Patterson 1991). This freedom is seen as natural and fundamental and indeed is considered the basic starting point, not only for understanding human relations and society, but for defining and justifying other concepts, such as justice, obligation, and rights. This is particularly so in the negative liberty of liberalism, which dominates Western culture. For instance, obligation can be justified only if it is taken on voluntarily, by free agreement, called "consent" or "social contract"; this ignores the historical bonds and "obligations" of women in the private sphere, which were not generally freely choosen (Hirschmann 1992). In liberal theory, the importance of equality is that we are equally free, and rights exist to protect individual spheres of action from outside interference. Yet, that sovereignty is denied to women. Indeed, women's equality has been so persistently and sytematically denied, the rights we have obtained have been so hard won, with such ambiguous results, that many feminist theorists are questioning these concepts altogether.

Similarly, in positive liberty theories, freedom is so all-encompassing that everything seems to come under its umbrella. Equality, obligation, and justice are all subsumed by and serve the ends of positive liberty; and they are defined to exclude women. For instance, in Rousseau's *Emile,* virtue is essential if we are to know our true will and hence be (morally) free; but virtue requires one set of rules for men—independence, strength, activity—and another for women, servitude and passivity. Equality is absolute among men but a "separate-but-equal" doctrine applies to women. Thus rather than deny these concepts to women outright, positive liberty redefines them for women; but the effect is the same.

Of course women are not the only group excluded from these theories of freedom; but the point is that to define the world in terms of a concept that is denied to a majority of the population, namely women, people of color, and the poor, that takes white, economically privileged men as the standard for "humanity," suggests fundamental difficulties in terms of representation and applicability. It suggests that one cannot merely take existing liberty theories, "add women, and stir." Rather, it suggests the need to rethink what we mean by freedom.

The Paradox of Social Construction

I START THIS rethinking by challenging the naturalist basis to freedom. In claiming that freedom discourse falsely universalizes a highly particularistic notion of humanity—white, economically privileged men—I invoke a notion sometimes called "social construction." The idea of social construction is that human beings and their world are in no sense given or natural but the product of historical configurations of relationships. The desires and preferences we have, our beliefs and values, our way of defining the world, are all shaped by the particular constellation of personal and institutional social relationships that constitute our individual and collective histories.

Theorists such as Foucault (1990), Derrida (1982), and Lyotard (1979) suggest that we must look at and try to understand these values, concepts, and pictures of reality in their historical contexts. The Wittgensteinian idea that language has meaning only in a "form of life"—in a set of practices that are widely shared among people and that serve as a frame of reference for understanding the words people use—is carried further by poststructuralists such as Foucault and Judith Butler (1990) who argue that even the most intimate and supposedly "internal" aspects of our being, such as our sexuality, must be understood in terms of the historical relations and actions that have imported meaning to our bodies. Context is what makes meaning possible; and meaning makes "reality." Contrary to a Marxist materialism, social constructionism rejects the idea that there is some "true" basic material reality that language and ideology merely subvert; rather, reality itself lies in the ideology and language. Context is—or constructs—our reality.

Thus the value that we place on freedom, as well as the meaning we give to the word, is in no way essential or natural but the product of particular historical relationships that have developed through time. In modern political theory, freedom is a given of the state of nature; it is essential to humanity, a natural right, a basic starting point. The problem is not whether we (men) are (should be) free—that is fundamentally assumed—but how freedom is defined, lived, and experienced. Social construction suggests that the "natural man" of social contract theory, with "his" "natural" freedom and equality, should really be seen as the construct of particular individuals located in particular time and place, specifically, bourgeois white males at the dawn of capitalism and liberal representative democracy. Developed in part as a response to absolutist political authority and emerging political movements for parliamentarian and representative government (motivated in turn by largely economic considerations—see Ashcraft 1986; Kramnick 1990; Macpherson 1962), the emphasis on the individual as the unit of analysis and freedom as noninterference by governments is an understandable (though not the only possible) reaction to contemporary historical and political conditions. Social constructionism does not reject individualism or negative freedom out of hand but merely points out that calling these conceptions natural and timeless obfuscates their origin and meaning, decontextualizes and dehistoricizes, and hides their biases thereby. It is in such hidden biases that the dangers of totalizing representation and the erasure of men and women of color, white women, workers, and the poor lie.

The idea of social construction is particularly important to feminism, for it is key to rejecting patriarchal arguments about men's and women's "natures." Yet, it also poses a paradox. If we are socially constructed, male domination is and has been an important part of that construction; this has resulted in laws, customs, and social rules that come from men and are imposed on women to restrict their opportunities, choices, actions, and behaviors. Further, this construction of social behaviors and rules takes on a life of its own and becomes reality. That is, these rules become constitutive not only of what women are allowed to *do* but to *be* as well: how women are able to think and conceive of themselves, what they can and should desire, what their preferences are. Because our conceptual and material world has been formulated and developed by these masculinist perspectives, such rules are not simply external restrictions on women's otherwise natural desires; rather, they create an entire cultural context that makes women seem to choose what they are restricted to (Coole 1993).

Some, like feminist philosopher Adriana Cavarero, believe this construction of reality takes root in our very language: "Woman is not the subject of her language. Her language is not hers. She therefore speaks and represents herself in a language not her own, that is, through the categories of the language of the other. She thinks herself as thought by the other" (de Lauretis 1989). This is a view shared by many French feminists as well, such as Luce Irigaray (1985) and Julia Kristeva (1986). If the language women speak is not "ours," if it is a language and conceptual vocabulary of identity and being that is specifically masculinist, then our very categories of meaning become barriers to women's self-defintion; our epistemology itself is a restraint because our ways of knowing and categories of knowledge themselves encode and derive from patriarchal constructions of women.

If this is so, then from a feminist perspective, some contexts will be better than others. That is, social constructionism suggests that we may be able to adapt a negative liberty model to feminist purposes by expanding the notion of what counts as a "barrier" to freedom. In particular, the existing patriarchal context can be seen as a socially constructed external barrier to women's freedom. The social and political structures of liberalism, its conceptual categories, even the concept of "freedom" itself, are premised on women's subservience to men, on the denial and obliteration of their humanity: in short, on their unfreedom. Feminism is what allows us to deconstruct the "self-evident" and "natural" claims of modernist ide-ologies as the social constructions of particular times, histories, contexts, classes, races, and genders. And this recognition enables us to make com-parisons: a woman who is not abused is freer than one who is; a woman who is able to obtain an abortion when she wants it is freer than one who cannot; a woman who can be open about her sexuality without fearing pro-fessional repercussions is freer than one who must hide. The essence of negative liberty as the absence of external impediments is thus preserved; but the meaning of "external impediment" is considerably expanded beyond what most negative libertarians conceive.

Indeed, this expanded notion of negative liberty would also highlight the ways in which things that are considered "internal" barriers within pos-itive liberty terms are externally generated, culturally mediated and cre-ated. For instance, battered women may stay with batterers because of "internal" barriers such as shame, self-blame, guilt, low self-image, or love and its attendant belief that change is possible as well as "external" barriers such as fear and economic dependence (Walker 1989). Social construc-tionism suggests that this internal-external dichotomy is itself a construc-tion; we have to acknowledge how external factors influence and generate inner feelings and motives, how they "construct" us in our very being. If we are who we are through social relations, and if those social relations send us extremely negative messages, it is only human to internalize them, to give them some credence, to accept them as "truth," and to be who they say we are. In a society where resources for battered women are a low fund-ing priority, where courts and police openly disbelieve women, where rela-tives and friends fail to help and protect; shame, guilt, and feelings of unworthiness and deservedness are predictable responses (Brown 1987, Pagelow 1981, Dobash and Dobash 1992). But they are not just internal. In a similar manner, Mrs. Bridge's self-effacement may be the product of an oppressive upbringing in a sexist society; Charlene's fear of being fired may be a reasonable reaction to heterosexism.

But a troubling paradox has revealed itself in my presentation. Namely, social constructionism should make my foregoing arguments impossible. If patriarchy constructs us to such an extent that it includes language and epistemology, how can we ever *know* that some contexts are better (or freer) than others? Indeed, how can we ever think (let alone "know") that we are not what it says we are? How can we ever figure out who "we" are or what "we want" if the language and concepts we need to use are antagonistic to the enterprise we seek to carry out? How is it possi-ble to talk about "women's freedom" outside of the conceptual vocabulary patriarchy provides?

Furthermore, if the social construction thesis is true, then aren't *all* contexts restrictive? Wouldn't a so-called feminist context restrict just as much—albeit in different ways—as a so-called patriarchal one? And isn't the assumption of feminist guides to comparison rather absolutist, denying the degree to which feminism itself, as it is understood at this time in the West, must have been socially constructed by patriarchy? Who is this "we" that is constructed, if it is not already what patriarchy has made of us? Where does this "we" come from that is able to make these claims, and how can we know it exists outside of the constructing context? And anyhow, what about men; aren't they just as socially constructed as women? How can "patriarchy" even be conceptualized if men themselves are constructed?

The paradox of social construction lies in the tension between the poststructuralist realization that we are who we are because of and through the social relations that exist currently and historically, and the feminist desire to claim that this construction has been conducted by men at women's expense. The argument that patriarchy involves an epistemology and language that pervade women's very being, their self-conceptions and desires, is powerful and persuasive; and yet it paradoxically allows women no other way to see themselves. Feminists need the idea of social construction to deconstruct the idea of freedom, to identify the ways in which patriarchy has limited not only our options and choices but our self-conceptions; yet it appears to make such deconstruction impossible.

Thus the claim that context is a barrier to women's freedom must be viewed with self-critical ambivalence, because it implicitly utilizes a concept of the subject that exists beyond, or outside of, not only this particular context but any context whatsoever. We need to recognize that this abstract "woman" whose "freedom" is restricted by her context is who she is *because* of that context; we cannot operate from some abstract ideal of what a woman is "really" like, what her desires and preferences "truly" consist in, without then challenging the entire framework of social construction, which is necessary to our critique of patriarchy in the first place. Furthermore, it turns women into complete victims, denying the reality that women, by living and acting within and on existing contexts, have always helped shape them. To deny this is to deny their humanity. As Vaclav Havel points out, people who adapt to oppressive conditions "help create those conditions . . . . They are objects in a system of control, but at the same time they are its subjects as well" (Havel 1987, 51–52).

If we are its subjects, then we have the power to change it. If we are who we are through the social relations that make us, then even as they limit our options, they create them. A problem with Cavarera's and the French feminists' view that women are alienated from the very language we speak is that it ignores this duality of social construction. Self-definition *always* takes place in and through language; women have participated in that language, and we have responded to it throughout history with our practices. If we are social constructions, then we have to look at the contexts that created us to understand ourselves. We are who we are because of those contexts. Those contexts may restrict, but they also make freedom possible.

Thus feminist freedom requires a double vision. While preserving an emphasis on social construction, feminists concerned with freedom also want to acknowledge that some groups of people systematically and structurally have more power to do the constructing than do others. That it may be more *difficult* for women to define themselves within a masculinist epistemology and language—as it is for people of color in a white language, and lesbians and homosexuals in a heterosexual language—is crucial to recognize. This greater difficulty means that women and other "excluded others" *are* less free within these contexts and within the terms of masculinist discourse itself. But "less free" does not mean "unfree"; "more difficult" does not mean "impossible." We need also to acknowledge that "excluded others" participate in social construction to varying degrees. Further, the meaning that has been created by these contexts enables us to understand who we *are* as much as who we are *not;* it conceptualizes our powers as well as our restrictions.

Because of this duality, it is not the case that all men are free and all women unfree; indeed, perhaps under patriarchy none of us is really free in the full senses meant by positive and negative liberty. Similarly, some women are better placed to support patriarchy than some men, by virtue of race, class, or other privileging factors; although patriarchy is about gender domination, it cannot be completely separated from other kinds of domination, such as race, class, physical ability, and so forth. White women benefit from the race privilege that being white accords, just as black men benefit from the privileges of gender. Both thus share responsibility within the system of white patriarchy.[2] However, feminists also wish to recognize that patriarchy is defined by the general dominance of men over women, across race and class; it is premised on women's powerlessness and men's power. And the power it confers includes the power to guide, direct, and shape social construction to a far greater degree than that available to the "resisting" classes. Freedom for these groups thus requires increasing their ability to participate in the processes of construction.[3] The paradox of social construction commits us to this double-edged sword.

The Need for New Contexts I: The Role of Equality

HOW CAN A feminist theory of freedom help realize this approach to social construction and create the spaces for women to participate more in its ongoing processes? To me, feminism suggests a way to use the tools patriarchy constructs to challenge and resist its power to restrain. To loosely paraphrase Marx, all contexts provide the means for their own transcendence. All contexts—their ideologies, their language, their meaning—

have "loopholes," or what Audre Lorde (1984) more eloquently calls "gaps and fissures," and even contradictions.[4] The fact that the dominant discourse has room, no matter how small, for feminists to be able to claim that women are less free than men *within* the terms of positive and negative liberty discourses provides the possiblity of moving outside those discourses and hence of transforming and transcending the context that yielded them. As contexts create us and make action possible, they supply the tools we need to at least change, if not dismantle, those contexts.

For instance, equality is central to the idea of freedom that emerges from the Enlightenment. Negative liberty theorists like Hobbes and Locke, in declaring all men to be free in the state of nature, declared that formal equality, of right and of liberty, were central to the social contract. Positive liberty theorists like Rousseau declared that equality of a more substantive kind was central to equal power among community members seeking liberty through self-rule. And virtually all liberty theorists—even Mill, although perhaps less blatantly—have denied this equality to women.

At the same time, however, it was the Enlightenment ideal of equality that provided early feminists such as Mary Astell and Mary Wollstonecraft the opening they needed to assert women's entitlement to be recognized as human subjects with agency and intellect. Indeed, the Enlightenment provided an entire conceptual vocabulary for women to make such claims, as well as for men to understand them (even if they chose to ignore them). In creating the idea and language of agency and equality for men, liberalism ironically offered feminists a way to challenge its denial of agency and equality to women; and this in turn provided a basis for challenging liberalism altogether. From Abigail Adams to Sojourner Truth to Margaret Fuller to Patricia Williams, feminists have used the existence of the notion of equality in patriarchal language to challenge and resist patriarchy and to try to achieve greater freedom for women. This equality evolved from women's demand for equality with men to feminist assertions (at least by implication) of equality among women.

What is the specific role that equality should play in a feminist conceptualization of freedom, however? Equality can help in a feminist assessment of which contexts are better than others; the specific measure should be whether a context constrains any group of people less or more than it does any other. For instance, if a society repeatedly, systematically constrains women more than men, blacks more than whites, lesbians more than heterosexuals, then there is a theoretical presumption in favor of the conclusion that the society as a whole provides a barrier to the more constrained group. If it does not, and all are equally limited in similar ways by a particular context, then there is a theoretical presumption in favor of the conclusion it does not constrain *per se* but only defines our choices, as poor as those choices may be. I state it in this manner of "presumption" because there can always be cases made to the contrary; but the presumption places the burden of proof on the person who defends unequal limitations on choice. For example, gravity limits us all; it is not the case that some are freer to fly than others, and the burden of proof is on those who seek to challenge this claim. On the other hand, racial economic policy in the United States may result in the majority of airplane riders being white, whereas the majority of bus riders are black; here, inequality is an indication that some are constrained in their liberty by social structural forces, and the burden of proof is on those who wish to deny this.

Such constraints are not necessarily obvious, they may be indirect and hidden. Laws against pregnancy- and childrearing-leave appear to limit us all equally, by referring to "pregnant persons" and "parents," but in fact single out a particular group because of social custom as well as biology. Certainly, the ability or inability to become pregnant should not be considered a restraint; yet its treatment within a larger social context of sexual discrimination results in social policy that in fact inhibits women's liberty. The barrier to freedom is thus not women's pregnant bodies but rather patriarchal social attitudes and customs pertaining to pregancy and women.

This requires, however, a different understanding of equality as well. Equality plays a relatively obvious role in positive liberty, of course; ever since Rousseau, positive libertarians have recognized that formal equality without substantive equality is a hollow sham: Substantive unequals are never equal under the law. But positive liberty's "second guessing" and "general will" indicate that this equality assumes—or even worse, requires—a profound sameness of the will. If equal resources and political position are necessary to equal political power, they also have a psychologically homogenizing effect, as disruptive and unbalancing particular wills give way to a universal general will or *Geist*. Particularly given the fact that in many such positive liberty theories, such as Rousseau's and Hegel's, this unity of will is produced by women's exclusion from political participation and their subordination to men, feminists should be suspicious of claims to universality and commonality. It is perhaps such history—as well as the inequalities and accompanying erasure of experience suffered by women of color in the name of "sisterhood" in the history of the feminist movement—that makes claims to difference and heterogeneity so important to contemporary feminism. Thus a feminist conception of equality must attend to issues of difference and diversity.

Some would suggest that difference is at the heart of negative liberty's conceptualization of equality as strictly formal and procedural. In theorizing "empty spaces" within which individuals should be "free" to act as they wish (Coole 1993), negative liberty supposedly gives priority to differences among people; it is recognition of these differences that motivates the definition of freedom as the absence of external impediments. Yet, negative

liberty incorporates its own conception of sameness; indeed, the universalism of liberal rights discourse and formal equality *denies* the reality of concrete differences among people and is fundamentally biased along lines of
race, class, and gender. For women, equality generally means "the same as
white men," ignoring that women experience a multiplicity of difference
from men and each other. Taking (white) men as the standard for equality
catches women in a double bind: either women are treated exactly the
same as men, thus denying their specific needs (as in *Cal Fed v. Guerra*), or
else they are treated as completely different from men and in need of special protection (*EEOC v. Sears*).[5]

Both of these approaches to difference and equality are inherently
masculinist because they pass off male experience as "gender-neutral."
This is not only self-contradictory but discriminates against women at the
very core of our legal system: Women cannot be equal to men *as women*. As
Kristin Bumiller (1988, 75–76) notes, the construction of "reality" as the
same for victim and nonvictim denies actual differences in needs and thus
perpetuates real, substantive inequality under the guise of procedural
equality. Women's claim for equal opportunity and equal rights to compete
in the marketplace without challenging how "the marketplace" is structured, for instance, left women with a double day, chasing after a definition
of success that is not only antifeminist but antiwoman. For instance, expectations of seventy-hour work weeks for partnership in a law firm are
premised on an economic and social model of the family in which one
person—usually a woman—is responsible for precisely those areas of life
that the business world excludes. This notion of success is not only sexist
but classist and racist as well, as (usually white) women who seek equality in
such a work environment must depend on an underclass of workers in
childcare and housekeeping, often third world women who are undercom-
pensated. By refusing to recognize childrearing and housework as socially
necessary, the social structure of "success" makes the achievement of affective life either exploitive or impossible. Furthermore, existing definitions
have denied the ways in which professions have been effectively closed off
to large segments of the population—particularly women of color—whose
family life did not necessarily conform to the white middle-class model.
The subject of success thus retains its privileged gender, race, and class
(see Hirschmann 1992, 245–246).

On this view, the problems of gender inequality lie not with women
per se (though they may participate in its perpetuation) but with the
socioeconomic model within which they seek both to work and to maintain their personal lives. Structural barriers to equality are thus built into
the system. As talk of the "glass ceiling" suggests, when women are continually and systematically harassed and discriminated against, it becomes
virtually impossible to achieve success on this masculinist model. As a
result, it becomes similarly impossible for women to achieve equality more

generally; equality requires that we be "the same," but structural elements guarantee our difference. As long as the individualist model dominates our conceptual vocabulary, however, it is difficult to see this contradiction, and our apparent "failure" leaves women guilty and frustrated: did we not "succeed" because we are, after all, not as good, unequal to men?

So the concept of equality necessary to freedom is different than that found in either positive or negative liberty and is one that must be reconceived through difference. I find Mary Parker Follet's notion of "related difference" particularly helpful. For Follet, differences exist and make sense only in relationship; we are different from other people; these differences have to mean something (they have to "make a difference") in order for us to recognize them as such. And this relatedness, in turn, is what gives us our individuality: "My individuality is difference springing into view as relating itself with other differences . . . the essence of individuality is the relating of self to other difference" (Follet 1920, 63). We are "individuals" only insofar as we are in relationship; it is somewhat nonsensical to say that a person totally isolated from others is an "individual," because the word is itself a social term that has a meaning only in a language, "individual" compared to what? Or to whom?

Follet locates difference as a source of power, both for the individual and the community. "Difference is not something static . . . [but is] involved in the world of becoming" (1920, 63). Differences among people provide the impetus to collective action; they stimulate individuals in social relations to work through their differences, whether that means working out conflict or striving to understand one another. Difference is thus an important force that moves societies forward. Of course, underlying her account is the belief that societies strive for some sort of unity; differences thus provide the spur to social evolution because they force us to struggle to understand differences and achieve a new unity. But unity does not mean uniformity; it requires heterogeneity. If differences do not exist, then society is unfree; either differences exist but are being squelched, or else the mechanisms and institutions of society have genuinely beaten individuality out of its citizens. Thus "each must discover and contribute that which distinguishes him from others, his difference. The only use for my difference is to join it with other differences" (1920, 29).

Follet's notion of equality that rejects false universalization and embraces difference can enrich a feminist conception of freedom. It reveals that both positive and negative liberty employ conceptions of equality that are based on sameness. The requirement of homogeneity ensures that some will always be freer than others because some systematically have greater power in the process of social construction; the "circulation" of power in a neutral "field" is revealed as a cover for systematic domination as long as difference is denied and excluded. Emphasizing difference provides a way to achieve a greater equality and reciprocity in social construction so that all have the freedom of self-definition insofar as that is possible. It also suggests why the participation of excluded peoples in social construction is important to freedom for us all by making difference a vital element, not only of community, but of individuality as well.

The Need for New Contexts II: Relationships and Material Experience

THUS FEMINISTS CAN derive valuable tools for the transcendence of existing contexts by using the dominant discourse against itself. This method can open up social construction to allow women to participate on more equal terms, as well as for the recognition of the ways in which women *already* participate. The paradox of social construction, however, raises questions about the efficacy of this method. If freedom and equality were conceptualized in ways that excluded women and were indeed founded on, and made possible by, that exclusion, then that might suggest automatic and insurmountable limits to feminist attempts to turn these concepts against themselves. Perhaps, as Audre Lorde observed, "The master's tools will never dismantle the master's house" (Lorde 1984).

This is why feminism often turns to other tools that stem from resistance to the dominant discourse's power, instead of directly out of it. For instance, the ethic of care and connection that Gilligan and others maintain as an empowering epistemological, moral, and political standpoint for women arose not out of the dominant discourse itself but in contrast to it, out of women's oppression and privatization within the patriarchal nuclear family. Feminists have used this ethic in recent years to highlight the sexism of the public-private dichotomy that spawned that ethic in the first place. Similarly, Patricia Hill Collins notes that white and black patriarchy has created mythologies of African American women as "jezebels, mammies, and matriarchs" as a means of dehumanizing and controlling them. But she points out that each of these images also has an affirmative component, which can be used by African American women to assert their humanity and power to resist sexism and racism: "African American women who value those aspects of black womanhood that are stereotyped, ridiculed, and maligned in scholarship and the popular media challenge some of the basic ideas inherent in an ideology of domination" (Collins 1990, 107).

This strategy can be identified and utilized through two sources available within patriarchal society: relationships among women, and material experience, which are the activities women have historically engaged in. Because women are an oppressed group that has intimately participated in, but not been the primary shapers of, our social contexts, our material experience has provided a powerful basis for change, what Nancy Hartsock (1984) has called a "feminist standpoint." Feminist standpoint basically involves a dual consciousness. Women are aware of the dominant ideology of patriarchy because it constructs our lives: Women are the literal embodiment and instruments of this ideology as caretakers and nurturers, as mothers and wives, as prostitutes, as cleaners of houses and makers of homes. Yet, at the same time, the material experience this ideology constructs for women provides the basis for seeing a disjunction between ideology and that experience. Even as women internalize cultural norms that the activites of childcare and domestic work are unimportant, women experience them as very important. Even though the prostitute lives her dehumanization, she experiences herself as a human being. Even though nurturance is considered natural, even biological and hence belonging to the realm of "being" rather than "doing," women experience it as an activity, one that involves an ethical system with its own integrity and that has much to say about human experience that the dominant discourse and public morality ignore. This dual consciousness that women experience as an oppressed group forms the basis for political change.

But this consciousness, or feminist standpoint, is only *effectively* realized in relationships with other women. That is, if material experience provides the concrete "data," relationships among women provide a context for giving meaning to the data. If women in patriarchal contexts are likely to internalize its image of their inferiority (as Wollstonecraft among others suggested), then conversely the realization that this inferiority *is* a constructed image, that it is false, that women's activities *have* value needs the support of other women's similar realization or consciousness: in other words, it requires a different context, one that can provide a different meaning to experience, one that utilizes a different conceptual vocabulary. Relationships among women provide this different context for the sharing of these realizations and hence the creation of a political, feminist standpoint. Although patriarchy has dehumanized, decentered, dismissed, and disrupted women's relationships with one another throughout history, it has nevertheless permitted those relationships to exist, generally by default: again, in its "gaps and fissures." In dismissing the private sphere and the work of women as inessential and in directing their attention to the public sphere, men have historically been unable to completely repress or stop women's relations and communities from evolving. These have often evolved as means of survival for women, ways that women have been able to help one another cope with their oppression, but they have simultaneously provided the basis for transcending it as well. And even though male domination often sets the parameters for these relationships— whether it is the oppressive conditions of a slave barracks, the Triangle Shirtwaist factory floor, a brothel, a tea for middle-class housewives, or the waiting room of a male gynecologist—such relationships have the potential to allow women to define themselves in ways that resist the patriarchal contexts that surround them. The most obvious contemporary example of this phenomenon is of course consciousness raising groups; but such groups have existed in subtler, less recognized forms throughout history.

In her book *Black Feminist Thought*, Patricia Hill Collins shows how these two elements—material experience and relationships among women—need to be understood together. As what she calls "outsiders within," African American women must adopt and internalize the language and epistemology of white patriarchy; in order to survive, to be "within" the dominant culture, they must daily experience its ideology, and their lives are importantly structured by it. Yet, they are also "outsiders" within that culture; and as such, they also can contest the truth-claims of this ideology. Black women can see the contradictions between the ideology and the reality of their experience, she argues, because they *live* that experience, and the contradictions affect them in immediate and concrete ways. The status of outsider, of being on the margins, provides an empowering standpoint, Collins argues, that allows black women to create what she calls "safe spaces," relationships and communities among women that can produce freedom. For these relationships in turn form the basis for affirmation and resistance by identifying and naming that dissonance between ideology and their lives, by talking about the ways in which white patriarchy does *not* describe who they are, and by being able to affirm each other in who they *are*. Such communities are both real—"relations between . . . daughters, sisters, friends . . . mothers and mother figures" who concretely and daily reaffirm and empower each other—and symbolic (Collins 1990, 96). For instance, she identifies blues and writing as two "safe spaces" where African American women have declared their rejection of patriarchal images and affirmed their identities (Collins 1990, 99–103).

For Collins, freedom is not *just* the absence of external restraints, "the capricious masters and endless work" of slavery, but consists further in the reclaiming of inner powers. By claiming "consciousness as a sphere of freedom," which can provide "the conceptual tools to resist oppression" (Collins 1990, 227–228), Collins endorses the need to actively change existing contexts and in the process to reshape and redefine the self. Because of the pervasiveness of the dominant ideology in constructing African American women, and because of the power of African American women's communities to resist, freedom is concerned with both internal and external factors; it attends to both emancipation and empowerment. Freedom, as Audre Lorde puts it, concerns not "merely the oppressive situations which we seek to escape, but that piece of the oppressor which is planted deep within us" (Lorde 1984, 123). Given this, the task of self-definition among oppressed peoples is not so much a right as it is a responsibility. But it is achievable only in relationships with those who are similarly oppressed. Collins's community of women sets up relationships of interdependence and expectation that require us to continue to work in and through such relationships, not only for others, but for ourselves. For it is only through such relationships that freedom can occur.

Relationship is also central to the notion of liberty found in the Milan Women's Bookstore collective's *Sexual Difference: A Theory of Social-Symbolic Practice,* which is one of the few contemporary works that attempts to theorize freedom in specifically feminist terms. Their book suggests that a feminist theory of freedom is based not on rights but on responsibility, not on separation but on connection, not on autonomy as rejection of or reaction to others but on relationship and interaction with others. Relationship is conceived not as a mere state of existence, nor as peripheral to what is important, but rather as a vital political practice; relationships are not only the context for the interpretation of material experience but themselves provide materiality. Although context is all important, the fact that the patriarchal context in which women live so profoundly restricts women's ability to define themselves suggests the need for some sort of radical break, a political and intellectual separatism that can yield a relational context that is not—or at least has the potential not to be—totally constituted by patriarchy.

In Italian feminism, the focus of such separatism was the "*autocoscienza*" group. Like consciousness raising in the United States, *autocoscienza* is a practice where women gather together in small groups to help themselves and each other to gain a deeper understanding of themselves in the patriarchal world order. Through an emotional and intellectual "separatism" such groups provide and engage in the construction of a new context of woman-to-woman support, a "safe space" for women to explore the dissonances between their experiences and the dominant discourse, to attempt to describe those dissonances, and from there to rearticulate and reformulate their "original" experiences and create new experiences and descriptions. Such groups thus move from a negative exploration—how their experience is *not* what patriarchy says it is, how it cannot even find adequate expression there—to a positive one, a new vocabulary of meaning that emerges from the new feminist context's reinterpretation of women's historical and current experiences.[6]

Like positive liberty, the Milan group emphasizes "freedom *to*" in its emphasis on self-definition and empowerment, rather than rights and opportunities. This requires the interaction and support of "the symbolic community of women" because it is only in this community that new meanings can be created. They assert that women have a "symbolic debt" (Milan 1992, 129) to engage in this community, to participate in creating new contexts by identifying with other women, and by working through the processes of deconstruction and re-creation. "We are not free with regard to payment of the symbolic debt," they say, "yet its payment is liberating for us" (138). At the same time, this "liberation" is very sympathetic to negative liberty's "freedom *from*." The need for community is stimulated by the enormity of the external barriers; if the freedom of self-definition is not possible within patriarchal language and contexts, then women need to create new ones. Furthermore, they maintain, engaging in such community allows women to see how they have created, and can create, the world; hence it enables women to identify their agency, their ability to act on and shape their contexts, to make choices and act on them. Without such community, then, no "individual" woman can ever be free because the existing patriarchal context is invested in obscuring women's agency, even from women themselves.

The notion of the individual necessary to their feminist conception of freedom as self-definition is thus more complicated, both politically and epistemologically, than either negative liberty's individualism or positive liberty's communitarianism. Isolated individuals cannot achieve freedom as such; as an "individual," I always exist and operate in a social structure that I help support by my actions. This structure provides meaning to all I do and say: "Language is part of the fabric of social relations, and these are not favorably disposed to women's experience" (28). Because all meaning requires context, and because contexts are created through social interaction and not individual will, negative liberty's "individualistic" approach requires a dependence on existing patriarchal contexts, which are premised on women's oppression.

The issue thus becomes *which* social structures I wish to promote: the existing patriarchal one, by invoking and supporting existing meanings, or a new woman-centered one that challenges and changes meaning? As the Milan authors put it, there is always a "debt" to be paid; the trick is not to pay it to the "wrong creditor" (129). In other words, there is always a context that is promoted through one's action; it is not the case that some contexts are ideological or political (like feminism or patriarchy) and some are pure or neutral (like liberalism or positivism). All contexts have substantive meaning; the key is to be aware of the context one supports and to make a choice between contexts insofar as that is humanly as well as historically possible. This awareness and choice is crucial for women; for "if the social translation of the human value of being a woman is not done by women, it will be done by men according to their criteria" (147).

Thus, shades of negative and positive liberty run through this conception of freedom. As with Collins's emphasis on communal self-definition, the idea of a "symbolic debt" to other women suggests the centrality of responsibility to feminist freedom, and requires us to begin our understanding of human freedom from the perspective of interconnection and relationship. Yet it is also important to acknowledge the centrality of individual difference and choice in the Milan formulation: "The individual must make her accounts and decide by herself what she wants, what is worthwhile for her"(119).[7] This choice is never abstract, for the "individual" making these choices exists in a particular context, which always limits choices even as it simultaneously produces them. Thus "a woman is free when she chooses to signify her belonging to the female sex, well knowing it is not an object of choice" (138). This notion of identity recognizes the centrality of context and relationship to who we are as "individuals." This context means that we do not create ourselves "from scratch" in an abstract state of nature; but we can choose to recognize what has been created. In this recognition—perhaps paradoxically—lies the possibility of change, self-creation, and choice.[8]

Conclusion

UNDERSTOOD IN THIS way, the practice of *autocoscienza* provides a powerful political tool for understanding the patriarchal bias of political theoretical concepts like freedom as well as the underlying epistemology. It makes possible the act of stepping outside the given context to see it more clearly; but it does so by providing an alternative context to step *into,* even if only momentarily (for example, while the *autocoscienza* group is meeting). Such moments change participants' vision of their contexts even as they must go back to them and live them; and this altered vision contains the potential for real, material change in the social relations that frame our construction.

So key to feminist freedom, and to the self-realization that lies at its core, is a notion of empowerment. Precisely because we are created and shaped by our contexts, a feminist practice of liberty must empower individuals to create and influence their contexts in more self-critical, self-reflexive ways. This requires negative liberty's absence of restraint, as well as positive liberty's community assistance; but it simultaneously requires an expansion of external restraint beyond negative liberty's conventional formulation, and a notion of community that pulls back from, or transforms, positive liberty's hierarchical social determination of desire. Equality is a vital component of relationships in this community; but the equality among individuals is one founded on difference, one that acknowledges and indeed depends on individuals' unique and particular ways of manifesting and living out the commonly shared and similarly encoded aspects of experience.

A notion of agency lies at the heart of a feminist theory of freedom; but this agency is not the abstract and individualist agency of negative liberty's state of nature any more than it is the selfless, collective agency of the general will. It involves a notion of self deeply situated in relationship; it involves recognition of the ways our powers and abilities have come from, and been made possible by, particular relationships and contexts. We are "autonomous" in the sense that we have powers and abilities, desires and wants and needs, but these are "relational," they come from, exist in the context of, and have meaning only in relation to others (Bakan 1966; Hirschmann 1992). Other and self are thus not opposed, but related. But to say they are "related" is not to say that they are "one," as positive liberty suggests, any more than they are two separate entities that must somehow be fitted together, as negative liberty asserts.

This focus on context requires an understanding of the ways in which the language, concepts and epistemology of the patriarchal world constrain women's choices in ways in which men's choices are not constrained. But it also must be understood as a context of relationships that help create individuals—women as well as men—capable of making choices for themselves and understanding themselves in and through those relationships that give us our "desires" and "will" in the first place. Feminist freedom requires us to recognize that things *simultaneously* create and destroy, prevent and promote, prohibit and require. By emphasizing the centrality of agency and choice, but by deeply locating agents and their choices in relationships and contexts that can empower as well as inhibit them, such a conceptualization requires that we collectively create a new context that will help people, particularly those on the margins like women, define themselves and become aware of their capacities and abilities. We must learn how to exercise our choice to affect our contexts themselves; for only then can the choices that occur within these contexts be conceived of as genuinely free.

Notes

1. Lewin (1992, 18). Thanks to the American Council of Learned Societies, which funded my fellowship at the Bunting Institute of Radcliffe College, where much of the present paper was written.

2. Furthermore, as Iris Young (1990) argues, we must keep in mind the distinction between responsibility and blame. While we may not be able to blame individual men for patriarchy because they are victimized by it—perhaps even (some? many?) white, economically privileged men—we can nevertheless hold men collectively responsible for it, because they benefit from the power it gives them over women, and they either tacitly or overtly refuse to resist those benefits, just as many whites, women as well as men, tacitly accept the benefits of race privilege. As some benefit more than others, some are more responsible than others.

3. I use the wording "participate in its processes" because I wish to avoid the impression that I think social construction is really as conscious and active as the term "construction" implies. I believe that many men actively engage in perpetuating sexism, for instance, but its existence is much more complex than conscious

conspiracy; perhaps it is its pervasiveness at the subconscious level that accounts for its tenacity.

4. In this, I reveal a long-standing discomfort with Audre Lorde's claim that "the master's tools will never dismantle the master's house" (Lorde 1984, 110). I believe that when the master's tools are appropriated by the slave, they are thereby transformed and have a revolutionary potential. They also have a serious potential to compromise and further enslave the slave, which makes these tools problematic and even dangerous; but my approach to social construction and context suggests that these tools are necessary to dismantling the master's house, and may even be the only ones available.

5. See Eisenstein (1988) and Scott (1988) for discussions of these cases.

6. My own reading of *autocoscienza* thus suggests a strong affinity with standpoint epistemology, which involves "achieving" (rather than passively "discovering") a feminist consciousness, or standpoint, as a liberatory strategy and as a necessary stage to realizing the feminist perspective latent in at least most women's daily experience (Hartsock 1984; Hirschmann 1992).

7. They even talk in terms of a "female social contract," which I find an unfortunate choice of terms, though this must be understood in terms of the reformulated conception of the "individual contracter" as a self located in relationship, rather than the abstract interest-maximizer of social contract theory.

8. There are a number of elements of *Sexual Difference* that I have left out of the discussion that I find rather problematic, particularly their notions of "disparity" and "entrustment." The former encapsulates their belief that, within patriarchy, "difference" definitionally constitutes "inequality." The way to combat this is not to deny that women are unequal in the name of sisterhood, for that will merely result in the silencing of certain experiences, such as women of color experienced in U.S. feminism. Rather, they urge women to acknowledge their inequality and to use the powers that patriarchy has allowed them to change it. This in turn, however, requires relationships of "entrustment" where women who are less powerful entrust themselves to women who have more of the powers that patriarchy confers; they offer the example of a woman client who hires a woman lawyer to represent her in court. I am uncomfortable with this notion of entrustment; rather than a palliative to the effacement of excluded groups within feminism, it seems a formula for its promulgation. I believe these concepts could work, however, if the Milan authors sought a reformulation of "equality" rather than rejecting it outright as a patriarchal ruse; indeed, I think they implicitly employ such a notion of equality in their emphasis on reciprocity in such relationships. However, this element of their work needs more analysis (Hirschmann 1992).

References

Ashcraft, Richard. 1986. *Revolutionary Politics and Locke's Two Treatises.* Princeton, N.J.: Princeton University Press.

Bakan, David. 1966. *The Duality of Human Existence: Isolation and Communion in Western Man.* Boston: Beacon Press.

Berlin, Isaiah. 1971. "Two Concepts of Liberty." In *Four Essays on Liberty*. New York: Oxford University Press.

Brown, Angela. 1987. *When Battered Women Kill*. New York: Macmillan.

Bumiller, Kristin. 1988. *The Civil Rights Society: The Social Construction of Victims*. Baltimore: Johns Hopkins University Press.

Butler, Judith. 1990. *Gender Trouble*. New York: Routledge.

California Federal Savings and Loan Association v. Guerra. 1987. 479 U.S. 272.

Collins, Patricia Hill. 1990. *Black Feminist Thought*. Boston: Unwyn-Hyman.

Coole, Diana. 1993. "Constructing and Deconstructing Liberty." *Political Studies* 41: 83–95.

de Lauretis, Teresa. 1989. "The Essence of the Triangle or, Taking the Risk of Essentialism Seriously: Feminist Theory in Italy, the U.S., and Britain." *Differences* 1 (2):3–37.

Derrida, Jacques. 1982. *Margins of Philosphy*. Trans. Alan Bass. Chicago: University of Chicago Press.

Dobash, R. Emerson and Russell P. Dobash. 1992. *Women, Violence, and Social Change*. New York: Routledge.

Eisenstein, Zillah. 1988. *The Female Body and the Law*. Berkeley: University of California Press.

Equal Employment Opportunity Commission v. Sears, Roebuck and Co. 1986. 628 F. Supp. 1264, 39 FEP 1672 (N.D. Illinois).

Follet, Mary Parker. 1920. *The New State*. New York: Atheneum.

Foucault, Michel. 1990. *The History of Sexuality*, Vol. 1, *An Introduction*. Trans. Robert Hurley. New York: Vintage.

Gilligan, Carol. 1982. *In a Different Voice*. Cambridge, Mass.: Harvard University Press.

Hartsock, Nancy. 1984. *Money, Sex, and Power: Toward a Feminist Historical Materialism*. Boston: Northeastern University Press.

Havel, Vaclav. 1987. *Living in Truth*. London: Faber and Faber.

Hirschmann, Nancy J. 1992. *Rethinking Obligation: A Feminist Method for Political Theory*. Ithaca, N.Y.: Cornell University Press.

Irigaray, Luce. 1985. *This Sex Which Is Not One*. Trans. Catherine Porter and Carolyn Burke. Ithaca, N.Y.: Cornell University Press.

Kramnick, Isaac. 1990. *Revolutionary Politics and Bourgeois Radicalism*. Ithaca, N.Y.: Cornell University Press.

Kristeva, Julia. 1986. *The Kristeva Reader*. Ed. Toril Moi. Oxford: Blackwell.

Lewin, Tamar. 1992. "Hurdles Increase for Many Women Seeking Abortions." *The New York Times*, March 15;1, 18.

Lorde, Audre. 1984. *Sister Outsider*. Freedom, Calif.: The Crossing Press.

Lyotard, Jean François. 1979. *The Postmodern Condition: A Report on Knowledge*. Trans. Geoff Bennington and Brian Massumi. Minneapolis: University of Minnesota Press.

Macpherson, C. B. 1964. *The Political Theory of Possessive Individualism: Hobbes to Locke*. Oxford: Oxford University Press.

Milan Women's Bookstore Collective. 1990. *Sexual Difference: A Theory of Social-Symbolic Practice.* Trans. Patricia Cicogna and Teresa de Lauretis. Bloomington: Indiana University Press.

Mill, John Stuart. 1991. *On Liberty.* New York: Oxford University Press.

Pagelow, Mildred. 1982. *Woman-Battering.* Beverly Hills: Sage.

Patterson, Orlando. 1991. *Freedom: Freedom in the Making of Western Culture.* New York: Basic Books.

Rousseau, Jean Jacques. 1979. *Emile.* Ed. Allan Bloom. New York: Basic Books.

Scott, Joan. 1988. "Deconstructing Equality-Versus-Difference: Or, the Uses of Poststructuralist Theory for Feminism." *Feminist Studies* 14 (1):33–50.

Taylor, Charles. 1979. "What's Wrong with Negative Liberty?" In *The Idea of Freedom: Essays in Honor of Isaiah Berlin.* Ed. A. Ryan. New York: Oxford University Press.

Walker, Lenore. 1989. *Terrifying Love: Why Battered Women Kill and How Society Responds.* New York: Harper and Row.

Wittgenstein, Ludwig. 1968. *Philosophical Investigations.* Trans. G. E. M. Anscombe. New York: Macmillan.

Young, Iris. 1990. *Justice and the Politics of Difference.* Princeton, N.J.: Princeton University Press.

4

What Is Authority's Gender?

Kathleen B. Jones

What is authority's gender? This question extends the question that Hannah Arendt posed in her classic essay "What is Authority?" Arendt rejected modern concepts of authority that identified authority with the legitimate power to rule another. My critique of authority is prompted by hers, yet moves well beyond Arendt's critical horizon. Like Arendt, I am wary of the identification of authority with domination. Yet, unlike Arendt, I am concerned not only with the antipolitical consequences of this identification but also with its specifically gendered implications.

Western political theorists have regarded authority as a distinctive type of social control or influence, a peculiar form of getting people to obey social prescriptions without resorting to overt coercion. If authority is defined as a relationship constituted by consent that gives someone the right to command another who has a duty to obey, then any justification of authority depends only on clarifying the criteria by which one recognizes authority as such in the first place. Within this logic, neither does one have to be persuaded to obey those in authority, nor is one coerced into obeying. One obeys those in authority because they are entitled to obedience (Friedman 1973, 131).

Although modern theorists have noticed an implicit tension between authority and autonomy, few have enabled us to think about authority beyond the scope of command-obedience relationships. With the singular exception of Hannah Arendt, who refused the equation of authority with either force or power, most theorists have accepted some version of the claim that authority describes a relationship occupying a discursive space somewhere beyond persuasion, only slightly short of force.

What does feminist theory have to offer as a perspective on authority? As the essays in this volume demonstrate, feminist theorists have provided critical analyses of most of the central concepts of political discourse. Their collective work has disclosed a host of gendered practices and meanings on which the traditional concepts of political analysis have been founded. Yet, beyond observations about authority's patrilineal origins, feminist theorists have rarely subjected the conceptualization of political authority itself to any careful critique of its gendered representations. Instead, feminists have assumed that what needs to be explained is women's exclusion from authority.

Feminist scholarship has focused on exploring the barriers to women's inclusion within existing authority practices, in part because feminism in the West has been linked most directly to liberal, democratic traditions. Within this tradition, democracy has been defined as equal access to public arenas of self-governance; reconciling authority with democracy depends upon removing arbitrary barriers to different persons' access to being in authority or participating in practices of self-rule. Consequently, Western feminists' arguments about women's relationship to authority imply that bringing women into the field of authority, or enabling women to command obedience, contributes automatically to the process of democratizing authority practices.

Feminist theory has certainly approached the problem of reconciling authority with democracy more broadly than traditional political theory has considered it, especially because feminists have recognized the internal connections between patterns of authority in the public realm and the social organization of gender within the private sphere. Building on John Stuart Mill's insight in *The Subjection of Women* that the development of a tradition and practice of democracy within the "public" realm depended on the development of democracy within the "private" sphere of familial relationships, yet moving well beyond Mill's assumption of the necessary foundation of democracy in a "family life" structured in terms of traditional, heterosexist relationships, feminists have developed an elaborate analysis of the scope of the "private" and its relationship to the "public."

Despite this innovative research, feminists have accepted the assumption that, within the context of liberal democracies, authority is a system of self-governance that can be made equally accessible to all. Consequently, even feminist theory reduces analysis of the relationship between gender and authority to an assessment of the factors contributing to the lower proportion of women than men who are found in authoritative, public roles.

Yet, the more one focuses on the tendency, even in liberal, democratic traditions, to identify authority with command, the more one concludes that the concept and practice of authority itself needs to be subjected to critical, feminist analysis. Hence, the critical question for me is: Does the conceptualization of authority in the Western, liberal democratic tradition as a command-obedience relationship rest on a gendered foundation? What is authority's gender?

Asking about authority's gender redefines the struggle for democracy in terms broader than demands for equal access to positions of rulership; it poses instead a more radical challenge to the compatibility of relationships of rule and hierarchy in a free society of equal, although different, persons. Unwilling to concede the validity of dominant conceptualizations of authority as systems of rule, this challenge to account for authority's gender provides a radically democratic moment for feminist politics. I consider this more radical moment to be an effort to create a public realm not as an escape from, but rooted in, what Hannah Arendt called the "human condition of plurality" (Arendt 1958, 222).

I argue for a radical shift in feminist analysis away from a narrow inquiry into those conditions that would enhance women's being in authority, or women's becoming more able to command, to a more inclusive investigation of whether the dominant conceptualization of authority as commanding sovereignty represents, as normative, a patriarchally gendered masculine practice of authority (Jones 1993, 219–229). Not only should women be included in authority, both the concept and practice of authority need to be reconstituted if the interests that women represent are to matter to democracy (Jonasdottir 1994).

Contemporary feminist theory defends women's right to be integrated into public life as *equal persons,* irrespective of sex (the position of privileging sex neutrality), while simultaneously claiming that democracy must support principles of plurality and recognize the value of the contributions that *different persons* make to the quality of public discourse and public life (the position of privileging plural differences). Feminist political theory has concerned itself with the question of whether and how the articulation of different political values and interests in our discourse about public life might decenter patriarchally masculinized constructions of political theory and political action and destabilize the still comfortable disassociation of women from public life. How does gender function as a discourse of power that defines who we recognize as leaders, rulers, or as those who are "in authority"?

Marks of Authority's Gender

THE STANDARD ANALYSIS of authority in modern Western discourse defines authority as a set of rules governing public life issued by those who are entitled to speak. In these terms, an authority is someone who is *official* (occupies a public, professional role recognized as having the capacity to issue rules), *knowledgeable* (has knowledge that meets certain epistemic criteria in order to issue rules), *decisive* (possesses singularity of will and judges dispassionately so that the rules will be enforced), and *compelling* (constructs political obedience to the rules ordering public life through institutionalized hierarchy). In other words, those who are "in authority" are perceived to be "in authority" because they exhibit the signs of office, knowledge, judgment, and will associated objectively and formally with the practice of ruling.

In the literature on rulership and leadership, the gender-neutrality of these four characteristics of *office, knowledge, judgment,* and *will* has been accepted axiomatically. For instance, Bell, Hill, and Wright (1961) contend that male domination is not a product of the way we conceptualize public leadership. "No matter what concept of leadership is adopted or what methods for locating leaders are employed," they write, "most studies document the fact of male dominance in public affairs in the United States" (1961, 34). In their view, overcoming obstacles to female leadership depends upon changing women themselves so that they no longer will be personally apathetic, lack interest in politics, or be mired in those situations that distract from their ability to become public leaders (35, 54).

Even the burgeoning feminist literature on political women supports similar conclusions. Although feminists tend to place more stress on structural obstacles to women's being better represented in positions of public authority than on sociopsychological explanations, the general assumption of much of the feminist literature on women and politics has been that the conceptualization of public authority is unproblematically gender-neutral. The issue for feminist researchers has been to demonstrate the existence and continued operation of sexism in the form of differential public career opportunities for women and men (Sapiro 1983, Welch 1977).

Although it is undeniable that women occupy disproportionately fewer appointive or elected public offices than men, and that there are specific political systems—notably those structured as multiparty parliamentary systems—that are more advantageous to women's success as candidates for public office, a broader philosophical question remains: What is our understanding of the meaning of being "in authority"? How do we conceptualize practices of rulership and legitimacy when we limit our understanding of being "in authority" to accepted notions of *office, knowledge, judgment,* and *will?*

Descriptions of those who act as public authorities—public spokespeople—and of the norms and rules that they articulate, generally have excluded characteristics culturally coded as "feminine." In Western political thought *office, knowledge, judgment,* and *will* have been connected more immediately to patriarchally gendered masculine rather than to feminine modes of being and action. The definition of authority itself as a set of practices designed to institutionalize social hierarchies and to ensure that political subjects obey leaders' commands depends upon the separation of "women-qua-women" from the process of authorizing.

Recognizing the gendered nature of the codes used to signal relationships of authority denaturalizes them and the assumption that masculinized bodies best represent the body politic. It enables also a consideration of ways that the dichotomy between compassion and authority, feeling and cognition, empathy and judgment contributes further to the association of the authoritative with what is patriarchally defined as masculine and the disassociation of what is patriarchally defined as feminine from public life. When we read political discourse through the lens of gender, the specific constellation of offices associated with public leadership, the kinds of knowledge qualified as legitimate knowledge, the definition of political judgment as the practice of a commanding, dispassionate gaze, and the monolithic nature of the willfulness of authorities become more noticeably defined in patriarchally masculinized terms.

My investigation of the gendered codes for recognizing an authority requires a strategic use of signs of sexual difference—those historical marks of embodiment, voice, role, and wisdom that have been taken to represent one sex or gender or another. I use "masculine" and "feminine" as categories of meaning, as names for specific marks of authority that have otherwise masqueraded as universal, objective, genderless signs of authority's presence. I am aware that using these terms necessarily risks reinforcing the very stereotypes about representations of "woman" that feminists have claimed to want to subvert.

Risk and danger are inherent in all discursive strategies. Any strategy "is a risk because its effects, its outcome, are always unpredictable and undecidable." The effects of a particularly risky strategy depend upon, among other things, historical circumstance, cultural context, and subject-position (Fuss 1989, 19). My intent is not to claim that some "masculine essence" hides out under the cover of Western political theory but to recover the ways that specific practices for legitimating authority depend upon excluding what has been called "the feminine" for establishing their own credibility. I want to provoke us to think about how the separation between things we call masculine and feminine is the effect, among other things, of a particular discourse about and marking of authority. In this exploration, I will focus especially on how particular notions of judgment construct a specifically gendered discourse on authority.

Judgment and the Dispassionate Gaze

WESTERN POLITICAL THEORY is a catalog of different systems for mapping the constellations of belief that locate authority in specific places, for marking its territory. One of the most influential modern typologies for distinguishing among the "marks" of authority is Max Weber's formulation. Weber cataloged three types of legitimate rule: rational, traditional, and charismatic. Each of these three kinds of claims to authority was, he argued, paralleled by a "type of obedience, the kind of administrative staff developed to guarantee it, and the mode of exercising authority" (Weber 1947, 325). Do any of these forms of rulership depend upon representations that privilege masculinity, or are they gender-neutral?

Weber argued that the hallmark of modernity was the gradual shift from personal to impersonal, rational rule. Instrumental rationality, the model of modern authority, was the pursuit of established ends by the most efficient means. The fundamental characteristics of rational legal authority were the "continuous conduct of rule-bound official business," where each office extended to a specified sphere of competence (jurisdiction), and where the "organization of offices follow[ed] the principle of hierarchy; that is, each lower office is under the control and supervision of a higher one" (Weber 1978, 213).

Weber made the emphasis on office over person one of the distinguishing characteristics of bureaucratic authority. It was this feature that permitted rational legal systems to administer authority over human beings with the highest degree of efficiency. "Bureaucratization," he wrote, "offers above all the optimum possibility for carrying through the principle of specializing administrative functions according to purely objective considerations . . . 'Objective' discharge of business primarily means a discharge of business according to *calculable rules* and 'without regard for persons'"(Weber 1978, 975). This disregard of the personal extended to the relationship between an office-holder and the office held. Weber argued that "in the rational type case, there is also a complete absence of appropriation of his official position by the incumbent" (Weber 1978, 219).

Locating authority in the office itself, rather than in the specific person who occupies it, appears to negate all the personal dimensions of authority. The separation of the personal, or charismatic, dimensions of authority from the practice of authority in rational legal systems seems to establish authority in the most gender-neutral terms. The more that ruling is depersonalized, the more its characteristics transcend the boundaries of sex. Anyone, regardless of sex, can occupy an authoritative office. Yet, the question of the gender of rational legal systems of authority depends upon the extent to which ruling constituted as "objective discharge of business . . . 'without regard for persons'" itself can be considered a gendered practice.

Some recent analyses of this conceptualization of ruling practiced as instrumental rationality have taken it to be indicative of patriarchally masculinized practices. Wendy Brown has argued, for instance, that "Weber's analysis of modern political and economic institutions reveals instrumental rationality to have been harnessed to specific projects of manhood . . . . These projects include a quest for freedom defined as liberation from constraint and power defined as domination" (Brown 1988, 152). Paying particular attention to the effects of connecting instrumental rationality with mechanisms of social control and domination on the reproduction of gender, Brown contends that "the complete realization of rationalized economic and political life, with its qualities of disciplined obedience and conformity, creates men who are calculable and predictable, models of behavioralist analysis, fully conditioned into automatons . . : . It is not the feminine alone that is imperiled under conditions of rationalization . . . The will to freedom, control, domination, and power . . . has engendered such total systems of domination in the form of capitalism and the bureaucratic state that *manhood itself, at the moment at which it is fully realized, is wholly crushed*" (Brown 1988, 162, emphasis added).

In other words, "the most rational form of exercising authority over human beings" rests upon the routinization of experience and the annihilation of any inner life, an inner life that Weber had identified as "the feminine" (Brown 1988, 128–129). Yet this routinization of experience also devirilizes most men by transforming them into uniformly disciplined cogs in what Weber termed a "ceaselessly moving mechanism." Regardless of their sex, bureaucratic leaders are masculinized because they alone are above the merely subjective pull of everyday life; whether they are males or females, their followers are feminized because they are subjected to the soulless commands of rationalized, instrumentalist, and institutionalized manliness.

In the Western liberal tradition a political authority is supposed to be a neutral, disinterested, and impartial judge, one who issues or interprets rules that are meant to be applied to any member of the polity equally. Uninfluenced by any particularized connection to or feelings about specific citizens/subjects, all of whom have consented, either explicitly or implicitly, to being ruled, and, therefore, are equally obligated to comply with the rules; an authority makes judgments that, in the political arena, become binding because they are issued by those who have entitlement to judge.

Determinations of entitlement vary constitutionally, but the effect of being entitled to rule in the tradition of positive law is to create an office of command whose purpose is to create a unity of will out of the diversity of wills consenting to being ruled in the first place. To judge authoritatively, to make legitimate decisions within this framework, means, among other things, to be able to treat persons as fungible objects where their peculiar characteristics—their specific identity, their irreducible distinctiveness—becomes irrelevant to the practice of authority. To judge authoritatively means to judge impartially, from a position "outside and above" the conflict itself (Young 1987, 60). From this position "outside and above," political authorities promulgate and enforce laws that are themselves assumed to be universal and impartial. Thus, one of the signs of being in authority is the ability to articulate universal and impartial rules, rules that replace disorder with order.

This discourse on rule-making normalizes authority as a distant, dispassionate, and disciplinary gaze. Such a discourse secures authority by opposing it to emotive connectedness or compassion. Within this discourse of judgment as impartiality, authorities order existence through general rules applied fairly, that is, equally to all. Actors and actions are defined by these rules. Compassion cuts through this orderly universe with feelings that connect us to the specificity and particularity of actors and actions. Compassion's "rules" are defined by the particularity of actors and actions. Being attuned to the particular makes compassion seem anarchical, even ruleless. Rational-legal authority's rules distance us from the person and the personal. Its rules treat everyone as anyone, not someone in particular. Compassion pulls us into a face-to-face encounter with a specific, concrete other. Rational-legal authority subjugates and domesticates desire, affect, and "those aspects of life associated with the body" (Young 1987, 64). Compassion subverts the universal point of view by refusing the totalizing and dehumanizing effects of a transcendent rationality in favor of desire's "going public" by joining forces with "reason."

Rational-legal authority enables groups of individuals, necessarily in conflict with one another, to resolve their conflicts by appealing to the rules that specify priorities of rights. The rules of authority provide sanctuary from the dangers of social intercourse, or from what Hannah Arendt called the uncertainty of action in a world of plural agents. From the vantage point or gaze of the rules, the uncertainty of living in a world of difference can be managed by the application of the correct abstract principle. Although it comes to be associated with systems of rule that are themselves genderless, this form of ordering social behavior is at least arguably "masculine." The modern normalization of authority as a disciplinary gaze represents, in classical psychoanalytic terms, the masculinization of this aspect of being in authority.

Both the omniscient watchfulness and apparently threatening nature of authority produces passive and compliant subjects. Michel Foucault has contributed significantly to the study of the complex ways that modern discourses and technologies of power—technologies that permit power to "gain access to the bodies of individuals, to their acts, attitudes and modes of everyday behavior"—create the subjugation of the subject through processes that "subject our bodies, govern our gestures, dictate our behaviors, etc."(Foucault 1980, 125, 97). The subject of modern discourses of power is produced as a subject *to be looked at, to be watched.*

Foucault's research on the rise of power as the "permanent exercise of indefinite discipline" (Foucault 1979, 217) has amply documented the ways that modern discourses of science, medicine, health, aesthetics, and so forth, contribute to the elaboration of a complex web of authority as control, producing modern subjects as subjugated subjects. Yet, Foucault did not always make clear the gendered nature of the subject-position produced by this discourse of power as domination and authority as the "sovereignty" of surveillance: The masculinization of authority follows from the feminization of subjects, subjects whose being disciplined through their bodies represents their "feminization."

In *Discipline and Punish,* Foucault suggested that the localization of power in monarchical sovereignty was superseded by the multiplication of power in what he called a "society of surveillance." The fact of power's dispersal seemed to undermine the existence of structured dimensions to power. Yet, if sovereignty lost its apparent indivisibility in the context of a "disciplinary modality of power," this is not, as Foucault himself recognized, because the internalization of the gaze has replaced all the other, older forms of power, "but because it has infiltrated the others, sometimes undermining them, but serving as an intermediary between them, linking them together, extending them and above all making it possible to bring the effects of power to the most minute and distant elements" (216).

The subject of disciplinary power takes the sovereign into herself making the existence of external controls seem redundant. Since the construction of *to-be-looked-at-ness* is precisely the way that disciplinary power works its effects on all its subjects, it would be accurate to claim that the "citizen" in the disciplinary state becomes feminized; correspondingly, judgment as the operation of the gaze becomes a masculinized, ocular-centric practice.

Moral Reciprocity and Compassionate Authority

TO JUDGE OUTSIDE and above, as if one were an unsituated, disembodied, and disinterested actor, has become the hallmark of rational decisionmaking. Modern theories of judgment postulate the autonomous individual as a moral agent who responds to the world in a moral way by applying universal, abstract rules to concrete, yet generalizable, situations. Moreover, to judge impartially is to treat others as if they were just like us, "entitled to the same rights and duties we would want to ascribe to ourselves" (Benhabib 1987, 87). To judge is to apply neutral rules to abstracted persons.

Judgment as the equal application of rules establishes justice as fairness—a formal, public practice of the granting of appropriate rights to and the demanding of corresponding obligations from isolated, undifferentiated subjects by impartial umpires who remain indifferent to the particularity of the subjects in question. The sphere of justice as this sort of practice is structured in opposition to the sphere of personal, intimate, caring relations. In the latter sphere, human relations are "governed by norms of *equity* and *complementary reciprocity.* Each is entitled to expect and to assume from the other forms of behavior through which the other feels recognized and confirmed as a concrete, individual being with specific needs, talents, and capacities" (Benhabib 1987, 87). Insofar as the dominant model of judgment remains impartiality, then practices of judgment

that attempt to judge from within, instead of only from without, are dele-
gitimated as practices of justice and consigned to the private sphere.

Yet, the standard of judgment established through norms of impartiality that treats others as "just like us" masks a bias that is masculinized in its
perspective and colonizing in its effects. Its own objectivity is called into
question by its interests in defining subjects as compliant, malleable selves.
The distinctiveness and potential for resistance of human subjects must be
ignored in order to affirm the correctness and power of the perspective of
the one who is judging. Subjects who are not like us, not like the judges,
must either be domesticated or extradited.

One of the features of feminist democratic theory is the centrality that
difference and plurality play in its elaboration of practices of justice and
judgment. Feminist moral theorists claim that to judge a situation exclusively "from outside," to interpret it from a distanced perspective without
any effort to empathize or to explore the situation also "from within," is
the height of patriarchalized masculinity's "arrogant perception" (Frye
1983). In feminist theories of justice, judgment requires moral reciprocity—taking the standpoint of the other or putting oneself imaginatively in
the place of the other (Benhabib 1987, 89). To be able to take up the
standpoint of the other requires knowledge of the situation *from the perspective of the other.* This means having access to knowledge of concrete others,
"knowledge of the agents involved in these situations, of their histories,
attitudes, characters, and desires" (Benhabib 1987, 90). Benhabib's notion
of "moral reciprocity," along with the understanding of judgment in the
work of other feminist writers on ethics, such as Tronto (1993), Young
(1987), and Held (1990), requires a de-centering of judgment exclusively
from the position of those who are "like us" and the taking up imaginatively of the perspective and position of the other. This imaginative taking
up of the position of the other is what is at work in what I call "compassionate authority."

A practice of judgment derived from the standpoint of the "concrete
other" does not simply reject but rather builds on the stance of judgment represented in conceptualizations of authority as traditionally rule-
governed behavior. Elisabeth Spelman has called this alternative practice
of judgment the moral practice of treating a person as the person one is.
Instead of seeing a person exclusively as the universal bearer of rights, this
alternative practice of judgment responds "to the person someone is or,
more exactly, the person who someone takes himself or herself to be"
(Spelman 1978, 151). For Benhabib, it is not a question of choosing
between the position of the "generalized" or the "concrete" other; rather,
we "recognize the dignity of the generalized other through an acknowledgment of the moral identity of the concrete other" (1978, 92).

If recognizing the concrete other requires being able to understand
accurately who the other is *as the other sees herself or himself,* then how do we

arrive at this position? Spelman has contended that the "concept of treating someone as a person implies that you have a certain authority about who you are, about the features of yourself which are central to the person you are" (1978, 152). We begin to arrive at the perspective of the other from which we should judge an action, or the appropriateness of the application of a rule, by ceding to the other some minimal sense that she is an important source of knowledge about herself.

Yet, Spelman also cautioned against claiming that a person's authority about who she is, or her control over her standpoint, is complete or unimpeachable. Both the possibility that we may be deceived about the persons we think that we are and the idea that knowledge of the self is constructed in the context of communicative interactions require us to see identity as socially constituted and, hence, subject to different interpretations.

Our identity is not whatever we declare it to be. Instead, identity is bound up with our own specific individual histories, as well as the complex web of cultural practices that we share with those with whom we most closely identify. In addition, specific political, economic, and social institutions, ideologies, and practices limit our knowledge of ourselves, structure cultural practices, and shape the range of possible identities available to us as concrete positions. These structured constellations of power precede and exceed the boundaries or the origins of the immediate group to which we claim to belong and limit any individual or group's ability to perceive and to critique its own position as such.

Having access to knowledge of the other from the perspective of the other reflects feminist efforts to conjoin justice with care, suggesting a model for judgment that Benhabib calls "communicative need interpretations." This model moves away from understanding judgment as the imposition of rules from outside and above a situation, calling instead for *dialogic* inquiry into "not only rights but needs, not only justice but possible modes of the good life." Emphasis on the dialogic characteristics of the practice of justice as communicative need interpretations has the advantage of supplanting the gaze of impartiality with the discourse of public speech. Unfolding in a space "created by commonality and uniqueness," this sort of ideal role-taking—being able to enter into the world of the other, imaginatively taking on the other's view—presupposes the transformation of the conditions and content of public speech and action so as to permit an openness to diversity that could enable "moral and political agents to define their own concrete identities on the basis of recognizing each other's dignity as generalized others" (Benhabib 1987, 92, 93; White 1991).

The norms of judgment implicit in caring for the concrete other, who is seen as a specific person with specific needs and interests, are the norms that Seyla Benhabib has identified as "friendship, love and care" (Benhabib 1987, 87). However valid these norms may be as representa-

tions of alternatives to distanced, impartial practices of judgment, the difficulty that remains is to determine how far we can extend these moral categories, derived from intimate relationships, into the arena of political
discourse and public action. To what extent, for instance, can the sort of
ethical commitment that we learn through what Sara Ruddick has called
"maternal stories" be extended beyond the horizon of intimate, interpersonal relations? Minimally, such an extension requires reworking both the
structure and the ethos of intimate relations, including the structure and
ethos of "the family." We may be capable of caring far more than we do at
present about the sufferings of those who are more distant from us in habit
as well as space. But we need to consider exactly how we can encourage the
development of expanded care-taking enterprises in ways that neither
overburden women, who have been disproportionately burdened with the
demands of care-taking, nor require us to reduce the feminist concern
with care-taking as a model of judgment to a "wholly impossible politics of
universal love" (Ferguson 1984, 172).

The kind of judgment found in compassionate authority depends
upon an "ideal of identifying with women's struggles quite different from
one's own" that does not reduce these other struggles to instances reflect-
ing one's own view of the priorities of struggle but responds instead "to
women in particular situations of struggle" (Ruddick 1989, 240). The
dilemma, of course, is how to respond to the particular while remaining
committed to some vision of a feminist future that subscribes to generalizable criteria for determining progress toward greater equality and dignity
for women and men.

Compassion enables the imaginative taking up of the position of the
other. It depends upon a willingness of the compassionate judge to judge
from a perspective other than what is good for "me and mine." Crossing
borders that bound the safe environs of one's own home, one's identity,
one's nation, moving in the world "as if" through other people's minds,
hearts, and bodies, and seeing the world from other's perspectives, as
much as that is possible, suggests that there are necessary connections
between compassionate authority and concepts of justice. Although most
discussions in political theory treat these concepts as analytically separate,
the rethinking of authority in ways that I have defined entails attention to
the interdependence of a variety of concepts not ordinarily linked.

A Response to Arendt's Critique of Compassion

IMAGINATIVELY TAKING UP the position of another links the idea of compassion with concern for the suffering of another. This linkage led Hannah
Arendt to argue that it was impossible to found authority on such a sentiment. Arendt feared that rather than reconstituting a public realm in

which action in concert was facilitated, identification with the "immediacy of suffering" that compassion excited led ultimately to boundless violence. For Arendt, because compassion inevitably deteriorated into pity, it was much more likely to lead to domination and the imposition of the will of leaders than it ever would lead to the sort of deliberative reflections that were, for her, emblematic of political life. "Because compassion abolishes the distance, the worldly space between men where political matters, the whole realm of human affairs, are located, it remains, politically speaking, irrelevant" (Arendt 1963, 81).

Yet, if Arendt was critical of compassion as a model for authority, she was equally hostile to the idea that command was the form that authority ought to take. Arendt's concern was to reconstitute authority so as to make it work to sustain better the sorts of relations that would enable deliberative reflection on the principles of public life consistent with the human condition of plurality. Arendt's rejection of domination as a model for political authority was the result of the same interpretation that led her to reject compassion. Neither command nor compassion respected the human condition of plurality; both depended on violence for the resolution of political conflicts.

I take Arendt's focus on plurality to be central to feminist theories of democracy. Yet, I disagree with her reading of the opposition between compassion and solidarity, as well as her contention that compassion leads inevitably to violence. There is a certain tension, then, in feminist usage of Arendt's analysis that must be acknowledged. Her theory of politics remains useful to feminism only if basic assumptions that she makes about the relationship between politics and social life and between compassion and tolerance are challenged.

Arendt argued that it was compassion, or more precisely, the confusion of pity for the masses with solidarity that accounted for the destructiveness and violence of revolutionary authority. Virtue, Arendt contended, can be embodied in lasting institutions; compassion cannot. Virtue facilitates political action. It operates in the sphere of choice and knows the limits of human existence. Pity, or the "passion of compassion," cannot focus on specific persons in their specific suffering; it comprehends the masses in their boundless suffering. It sees "a multitude—the factual plurality of a nation or a people or society—in the image of one supernatural body driven by one superhuman, irresistible 'general will'" (Arendt 1963, 54). Pity, as the sentimental perversion of compassion, undermines solidarity. Solidarity enables the deliberate and dispassionate establishment of "a community of interest with the oppressed and exploited." Arendt calls solidarity a "principle that can inspire and guide action." Although it may be "aroused by suffering, it is not guided by it, and it comprehends the strong and the rich no less than the weak and the poor; compared with the sentiment of pity, it may appear cold and abstract, for it remains committed to 'ideas'—to greatness, or honor, or dignity—rather than to any 'love' of men" (Arendt 1963, 84).

For Arendt, the problem with compassion is it soon deteriorates into pity and becomes unable to distinguish among the masses. Moreover, pity recognizes no commonality between the strong and the weak; it can only comprehend suffering in terms of quantity, not kind. Pity responds only to the massiveness of the sheer number of sufferers, not the particularity of their pain or struggle. Accepting no limitation to their own willfulness to attempt to put an end to suffering itself, compassionate political interventions become responses to the "urgency of the life process itself" (Arendt 1963, 55). Unable to "establish and hold fast to rapports with persons in their singularity," and masking the power relations that it nevertheless wants to sustain behind its show of emotion, compassion is disingenuous. Without the "presence of misfortune, pity could not exist, and it has therefore just as much vested interest in the existence of the unhappy as thirst for power has a vested interest in the existence of the weak" (Arendt 1963, 85, 84).

For Arendt compassion must be constrained by the inevitable limitations of ourselves as "organic bodies, subject to necessary and irresistible processes" (Arendt 1963, 110). The inevitable struggle with "necessity" meant that any effort to end forever the "suffering" or the unhappiness of humankind by political means could only be doomed to failure. Violence existed as the ever present horizon of any political intervention intended to guarantee a conflictless human existence. The threat of violence as a "raging force . . . nourished by the necessity of biological life itself . . . as irresistible as the motion of the stars, a torrent rushing forward with elemental force, engulfing a whole world" marked the boundary of compassion's public life (Arendt 1963, 108–109).

Arendt feared the implications of any wish to escape our bodies, or the suffering and pain that being embodied entails when that wish became attached, as a "principle," to the public realm. For Arendt, the history of the struggle to end suffering by political means was the history of the deterioration of authority into "rulership." "All rulership has its original and its most legitimate source in man's wish to emancipate himself from life's necessity, and men achieved such liberation by means of violence, by forcing others to bear the burden of life for them" (Arendt 1963, 110).

For instance, whereas some modern theorists—some recent feminists among them—would applaud the inventions of science, seeing in technology the means to end human suffering, for Arendt, the "rise of technology" was not the harbinger of an age or a world that enhanced freedom. Freedom could not be the end of suffering or the limitations of embodiment but could only come from engaged political action in the public realm. For Arendt, the modern age of science, with its promise to create "artificial" life, and the modern world "born with the first atomic explosions" were mirror images. Each had contributed to "modern world alienation, [with] its twofold flight from the earth into the universe and from the world into the self" (Arendt 1958, 2, 6).

Is it possible to reconcile freedom and rational discourse with compassion and remain able to distinguish political authority from compulsion or the demand for blind obedience? What Arendt translates as the "barbarian vice of effeminacy" and rejects as a principle of authority may yet provide an important way to make authority more compatible with agency.

In Arendt's terms, human understanding is understanding the limits of human action in the world. It means living in a world in which one has to make choices and suffer the consequences. Action is earth-bound. Yet, authority seems to lift one beyond one's emotions, beyond "merely" private, "merely" personal feelings. Authority is embodied in the judge who orders the sentence of death despite sympathy for the accused.

Arendt's interpretation of Captain Vere's actions in Herman Melville's *Billy Budd* best represents her view here. She argues that Vere must condemn Budd for the crime of murder, even though he knows Budd is innocent in some larger sense of the term. Authority cannot be modified by compassion in this instance. To allow compassion to rule would be to allow unreflective immediate action to be substituted for the processes of persuasion, negotiation, and compromise. It would be to substitute faith for reason. Arendt contends that it is the very directness of the compassionate response that removes it, or ought to remove it, from the realm of politics, and hence the realm of lasting institutions, to practices that will endure.

Yet, Vere's response to Budd is not unmediated, as Arendt claims. Vere's response to Budd is mediated by his understanding that his relationship to Budd is like that of a father to a son. Arendt contends that this sort of connection, born of compassion and caring, is particularized and that it would soon deteriorate if brought into the open, into the public realm, into the "boundlessness of an emotion that . . . [would] respond only too well to the boundless suffering of the multitude in their sheer overwhelming numbers . . . drown[ing] all special considerations, the considerations of friendship, no less than considerations of statecraft and principle" (Arendt 1963, 85).

Yet, compassion and caring are not without their own rules, their own principles and rational interests. Vere's caring for Billy Budd provides him with the knowledge that the law he is required to apply is more barbaric than the act that it punishes. As an ironic commentary on Arendt's interpretation that following the rule of law secures the public space for rational, persuasive discourse, Vere declares that among his reasons for condemning Budd is that the people, "long molded by arbitrary discipline, have not the kind of intelligent responsiveness that might qualify them to comprehend and discriminate" (Melville 1961, 68–69). Finally, too, the death of Billy Budd, while ostensibly carrying out the "measured forms" of politics, achieves no positive, augmenting, political value. It does not facilitate action but conformity.

The importance of connecting compassion and authority is that it reminds us that the order that authority as sovereignty imposes can never represent the world in all its complexity. Compassion can respond to the gesture of those who are inarticulate, thereby helping, in William Connolly's words, "that which is subordinate to find its own voice and, perhaps, to expand the space in which [the subordinate] can be for itself rather than only for the order" (Connolly 1987, 23).

The "rational" modes of speech taken to be constitutive of authority exclude certain critical human dimensions, voices, and "interests" from the discourse of rationality and from circulation in the public realm. Indeed, the structure of authority as commanding sovereignty in the public realm is connected internally to this exclusion. These dimensions, voices, and interests cannot be translated simply into the language of dispassionate, discursive speech. Nevertheless, their expressiveness is essential to understanding nuances of meaning and to recognizing what has been silenced by modes of political speech that know only the imperative mood and the future tense.

Compassion as attention to the need of a particularized other is an attention oriented to the other person's needs that resists translating these specific needs and particular desires into reflections of one's self: a "knowing the other without finding *yourself* in her" (Ruddick 1989, 121). It represents the capacity to attend to another's suffering in a way that preserves the other's suffering in all its particularity. The practice of "solidarity," a practice that recognizes the uniqueness of different women's and men's "particular situations of struggle" and suffering, enables the extension of compassion's scope beyond the "private" sphere from which it emerges into the public realm (Ruddick 1989, 240).

Compassion preserves the particularity of the other's suffering; it is "other-directed," identifying the needs of others *as distinct from* one's own. Yet, because another's problems are *distinct* from my own does not mean that I cannot, through compassion, perceive another's suffering *as if* it were my own and work in solidarity with unique others towards certain goals. Such a discourse of solidarity that respects difference seems to be precisely what feminists have been stressing is necessary to reflect the practice of building a world that is friendly to women in all their diversity.

The tragedy of the human condition is that, as Arendt recognized, we live in a plural world—a world in which we are all the same, that is, human, and at the same time utterly, isolatingly unique. The promise of the human condition is that our very plurality—being born and beginning again and again—provides the opportunity for our speaking and acting to live together, building a world together, learning to be at home in this world, whose durability will outlast our immediate actions only if our actions move beyond the range of the useful (Arendt 1958, 173). Although we can never *be* another person, our capacity for speech and action enables us to bridge this distance between each of us, to understand one another, to achieve what Nancy Fraser has called an "ethic of solidarity" (Fraser 1984, 425–429; see also Love 1991, 102–122; White 1991).

Arendt had argued that it was humanly impossible to establish solidarity by bringing compassion into the public. "Whatever the passions and emotions may be, and whatever their true connection with thought and reason, they certainly are located in the human heart . . . . The qualities of the human heart need darkness and protection against the light of the public to grow and to remain what they are meant to be, innermost motives that are not meant for public display" (Arendt 1963, 91). Carried into the public realm, into the light of the world, Arendt argued, the conflicts that emotions express become "murderous because they [are] insoluble" (Arendt 1963, 93). Yet, Ruddick has contended that the reasoning of the emotions can provide a lucid kind of knowledge that not only can withstand but even requires "going public" to work its transformative effects (Ruddick 1989, 237). For Ruddick, compassion does not have to be expressed immediately; it can become the motivating force behind "active responsibility and engagement." Moreover, the language of compassion, taken into the public realm, can be made the language, not of violence, but of protective peace-making.

Acting on the promise of natality requires compassionate authority, attentive love toward the world. Although Arendt endorsed the action of world-protection and complained most vehemently about those human endeavors that seemed rooted in the denial of birth and the rejection of the earth as our home, she distrusted the modeling of political relationships on the household. Yet, it is an ironic commentary on Arendt's work that someone who so radically distinguished between the social and the political, and between the private and the public, nonetheless wrote about understanding the "world" as the "man-made home erected on earth," and eloquently contended that "without being at home in the midst of things whose durability makes them fit for use and for erecting a world whose very permanence stands in direct contrast to life, this life would never be human" (Arendt 1958, 135).

Compassion has the potential for humanizing authority. If women do not represent those who speak authoritatively, in a commanding voice, perhaps the hesitancy of this different kind of speech reveals the ambiguity, and the choices, behind all systems of rule. By reminding us of this ambiguity, the voice and gesture of compassion shocks us into a memory of what has been hidden by the ordered discourse of authority: the utter contingency of our being born and our original dependency upon the body of a woman for the possibility of our acting at all.

It is of course possible to go too far in the other direction. Refusing to engage in any political judgment because all judgment smacks of discipline and assumed mastery is dangerous because it leaves untouched the "immediate plight of women," or of anyone suffering under the weight of existing injustices and constraints. Rejecting the idea of Enlightenment truth as a final, fixed point does not necessarily require that we repudiate any efforts aimed at "progress" in human rights, liberatory practices, or the pursuit of a more just, less authoritarian order. We may criticize the limits of certain strategies of resistance—the fact that choices close down other options, close off certain ways of living—but we cannot afford to choose not to choose. In Stephen White's (1991) words, we have the responsibility to otherness and the responsibility to act.

The riskiness of acting in the public realm is the combined result of the fact that all human action is performed in a space "where everything and everybody are seen and heard by others," and that action is ultimately unpredictable and irreversible (Arendt 1958, 77). There can be no false comfort that we will not do more violence than we intend when we aim for the "good." My defense of compassionate authority provides no more certainty that any harmonious feminist community will necessarily result. What my defense does is provide a way of thinking about ways that compassion can have public resonance because it suggests a way towards establishing a *dialogue* about solidarity with one another's needs.

Having accepted responsibility for acting does *not* annihilate the imperative to act; instead it serves as its foundation. The responsible, politically engaged, yet compassionate individual judges and acts without the protection of an armament of frozen, canonized, moral principles; hence she is subject to the painful knowledge that the chosen action may not be right or may not be right forever. What is gone in the modern world is the security of self-righteousness and the certainty of authority. But if security and certainty have disappeared, the need for authority as meaningful order has not. Its achievement may be made more ambiguous and humbled by the dynamics of modernity. It nonetheless can and must be re-grounded.

References

Arendt, Hannah. 1958. *The Human Condition.* Chicago: University of Chicago Press.

Arendt, Hannah. 1963. *On Revolution.* New York: Viking Press.

Bell, Wendell, Richard J. Hill, and Charles R. Wright. 1961. *Public Leadership.* San Francisco: Chandler Publishing Co.

Benhabib, Seyla. 1987. "The Generalized and the Concrete Other: The Kohlberg-Gilligan Controversy and Feminist Theory." In *Feminism as Critique: On the Politics of Gender.* Ed. Seyla Benhabib and Drucilla Cornell. Minneapolis: University of Minnesota Press.

Brown, Wendy. 1988. *Manhood and Politics: A Feminist Reading in Political Theory.* Totowa, N.J.: Rowman and Littlefield.

Connolly, William. 1987. "Modern Authority and Ambiguity." In *Nomos xxix: Authority Revisited*. Ed. Rolland Pennock and John Chapman. New York: New York University Press.

Ferguson, Kathy. 1984. *The Feminist Case Against Bureaucracy*. Philadelphia: Temple University Press.

Foucault, Michel. 1979. *Discipline and Punish: The Birth of the Prison*. Trans. Alan Sheridan. New York: Vintage.

Foucault, Michel. 1980. *Power/Knowledge: Selected Interviews and Other Writings. 1972–1977*. Ed. Colin Gordon. New York: Pantheon.

Fraser, Nancy. 1984. "Toward a Discourse Ethic of Solidarity." *Praxis International* 4:425–429.

Friedman, Richard. 1973. "On the Concept of Authority in Political Philosophy." In *Concepts in Social and Political Philosophy*. Ed. Richard Flathman. New York: Macmillan.

Frye, Marily. 1983. *The Politics of Reality: Essays in Feminist Theory*. Trumansburg, N.Y.: Crossing Press.

Fuss, Diana. 1989. *Essentially Speaking: Feminism, Nature, and Difference*. New York: Routledge.

Held, Virginia. 1990. "Feminist Transformations of Moral Theory." *Philosophy and Phenomenological Research* 1 (Supplement):321–344.

Jonasdóttir, Anna G. 1994. *Why Women Are Oppressed*. Philadelphia: Temple University Press.

Jones, Kathleen B. 1993. *Compassionate Authority: Democracy and the Representation*. New York: Routledge.

Love, Nancy. 1991. "Politics and Voice(s): An Empowerment/Knowledge Regime. *Differences* 3:85–103.

Melville, Herman. 1961. *Billy Budd and Other Tales*. New York: Signet.

Ruddick, Sara. 1989. *Maternal Thinking: Toward a Politics of Peace*. New York: Ballantine Books.

Sapiro, Virginia. 1983. *The Political Integration of Women: Roles, Socialization and Politics*. Champaign, Urbana. Ill.: University of Illinois Press.

Spelman, Elizabeth. 1978. "On Treating Persons as Persons." *Ethics* 88: 150–161.

Tronto, Joan. 1993. *Moral Boundaries: A Political Argument for an Ethic of Care*. New York: Routledge.

Welch, Susan. 1977. "Women as Political Animals." *American Journal of Political Science* 21:711–730.

Weber, Max. 1947. *Theory of Social and Economic Organizations*. Glencoe, Ill.: Free Press.

Weber, Max. 1978. *Economy and Society: An Outline of Interpretive Sociology*. Ed. Guenther Roth and Claus Wittich. Berkeley: University of California Press.

White, Stephen. 1991. *Political Theory and Postmodernism*. Cambridge: Cambridge University Press.

Young, Iris. 1987. "Impartiality and the Civic Public: Some Implications of Feminist Critiques of Moral and Political Theory." In *Feminism as Critique*. Ed. Seyla Benhabib and Drucilla Cornell. Minneapolis: University of Minnesota Press.

5

Autonomy in the Light of Difference

Christine Di Stefano

Along with other prized concepts of modern liberal political culture, autonomy has been subjected to feminist critical scrutiny.[1] Because of its centrality to standard feminist political goals—control over our bodies, our labor and economic resources, our life decisions—autonomy would not seem to require much "revisioning." But in fact contemporary Western feminism exhibits a complex ambivalence toward autonomy, which is unappreciated by most traditional contemporary theorists of autonomy who assume or argue, usually with minimal, if any, demonstration, that autonomy is just what feminists want for women. A closer look reveals a more nuanced picture. How has autonomy fared under the feminist gaze?

Trouble with Autonomy: Preliminary Observations

ACKNOWLEDGING THAT NARRATIVE beginnings are invariably arbitrary and that they prefigure the structure of resolution or closure proffered in endings, I take as my point of departure *The Second Sex*, in which Simone de Beauvoir highlighted and pursued relentlessly the heteronomous construction of "Woman" (de Beauvoir 1974). From this vantage, twentieth-century Western feminism enacts the articulation of widespread disappointment and rage with respect to women's longstanding experiences of being governed and defined by others, of being subjected to various imposed forms of social, political, and cultural rule that prescribe and enforce their unequal and deficient status relative to men. Beauvoir's genealogy of Western femininity identified and analyzed the various mechanisms and symbolics involved in the production of the feminized Other. In spite of her repeated insistence that women should assertively claim the benefits and responsibilities of male-monopolized subject-status for themselves, however, her analysis also intimated a contrary conclusion. To the extent that the feminized Other functions as a prop for the virile, autonomous self, this might also suggest that the ideal of autonomy is problematic by virtue of its intimate and longstanding imbrication in feminized alterity. In effect, Beauvoir's analysis of Western femininity induced the suspicion among some readers that masculinized autonomy and feminized heteronomy function as a couplet; that feminized heteronomy cannot be jettisoned without remainder, without influence on our conception of the autonomous subject.

This complicated theoretical legacy continues to inflect Western feminist thinking about autonomy and related models of subjectivity, agency, empowerment, and emancipation. In the aftermath of *The Second Sex*, feminists have questioned autonomy as a normative standard of mature selfhood and emancipation even as we continue to invoke it as a desideratum. Within contemporary Western feminist discourse, the legacy of autonomy exhibits positive as well as negative valences.

For instance, echoing the traditional liberal view of autonomy as the ability to disengage from social context and relationship, Candace Watson has argued that women can best discover sexual autonomy by retreating from heterosexual relations with men. "To some extent," she writes, "sexuality can be lived separate from its [oppressive] social context. . . . Through masturbation, the celibate woman can celebrate her sexuality apart from the aspects of its social expression" (Watson 1987, 257–258).

In a diametrically opposed account, Jean Baker Miller depicts autonomy as an "inappropriate carryover from men's situation." Her quarrel with autonomy is that "it carries the implication—and for women therefore the threat—that one should be able to pay the price of giving up affiliations in order to become a separate and self-directed individual . . . the word *autonomy* seems possibly dangerous; it is a word derived from men's development, not women's" (Miller 1976, 94–95).

Other feminists question autonomy even as they continue, seemingly in spite of themselves, to invoke it as a normative standard of emancipation. In her review of feminist contributions to the conceptualization of citizenship, Kathleen Jones asserts: "Our general emphasis on relationships as definitive of personality and selfhood implies a renewed critique of the concept of autonomy embedded in Western political philosophy" (Jones 1990, 787–788). Yet several pages on, she makes reference to "the potential conflict between personal autonomy and the search for community reflected in radical political movements for social change" (Jones 1990, 809). In this example, autonomy emerges simultaneously as a question and as an unquestioned norm for feminists.

In other cases, autonomy eludes contestation from feminist theorists who are otherwise engaged in the interrogation of ostensibly humanist concepts. Elizabeth Gross contrasts two strands within feminist theory and politics, one motivated by the aim of "equality," the other by the ethos of "female autonomy." According to Gross, "equality" should be handled with skepticism, for it commits its feminist users to pre-established, male-defined norms, whereas autonomy—"women's right to political, social, economic and intellectual self-determination"—"implies the right to see oneself in whatever terms one chooses" (Gross 1987, 193). In direct contrast to Miller, Gross argues that the notion of autonomous self-determination is gender-neutral. Gross also assumes that "equality" and "autonomy" can be disentangled from each other, as if they do not inhabit and comprise a unified conceptual world.[2]

Jean Grimshaw is less sanguine about the salutary effects of autonomy for women; but she is also committed to the project of salvaging a modified autonomy to serve women's needs. Grimshaw takes issue with pro-autonomy feminists such as Weston who distinguish between an "inner" and an "outer" self. The "outer" self is the self that has been coerced through force, conditioning, or psychological manipulation; we may call this the false feminine self. The "inner" self, by contrast, "is seen to be an authentic female self, whose recovery or discovery it is one of the aims of feminism to achieve" (Grimshaw 1988, 93). Grimshaw points out that this kind of thinking is based on a contestable set of assumptions regarding the self: first, "that it is, at least potentially, a unitary, rational thing, aware of its interests" (Grimshaw 1988, 95); second, that divisions within the (otherwise unified) psyche or self result from socialization and conditioning; and third, that the task of undoing feminine conditioning can be achieved through rational processes of analyzing and contesting male domination (Grimshaw 1988, 95). These assumptions congeal into the familiar rendition of autonomy as authenticity, of autonomy as originating within a self which is unpolluted by conditioning or manipulation:

> To be autonomous or authentic one should be strong, independent, rational, coherent or consistent, able to distinguish clearly those aspects of one's previous self which derive from male-dominated conditioning and reject them. If one is ambivalent, conflicted, uncertain, confused, unwilling to make wholesale rejections, one stands to be accused, whether by oneself or by others, of bad faith, of lack of courage, of 'selling out,' of tokenism (Grimshaw 1988, 97).

As a result of this way of thinking about autonomy, some women will feel "put down" by the characterization of their lives as a bundle of coerced and wasted efforts. Even those women who identify as feminists may feel vulnerable to charges of being politically retrograde if they have not completely remade themselves and their lives along unambiguous feminist contours.

On Grimshaw's reading of these problems, the solution lies not with a rejection of autonomy but with its modification. The feminist challenge is "to offer an interpretation [of autonomy] which neither assumes the original unitary self . . . nor ignores the needs of women" (Grimshaw 1988, 105). These needs include the desire of many women "to relate confused fragments of ourselves into something that seems more coherent and of which we feel more in control" (1988, 106). Returning to Watson's model, for example, we might envision sexual autonomy not as a return to one's obfuscated self discovered by means of solitary introspection/masturbation but rather as the quest for other possible selves which might be elicited in new sexual-social habitats.

Finally, recent theoretical work of Foucaultian and Lacanian inspiration on the status of the subject suggests that autonomy should be reconceived as an illusory effect rather than as a substantive achievement or foundational grounding. For example, Judith Butler describes autonomy as "the logical consequence of a disavowed dependency, which is to say that the autonomous subject can maintain the illusion of its autonomy insofar as it covers over the break out of which it is constituted" (Butler 1992, 12). Here we approach the vanishing point of autonomy as a normative political concept. Revisioning the political may involve the thoughtful appraisal of conceptual loss rather than the reconstruction and revival of moribund vocabularies.[3]

These examples illustrate a portion of the diversified range of thinking about autonomy among feminists. Feminist debate regarding the status of autonomy is embedded within a thicket of questions: Is autonomy part of the dominant and domineering gendered political discourse which privileges elite men's behavior and norms? Alternatively, is it an emancipatory concept from which many women and some men have been unfairly excluded and to which they do and should aspire? Is the deployment of autonomy within feminist discourse yet another attempt to stuff unruly feminine matter into civilizing conceptual straightjackets? To what extent is the celebrated self-mastery of the autonomous subject implicated in the construction of and mastery over heteronomous others? If some women refuse heteronomy in the name of autonomy, who will take their place?[4] Among women as a differentiated cohort of persons, which of them are more or less likely to see themselves as candidates for autonomy and why? Can the vanishing point of autonomy actually be thought through? What lies on the other side, particularly as this relates to questions of political agency? Can autonomy be revised in the light of feminist dissatisfaction with and yearning for autonomy?

The Incredibly True Adventures of the Concept of Autonomy

THE "MALESTREAM" CONCEPT of autonomy captures, in an especially compelling and efficient way, the modern discovery and valuation of freedom, reason, and agency housed within a conception of the self as an independent and reflexive rational chooser. It connotes what Stephen Macedo describes as "the active power of persons to shape who they are, to understand, control, and shape their desires. . . . When a person also has the resolve, the fortitude, to act from the results of such delibera- tions, we may think of him or her as autonomous" (Macedo 1991, 225). A number of themes recur in the literature: self-definition, self-mastery, self-determination, self-directedness, self-rule, self-respect, living in har- mony with one's (true) self, authenticity, and procedural independence in defining and identifying with the substance of these terms. Several contemporary theorists of autonomy elaborate this concept within the terms of a "unified life" or "life plan." According to Robert Young: "To the extent that an individual is self-directed he (or she) brings the entire course of his life into a unified order" (R. Young 1989, 78). Gerald Dworkin describes autonomy as a "global concept": "the question of autonomy is one that can only be assessed over extended portions of a person's life. It is a dimension of assessment that evaluates a whole way of living one's life" (Dworkin 1989, 60). Autonomous lives, then, are orderly, consistent, holistically patterned, rationally and deliberately con- structed by an author-self. Even though autonomy is procedural in the sense that the substantive desires of the self are chosen, autonomy imposes certain limits on such choices by insisting that they cohere with one another over time. The autonomous self functions ideally as an effi- cient chooser. Among the cognitive and psychological vices to which autonomy is vulnerable, ambivalence is a notable target of criticism (R. Young 1989, 78).

According to Joel Feinberg, the concept of personal autonomy has four distinct and related meanings: the capacity to govern oneself; the actual condition of self-government; an ideal of character derived from the condition of self-government and its associated virtues; and the sover- eign authority to govern oneself within certain boundaries (on analogy with the sovereign state). Consider now Feinberg's elaboration of the par- allel senses of the term "independent" that correspond to these four dimensions of personal autonomy: "the *capacity* to support oneself, direct one's own life, and finally be responsible for one's own decisions; the *de facto condition* of self-sufficiency; the ideal of self-sufficiency; and . . . the right of self-determination" (Feinberg 1989, 28). "Capacity" in this con- text conjures up several distinct reminders for feminists. The first is that women's capacities for political self-rule have been historically and vari- ably defined to exclude them from the franchise and other democratic mechanisms of representation and self-rule. The second is that such "capacities" are sometimes difficult to know and assess in light of the engendered nature of selfhood and socialization. Feminine socialization has actively discouraged women's capacities for self-support, self-direction and self-responsibility. Third, we recall that women's capacities for self-support are systematically thwarted within the frame of contemporary economic and social arrangements, which continue to rely on a sexual division of labor within households as well as official economies and thereby depress women's abilities to compete with men in the official economy. The *de facto* condition of self-sufficiency highlights, as a counterfactual, a host of familiar and depressing facts including women's vulnerability to physical violence and to poverty. Finally, *de jure* sovereignty and the "right" of self-determination have, most especially via liberal legal discourse, served as a resource for women who have claimed (with alternating periods of success and failure) bodily boundaries within which the state and social opinion may not tread, particularly as these frame issues of reproductive decisionmaking.

The celebrated ideal of autonomy as self-sufficiency, then, operates in two ways. First, it functions as a reminder of women's heteronomy within the contemporary frame of gendered social relations and therefore as a critical resource for the contestation and dismantling of those relations. Autonomy provides a powerful instrument of censure and indictment for a system of gender socialization and enforcement that pre-decides significant aspects of the lives and psyches, and therefore, of the interests and decisionmaking capacities, of persons. The discourse of autonomy has been used, with some success, to create "space" for women as free agents with the capacity for and the right to self-determination. Second, the ideal of self-sufficiency emerges as a question: what does this ideal really mean? Few persons in this, or any other known, society are truly self-sufficient. Is this what women (should) want? In this light, autonomy sits uneasily with feminist criticisms of the modern liberal self, particularly as this involves notions of individualist self-sufficiency and auto-determination.

With few notable exceptions, the mainstream literature on autonomy invokes and presupposes a version of the human subject that is remarkably under-specified. Lorraine Code does not exaggerate when she asserts that "autonomous man is . . . self-sufficient, independent, and self-reliant, a self-realizing individual (Code 1987, 358). This self-to-the-left-of-the-hyphen is, for the most part, uninterrogated. The self-realizing person is a locus of will and intention whose touchstone-effect is a presumably real or authentic self (Meyers 1989). Certifiably autonomous choices *conform with* an autonomous self and help to *produce* an autonomous self. What else do we know about this self?

Thanks to Feinberg's detailed portrait of the autonomous person, we have a bit more to work with than empty, circular references to authenticity, self-definition, and self-realization.[5] His outline of autonomy as "an ideal complex of character traits" lists twelve virtues: self-possession, individuality, authenticity or self-selection, self-creation or self-determination, self-legislation, moral authenticity, moral independence, integrity, self-control, self-reliance, initiative, and responsibility for self (Feinberg 1989).

According to Feinberg, "self-possession" indicates that the autonomous person belongs to no one but himself. "Individuality" suggests that the autonomous person "is not exhaustively defined by his relations to any particular other" (1989, 31). "Self-selection" means that "his tastes, opinions, ideals, goals and preferences are all authentically *his*" (1989, 32). "Self-legislation" is the idea that one follows only those rules one has given to oneself or agreed to in an uncoerced manner. "Moral authenticity" refers to the notion that one's moral convictions are freely and consciously adopted rather than merely inherited. "Moral independence" signals our ability to be independent judges of our moral commitments. "Integrity" suggests consistency and faithfulness to one's principles over time. "Self-control" implies that the self is governed from the "inside" and not from the "outside." "Self-reliance," as Feinberg admits, runs the risk of anti-sociability. It is, nevertheless, an indispensible feature of the autonomous personality. "Initiative" depicts an active person who initiates her own activities and projects rather than taking cues from others. And "responsibility for self" conveys the notion that the autonomous person is responsible for the consequences of her actions.

As Feinberg admits, this sketch is by no means an automatically "attractive ideal." One can be faithful to it and come up with a person who is selfish, who has no moral, political or social commitments whatsoever, or, alternately, who subscribes to immoral principles. What is particularly interesting is that Feinberg's attempts to "reshape" his sketch of the autonomous personality so as to make it more "attractive" involve a taming of some of the very notions that feminists have found troubling, particularly as these connote or require an atomistic conception of the person (C. Keller 1986; Nedelsky 1989, 1990; Wolgast 1987). For example, Feinberg admits that self-creation and authenticity cannot literally be true: "Self-creation is possible but not *ex nihilo*" (Feinberg 1989, 34). Feinberg also limns the boundaries of a too-separative ego who, in the absence of countervailing interests or pressures, is liable to be completely disembedded from any social context: "The ideal of the autonomous person is that of an authentic individual whose self-determination is as complete as is consistent with the requirement that he is, of course, a member of a community" (Feinberg 1989, 45).

"Of course," we murmur in approving response, wondering what all has just been bundled up in this brief acknowledgment of community as a limiting counterpoint to complete self-determination. And, indeed, feminists would be correct to maintain their suspicions. Among the twelve virtues explored by Feinberg, for instance, several are particularly troublesome and cast into doubt the gender-neutrality of Feinberg's explication. Individuality has been questioned as an empirical and normative marker of mature selfhood, while psychoanalytic accounts of subject formation suggest that the notion of self-selection is naive (Benjamin 1988;

Chodorow 1978, 1989; Flax 1990). Self-creation appears bizarre from the perspective of women's reproductive experience and labor (O'Brien 1981). Kantian self-legislation generates two diametrically opposed versions of morality that some feminists would take issue with—anarchistic moral isolation and relativism on the one hand (Murdoch 1970), and universal moral objectivity on the other (Gilligan 1982, 1986, 1987). Self-control contains disturbing echoes of the white male Protestant ethic, along with reminders that the "stuff" (internal and external nature) requiring control has been symbolically coded as feminine (Dinnerstein 1976; E. Keller 1985; Merchant 1980). Finally, self-reliance as a primary value or virtue may interfere with the development of alternative moralities of social connectedness and responsibility to others (Elshtain 1990; Gilligan 1986; James 1993; Noddings 1984; Ruddick 1989; Tronto 1993).

Where do we locate autonomy and how do we endorse decisions and actions as authentically "autonomous"? Within the mainstream literature on autonomy, the attempt to find it a resting place creates a problem of infinite regress with respect to a self whose decisions may not be trusted to be his or her "own." A recurring problem with autonomy has to do with the challenge of determining how we know when our choices are "really" our "own." Gerald Dworkin's effort to develop a procedure for answering this question involves the distinction between higher-order and lower-order desires (Dworkin 1989). Higher-order desires denote our approval of and identification with lower-order desires, the desire to desire what we desire. Higher-order reflections about our lower-order motivations introduce an element of reflection and distance on what it is that we think we want. However, as some critics have asked, what makes us think that we can trust second-level scrutiny of first-order desires? This question introduces the prospect of infinite iteration, moving to ever "higher" levels of reflection on the question of whether we desire to desire what we desire to desire, and so on. The subject-result of such efforts is referred to as a "split-level" self, although the irony and deconstructive implications of this term seem to have been lost on its users, who deploy it quite earnestly (Christman 1989).[6]

Autonomy as consistent self-identity over time seems to require a splitting within that, nevertheless, secures the integrity of the autonomous self by means of privileging its higher-order reflections over lower-order desires. Jennifer Nedelsky (1989, 1990) and other feminist theorists take issue with such figurations of autonomy by pointing out that the self is relational and embedded rather than bounded and separate. But boundaries figure here in a further sense, for the split-level self is *internally* differentiated and divided. When this differentiation is inspired and framed by the philosophical quest for integrity, wholeness and consistency, the guarantee for identity is projected onto a vertical topography of the self: higher-order choices subsume lower-order desires. But on closer inspection, this guarantee takes the form of a perpetual deferral, for there is always another, "higher" plane of reflection from which to scrutinize the last decision. Legitimation of the autonomous self extends into infinity. And with that "holy" movement upwards, a parallel dissection of the "lower" self into proliferating layers of heteronomous waste proceeds apace.

The figuration of the subject of autonomy as an embattled split-level self striving to protect itself from heteronomous influences is captured strikingly in the image of the "inner citadel" (Christman 1989). Deriving from the Latin *citas*, "citadel" is implicated in "citizenship," "a state or city," and "a small city." More conventionally, it can mean "a fortress on a commanding height for defense of a city," "a fortified place or stronghold," "a refuge, place of retreat," and (my personal favorite) "the heavily armored central structure of a warship, on which the guns are mounted" (Webster 1983). In the figure of the split-level self, we observe that the guns have turned against the ship on which they are mounted. The borders delineating good "inside" from dangerous "outside," "autonomous" choice from "heteronomous" influence are decomposing and reconfiguring themselves. We are witnessing an unacknowledged version of deconstruction in process. The split-level subject, I am suggesting, is an impossible subject, a subject whose psychological viability can only be maintained by premature closure on processes of critical reflexivity that are also the very sign of its status as a certifiably autonomous subject. We might say, with Julia Kristeva, that this subject is a product of "feigned ignorance" (Kristeva 1993, 149). In that case, just what is being ignored?

A Feminist Alternative? Relational Autonomy

IN THIS BRIEF and selective review of the mainstream philosophical literature on autonomy, two distinctive strands of feminist criticism have been briefly introduced. One takes issue with the figuration of the autonomous subject as isolated and bounded and proposes to rethink autonomy in terms of human connections, to "tame" the subject of autonomy. The other strand, although similarly skeptical towards the discrete citadel figure, proposes an alternative revision, designed to cultivate an awareness and appreciation of the strangeness and instability within the subject of autonomy.

Feminists have compelling reasons for critically engaging with the concept of autonomy. One path of engagement, indebted to object-relations theory, has worked to expose the autonomous subject as a hyper-masculine fiction and to develop a feminized revision of autonomy by means of a substitute model of the subject as a relationally embedded entity positioned within a web-like set of relationships. From this vantage, the feminist quarrel with autonomy is that it introduces and incites opportunities for conflict among separate and competing egos; that it misrecognizes the relational context for identity and independence; and that it perpetuates a willful ignorance and perverse denial of the role of maternal and caring labor in the creation of potentially autonomous subjects. According to this view, mainstream accounts of autonomy obscure pre-existing relations of interdependence that nourish the requisite capacities for the development of autonomy competency skills. We may call this the benign counter-narrative of autonomy.

As Nancy Chodorow and others of the object-relations theory persuasion have argued, issues of difference, separation, and integrity of a core self that inhere in modern individualist conceptions of autonomy resonate with gender-specific processes of acquiring and establishing a sense of identity within modern nuclear family settings in which females mother. Whereas masculine gender identity is acquired through gestures of separation from the maternal care giver, feminine gender identity involves a more complex process of negotiation between daughters and mothers who are both "like" and "unlike" each other. Separateness and distinctiveness are prized as constitutive attributes of an "independent" masculine self which is encouraged to repress reminders and memories of its earlier embeddedness in a maternal universe of diffuse connection:

> Difference is psychologically salient for men in a way that it is not for women, because of gender differences in early formative developmental processes and the particular unconscious conflicts and defenses these produce. This salience, in turn, has been transmuted into a conscious cultural preoccupation with gender difference. It has also become intertwined with and has helped to produce more general cultural notions, particularly, that individualism, separateness, and distance from others are desirable and requisite to autonomy and fulfillment. Throughout these processes it is women, as mothers, who become the objects apart from which separateness, difference, and autonomy are defined (Chodorow 1989, 112).

Chodorow's discussion here highlights two related themes that are of concern to feminists engaged with the reappraisal of autonomy. We notice that autonomy seems to carry specifically gendered connotations (indeed, precisely those antisocial connotations that Feinberg attempts to modify). Furthermore, we observe that the process of acquiring, defining, and defending (masculinized) autonomy implicates women as "objects" and therefore as heteronomous "others." Object relations theory argues that the acquisition of autonomous selfhood is framed and constituted by gestures of separation from the maternal presence, which comes to represent the danger and ecstasy of blissful merger. Autonomy, along with objectivity, is effectively masculinized as the vigorous and oppositional stance of separation from the mother (E. Keller 1985, 74–114).

Feminist object relations theory highlights the ways in which gendered symbolics and social arrangements produce two different kinds of self: a masculine "separative" self and a feminine "soluble" self (C. Keller 1986). Whereas the soluble self exhibits a tendency to "dissolve emotionally and devotionally into the other," the separative self "makes itself into the absolute in that it absolves itself from relations" (C. Keller 1986, 13, 26). The point of cultivating an awareness of these distinctive versions of self is not to substitute the soluble self for the separative self; it is rather to question the exemplary status of the separative self as the subject of autonomous self-governance.

To the extent that concepts of "autonomy" and "self" are mutually constitutive, the object relations insistence that psychological life begins with and in connection rather than separation is significant. The self of object relations theory is inexorably, and not merely contingently, social; it is constructed within a relational matrix of exchanges that come to constitute selfhood. "We are all," writes Chodorow, "to some degree incorporations and extensions of others" (Chodorow 1989, 107). "Even the apparent boundaries of the individual do not separate in any simple way the pristine individual from the rest of the world" (Chodorow 1989, 157). The object relations account problematizes the very notion of the self as an independent touchstone for autonomy. For this self is complexly constituted, relationally embedded, and not necessarily whole or unitary except in provisional, fictitious, or exaggerated poses of separation, independence, and identity.

But if these feminists are critical of accounts of autonomy that belie the embedded nature of the self and promote masculine constructs of separative selfhood, they are unwilling to give up altogether on autonomy. Rather, autonomy has been revised to acknowledge connective notions of selfhood. Chodorow, for example, invokes "a relational rather than a reactive autonomy" (Chodorow 1989, 107) and she substitutes a notion of "confident distinctness" for separateness in her redescription of the identity of the self. The vocabulary of individuality and agency is detached from its masculine habitat and re-embedded within a different script for self-development. Evelyn Keller proposes a substitute version of "dynamic" autonomy, which she contrasts with the old "static" account:

> Dynamic autonomy reflects a sense of self . . . as both differentiated from and related to others, and a sense of others as subjects with whom one shares enough to allow for a recognition of their independent interests and feelings. . . . It develops not simply out of the feeling of competence, of being able to affect others and one's environment in ways that feel satisfying, but also, and essentially, out of the experience of continuity and reciprocity of feeling . . . (E. Keller 1985, 99).

This refiguration of the autonomous self as not merely *also* connected (à la Feinberg) but as *already* connected—as an amalgam of relations with other similarly constituted selves—is an attractive revision in many respects. But is it perhaps too attractive? And is it perhaps insufficiently revisionist? One gets the sense that feminists want to have our cake and eat it too. We want to expose and criticize the mobile, masculine autonomous self—that "separate, self-enclosed subject, remaining self-identical throughout its exploits in time," whose "relations do not affect its essence," who "proves its excellence through . . . tests of separation" (C. Keller 1986, 9)—and we propose to redefine autonomy outside of this gendered context. But our refurbished accounts of autonomy often read as if elements of the feminine connected self have been grafted onto selected aspects of the old, masculine, disembedded self. Object relations theory promises to deliver on the claim that autonomy and connection can be reconciled by means of a different notion of the self. The risk entailed in this promise is that we will succumb to the ruse of a nominalist masquerade: I'm autonomous, you're autonomous.

To what extent does the self-in-relation serve as a sufficiently different point of departure for the revisioning of autonomy? Can we identify other terms of critical engagement with the subject of autonomy that might yield productive insights? For object relations theorists the masculine subject of autonomy stands revealed as an impossibly solitary, self-sufficient being. This reading of the classical subject of autonomy is not incorrect, but neither is it complete.

Otherizing the Subject of Autonomy

WHEREAS OBJECT RELATIONS theory attempts to bring the isolated subject of autonomy into the field of relations with others to whom it is too distantly related and to cultivate our attunement to unacknowledged connections, Julia Kristeva uncovers a world of differences *within* the subject of autonomy. Her theory of abjection offers a powerful and disturbing provocation to political and philosophical theories of autonomy that rely on uninterrogated notions of the self by cultivating our attunement to the unacknowledged otherness *within*. Kristeva's strategy is to "break down the identity of the autonomous subject" (Oliver 1993, 1), whereas Chodorow's is to build it up.

Kristeva's counter-narrative suggests that autonomy is deceptively peaceful, that it relies on the repression of a relational field of conflict, violence, confusions, and heterogeneity located within the subject. In effect, Kristeva invites us to take a closer look at the inner citadel. Kristeva would have us interrogate autonomy, not in the premature effort to discern that which links us to one another (although this issue is also important for Kristeva, as I discuss below), but in order to re-cognize that which divides us from within. While object relations theorists propose that we de-otherize those others to whom the autonomous subject is too-distantly related, Kristeva proposes that we put the other back in to the subject (Oliver 1993, 13). Abjection plays a major role in this theoretical project of otherizing the subject.

Abjection has to do with invented borders, installed boundaries, "devices of discrimination," inevitably frail identities, and those differentiations which produce and protect such identities: the distinction between inside-outside, pure-impure, self-other, and other forms of dichotomized difference which produce identity. It is implicated simultaneously in the creation of boundaries and in archaic memories of the nonexistence, fragility, and violation of those boundaries: "We may call it a border; abjection is above all ambiguity" (Kristeva 1982, 9). The feeling of abjection may be induced by whatever "disturbs identity, system, order. What does not respect borders, positions, rules. The in-between, the ambiguous, the composite" (Kristeva 1982, 4). Abjection attracts and repels simultaneously: "the abject simultaneously beseeches and pulverizes the subject" (Kristeva 1982, 5).[7]

The domain of abjected alterity comes into view by means of Kristeva's elaborated approach towards language, a social practice that presupposes two modalities of significance, the semiotic and the symbolic. She defines the semiotic as "a modality avowedly heterogenous to meaning, but always aspiring to, negating, or exceeding meaning" (Kristeva 1993, 156). The semiotic issues from the felt processes of the drives (appropriation-rejection, orality-anality, love-hate, life-death) and may be traced to the archaic, pre-oedipal period of the body. The symbolic, on the other hand, constitutes itself by cutting itself off from the semiotic state: "Language as symbolic function is constituted only at the price of *repressing both the drives and the continuous relation to the mother*" (Kristeva 1993, 159). Kristeva insists that both modalities of significance are combined, albeit in different proportions, in different types of discourse. Scientific discourse minimizes, but can never eliminate, the semiotic element; whereas in poetic language the semiotic tends to predominate. Without the symbolic function, however, there would be no poetic *language* at all.

In Kristeva's account of language, at least two subjects are revealed— the transcendental ego of symbolic language and the subject-in-process of poetic language. Whereas the latter is sustained by "the *reactivation of the repressed drive- and mother-related material*" (Kristeva 1993, 159), the former assumes a position of mastery with respect to processes of signification that rest upon unacknowledged and repressed exclusions. This transcendental ego—whose resemblance to the mainstream subject of autonomy is unmistakable—is out of touch with the fragility of the symbolic function and with the sacrifice that brought it into being.

The abject, then, represents the positing of an object beyond the borders of theoretical reason: "Abjection preserves what existed in the archaism of pre-objectal relationship, in the immemorial violence with which the body becomes separated from another body in order to be—

maintaining that night in which the outline of the signified thing vanishes and where only the imponderable affect is carried out" (Kristeva 1982, 10). Language, which enables the subject to differentiate from the other, does so by repressing archaic maternal authority. This maternal authority is implicated in the semiotic, presymbolic mapping of "the self's clean and proper body." Abjection confronts us "with our earliest attempts to release the hold of *maternal* entity even before ex-isting outside of her, thanks to the autonomy of language" (Kristeva 1982, 13). It is implicated in "a violent, clumsy breaking away, with the constant risk of falling back under the sway of a power as securing as it is stifling" (Kristeva 1982, 13). What has been the mother, "will turn into an abject. Repelling, rejecting; repelling itself, rejecting itself. Ab-jecting" (Kristeva 1982, 13).

Abjection lies at the foundation of our symbolic and social being, at the "dawn" of the speaking being. The abjectification of the maternal body occurs in the context of a fragmentary infant subject who comes into being as a subject through mimetic identification with an image of itself. But even before mimesis, argues Kristeva " 'I' am not but do *separate, reject, abject*" (Kristeva 1982, 13). Abjection is located in "the bottomless 'primacy' constituted by primal repression," where "'subject' and 'object' push each other away, confront each other, collapse, and start again—inseparable, contaminated, condemned, at the boundary of what is assimilable, thinkable: abject" (Kristeva 1982, 18). The vocabulary of "subject" and "object" misleads, however, for abjection has to do with the felt affect of that which is not yet a thing/object for me. The archaism of abjection involves that "primal" repression prior to ego, objects, and representations, the offspring of "secondary repression." Abjection is the return of a marked-off primary repression that "notifies us of the limits of the human universe" (Kristeva 1982, 11). The abject is "a wellspring of sign for a non-object" (Kristeva 1982, 11). Or we may think of it as "that pseudo-object that is made up *before* but appears only *within* the gaps of secondary repression. *The abject would thus be the 'object' of primal repression*" (Kristeva 1982, 12). The way to abjection—to "the fragile border . . . where identities . . . do not exist or only barely so—double, fuzzy, heterogeneous, animal, metamorphosed, altered, abject" (Kristeva 1982, 207)—therefore, lies with poetic language.

But what can it mean to *theorize* on behalf of poetic language "that defies knowledge," on behalf of "the impossibility of a signified or signifying identity" (Kristeva 1993, 172)? Kristeva is not unaware of the difficulties involved; nor does she offer a simplistic solution. Kristeva takes issue not only with "a linguistics lowered from the phenomenological heaven" (i.e., scientific discourse) but with those who would equate theoretical discourse with mimeticism ("the philosopher starts to go in for literary tics") (Kristeva 1993, 173). In other words, Kristeva proposes that we refuse the either/or choice between strictly symbolic and strictly poetic language, that we position ourselves *between* overly stable and completely dissolved identities, between tyranny and delirium, between oppression and madness (Oliver 1993). The abject marks the unstable and uncomfortable space of this in-between-ness.

But why should we want to go; why should we listen for that "black laughter"? Kristeva herself poses the same question: "in these times of dreary crisis, what is the point of emphasizing the horror of being?" (Kristeva 1982, 208). Kristeva's answer underscores the significance of abjection for students and practitioners of political theory. Abjection, she suggests, is the "other facet of religious, moral, and ideological codes on which rest the sleep of individuals and the breathing spells of societies" (Kristeva 1982, 209). In short, abjection is implicated in the mystification, or misrecognition, of "power."

Furthermore, those of us who so misrecognize power are cast in the position of the deject: "A deviser of territories, languages, works, the *deject* never stops demarcating his universe whose fluid confines—for they are constituted of a non-object, the abject—constantly question his solidity and impel him to start afresh" (Kristeva 1982, 8). Endless demarcation of the boundaries of the subject; obsession with location and foundations; repeated efforts to fortify the "inner citadel" against heterogeneous forces and heteronomous influences; the very distinction between autonomy (rule from the good inside) and heteronomy (influence from the bad outside): there is an unmistakable tone of *dejection* in the literature on autonomy, a tone that conforms with its deject-subject, autonomous man.[8] The question to consider at this point is how best to engage and challenge this deject-subject. Do we help "him" to further demarcate the fluid boundaries of his universe by inviting him to map his connections with others? Do we draw attention to the demarcating impulse itself, to "the abject origin of images from which subjects emerge" (Fisher 1992, 101)? Or do we perhaps pursue both projects, subjecting each to the critical gaze of the other in turn?

Kristeva's work inspires an ethic of attunement to others that relies on a posture of attentiveness to the otherness within the self. The encounter with otherness invariably calls up disturbing reminders of the abject:

> Strange indeed is the encounter with the other—whom we perceive by means of sight, hearing, smell, but do not "frame" within our consciousness. The other leaves us separate, incoherent; even more so, he can make us feel that we are not in touch with our own feelings, that we reject them or, on the contrary, that we refuse to judge them—we feel "stupid," we have "been had.". . . Confronting the foreigner whom I reject and with whom at the same time I identify, I lose my boundaries, I no longer have a container, the memory of experiences when I had been abandoned overwhelm me, I lose my composure. I feel "lost," "indistinct," "hazy" (Kristeva 1991, 187).

If we are to get along, Kristeva is saying, we must negotiate the terrain of otherness. But what Kristeva means by "getting along" is something other than tolerating "differences" that stand in the way of recognizing a more "common" humanity. Instead of "welcoming the foreigner within a system that obliterates him," we would do better to promote "the togetherness of those foreigners that we all recognize ourselves to be" (Kristeva 1991, 2–3). According to Kristeva, this can only happen "*when the citizen-individual ceases to consider himself as unitary and glorious* but discovers his incoherences and abysses, in short his 'strangenesses'" (Kristeva 1991, 2; emphasis added).

Kristeva has declared war on the figure of autonomous man—transparent to himself, unified, sole author of a coherent life-plan which is his alone to shape, whose tenuous solidarity with others depends on his recognition of their own capacities for rational self-mastery, which are roughly equal to his. But it is also possible to discern in her work the effort to salvage, to reinvigorate autonomy. Uncanny strangeness, sustained encounters with the abject, "repeat the difficulty I have in situating myself with respect to the other *and keep going over the course of identification-projection that lies at the foundation of my reaching autonomy*" (Kristeva 1991, 187; emphasis added). If identification and projection are the ineliminable, heterogenous, and unstable foundation of identity, then it might be said that a reconfigured, more modest, but no less vigorous autonomy consists in the ongoing conversion of such difficulties into opportunities.[9]

Revisioning Autonomy: The Challenge Ahead

FOR ALL OF the differences between the counter-narratives of autonomy proffered by feminist object relations theory and Kristeva, each shares the elaborated intuition that the trouble with autonomy is that it relies on a repression of the maternal. In the former case, the maternal has the status of a recuperable "object"; whereas for Kristeva, the pre-object status of the archaic maternal body and of archaic maternal authority casts it further from our reach as ineluctably "other." Out of reach, however, does not mean not worth reaching for. In my estimation, the differences between these accounts, although significant, should not obscure what they share: a specifically feminist mode of engagement with autonomy, attuned simultaneously to the gendered symbolics of autonomy and to the need to rethink autonomy in the light of its unacknowledged exclusions.

Object relations theory seeks an accommodation between women and autonomy that proceeds by gendering the mainstream account of autonomy and problematizing its claims to universal discursive appeal. Once the subject of autonomy is revealed as a masculine figuration, an opening is created for an alternative feminine figuration of the autonomous self-in-connection. Relational autonomy is autonomy "made safe" for women.

The appeal of this revision is that it brings autonomy within women's reach. The danger of this revision is that it is insufficiently radical. To the extent that the self-in-connection is a simple inversion of the separative self, we run the combined risk of "switching labels" on standard gender-coded behavior (redescribing feminine behavior as "autonomous" and as normatively praiseworthy) and creating a one-dimensional one-world utopia. Kristevan theory, on the other hand, lacks the everyday appeal of familiar, gender-coded recognition; it problematizes identity and agency to a far more significant degree and puts us in touch with unconscious and uncomfortable registers of memory. The road to autonomy—understood as simultaneously fragile, partial, impossible, and normatively desirable—begins with the effort "to imagine and make oneself other for oneself" (Kristeva 1991, 13).

Feminists committed to the project of revising autonomy must also be prepared, as we have seen, to rethink reigning assumptions about the theoretical status of selves. The relation between subjects and their others is significantly at stake in this enterprise. Whether identity is postulated as a formation based on (repressed) connections or as a formation based on (repressed) exclusions, the unified, discrete subject of autonomy no longer serves as a credible model of emancipated self-rule. Revisioning autonomy in the light of this discomfiting and exhilirating awareness is the challenge-in-process.

Notes

1. Earlier versions of this paper have been delivered as conference papers and public lectures. Portions of this paper have been published (Di Stefano 1994). Special thanks are extended to Timothy Kaufman-Osborn and Lynda Lange for giving me the opportunity to share my thoughts on autonomy with their students and colleagues at Whitman College and the University of Toronto, respectively. I am also grateful to the Humanities Institute at the University of California at Davis, which provided shelter, salary, and intellectual stimulation during a year's sabbatical leave. Several colleagues at the Institute were especially generous with critical comments on my early and awkward efforts to revision autonomy: Fred Block, Kay Flavell, Nancy Folbre, Dena Goodman, and Linda Kauffman. James Glass provided useful commentary and criticism on a draft of this paper presented at the 1993 Annual Meeting of the American Political Science Association. Without the vote of confidence conferred by the APSA Organized Section on Women and Politics Research, which awarded a best paper prize to my first effort to revision autonomy, I am not at all sure that I would have continued with the project. Finally, I am especially grateful to Nancy Hirschmann for her very helpful comments and editorial suggestions on this chapter.

2. See Lukes (1973) for the argument that "equality" and "autonomy" share an intimate history with each other.

3. For a fascinating philosophical investigation into the varieties of conceptual loss, see Diamond (1988).

4. This question builds on the insight derived from Beauvoir and discussed above. If autonomous subjects require the existence of heteronomous subjects in order to assure the conditions of autonomy, then feminist claims to autonomy beg the question of the displacement of heteronomy onto other subjects. These "other" subjects might be women who do not identify with the aspirations of contemporary Western feminism; they might be men and women of the underclasses and/or racialized or sexualized minorities within postindustrial societies; they might be men and women of the "developing" areas of the world. The possibilities are endless. Another possibility to consider is that the surplus heteronomy released as a result of Western feminism's grab for autonomy might be displaced onto the terrain of "nature."

5. However, Feinberg does not completely escape the problem of circularity either. This is the problem with the "self"-referential vocabulary of autonomy discourse. Other useful and fascinating portraits of the autonomous self are provided by Benson (1983) and R. Young (1986). Feminists who are skeptical about the gender-neutrality claimed for autonomy can have a field day with these portraits.

6. For further discussion of the split-level self, see Christman (1988). For a critique of the split-level self and a response, respectively, see Friedman (1986) and Christman (1987).

7. As Kristeva herself points out, abjection is difficult to approach directly, to pin down by means of neat analytical formulations and definitions. It is above all a feeling or a bundle of feelings—often more visceral than cognitive—that includes attraction, repulsion, fascination, and horror. In many cases, we cannot come up with a "rational" explanation for these feelings. What is it, for example, about the "skin" on the surface of boiled milk that makes some of us so squeamish? Why do we return to this and other domestic scenes of horror for repeat command performances? Food loathing (aversion to particular foods) is an elementary and familiar form of abjection. Various codings of abjection may be read out of rituals and taboos. Moviegoers will recognize the abject in the "Alien" series, particularly in those scenes where parasitical baby aliens burst forth from the mangled bodies of their human and animal hosts. The abject may be encountered in human excremental waste; in menstrual blood; in "the corpse, seen without God and outside of science" (Kristeva 1982, 4); and in crimes that reveal the fragility of law. Sublimated versions of abjection abound in religion, in literature, and (most likely although as yet underanalyzed) in political theories. Iris Young (1990) and others (Fuss 1991; McAfee 1993) have read abjection out of contemporary attitudes of racism, misogyny, xenophobia, and homophobia. It is pervasive, yet difficult to articulate. What all of these examples invoke, in some manner, are thematics of boundary violation.

8. The mutually constitutive parallels between Kristeva's refiguration of autonomy and her characterization of theoretical reason are instructive. In contrast to the notion that theoretical success is best measured by criteria of explanation, i.e., by our ability to account for a variety of phenomena within a unified field of vision, Kristeva urges an alternative view: "to refuse to abandon theoretical reason, and instead to force it to increase its power by positing for it an object beyond its limits" (Kristeva 1993, 173). The subject of theory (a.k.a. the theorist), who is also the subject of autonomy, is advised to forego the maneuvers of the deject-subject, to attend instead to the "strangenesses" within and without. Theory

here is refigured to honor the quest for the unthinkable, and reason is advised of its limited reach.

The sentence from which this excerpt was taken is worth citing in full: "One must perhaps be a woman—that is, the ultimate guarantee of sociality, transcending the collapse of the symbolic, paternal function, and at the same time the inexhaustible generatrix of its renewal and expansion—one must be a woman, I say, to refuse to abandon theoretical reason, and instead to force it to increase its power by positing for it an object beyond its limits" (Kristeva 1993, 173). This excerpt has caught the attention of many feminist readers. What does it mean? I doubt that Kristeva is saying that all women and only women are capable of rigorous theorizing. Rather, she has sought to ally the *position* of woman with a particular characterization of theoretical reason that departs from the paradigm of theory-as-mastery. This alternative characterization is robust, yet humble.

9. A number of feminists have raised critical questions about the usefulness of Kristeva's work for efforts to develop accounts of women's agency. In this paper, I have tried to flesh out what is innovative and suggestive about Kristeva's counter-narrative of autonomy, particularly as this compares with the object relations account. Whether or not the feminist revisioning of autonomy rests complete with object relations and Kristevan theories is beyond the scope of this paper. For feminist-inspired criticism of Kristeva, see Butler (1993), Fraser (1992), A. Jones (1984), Kuykendall (1989), and Smith (1989).

References

Beauvoir, Simone de. 1974. *The Second Sex*. Trans. and ed. H. M. Parshley. New York: Random House.

Benjamin, Jessica. 1988. *The Bonds of Love: Psychoanalysis, Feminism, and the Problem of Domination*. New York: Pantheon.

Benson, John. 1983. "Who Is the Autonomous Man?" *Philosophy* 58:5–17.

Butler, Judith. 1992. "Contingent Foundations: Feminism and the Question of 'Postmodernism'." In *Feminists Theorize the Political*. Ed. Judith Butler and Joan W. Scott. New York: Routledge.

Butler, Judith. 1993. "The Body Politics of Julia Kristeva." In *Ethics, Politics, and Difference in Julia Kristeva's Writing*. Ed. Kelly Oliver. New York: Routledge.

Chodorow, Nancy. 1978. *The Reproduction of Mothering*. Berkeley: University of California Press.

Chodorow, Nancy. 1989. *Feminism and Psychoanalytic Theory*. New Haven, Conn.: Yale University Press.

Christman, John. 1987. "Autonomy: A Defense of the Split-Level Self." *Southern Journal of Philosophy* 25:281–293.

Christman, John. 1988. "Constructing the Inner Citadel: Recent Work on the Concept of Autonomy." *Ethics* 99:109–124.

Christman, John, ed. 1989. *The Inner Citadel: Essays on Individual Autonomy*. New York: Oxford University Press.

Code, Lorraine. 1987. "Second Persons." In *Science, Morality, and Feminist Theory.* Ed. Marsha Hanen and Kai Nelson. Calgary: University of Calgary Press.

Diamond, Cora. 1988. "Losing Your Concepts." *Ethics* 98:255–277.

Dinnerstein, Dorothy. 1976. *The Mermaid and the Minotaur: Sexual Arrangements and Human Malaise.* New York: Harper and Row.

Di Stefano, Christine. 1994. "Trouble with Autonomy: Some Feminist Considerations." In *Feminism.* Ed. Susan Moller Okin and Jane Mansbridge. Cheltenham, England: Edward Elgar.

Dworkin, Gerald. 1989. "The Concept of Autonomy." In *The Inner Citadel: Essays on Individual Autonomy.* Ed. John Christman. New York: Oxford University Press.

Elshtain, Jean Bethke. 1990. *Power Trips and Other Journeys: Essays in Feminism as Civic Discourse.* Madison: University of Wisconsin Press.

Feinberg, Joel. 1989. "Autonomy." In *The Inner Citadel: Essays on Individual Autonomy.* Ed. John Christman. New York: Oxford University Press.

Fisher, David. 1992. "Kristeva's *Chora* and the Subject of Postmodern Ethics." In *Body/Text in Julia Kristeva: Religion, Women, and Psychoanalysis.* Ed. David R. Crownfield. Albany, N.Y.: State University of New York Press.

Flax, Jane. 1990. *Thinking Fragments: Psychoanalysis, Feminism, and Postmodernism in the Contemporary West.* Berkeley: University of California Press.

Fraser, Nancy. 1992. "The Uses and Abuses of French Discourse Theories for Feminist Politics." In *Revaluing French Feminism: Critical Essays on Difference, Agency, and Culture.* Ed. Nancy Fraser and Sandra Bartky. Bloomington: Indiana University Press.

Friedman, Marilyn A. 1986. "Autonomy and the Split-Level Self." *Southern Journal of Philosophy* 24:19–35.

Fuss, Diana. 1991. "Introduction." In *Inside/Out: Lesbian Theories, Gay Theories.* Ed. Diana Fuss. New York: Routledge.

Gilligan, Carol. 1982. *In a Different Voice: Psychological Theory and Women's Development.* Cambridge, Mass.: Harvard University Press.

Gilligan, Carol. 1986. "Remapping the Moral Domain." In *Reconstructing Individualism: Autonomy, Individuality, and the Self in Western Thought.* Ed. Thomas C. Heller, Morton Sosna, and David E. Wellbery. Stanford, Calif.: Stanford University Press.

Gilligan, Carol. 1987. "Moral Orientation and Moral Development." In *Women and Moral Theory.* Ed. Eva Feder Kittay and Diana T. Meyers. Totowa, N.J.: Rowman and Littlefield.

Grimshaw, Jean. 1988. "Autonomy and Identity in Feminist Thinking." In *Feminist Perspectives in Philosophy.* Ed. Morwenna Griffiths and Margaret Whitford. Bloomington: Indiana University Press.

Gross, Elizabeth. 1987. "Conclusion: What Is Feminist Theory?" In *Feminist Challenges: Social and Political Theory.* Ed. Carole Pateman and Elizabeth Gross. Boston: Northeastern University Press.

James, Stanlie M. 1993. "Mothering: A Possible Black Feminist Link to Social Transformation?" In *Theorizing Black Feminisms: The Visionary Pragmatism of Black Women.* Ed. Stanlie M. James and Abena P. A. Busia. New York: Routledge.

Jones, Ann Rosalind. 1984. "Julia Kristeva on Femininity: The Limits of a Semiotic Politics." *Feminist Review* 18:56–73.

Jones, Kathleen. 1990. "Citizenship in a Woman-Friendly Polity." *Signs: Journal of Women in Culture and Society* 15:781–812.

Keller, Catherine. 1986. *From a Broken Web: Separation, Sexism, and Self.* Boston: Beacon Press.

Keller, Evelyn Fox. 1985. *Reflections on Gender and Science.* New Haven, Conn.: Yale University Press.

Kristeva, Julia. 1982. *Powers of Horror: An Essay on Abjection.* Trans. Leon S. Roudiez. New York: Columbia University Press.

Kristeva, Julia. 1991. *Strangers to Ourselves.* Trans. Leon S. Roudiez. New York: Columbia University Press.

Kristeva, Julia. 1993. "The Speaking Subject Is Not Innocent." In *Freedom and Interpretation: The Oxford Amnesty Lectures 1992.* Ed. Barbara Johnson. New York: Basic Books.

Kuykendall, Eleanor. 1989. "Questions for Julia Kristeva's Ethics of Linguistics." In *The Thinking Muse: Feminism and Modern French Philosophy.* Ed. Jeffner Allen and Iris Marion Young. Bloomington: Indiana University Press.

Lukes, Steven. 1973. *Individualism.* Oxford: Basil Blackwell.

Macedo, Stephen. 1991. *Liberal Virtues: Citizenship, Virtue, and Community in Liberal Constitutionalism.* Oxford: Clarendon Press.

McAfee, Noëlle. 1993. "Abject Strangers: Toward an Ethics of Respect." In *Ethics, Politics, and Difference in Julia Kristeva's Writing.* Ed. Kelly Oliver. New York: Routledge.

Merchant, Carolyn. 1980. *The Death of Nature: Women, Ecology, and the Scientific Revolution.* San Francisco: Harper and Row.

Meyers, Diana T. 1989. *Self, Society, and Personal Choice.* New York: Columbia University Press.

Miller, Jean Baker. 1976. *Toward a New Psychology of Women.* Boston: Beacon Press.

Murdoch, Iris. 1970. *The Sovereignty of Good.* London: Routledge.

Nedelsky, Jennifer. 1989. "Reconceiving Autonomy: Sources, Thoughts, and Possibilities." *Yale Journal of Law and Feminism* 1 (7):7–36.

Nedelsky, Jennifer. 1990. "Law, Boundaries, and the Bounded Self." *Representations* 30:162–189.

Noddings, Nel. 1984. *Caring: A Feminine Approach to Ethics and Moral Education.* Berkeley: University of California Press.

O'Brien, Mary. 1981. *The Politics of Reproduction.* Boston: Routledge and Kegan Paul.

Oliver, Kelly. 1993. "Introduction: Julia Kristeva's Outlaw Ethics." In *Ethics, Politics, and Difference in Julia Kristeva's Writing.* Ed. Kelly Oliver. New York: Routledge.

Ruddick, Sara. 1989. *Maternal Thinking: Toward a Politics of Peace.* Boston: Beacon Press.

Smith, Paul. 1989. "Julia Kristeva Et Al.; or, Take Three or More." In *Feminism and Psychoanalysis.* Ed. Richard Feldstein and Judith Roof. Ithaca, N.Y.: Cornell University Press.

Tronto, Joan C. 1993. *Moral Boundaries: A Political Argument for an Ethic of Care*. New York: Routledge.

Watson, Candace. 1987. "Celibacy and Its Implications for Autonomy." *Hypatia: A Journal of Feminist Philosophy* 2:257–258.

Webster's New Universal Unabridged Dictionary. 1983. Second ed. New York: Simon and Schuster.

Wolgast, Elizabeth. 1987. *The Grammar of Justice*. Ithaca, N.Y.: Cornell University Press.

Young, Iris Marion. 1990. *Justice and the Politics of Difference*. Princeton, N.J.: Princeton University Press.

Young, Robert. 1986. *Personal Autonomy: Beyond Negative and Positive Liberty*. London: Croom Helm.

Young, Robert. 1989. "Autonomy and the 'Inner Self'." In *The Inner Citadel: Essays on Individual Autonomy*. Ed. John Christman. New York: Oxford University Press.

6

Reconstructing Democracy

Jane Mansbridge

*E*ach generation, culture, and subculture reconstructs the ideas and practice of democracy to fit its insights and needs.[1] Today's feminist reconstruction of democracy has just begun. Although the experiences and thought of middle-class Euroamerican women heavily influenced the early stages of this process in the United States, more recently African-American feminists, international feminists, and postmodern feminists have reconstructed these earlier reconstructions, now stressing the need to fight, conceptually and institutionally, the tendency in any democracy for members of a dominant group to assume away the needs and perceptions of subordinates.

This essay draws from the existing collection of feminist insights in its own preliminary attempt to reconstruct the democratic processes of power and persuasion. It argues that two different sets of insights, deriving from women's experiences with human "connection" and domination, illuminate the two democratic processes of persuasion and power. In the resulting fourfold set of relations I will have most to say on the relation between connection and persuasion. My larger point, however, is that any effective theory or practice of democracy needs to encompass both persuasion and power and can be effectively reconstructed only by drawing from the experiences of both connection and domination.

Power and Persuasion

ACTUAL DEMOCRACIES USUALLY bring about change through some mixture of power and persuasion. Power—which I will sometimes call "coercive power"—involves either the threat of sanction ("Leave this room or I'll shoot you") or the use of force (I pick you up and carry you out of the room). The threat of sanction involves the other's will; force does not. If I threaten, "Leave this room or I'll shoot you," you *can* say, "Shoot me," in which case I will not get what I want, which is for you to leave the room. Your will is involved, in the first instance, in a way that it is not if I carry you out of the room.[2]

Some subtle forms of force and the threat of sanction take the form of "systemic power," as when, in one example of force, women must explain some of their experiences through a language crafted without reference to those experiences (see Hurston 1990). In systemic power, the force involved can produce its effects without anyone being conscious of its action and therefore resisting. Foucault's maxim, "where there is power, there is resistance," thus applies only if he meant by "power" the threat of sanction rather than force (Foucault 1978, 95).[3]

In contrast to the threat of sanction and force, persuasion consists of presenting reasons in a process that mixes cognition and emotion. Genuine persuasion is distinguished from manipulation by its intent to further the goals of the person receiving the communication, including goals held in common with the persuader. You act differently after I persuade you, but you still act both willingly and in your own interests broadly speaking (that is, including your principles and the interests of others that you have made your own).

Different democratic ideals apply to these two processes. Ideally, the exercise of democratic *persuasion* should be as insulated as possible from the use of force and threat of sanction. The exercise of democratic *power* should derive as much as possible from procedures on which there is close to universal agreement and should allocate the resources for power as close to equal as possible among the members (Mansbridge 1995).

Democracies can settle some conflicts through mutual persuasion. By providing and absorbing logical arguments, new information, and new cognitive and emotional insights, members of a polity can help transform their own and others' preferences, creating previously unrealized areas of agreement. The process of persuasion in deliberation can even change the participants' characters, and therefore their interests, in ways that promote agreement.

Yet in the many moments in democratic life in which members' interests conflict so deeply that they cannot be resolved through persuasion, democrats must choose between remaining with the status quo or letting some members exercise coercive power over others (threatening them with sanctions or exercising force). If we cannot act collectively in such moments (by letting some exercise legitimate coercive power over others), the status quo will prevail, and often prevail unjustly. The goal of democracies ought to be, therefore, to make the processes of persuasion as genuine as possible by reducing the degree to which they are influenced by force and the threat of sanction, and to make the processes of exercising power as derivative as possible from agreed procedures and as equal as possible among the members. Feminist insights into connection and domination must inform the use of both persuasion and power.

Reconstructing a Theory of Democratic Persuasion Through Experiences of "Connection"

CONTEMPORARY FEMINIST INSIGHTS into human connection stem both from experiences that are more typical of women than men and from a conceptual tradition, dating from before the suffragist era, in which the culture coded tenderness, nurturance, and a "giving" concern for others as particularly female. Insights associated with these experiences and this culture help us reconstruct democratic ideals to make persuasion more central in democratic practice and theory.

The feminist emphasis on "connection" coincided with and undoubtedly stemmed in part from women's historical position of powerlessness. In 1818, Hannah Mather Crocker, an early feminist, had no trouble making two separate claims. First, she argued for equality, saying that God had "endowed the female mind with equal powers and faculties" to those of men. Second, she argued for women's special contribution to democracy, saying that "it must be the appropriate duty and privilege of females, to convince by reason and persuasion" (Crocker 1968, 40).

Crocker's stress on women's special capacities for persuasion drew heavily from the culture around her. Not having the same economic, social, or political power resources as men (that is, the resources with which to impose force or threaten sanctions), women of all classes and races recognized that they must develop not only the few power resources they had but also the arts of persuasion. Both Abigail Adams's letter asking her husband to "remember the ladies" (Butterfield 1975, 121) and Lydia Brown's account of the life of a woman slave (Carby 1987) rely solely on persuasion because their authors had little power relative to those they were trying to persuade.

The suffragists also relied on persuasion because they had little political power. Yet the style came easily to them, for many suffragists believed that women would bring virtue into politics by extending to the public sphere the methods they had used as mothers.[4] Chief among these methods was a reliance on persuasion rather than power.

Although persuasion had played a critical role in human decision since long before Aristotle's *Rhetoric* (Aristotle 1941), and the desire to eliminate power from communal life was a frequent motif in nineteenth-century liberal and socialist writing, the theme of substituting persuasion for power has had particular resonance for women in the United States. Both because women have had less access than men to the resources for threatening sanctions or exerting force, and because both women and men have attributed to women a greater capacity for interpersonal sensitivity, women have often considered the arts of persuasion particularly their own.

In the period between the two waves of American feminism, for example, the major female organizational theorist and the major female philosopher in the Anglo-American tradition both emphasized persuasion over power. Mary Parker Follett, an important organizational theorist of the 1930s, argued against "domination" ("a victory of one side over the other"), and even against "compromise" ("each side gives up a little in order to have peace"), in favor of what she called "integration," which allows neither side "to sacrifice anything." Follett exemplified integration with a tale of wanting to shut the window in a public library while another reader wanted it open and finding the solution in opening the window in the next room where no one was sitting. "There was no compromise," she wrote, "because we both got all we really wanted. For I did not want a closed room, I simply did not want the north wind to blow directly on me; and he, the man in the room with me, did not want that particular window open, he merely wanted more air in the room" (Follett 1949, 62; 1942, 32).[5] To signal an alternative to domination, Follett coined the distinction between "power-over" and "power-with" (Follett 1942, 101, 109).

Dorothy Emmet, the first female president of the British Aristotelian society, later picked up Follett's distinction. She described "power with" as "the capacity to make things happen effectively, in which people can grow in collaboration" (Emmet 1953–1954, 9), elaborated a typology of forms of power, few of which were coercive, and concluded that "political power is not only the power of coercion" (1953–1954, 15).

When the second wave of feminism emerged in the United States in the late 1960s, many activists concluded that along with having interests that conflicted with those of men, women also had a "culture" distinct from, and in some ways better than, that of men. This culture emphasized connection and relationship over individualism and rights. By 1970 the term "women's culture" had become part of the language of the women's movement. Political activist Marlene Dixon wrote in one feminist publication:

> Women are trained to nuances, to listening for the subtle cues which carry the message hidden under the words. It is part of that special skill called 'intuition' or 'empathy' which all female children must learn if they are to be successful in manipulating others to get what they want and to be successful in providing sympathy and understanding to their husbands and lovers (Dixon 1970, 8).

In this passage Dixon derived the special skills of "listening," "intuition," and "empathy" from women's relative powerlessness. Three years later, the political activist Jane Alpert—predating by seven years the work of Sara Ruddick (1980) and Jean Elshtain (1981)—linked intuition and empathy to mothering:

> Feminist culture is based on what is best and strongest in women, and as we begin to define ourselves as women, the qualities coming to the fore are the same ones a mother projects in the best kind of nurturing relationship to a child: empathy, intuitiveness, adaptability, awareness of growth as a process rather than as goal-ended, inventiveness, protective feelings towards others and a capacity to respond emotionally as well as rationally (Alpert 1973, 6).

In these years, Berenice Carroll (1972, 588) and Nancy Hartsock also suggested that feminism could lead to the "redefinition of political power itself" as not domination but "energy, strength, and effective interaction" (Hartsock 1981, 10, 9).[6]

Similar ideas entered the academy through the psychoanalytic theories of Dorothy Dinnerstein (1976), Nancy Chodorow (1978), and, a few years later, Carol Gilligan's influential study of moral reasoning, which adopted much of Chodorow's analysis. Investigating women's reactions to moral dilemmas, Gilligan concluded that in contrast to men, women define themselves "in a context of human relationship" and judge themselves according to their ability to care (Gilligan 1982, 17). Dinnerstein, Chodorow, and Gilligan inspired an outpouring of theoretical writing, including that of Sheila Ruth, an English philosopher, who concluded that male philosophers tended to shun or show contempt for female connection: "Flight from woman is flight from feeling, from experiencing, from the affective; it is flight into distance" (Ruth 1981, 47). Nel Noddings argued that the approach to ethics through law and principle "is the approach of the detached one, the father," whereas the caring approach, the "approach of the mother," is "rooted in receptivity, relatedness, and responsiveness" (Noddings 1984, 2).

Research on Gilligan's specific claim regarding gender differences in moral reasoning reveals that such differences appear, if at all, only among highly educated men and women. Yet these differences map well onto popular stereotypes of male and female behavior. When researchers describe two orientations to moral conflict, one based on relationships and one on rights, both men and women tend to rate the "care" orientation as more feminine and the "rights" orientation as more masculine. Empathy is indisputably coded as female, despite evidence showing no physiological differences between males and females in response to perceiving another's joy or pain.[7]

The question of the existence and provenance of gender differences in "care" or "connection" is now hotly disputed among feminists, both in the United States and internationally. Epstein (1988), for example, has argued strongly against the existence of major differences between men and women, against the probable biological or psychoanalytic provenance of most currently observable differences, and against a strategic stress on "difference," on the grounds that such an emphasis merely reinforces sexist stereotypes and gender inequality.

In my own view, the actual behavioral differences between men and women are usually far less than most people think. Male power, together with the inevitable salience of gender in human reproduction and sexuality, has produced in all societies strong patterns of "gratuitous gendering," which arbitrarily divide a great deal of social, economic, political, and linguistic life into the categories of "male" and "female." The same processes have exaggerated the salience of these divisions, allocated a generally lower status to traits coded as female, and given biological gender differences a positive normative status in spite of human culture being designed in part to bring biological impulses under conscious control (Mansbridge 1993).

Because so few empirical studies have found a relation between gender and a "care" versus a "rights" orientation, and because in some studies that show such a relation the experimenter may have given subtle clues as to what was being measured, I find it most useful to treat the literature on gender and "connection" not as necessarily demonstrating any large difference between the actual behavior, or even the normative orientations of most men and women in American society, but as drawing attention instead to the deeply gender-coded nature in this society of the dichotomy of separation versus connection.

Given this strong existing gender-coding, however, I also maintain that feminist analyses of maternal and other forms of intimate connection can generate insights that help reconstruct the concept of democracy. In part because the dichotomy "reason-emotion" has been gender-coded as "male-female," affective, relationship-based, and connection-oriented approaches to understanding democratic ideals and practice have been given short shrift in democratic theory, and cognitive, rights-based, individual-oriented approaches have predominated.

Anglo-American democratic theory, for example, often portrays the polity as constructed by free and unencumbered individuals who associate to promote their own self-interests. Such a theory cannot easily draw inspiration from or use metaphors derived from the experiences of empathetic interdependence, compassion, and personal vulnerability that the culture usually codes as "female." Seyla Benhabib, along with other feminist theorists, points out that Hobbes's image of the founders of the polity springing up "suddenly, like mushrooms, come to full maturity, without all kind of engagement with one another" is the "ultimate" male picture of autonomy (Benhabib 1987, 84). Yet, as Jennifer Nedelsky suggests, "What actually enables people to be autonomous . . . is not isolation, but relationships. . . . The most promising model, symbol or metaphor for autonomy is not therefore property, but childrearing" (Nedelsky 1989, 12). Virginia Held, comparing mothering to contract as a founding metaphor, similarly concludes that in reality "the starting condition is an enveloping tie, and the problem is individuating oneself" (Held 1990, 300).

Democratic theory and practice as it has evolved in the United States in the last half century has a particular need for these feminist correctives based on "connection." Although the ancient Greek and early modern democrats probably saw democracy as primarily a deliberative process, whose method was mutual persuasion and whose goal was producing a common good, a competing understanding, which began in the seventeenth century, has now become dominant. In this "adversary democracy," the method for settling disputes is only legitimate power based on the conclusion that politics involves only conflicting interests (Mansbridge 1983).

No existing democracy has in practice given up trying to create, through mutual persuasion, "just" substantive outcomes consonant with a "common good." Existing democracies are in practice all ad hoc mixtures of institutions based on persuasion, designed to further the good of all, and institutions based on power, designed to make the fight for comparative advantage relatively fair. But the twentieth-century theory of adversary democracy, and all practices based implicitly on that theory, postulate a radical separation of citizens grounded in their conflicting interests. The postwar pluralist approach to politics that emerged in the United States in the first half of this century, for example, saw politics primarily in terms of self-interest and the exercise of power (Lasswell 1936, Schumpeter 1942, Truman 1959). So too did the Marxist opponents of pluralism. By contrast, feminist premises of connectedness remind us of the possibility of "unitary democracy" (Mansbridge 1983), where mutual persuasion helps realize shared goals and interests.

The processes of persuasion may be related to a more consultative, participatory style that seems to characterize women more than men in the contemporary United States. Civil rights activist Ella Baker consistently promoted participatory institutions, in contrast to the internal hierarchies of power favored by most male leaders (Payne 1989). The black women leaders of the hospital union studied by Karen Sacks (1988) preferred to act as "center women," in Sacks's phrase, letting the men exercise public power as "spokesmen." Patricia Hill Collins (1990, 206ff.) concludes that an "ethic of care" typifies the behavior and norms of both black and white women in the United States as well as of men and women in Africa. An analysis of many studies on leadership concludes that in the contemporary United States women are more likely than men to adopt a "consultative" style of leadership (Eagly and Johnson 1990). This style, as Marlene Dixon (1970) suggested, accords serious value to "listening."

A consultative tradition contributes to understanding the practice of democracy, as does the special attention to relationships that women in the United States today evince in their friendships (Mansbridge 1993, n. 19) and perhaps in their moral reasoning. Successful negotiators take into realistic consideration the worth for both parties of their ongoing relationship, which shortsighted tactics aimed only at winning can undermine (Ury and Fisher 1981). Because democracies are almost always composed of ongoing relationships among groups (although not always among individuals), one would expect an explicit concern for ongoing relationships to shift toward commonality, the perceived balance of conflicting versus common interests.

If women in the late twentieth-century United States tend to have a greater concern for relationships than men, and if they prefer a more consultative style that de-emphasizes the threat of sanction and force, these concerns should affect the theory and practice of democratic deliberation by giving greater weight to the ongoing relations of the collective, making deliberations less hierarchical and refining the practice of active listening.

The practice of consultative democratic deliberation would require that men as well as women develop the conscious practice of emotional empathy, a characteristic now coded as female. Empathy makes it easier to understand others' needs, and by reflected understanding, one's own. Empathy helps surmount conflicting interests by allowing participants to make another's good their own. Empathy even helps in reaching agreement on principled convictions, because understanding the others' feelings makes it easier to forgive their intransigence or slips of logic and to make one's point again in language they can hear. Empathy is critical in good negotiations, because making suggestions that meet another's needs at less cost to one's own requires emotional and cognitive insight into the other's needs.

Empathy can either help or hinder respect for difference. Human beings understand others primarily by trying, emotionally and cognitively, to put themselves in the others' place. Because, unlike subordinates, members of dominant groups have not had a lifetime of learning the foibles of the other, they sometimes conclude from their efforts at empathy that others are very like themselves. Simone Weil (1962) and Iris Murdoch (1971) therefore stress the need to give "attention," noticing what the other does and asking explicitly for direction (Ruddick 1980, 359; Jones 1993, 143). Although one may not succeed in putting oneself in another's place, one must make the effort to notice, ask for help, and act upon revealed differences as well as similarities. The Enlightenment ideal of universalistic impartiality, which entails treating everyone according to the same rules, tends to the contrary to "eliminate otherness" (Benhabib 1987, 81) by assuming that other individuals and groups do (or should) act like the dominant norm. Empathizing with the experience of not being the "norm" (Lorde 1984), and realizing that others may feel differently and act under different constraints, requires the conscious exercise of both cognitive and emotional faculties.

Deliberation and deliberative appeals for the public good require an emotional and cognitive probing of one's own feelings of empathy, admiration, revulsion, or horror (Lindblom 1990, 32; Barber 1984, 174). We activate commitment to principle in part by appealing to people's emotional attachments to the aspects of their identity most linked to that principle. We activate feelings of empathy and responsibility—to all humanity, nation, ethnicity, or kin—by appealing emotionally to parts of the psyche we do not yet understand. Yet many democratic theorists, perhaps influenced by the enduring coding of "emotion as female" and "reason as male,"[8] think of deliberation only as "reasoned deliberation," making its emotional components illegitimate or leaving them unexplored. Female philosophers and feminist theorists have begun to point out the impossibility of separating emotion from cognition and to rehabilitate the role of emotions in political thinking (Nussbaum 1995, Rorty 1985).

Appeals to emotion *can* be dangerous. Emotional evocation opens the door to demagoguery as orators asking for sacrifice in the name of a public good call up visual images of the homeland, chords of buried anger, yearnings for a settled peace, and self-images of righteousness. The feminist project of giving moral status to the emotions can readily be used, sometimes legitimately, to justify favored treatment for those closest to us (Mansbridge 1993).

Emotional appeals must therefore stand up to reflection in tranquility. Later regret throws suspicion on (although it does not automatically invalidate) an emotionally cued deliberative decision. An emotional appeal should not impair one's ability to subject the factual or cognitive components of the deliberative process to the usual cognitive tests. If one feels awkward bringing up a fact or causal analysis that runs counter to prevailing sentiment, the ratio of emotion to cognition in the deliberative setting is probably too high. As we use our experience to elaborate standards for distinguishing beneficial from harmful uses of emotion, we must avoid the traditional, frequently male, mandate to "keep emotions out of it." Interpreting the ideal of "reasoned" or "rational" deliberation to delegitimate appeals to emotion makes it almost impossible to foster empathy, probe our own needs, or appeal for selfless behavior.

The issues of ongoing relationships, listening, empathy, and emotional commitment are as yet underdeveloped in democratic theory. Pamela Conover (1988) suggests that among political scientists eager to be seen as tough-minded, altruism in general has come to seem sissified. The same is probably true, to a lesser degree, for democratic theorists. In making the case for empathy, listening, ties of love and duty, mutual vulnerability, and even common interest in democratic politics, proponents of these values are hampered by the way Western culture has coded those values as female.

In practice, applying the insights of "connection" to the exercise of democratic persuasion means cultivating the capacities for empathy, listening, and forbearance in the face of human weakness. It prescribes an attention that notices and respects difference, reasonable estimates of the importance of ongoing relationships, sufficient understanding of one's own and others' emotions to give them rein but judge them at the same time, cognitive agility in reviewing and opening options, and as accurate as possible a sense of what oneself and others really want.

Reconstructing Democratic Power with the Insights of Connection

UNTIL NOW, FEMINIST theorists have tacitly argued as if concern for connection and relationships were antithetical to the use of coercive power. The work of feminists writing about connection and persuasion fills many pages, but no one makes the link between connection and power in this sense of the threat of sanction and use of force. I consider this a problem with existing feminist thinking about democracy. Even when we take as our concern only the intrinsic value of preserving and enhancing our ongoing relationships with others (with no interest in the instrumental value of these relations), an analysis grounded in experience must encompass the inevitable use in almost every human relationship of the threat of sanction and the use of force. Rather than branding this kind of power illegitimate, feminist theorists and practitioners of democracy must recognize its uses and find ways to make it more legitimate and less harmful.

As in most theoretically underexplored territory, the best way to begin is with the everyday experiences we know best. These will necessarily be small-scale experiences, often dyadic ones. These "micro" experiences may not generalize well to the "macro" level of national and international democratic politics. But relatively few of us have experiences at the national and international level that involve a thorough, multi-layered, and personally experienced understanding of the complexities of an interaction or decision. And we often need such personal experience before we can subject any interaction to the kind of scrutiny that asks questions not previously asked. Indeed, the vaunted difficulty of generalizing from the micro to the macro (as the ancient Greeks did when they described the *polis* as a kind of "friendship") draws heavily from a tradition, which itself evolved from the ancient Greeks, of excluding the "domestic," the realm of women, from the "political," the realm of men.

The goal, then, is to scrap the simple identification of "good" democracy with persuasion instead of power, and try to make coercive power—the threat of sanction and the use of force—relatively compatible with a mutually respectful, empowering, egalitarian and participatory ongoing relationship. What happens if, in this quest, we look to our closest relationships, which we know best? If the "use of force" can mean not only physical force but also placing others in a position that restricts or redirects their options without consulting their will, we must conclude that no ongoing relationship other than the most shallow can avoid each partner directing the other's life in various ways. Any one partner will make decisions without engaging the other's will and so place the other in a new, and unwilled, situation in which change from the new status quo will be costly. When I sit on the left side of the sofa, that seat is now filled, either directing my partner to the sofa's right side or requiring a request that I move. This subtle use of force matters, for purposes of this discussion, only when our interests conflict, as when the reading light is better on the left. As for the threat of sanction, if I am openly irritated when my partner comes home late, that irritation produces a sanction now and threatens sanctions the next time. The deeper the relationship and the more entwined the lives, the greater the mutual use of force and the more powerful the threat of sanction. Separation undermines the possibility of using force and threatening sanctions; connection makes both necessary and inevitable.

Even in intimate relationships, however, several conditions make the use of force and threat of sanctions relatively legitimate. First, the balance of power must be more or less equal between the parties. Second, the force or sanction must not undermine our deepest interests, say in self-respect or in emotional and physical flourishing. Third, the force and threat of sanction must be relatively above-board, and when submerged can be harmlessly brought to the surface for examination. Fourth, we must have mechanisms for bringing to light and examining the force and threat of sanction that pervade the relationship in order to judge the underlying equality of our resources for this kind of power. Fifth, we should be able to agree on standards for judging the equality in those resources. And sixth, we must have mutually trusted counselors to whom we can turn to help us decide wisely, and eventually agree, on the legitimacy and illegitimacy, helpfulness and harm, of any given threat or use of force.[9]

Some of these conditions also justify the use of force and threat of sanction in a democracy. First, the use of force and threat of sanction embodied in the vote is supposed to be more or less equal among citizens. Although inequalities in power resources pervade all actual democracies, they are normatively suspect. Second, the force or sanction that one group of citizens may use should not undermine the deepest interests of others. "Minority rights" have the institutional function of preserving those deep interests against the power of others.

The other conditions are not recognized in democratic theory or practice. Democracies do not at present have strong norms insisting that force and threat of sanction be relatively above-board or able to be harmlessly brought to the surface for examination. We do not have institutions for bringing to light and examining existing force and sanctions to judge the underlying equality among citizens' resources for this kind of power. The press and courts could play this role but do not now see it as their mandate. We do not have relatively agreed on standards for judging equality in the power resources of our citizens. And we do not have trusted institutions to help citizens and their representatives make wise decisions about, and possibly agree on, the legitimacy and illegitimacy, helpfulness and harm, of any given threat or use of force. Although equality in power resources may be a democratic ideal, it is so far from the reality in any existing polity that even investigating the question seriously would undermine one major function of democracy, which is to make some form of relatively legitimate decision for the collective so that it can act rather than remain at the status quo.

Here, however, a democratic theory with some link to the experience of ongoing intimate relationships can make a contribution. Power as the use of force and threat of sanction must be part of any active, ongoing relationship. Both good relationships and also good democratic institutions should make the use of power *mutually empowering* so that each individual experiences the ability to cause outcomes by shaping others' lives and threatening sanctions. At the same time, both good relationships and democratic institutions should find uses of power and stances toward those uses that strengthen close relations rather than disrupting them. Ancient Greek democrats believed that each citizen should rule and be ruled in turn. This vision, rather than one that eliminates "rule" entirely, should be our own ideal of democracy, with due restrictions on the way anyone can exercise that rule. One side "winning" disproportionately always undermines an ongoing relationship. If there can be no rotation of power among individuals, as in ancient Greece, the polity must at least try to create for all its members a vicarious sense of rotation through representation as well as some experience of empowering responsibility through decentralization and citizen activities such as jury duty.

Mutual empathy and a strong sense of ongoing relationship also cushion the exercise of power. When the losers in majority rule feel some obligation to support the winners, and possibly, through empathy or principle, even feel it is time for these winners to have their turn, a relatively just rotation in rule can find a niche within a community of mutual protection and concern. All-out war between political parties undermines the ongoing relationship; the practice of a "loyal opposition" sustains it. Unusual as this mutual recognition and respect may be on a larger scale, it often arises in small collectives familiar with encompassing in their ongoing relationships the legitimate use of force and threat of sanction. Rather than treating as illegitimate all instances of this kind of power, feminist theory, drawing on the experience of intimate connection, could flesh out the ways power as the use of force and threat of sanction can be most compatible with, and even promote, the goals of individual equality and empowerment.

In practice, applying the insights of "connection" to the exercise of democratic power means retaining the equal respect crucial to the relations of friendship by making the balance of coercive power as equal as possible among the partners, developing standards for judging that equality, insisting that the exercise of power not undermine anyone's deepest interests, bringing the exercise of power to light and keeping it there, and developing a deliberative arena that can judge the legitimacy of different acts of coercive power.

Reconstructing Democratic Persuasion and Power Through the Experience of Domination

A FEMINIST CONCEPTION of democracy can never be cheerfully sanguine about the possibilities for persuasion unmixed with coercive power in any actual political setting. Women know from experience that the gender inequalities in power in any formal political arena are only the public tip of a mass of subtle and unsubtle power inequalities in language, speech, agenda-setting, and the ability to define both the norm and the "other."

In language and speech, girls and women in the United States today speak noticeably less than boys and men both in mixed private settings (Haas 1979; Epstein 1988, 217ff.) and in public. In New England town meetings, women speak only half as often as men (Bryan 1975; Mansbridge 1983, 106; also Kathlene 1990, 246–247) and tend to give information or ask questions rather than stating opinions or initiating controversy (Mansbridge 1983, 106). In private, men are more likely to interrupt women than the other way around (Zimmerman and West, 1975).

As for the broader ability to define the norm, Catharine MacKinnon has put the case most forcefully:

> Men's physiology defines most sports, their needs define auto and health insurance coverage, their socially-designed biographies define workplace expectations and successful career patterns,... their military service defines citizenship, their presence defines family, their inability to get along with each other—their wars and rulerships—defines history, their image defines god, and their genitals define sex (MacKinnon 1987, 36).

In the realm of language, male nouns and pronouns usually become the generic. Less obvious, all words imply the dominant or majority subcategory in the category covered by that word, thereby excluding by implication the less powerful or the minority. The use of man to mean "human beings" theoretically includes women, except that the word "men" has connotations and establishes expectations that exclude women. Similarly, the word "women" theoretically includes African American women, except that because white women comprise in the United States the great majority of women, the word in that context has connotations that exclude experiences characterizing the majority of African American women. In the same way, the phrase "African American women" implies "heterosexual African American women," and the phrase "heterosexual African American women" implies "able-bodied heterosexual African American women" (Bartlett 1990, 848; Harris 1990; Spelmann 1988). Each category, conjuring up its dominant or majority referent, implicitly excludes those whose experiences differ from that majority.

Dominance through language thus cannot be avoided. It requires conscious effort to include in one's thinking those who do not fit the dominant or majority image, particularly when the interests of members of that group conflict with the interests of the dominant group. Because we must use words and cannot maintain in consciousness the potentially infinite regress of the implicitly unincluded, we must recognize that all communication encodes power and be sensitive both to the worst abuses and to those who bring that power to the surface for conscious criticism.

Consciousness of domination also alerts feminist theorists to the need to create democratic processes that can bring instances of subtle, private, and hidden power to the surface for conscious criticism. Democratic deliberation, for example, must be designed to reveal underlying conflict as well as facilitating agreement. Yet leaders committed to using persuasion rather than power often exaggerate the degree of common interest between themselves and those they try to persuade. Larger patterns of domination in any society unbalance the critical process in ways that subordinates may not notice or that put subordinates on the defensive. Many arenas of debate encode subtle expectations of appropriate demeanor, language, and style of argument that make it hard for a subordinate group to formulate its own thoughts, hard for a dominant group to hear what subordinates are saying, and hard for subordinates to believe, when they have begun to formulate their thoughts, that the dominant group will even try to hear.

Michel Foucault's stress on permeating power relations, in explicit contrast to views of power centered in the state, captures the depth of the problem that women, and others disadvantaged in a system of domination, must face. Foucault rejects views of power as purely repressive, views that imply one could in theory remove the repression and find authentic consciousness underneath. In Foucault's understanding, power even when repressive incites and induces the active powers or abilities of the repressed, so that the flow of ability within every self and the power we can exercise in the world are created and shaped by both the repressive power itself and the resistance that forms to it.[10] This insight resonates with feminist realizations that anything we do is in part created by and deeply intertwined with existing coercive powers.

Yet, Foucault's concept of resistance does not fully meet feminist analytic needs. First, the purely negative concept of resistance requires rejecting any notion of a "legitimate" basis for consent (Sawicki 1991, 21) and consequently any search for normative criteria by which to approve or disapprove the use of collective power. Second, the heroic, even male-coded, connotations of a firm, immobile stand ("refusal") imply contempt for the tactic, with which all weaker parties are familiar, of yielding to opposing forces in order perhaps later to advance. Third, Foucault's great interest in the modern forms of impersonal domination does not capture well the highly personal pervasive power that many oppressed groups, including women, experience (Scott 1990, 21 n. 3, 62 n. 31). Finally, when power works to shape the will itself, it will not always provoke resistance. Before the feminist movement, for example, I believe I could not have wanted what I later found good for me. For reasons involving what it seems reasonable to call "power" (at least in the sense of force), the possibilities, causal explanations, and new ideals that might have suggested another course were then not conceptually available. Accordingly, as democracies try to equalize the resources with which to impose and resist the use of force and threat of sanction, they must find ways of making as visible as possible the invisible workings of force.

In practice, there are no deliberative spaces into which power does not enter. And because traditional public deliberative arenas are the most likely to draw on symbols that support a dominant order, democracies cannot rely on these arenas to produce the ongoing critique of power that they need. For democratic participation to help those subject to domination understand their interests better, the participants need, among other things, protected enclaves, in which they can explore their ideas in an environment of mutual encouragement. They can then oscillate between these enclaves and more hostile but also broader surroundings in which they can test their ideas against the reigning reality.

The black colleges that began the sit-ins of the Southern civil rights movement in the United States, the black churches in the South, and the early women's consciousness-raising groups and Women's Centers provided "free spaces" in which like-minded people, especially those subordinated in the larger public discourse, could develop their own analyses for themselves (Allen 1970, see also Scott 1990 on "sequestered spaces" and Fraser 1992 on "subaltern counterpublics"). In these spaces, marginal groups could develop what Zora Neale Hurston called "new words" (Hurston 1990, 31, 109) and new ways of thinking.

Using such enclaves for effective deliberation requires a division of labor. Some individuals work best immersed in the enclave, developing the new words and pushing the new ideas as far as they can go, testing in their lives and talk some critical frontiers of change—but talking primarily with one another. Others—often those the dominant society rewards most heavily—work well as translators, with one foot in the world of immersion, one in the mainstream. Still others stand astride the border shooting at the mainstream, drawing ammunition from the raw, creative world of immersion.

Even the most just societies need these enclaves of protected discourse and action because each institution of new forms of power and participation unsettles past patterns of power in ways that are not simply just. Each balance of power creates a new underdog, each settlement a new group who would benefit from unsettling (Honig 1994). Each settlement accordingly creates not only the necessary capacity for action but also the need to protect and facilitate in some way those who have lost.

Just as feminist theory based on the greater self-consciousness of women regarding intimate connection makes available metaphors and experiences in which individuals are not so starkly pitted against one another as in the reigning liberal theory of "adversary" democracy, so feminist theory based on the experience of pervasive domination highlights the need for democratic practices and institutions to help unravel the interlocking systems of private and public power on which domination rests.

In practice, applying insights from the experience of domination to the exercise of democratic persuasion means recognizing that coercive power, the threat of sanction and the use of force, is everywhere. Its manifestations need to be fought, in the formal political arena and elsewhere, as elements of an interlocking system. When one's analysis suggests an ongoingly effective cause, such as the organization of the economy or of sexuality, that cause should become a focus of political action. Democracies should also look inventively for formal democratic institutions, such as group representation, that can increase the power of dominated groups (Young 1990). But the battle against domination cannot be restricted to the formal institutions of government. It must be waged on all fronts, including within the self.

Notes

---

1. I would like to thank the Center for Urban Affairs and Policy Research for support that allowed me to write this article. Although this is an original article, I have drawn in it from Mansbridge (1990b, 1993, and 1995).

2. By "power" in this essay I mean "power over"—causing an outcome through the use of force or threat of sanction on another human being. "Power" more broadly defined, to mean "the actual or potential causal relation between the interests or preferences of an actor or set of actors and the outcome itself" (adapted from Nagel 1975), includes persuasion, because it covers all forms of

cause, including anticipated reactions. This broader definition includes what many feminists and others call "power to" or "power with," as well as "power over" (Follett 1942, Emmett 1953–1954, Connolly 1974, Hartsock 1981, Starhawk 1987). I have adapted my distinctions regarding persuasion, force, and threat of sanction from Bachrach and Baratz (1963) and my association of force and threat of sanction with conflicting interests and persuasion with common interests from Lukes (1974). For more on these distinctions, see Mansbridge (1983, 1994). For the importance of persuasion in democracy, see in addition Mansbridge (1986, 1990a, 1990b, 1992, 1993).

3. He continued, "This resistance is never in a postion of exteriority in relation to power." Later, however, he suggested that this maxim holds only insofar as "power" is defined as engaging the subject's will: "power is exercised only over free subjects and only insofar as they are free" (Foucault 1982, 220). One could conclude that when power works to shape the will itself (in its incarnation as "force"), it will not always provoke resistance. It is a common mistake to assume that every form of power requires resistance (see, e.g., Weber 1978, 53).

4. Although Kraditor (1971) stresses the predominance of arguments from women's special virtues ("difference" arguments) toward the end of the suffrage movement, more recent historians (cited in Cott 1986, 50–51) demonstrate that both "sameness" and "difference" arguments flourished throughout the period from 1792 to 1921. Lerner cites evidence of European women's attempts to show female superiority to men in "sensibility and caring" as well as other virtues, beginning with Christine de Pizan in 1405 (Lerner 1993, 260–262). Cott (1986) provides an excellent short account of "sameness" versus "difference" strands in the first wave of feminism in the United States.

5. Follett is sometimes misinterpreted on this point. She made it clear by saying "definitely . . . I do not think integration is possible in all cases" (Follett 1942, 36) and argued that in trying to "find the real demand as against the demand put forward," the first rule for obtaining integration is to "face the real issue, uncover the conflict, bring the whole thing into the open" (1942, 38). More recently, Ury and Fisher's best-selling book on negotiation draws explicitly on Follett's theory and her example of the window in the next room (Ury and Fisher 1983, 41), without attributing either the theory or the example to Follett—perhaps because the book has no footnotes.

6. Although arguments for women's culture did not appear in print until around 1970, they were part of many activists' conceptual apparatus earlier in the movement. Echols (1989) is mistaken in thinking that these ideas were later accretions. See also in later years, Sara Ruddick on an ideal of "maternal power," which is "benign, accurate, sturdy and sane," interested in preservation and growth (Ruddick 1980, 345, 354), and Kathy Ferguson on using the "values that are structured into women's experience—caretaking, nurturance, empathy, connectedness" to create new organizational models not dependent on domination (Ferguson 1984, 25, 119–203).

7. For research based on Gilligan's approach, see Johnston (1988) and Lyons (1988). For empirical criticism of the Gilligan thesis, including the issue of gender differences in empathy, see Ford and Lowery (1986) and sources in Mansbridge (1993, notes 18, 31–34). For philosophical criticism of that thesis, see Tronto (1989), Flanagan and Jackson (1987), and Okin (1990).

8. The dichotomy between reason and emotion maps onto the male-female dichotomy more perfectly in the United States than in any other measured culture. When university students from twenty-eight countries rated adjectives as being "more frequently associated with men rather than women, or more frequently associated with women than men," a majority of students in all but one country (Pakistan) associated the adjective "emotional" with women and in all but five associated the adjective "rational" with men. English-speaking countries produced stronger dichotomies than others and the United States the strongest dichotomy of all. In the United States alone, every student gave "emotional" an association with women and a high percentage gave "rational" an association with men (data from Williams and Best 1982, Appendix A).

9. To some degree we may tacitly or explicitly agree in advance on conditions for the use of force and threat of sanction. The legitimacy of this agreement may be judged in part by the degree to which the deliberation resulting in agreement was free from the use of force or threat of sanction. Such prior agreement, however, is not the only source of legitimacy (Mansbridge 1995).

10. Foucault himself, however, would probably have refused on principle to distinguish "repressive power" from other forms. On Foucault's many uses of "power," see Fraser (1989) and McCarthy (1990).

References

Allen, Pamela. 1970. *Free Space: A Perspective on the Small Group in Women's Liberation.* New York: Times Change Press.

Alpert, Jane. 1973. "Mother Right: A New Feminist Theory." *Off Our Backs* 3 (8 May):6.

Aristotle. 1941. *Rhetorica.* In *The Basic Works of Aristotle.* Ed. and intro. Richard McKeon. New York: Random House.

Bachrach, Peter and Morton Baratz. 1963. "Decisions and Non-decisions: An Analytic Framework." *American Political Science Review* 57:632–644.

Barber, Benjamin R. 1984. *Strong Democracy: Participatory Politics for a New Age.* Berkeley: University of California Press.

Bartlett, Katharine T. 1990. "Feminist Legal Methods." *Harvard Law Review* 103:829–888.

Benhabib, Seyla. 1987. "The Generalized and Concrete Other." In *Feminism as Critique.* Ed. Seyla Benhabib and Drucilla Cornell. Minneapolis: University of Minnesota Press.

Bryan, Frank M. 1975. "Comparative Town Meetings: A Search for Causative Models of Feminine Involvement in Politics." Paper delivered at the Annual Meeting of the Rural Sociological Society.

Butterfield, L. H., Mark Friedlaender and Mary-Jo Kline, eds. 1975. *The Book of Abigail and John: Selected Letters of the Adams Family, 1762–1784.* Cambridge, Mass.: Harvard University Press.

Carby, Hazel. 1987. *Reconstructing Womanhood: The Emergence of the Afro-American Novelist.* Oxford: Oxford University Press.

Carroll, Berenice. 1972. "Peace Research: The Cult of Power." *Journal of Conflict Resolution* 4:585–616.

Chodorow, Nancy. 1978. *The Reproduction of Mothering: Psychoanalysis and the Sociology of Gender*. Berkeley: University of California Press.

Collins, Patricia Hill. 1990. *Black Feminist Thought*. London: Allen and Unwin.

Connolly, William E. 1974. "Power and Responsibility." In *The Terms of Political Discourse*. Lexington: D. C. Heath.

Conover, Pamela Johnston. 1988. "Who Cares? Sympathy and Politics: A Feminist Perspective." Paper presented at the annual meeting of the Midwest Political Science Association.

Cott, Nancy. 1986. "Feminist Theory and Feminist Movements." In *What Is Feminism?* Ed. Juliet Mitchell and Ann Oakley. New York: Pantheon.

Crocker, Hannah Mather. 1968. "Observations on the Real Rights of Women." In *Up from the Pedestal*. Ed. Aileen Kraditor. Chicago: Quadrangle Books.

Dinnerstein, Dorothy. 1977. *The Mermaid and the Minotaur: Sexual Arrangements and Human Malaise*. New York: Harper Colophon.

Dixon, Marlene. 1970. *It Ain't Me Babe*. April 7.

Eagly, Alice H. and Blair T. Johnson. 1990. "Gender and Leadership Style: A Meta-Analysis." *Psychological Bulletin* 108:233–256.

Echols, Alice. 1989. *Daring to Be Bad: Radical Feminism in America 1967–1975*. Minneapolis: University of Minnesota Press.

Elshtain, Jean Bethke. 1981. *Public Man, Private Woman: Women in Social and Political Thought*. Princeton, N.J.: Princeton University Press.

Emmet, Dorothy. 1953–1954. "The Concept of Power." *Proceedings of the Aristotelian Society* 54:1–26.

Epstein, Cynthia Fuchs. 1988. *Deceptive Distinctions: Sex, Gender, and the Social Order*. New Haven, Conn.: Yale University Press and Russell Sage Foundation.

Ferguson, Kathy E. 1984. *The Feminist Case Against Bureaucracy*. Philadelphia: Temple University Press.

Flanagan, Owen and Kathryn Jackson. 1987. "Justice, Care, and Gender: The Kohlberg-Gilligan Debate Revisited." *Ethics* 97:622–637.

Follett, Mary Parker. 1942. *Dynamic Administration: The Collected Papers of Mary Parker Follett*. Ed. Henry C. Metcalf. New York: Harper.

Follett, Mary Parker. 1949. "Coordination." In *Freedom and Coordination: Lectures in Business Organization*. London: Management Publications Trust.

Ford, Maureen R. and Carol R. Lowery. 1986. "Gender Differences in Moral Reasoning: A Comparison of the Use of Justice and Care Orientations." *Journal of Personality and Social Psychology* 50:777–783.

Foucault, Michel. 1978. *The History of Sexuality*. Trans. Robert Hurley. New York: Pantheon.

Foucault, Michel. 1982. "The Subject and Power." Afterword in *Michel Foucault: Beyond Structuralism and Hermeneutics*. Ed. Hubert Dreyfus and Paul Rabinow. Chicago: University of Chicago Press.

Fraser, Nancy. 1989. "Foucault on Modern Power: Empirical Insights and Normative Confusions." In *Unruly Practices*. Minneapolis: University of Minnesota Press.

Fraser, Nancy. 1992. "Rethinking the Public Sphere: A Contribution to the Critique of Actually Existing Democracy." In *Habermas and the Public Sphere.* Ed. Craig Calhoun. Cambridge: MIT Press.

Gilligan, Carol. 1982. *In a Different Voice.* Cambridge, Mass.: Harvard University Press.

Haas, Adelaide. 1979. "Male and Female Spoken Language Differences: Stereotypes and Evidence." *Psychological Bulletin* 86:616–626.

Harris, Angela. 1990. "Race and Essentialism in Legal Theory." *Stanford Law Review* 42:581–616.

Hartsock, Nancy. 1981. "Political Change: Two Perspectives on Power." In *Building Feminist Theory: Essays from Quest, A Feminist Quarterly.* Ed. Charlotte Bunch. New York: Longman.

Held, Virginia. 1990. "Mothering Versus Contract." In *Beyond Self-Interest.* Ed. Jane J. Mansbridge. Chicago: University of Chicago Press.

Honig, Bonnie. 1994. *Political Theory and the Displacement of Politics.* Ithaca, N.Y.: Cornell University Press.

Hurston, Zora Neale. 1990. *Their Eyes Were Watching God.* New York: Harper and Row.

Johnston, D. Kay. 1988. "Adolescents' Solutions to Dilemmas in Fables." In *Mapping the Moral Domain: A Contribution of Women's Thinking to Psychological Theory and Education.* Ed. Carol Gilligan, J. Victoria Ward, and Jill McLean Taylor. Cambridge, Mass.: Harvard University Press.

Jones, Kathleen. 1993. *Compassionate Authority: Democracy and the Representation of Women.* New York: Routledge.

Kathlene, Lyn. 1990. "The Impact of Gender on the Legislative Process: A Study of the Colorado State Legislature." In *Feminist Research Methods.* Ed. Joyce McCarl Nielsen. Boulder, Colo.: Westview Press.

Kraditor, Aileen. 1971. *The Ideas of the Woman Suffrage Movement.* Garden City, N.Y.: Doubleday.

Lasswell, Harold. 1936. *Politics: Who Gets What, When, How.* Cleveland: World Publishing.

Lerner, Gerda. 1993. *The Creation of Feminist Consciousness from the Middle Ages to 1870.* New York: Oxford University Press.

Lindblom, Charles E. 1990. *Inquiry and Change: The Troubled Attempt to Understand and Shape Society.* New Haven, Conn.: Yale University Press.

Lorde, Audre. 1984. *Sister Outsider.* Freedom, Calif.: Crossing Press.

Lukes, Steven. 1974. *Power: A Radical View.* London: Macmillan.

Lyons, Nona Plessner. 1988. "Two Perspectives: On Self, Relationships, and Morality." In *Mapping the Moral Domain: A Contribution of Women's Thinking to Psychological Theory and Education.* Ed. Carol Gilligan, J. Victoria Ward, and Jill McLean Taylor. Cambridge, Mass.: Harvard University Press.

MacKinnon, Catherine. 1987. *Feminism Unmodified.* Cambridge, Mass.: Harvard University Press.

Mansbridge, Jane J. 1983. *Beyond Adversary Democracy.* Chicago: University of Chicago Press.

Mansbridge, Jane J. 1986. *Why We Lost the ERA.* Chicago: University of Chicago Press.

Mansbridge, Jane J., ed. 1990a. *Beyond Self-Interest.* Chicago: University of Chicago Press.

Mansbridge, Jane J. 1990b. "Feminism and Democracy." *The American Prospect* 1:27–29.

Mansbridge, Jane J. 1992. "A Deliberative Theory of Interest Representation." In *The Politics of Interests: Interest Groups Transformed.* Ed. Mark P. Petracca. Boulder, Colo.: Westview Press.

Mansbridge, Jane J. 1993. "Feminism and Democratic Community." In *Democratic Community: NOMOS XXXV.* Ed. John Chapman and Ian Shapiro. New York: New York University Press.

Mansbridge, Jane J. 1994. "Politics as Persuasion." In *The Dynamics of American Politics.* Ed. Lawrence C. Dodd and Calvin Jillson. Boulder, Colo.: Westview Press.

Mansbridge, Jane J. 1995. "Using Power/Fighting Power: The Polity." In *Democracy and Difference.* Ed. Seyla Benhabib. Princeton, N.J.: Princeton University Press.

McCarthy, Thomas. 1990. "The Critique of Impure Reason: Foucault and the Frankfurt School." *Political Theory* 18:437–469.

Murdoch, Iris. 1971. *The Sovereignty of Good.* New York: Schocken.

Nagel, Jack H. 1975. *The Descriptive Analysis of Power.* New Haven, Conn.: Yale University Press.

Nedelsky, Jennifer. 1989. "Reconceiving Autonomy." *Yale Journal of Law and Feminism* 1 (1):7–36.

Noddings, Nel. 1984. *Caring: A Feminine Approach to Ethics and Moral Education.* Berkeley: University of California Press.

Nussbaum, Martha Craven. 1995. "Emotions and Women's Capabilities." In *Women, Culture, and Development.* Ed. Martha Craven Nussbaum and Johnathan Glover. Oxford: Oxford University Press.

Okin, Susan Moller. 1990. "Thinking Like a Woman." In *Theoretical Perspectives on Sexual Difference.* Ed. Deborah L. Rhode. New Haven, Conn.: Yale University Press.

Payne, Charles M. 1989. "Ella Baker and Models of Organizing." *Signs* 14 (4):885–900.

Rorty, Amélie Oksenberg. 1985. "Varieties of Rationality, Varieties of Emotion." *Social Science Information* 24:343–353.

Ruddick, Sara. 1980. "Maternal Thinking." *Feminist Studies* 6: 342–367.

Ruth, Sheila. 1981. "Methodocracy, Misogyny, and Bad Faith: The Response of Philosophy." In *Men's Studies Modified: The Impact of Feminism on the Academic Disciplines.* Ed. Dale Spender. New York: Oxford University Press.

Sacks, Karen Brodkin. 1988. *Caring by the Hour: Women, Work, and Organizing at Duke Medical Center.* Urbana, Ill.: University of Illinois Press.

Sawicki, Jana. 1991. *Disciplining Foucault: Feminism, Power, and the Body.* London: Routledge.

Schumpeter, Joseph A. 1942. *Capitalism, Socialism, and Democracy.* New York: Harper and Row.

Scott, James C. 1990. *Domination and the Arts of Resistance: Hidden Transcripts.* New Haven, Conn.: Yale University Press.

Spelman, Elizabeth. 1988. *Inessential Woman: Problems of Exclusion in Feminist Thought.* Boston: Beacon Press.

Starhawk. 1987. *Truth or Dare: Encounters with Power, Authority, and Mystery.* San Francisco: Harper and Row.

Tronto, Joan C. 1989. "Women and Caring: What Can Feminists Learn About Morality from Caring?" In *Gender/Body/Knowledge.* Ed. Alison M. Jaggar and Susan R. Bordo. New Brunswick: Rutgers University Press.

Truman, David. 1959. *The Governmental Process.* New York: Knopf.

Ury, William and Roger Fisher. 1983. *Getting to Yes.* New York: Penguin Books.

Weber, Max. 1978. *Economy and Society.* Berkeley: University of California Press.

Weil, Simone. 1962. "Human Personality." In *Collected Essays.* Ed. and trans. Richard Rees. London: Oxford University Press.

Williams, John E. and Deborah L. Best. 1982. *Measuring Sex Stereotypes.* Beverly Hills: Sage Publications.

Young, Iris Marion. 1990. *Justice and the Politics of Difference.* Princeton, N.J.: Princeton University Press.

Zimmerman, D. H. and C. West. 1975. "Sex Roles, Interruptions, and Silences in Conversation." In *Language and Sex: Difference and Dominance.* Ed. B. Thorne and N. Henley. Rowley, Mass.: Newbury House.

7

Care as a Political Concept

Joan C. Tronto

Much of the exciting and original work in feminist political theory has begun as critique. Feminists have explored the terrain of traditional political theory and have found many of the traditional concepts laden with sexist and masculinist biases. Nevertheless, as valuable as this work has been, we cannot move forward from negative critique to constructive theory unless and until we entertain the possibility that not all relevant concepts that we shall need to offer a feminist political theory already appear within the lexicon of political theory. We must expand the terrain to include concepts that are traditionally excluded from politics in order to see how their inclusion changes the contours of political life. I propose in this essay to explore how the shape of political theories might change were we to think of care as a political concept.[1]

In the first section of the chapter, I shall explore ways in which care now appears to be an apolitical concept. In the second section, I shall propose how a different conceptualization frees care from its apolitical context and opens new analytic issues in understanding care as a political concept. In the third section, I shall review the initial criticisms of the apolitical nature of care laid out in the first section of the chapter and consider whether these objections have been met. I shall conclude by offering some possible claims about political life that might emerge from a care perspective.

Thinking About the Apolitical Nature of Care

WE NOTE AT the outset that political theorists, and for that matter, social theorists, do not have a clear concept of care. It has not been a sufficiently important concept or issue for most philosophers, political theorists, or social theorists to consider. Indeed, the very way that the discussion of care has entered contemporary moral and political theory, as part of a debate called "justice versus care,"[2] presumes a contrast between a quintessentially political standard, justice, and a standard of questionable value in political theory. Surely, critics of care have said, it is not possible to displace justice—as it has traditionally been understood—as the ultimate standard for political judgment.

Whatever account is offered about the nature of care, care surely seems to be outside of the political realm, either because it is "below" or "above" politics. As we look more closely at these two positions, we shall see that they reveal how steadfastly gendered assumptions profoundly shape our political views.

There have been several versions of the view that care is "below" politics.[3] The most important of these views derives from one way of reading Aristotle's *Politics*.[4] Aristotle seems to make two related arguments about why "care" should be excluded from political life. In the first case, it is prepolitical; in the second case, it is apolitical and prevents the development of proper political attitudes.

That care is prepolitical might be argued from the position that there are some things that the statesman must take for granted: "Just as statesmanship has no need to make men, who are the material which nature provides and which statesmanship takes and uses, so nature can be expected to provide food, whether from land or sea or from some other source, and it is on this basis that the manager can perform his duty of distributing these supplies" (Aristotle 1962, 86; 1258a). What is interesting in this passage is that "nature" provides for human citizens and for food, and the process of converting these "natural" provisions into citizens and wealth are not the concerns of politics. Although these household activities may be necessary for human life, they only contribute in a preliminary way to the end of living a good life, which is the concern of the political realm (54; 1252a).

For Aristotle, the household cannot be a part of political life because it necessarily involves relationships among superiors and inferiors rather than relationships among equals or potential equals. Recall that the relationships of inequality are those of master and slave, husband and wife, and parent and child. In describing these relationships, Aristotle points to the narrowness of function and to the inadequacy of the reasoning capacity in natural slaves, all women and hence all wives, and children (i.e., sons). It is difficult to sort out to what extent Aristotle thought that the flaws of women and slaves derived from "nature" or from "function," in part because these categories overlap in Aristotle's thought. Nevertheless, Aristotle discounts the possibility of women's political roles because of their domestic duties (118; 1264b) and speaks of the corrosive effect of banausic professions on the capacity of men to pursue virtue (415; 1328b). It is clear that he excludes slaves and wives because they are inadequate to the tasks of prudential reasoning, to a large part because of the kinds of activities in which they engage. For Aristotle, who places a high value on the realm of political activity and sees it as a realm in which men can exercise their moral capacities, women and slaves spend their lives engaged in activities that do not allow them to develop adequate skills for these realms of life. Hence, there is something inherent in banausic and domestic duties, in care activities, that makes someone who engages in them incapable of political life.

What precisely is wrong with the life of care, then? From Aristotle's account, caring is about a narrow and technical world, a world of dependence, and a world in which judgment is too focused and narrow. Care is about the immediate and prevents anyone from thinking more broadly than about immediate concerns. Care is parochial. Care is undiscriminating. Care is attached to lower, rather than higher, human pursuits, such as meeting basic physical needs. Only if one transcends these concerns is one able to become involved in politics (see also Spelman 1988).

Care can also be excluded from politics because it appears to be "above" politics. This second version of care's exclusion is perhaps best introduced by noting its origins in the Christian roots of our political theory traditions. Care understood as the ideal accomplishment of the spiritual elite was perhaps a rare gift, but certainly no normal part of the earthly realm, after St. Augustine's delineation of the two cities (Augustine 1972). Christian notions of charity have long involved a notion of sacrificing the self for others, of taking the concerns of the other first. Indeed, on the most basic level Christianity seems to be a religion about caring; Jesus himself was seen as deeply caring, including in a physical sense, for the well-being of others. But for the most part, the Christian tradition of *agape* has not been primarily motivated toward the immediate physical and material needs of some people but toward a generalized love for all others. Although this idea has been used politically with powerful results—consider Martin Luther King Jr.'s version (Cannon 1988)—Christian charity has been for the most part so extensive in its range that it cannot belong in the rough-and-tumble, dirty-hands world of politics.[5]

If we conceive of care as charity above politics, then what care requires also disqualifies its practitioners from politics. To realists such as Augustine and Max Weber, to enter the political world with idealist notions of human kindness is not only naive but dangerous. Those who routinely engage in altruistic, other-regarding acts are excluded from proper inclusion in the political world by their innocence and gullibility. They will not know how to act when political action requires violence or coercion.

By this account, caring ill prepares its practitioners for politics because it renders them not banausic but indiscriminately kind. Just as those who are too close to necessity are unable to make political judgments, so can those who are forgiving never act properly in politics.

In short, then, whether care is below or above politics, it seems to be a quintessentially prepolitical or apolitical concept. Contemporary writing has largely followed this bifurcated account of care. On the one hand, care is about a type of dependence, often brought about by incapacity, and the work involved in coping with such dependent people (e.g., Ungerson 1990; Finch and Groves 1983; Abel and Nelson 1990). On the other hand, care is connected to the quality of our souls as we make a series of personal commitments to decide "the importance of what we care about" (Frankfurt 1988).

Such views ignore, however, that care is a complex process that ultimately reflects structures of power, economic order, the separation of public and private life, and our notions of autonomy and equality. Since contemporary views are limited by the initial assumptions made about the context of care, they cannot arrive at a political understanding of care. It will become clear in this paper how vitally care might reshape our political discourse and how its current narrow vision may have been constructed.

Care as a Political Concept

THE ACTIVITIES THAT constitute care are crucial for human life. Berenice Fisher and I devised this definition: care is *a species activity that includes everything that we do to maintain, continue, and repair our 'world' so that we can live in it as well as possible.* That world includes our bodies, our selves, and our environment, all of which we seek to interweave in a complex, life-sustaining web" (Fisher and Tronto 1991, 40).

Our definition of care includes the intellectual and practical aspects of the usual meaning of care, but our concept also exposes some of the hidden dimensions that are often included in concepts of care. In the first place, though we do not exclude the possibility that caring is an individual psychological quality, we refuse to limit our understanding of care in this way. By identifying caring as a "species activity" we hope to offset the usual association of care with the activities and mental states of individuals. Although it is possible to conceive of caring in individualistic terms, to do so makes it extremely difficult to use caring as a political concept.

Second, although care does involve an assessment of needs, and the concrete ways in which such needs are met, caring is not simply an abstract process of trying to determine how to meet needs (cf. Heller and Feher 1991). A group of government officials engaged in a policy debate about how to provide housing for the homeless is a part of the activity of caring, but it is not the entirety of care. In order to capture this aspect of our account of caring, Fisher and I provided a more careful delineation of the component parts of caring so that we could include all of the elements of care.

We began by delineating four component phases in the process of caring: *caring about*, that is, becoming aware of and paying attention to the need for caring; *caring for*, that is, assuming responsibility for some caring; *caregiving*, that is, the actual material meeting of the caring need; and *care-receiving*, that is, the response of the thing, person, group, and so forth, that received the caregiving, and the assessment of this response. We argue that any total account of care includes all four of these phases and that given the complexity of these different phases, they will frequently bear a complex relationship with one another: care processes can become fragmented, parts of a care process may come into conflict with each other. By allowing that care is a complex process with many components we do not romanticize the care process; care is more likely to be filled with inner contradictions, conflict, and frustration than it is to resemble the idealized interactions of mother and child or teacher and student.

Furthermore, we described caring as a process that can occur in a variety of institutions and settings. Care is found in the household, in services and goods sold in the market, and in the workings of bureaucratic organizations in contemporary life. Care is not restricted to the traditional realm of mother's work, to welfare agencies, or to hired domestic servants but is found in all of these realms. Indeed, concerns about care permeate our daily lives, the institutions in the modern marketplace, and the corridors of government. Because we tend to follow the traditional division of the world into public and private spheres, and think of caring as an aspect of private life, care is usually associated, as in Aristotle's dichotomy, with activities of the household. When we allow that government is performing acts of care, in the United States at least these acts are usually thought of as the government acting as a surrogate family, with all of the implied paternalism there involved (cf. inter alia, Abramovitz 1988). We do not think systematically about these concerns and therefore do not acknowledge their public face.

Finally, this account of care describes care as a practice (cf. Ruddick 1990a). It is a complicated matter to care well; caring involves thoughtfulness, deliberation, and good judgment. It requires self-knowledge, adequate resources, and knowledge of the situation in which one cares. It requires that immediate needs be balanced with long-term needs, that those who care think through their priorities and resolve conflicting demands for care.

How would our thinking about political life change were we to use care as a political concept? The inclusion of care would change our sense of political goals and provide us with additional ways to think politically and strategically. Thus, care serves as a political concept in both of the usual senses in which we use the language of politics: care is both a goal (a collective ideal) and a strategy (a way to affect the outcome of political conflict).

Care as a political goal is not an entirely new notion. That a society flourishes when its citizens are well cared for is not a claim that strikes us as outrageous or unusual. Despite that, relatively few political theorists have paid much attention to the notion that care is an important activity in political life.[6] Most have assumed that in a well ordered polity, the quality of private life will also be appropriate and well regulated. As a result, the care upon which society rests is controlled from a distance.

By contrast, contemporary feminist thought posits ways in which the construction of private life as separate from public life has led to the diminution of values of care, which now need to be revitalized. Putting care first reshapes our view of the relation between public and private life and transforms political values. For example, a politically visionary dimension of caring can be drawn out of the work of Sara Ruddick, who argues that maternal thinking, a type of care, can lead to a powerful form of peace politics (Ruddick 1990a, 1990b). Ruddick argues that the concrete focus on the preservation and growth of particular human bodies, especially those of one's own children, can lead to a concrete appreciation for the fragility and preciousness of human life. Someone who has experienced human life in this concrete way will be less able, Ruddick argues, to make the kinds of judgments and decisions necessary to think about human life simply as a resource that is as expendable as are other resources, for example, in waging war. If a group of people schooled in Ruddick's "maternal thinking" had been placed in the original position behind John Rawls's (1972) veil of ignorance, they might have reasoned (Ruddick 1990b) to very different conclusions than Rawls's two principles of justice about liberty and the distribution of goods by the difference principle (Okin 1989; Sevenhuijsen 1993).

Other feminists have suggested that the approach of care makes ecological concerns central to political life, not simply another set of separate interests to be pursued or ignored (Diamond and Orenstein 1990). By the same token, once we have expanded our notions of caring by looking at the effects our activities have upon the environment, it would be difficult not to notice the effects that our activities have upon other people and life forms beyond our own family, community, and country.

In addition to thinking of the provision of good care as a goal for society, however, considering care as a strategy has even greater political significance. Feminist theorists have used care strategically in a number of ways.[7] When we think of care in strategic terms, we admit that the question of what care is, who should provide care, and who should bear the various burdens of care are contested questions. These are issues that are at the heart of much contemporary political conflict.

By suggesting that care be included as part of our vocabulary of politics, several strategic possibilities open up to feminists. In the first place, the prospect for a broader base for political participation opens. Many women view themselves as excluded from political life (Fowlkes 1992). In order for women to become active, they need to sense that their concerns are part of the public concerns. By focusing on a vocabulary of care, feminists would be able to point to the importance of women's traditional activities without being forced to the logical position that women should continue to perform those traditional duties (Hirschmann 1992).

Second, care provides a way to overcome the piecemeal and fragmented way in which Americans now think about politics. Because care is integrative, it is possible to open a discussion of the needs of humans in broader terms once we start from the care perspective. To make certain that all people are adequately cared for is not a utopian question, but one which immediately suggests answers about employment policies, nondiscrimination, equalizing expenditures for schools, providing adequate access to health care, and so forth. Furthermore, care provides a framework in which we can see the absence of solutions to these problems.

Another strategic use of this concept of care is that it clarifies how to change the boundary between public and private life. The separation of life into spheres that are public and private is a hallmark of Western political thought (Elshtain 1981; Seery 1990). Nonetheless, the precise boundary between public and private changes constantly, and the work of changing that boundary is always a political struggle. For example, one of the tasks of Marxist and worker activists has been to make the claim that "private" corporations are actually public entities and should be held accountable in a public sphere for some of their activities. Some aspects of care have been more easily understood to fall within the realm of the public sphere. Hence, public education has been long understood to be a public activity despite its association with caring in a traditional sense. In contrast, for example, in the United States child care is considered wholly private, and the public implications of its provision are largely ignored. As a result, individual parents struggle to jerry-rig a system that can work for them, rarely thinking in a systematic way about the variety of care needs that are involved in this complex issue, and rarely thinking about what more public, rather than privately arranged, solutions might be. Or, to consider another example, insofar as care is distributed by the market, then the kind of care that people could provide for themselves (Waerness [in Ungerson 1990] calls such care "personal service") is disproportionately available to the wealthy and not to the poor. Seeing all forms of care as part of a whole, understanding the relationship of personal service in relation to caregiving activities, allows us to focus attention on how the boundary between public and private life is being constructed to benefit some and not others. These are essential political issues.

Care can also be valuable in providing a framework within which conflict can be more clearly theorized. Such clarity arises from the fact that, though caring is ideally integrated into a whole process, caring can be a source of deep conflict on many levels. In this sense as well, caring is quintessentially political. Let me briefly mention several ways in which caring can result in conflict and in which understanding the nature of care illuminates many forms of conflict.

First, any given caring activity can be well or poorly done, and its adequacy can be the source of friction and conflict. Conflict between caregivers and care-receivers are likely to result from the perceived adequacy of care. Second, insofar as caring depends for its accomplishment on resources, the allocation of resources is always a political process. Third, since care requires an integration of attentiveness, responsibility, as well as actually providing care, a disintegrated care process is likely to result in conflict. For example, if the rules of operation are determined by the higher-ups in an organization, but the actual caregivers find these rules inappropriate, conflict, visible or invisible, is likely to result. Fourth, caregivers themselves need care, and the potential for conflict among roles, about allocating resources, and so forth is likely to arise there as well.

Another key to effective political strategy is having a clear account of current political life; more precise political analysis will also result from using care as a political concept. The four phases of caring allow us to ask the basic questions about political life: To paraphrase Lasswell (1936), who gets what *care*, where, when, how, and why? Who can command care and resources for care?[8] Indeed, if the powerful consist of those who can command society's resources, then looking at the way some can command the care of others might be an important new way to analyze power.

One of the most powerful effects of defining care as political is that it allows us to focus a discussion on caring needs as a public discussion. At the present, which needs are met, how, and by whom are questions left to individuals, families, the market, and occasionally, the state. What making care into a political concept would require is that we have a public debate about needs, about which needs are met, how adequately, and so forth.[9]

Once we begin to discuss questions of caring in an open political forum, I submit that one last question that has been fundamental for feminist political thinkers and for all political theorists (cf. White 1991) would be more easily addressed: the question of otherness. Care may be an extremely important political idea for allowing a more open approach to the problem of otherness. Here I mean to invert entirely the usual critique of care as parochial, which views care as a lesser type of political thinking or moral argument because it starts from a parochial and local concern. It is often argued that only universal, disinterested, political thought, can save us from treating others poorly.

This argument would perhaps be convincing if it really were true that universalistic political theory were universal. Historically, though, political thinkers have begun by excluding some humans from those who fall within their political theories and thus the creation of "others" is part of all traditional political theories. Treating "the other" as a lesser human being is another part, of course, of the first political act; others are almost always described in terms of their difference from, and deficiencies from the standpoint of, those who have excluded them and called them "other."

The complex logic of caring processes demands that we explore "others" more honestly. Because it is both a universal quality of human existence and one that is realized in particular—culturally specific and different—ways, care requires that our political thought be based more thoroughly upon an accurate account of human life. That humans are dependent during part of their lives is a politically significant fact. When we try to pretend that humans have not undergone a period of dependence, we distort "the human condition" to try to cope with this exclusion. We create "others," I would suggest, when we understand the rage and hostility around the need we have to ignore or to forget (in a Nietzschean, bad faith sense) our dependence upon those "others." I do not mean to suggest that introducing a concept of care into our political vocabulary will lead to a solution of the problem of otherness. Nevertheless, because caring provides a way to describe and to account for some of the deep-seated emotions that give rise to the creation of otherness, it provides us with a start towards its analysis.

To summarize, caring can be a powerful strategy for change in our current polity. A political concept of care that aims at seeing all of the elements of the process of caring, and that concerns details that are of practical significance in the lives of all citizens, holds the prospects for becoming a powerful lens through which we can judge the political world. As Piven and Cloward (1977) mentioned in their description of poor people's movements, social movements and large infusions of new activists into the political world are possible only when society as it is organized appears suddenly to be disorganized. Under these conditions, more than piecemeal change is possible.

In truth, the daily experience of care is often tragic. Our care may fail; we can probably never care enough to solve all of the caring needs around us; there are more needs for care than can ever be met. Nevertheless, a frank understanding of the ways in which our life experiences of care help to shape us, an understanding of the importance of making public our attempts to meet the needs of all to be cared for and to engage in caring practices, would radically transform our sense of politics.

Using Care to Change Our Conception of Politics

GIVEN CURRENT UNDERSTANDINGS of care, thinkers have been unable to distinguish the kind of work and thinking that are involved in care from the highly particular, or wildly generous, occasions on which they think about care. As a result, most thinkers have mistaken these specific *contexts* of care for the *content* of care.

The grounds that are offered as to why care is apolitical or prepolitical, that care is either below or above politics, seem more tied to the context of care than to care itself. Nevertheless, these two sets of traditional arguments against care do provide the basic and important cautions that we must keep in mind if we wish to use care as a political concept. The concern that care is banal and below politics gives rise to the critique that care is parochial and too narrow in its focus. The concern that care is above politics and too much like charity gives rise to the critique that care is paternalistic or maternalistic in its approach. We must consider these two serious objections carefully.

The greatest limit to care is that insofar as it is an extremely concrete process, thinkers who write about care often wonder if it is too narrow to be expanded beyond extremely parochial borders (Dietz 1985; Tronto 1987). Nel Noddings (1984, 1990) is the extreme illustration of this point; Noddings was initially unwilling to allow that caring even occurred in institutional settings. She has since recognized the need to consider that caring is constrained and shaped by social institutions, but she has not yet expanded the realm of caring itself.

The problem with the narrowness of caring is that it permits individuals to be extremely self-righteous and narrow-minded in their understanding of what caring needs are most important. Not all of the caring work that needs to be done in the world will ever be done. As a result, all of us must always engage in a process of setting caring priorities. If those who are the most wealthy and powerful are allowed simply to pay special attention to their own needs because those are the ones that they are closest to and most well acquainted with, the problems of unequal resource distribution could actually be justified, rather than overturned, by the focus on care.

Several arguments limit the force of this objection. In the first place, because caring is context specific and concrete, the problem of parochialism is so obvious that no one will think about care without wondering about its parochialism. In this regard caring contrasts favorably I think with theories that claim to be universal but are not. When some theories claim to be universal, only to have others laboriously recognize and pull out the elements within them that are not universal, they in the meantime are capable of functioning ideologically as if they *were* universal. The task of dislodging a theory that functions as if it were universal, as opposed to the task of pointing to the limits of a theory that begins with the assumption that it is partial, is quite different. The latter task is more easily accomplished, and as a result, partial theories that are known to be such are more likely to be attentive to the kinds of evidence that are raised pointing to their partialities.

On another level, though, caring is not only a parochial theory. Although caring is partial in the sense that it is concrete, culturally specific, and historically variable, there is another sense in which care is universal. All humans are born, die, and require some basic necessities in order to survive. All humans require the assistance of others in meeting these basic necessities.

As a third response, we should note that admitting care to our political framework is not meant to displace justice and judgments made on the basis of justice. Care does not require that we surrender a commitment to universal principles, simply that we recognize that as they have been thus far constructed, they do not cover all possible conditions in the world.

Finally, though, it is important to remember, as Virginia Held (1993) has argued, that one important reason why caring practices are now so parochial is because they exist in a society that makes a rigid separation between public and private life, a society in which sexism and racism comprise elements of our social values.[10] In a society in which caring were conceived anew and in which issues of justice were more seriously addressed and remedied, these problems might seem to arise not from the nature of care but from the context within which care must now take place.

A second objection, this one derived from the image of caregivers as above care-receivers (and from the fact that care-receivers are often dependent on caregivers), is that the nature of caring is inherently unequal. Does the nature of care mean that care-receivers are not equal to caregivers? If so, how can a society that embraces the importance of care assume that people are equal and escape from treating some as the wards of paternalistic or maternalistic others? If some can withhold care from others, then do they not have power over their wards? How can equality flourish in such a society?

Care does challenge the modern notion of formal abstract equality; however, it also opens up the opportunity for a richer, more genuine, and more pluralistic account of equality and democratic life. When we include care and those who engage in care in the political arena, we recognize that citizens are not self-sufficient. All people depend upon others; for example, people depend upon the others in their households to meet their basic physical needs. Recognition of our mutual states of dependence and conditions of vulnerability provides a different basis for equality.

Care allows us to reconceive equality in such terms of mutual interdependence. Care is both universal and particularistic. Care is universal because all humans need care at some point in their lives; at the very least, people need care as infants, when they are infirm, and often when they are dying. Care is particularistic because answers to such questions as "what kinds of care? how much? who is providing it?" are deeply tied not only to culture but to gendered, classed, raced, and other structural features of any culture. But even a cursory glance at care reveals that it belies the myth that humans are independent, separate beings. While there may be times in our lives when humans are independent and autonomous, there are other times in our lives in which we are not independent. Further, in modern societies, we are often dependent in myriad ways upon others to help us meet our most basic needs for food, sleep, protection from the elements, hygiene, and so forth. For the most part, though, we choose to view these forms of dependency as a result of family life (constructed as if it were outside of politics) or as a result of unproblematic market relations. We do not view these relationships as a set of interconnected political relations, nor do we view them as defining who we are as humans. Nevertheless, to view these relationships in terms of their importance for our everyday existence, we would have to acknowledge our dependence upon many other people. The notion that we are independent would itself become questionable.

But this fact poses a challenge to democracy: If the myriad caring relationships are unequal, then how can we argue at all for human equality?[11] Political theorists have long recognized the danger of challenging the formal assumption of equality. If we are not all considered formally equal, then what prevents the emergence of a hierarchical order based upon some form of superiority presumed to exist? For example, the knowledge of caregivers could make them into a superior class.[12] How might we prevent paternalism?

What we can argue, I think, is that over the course of a human life, we will find ourselves in different degrees of dependence, independence, and interdependence. All of us are cared for and most of us must also provide care in different ways and at different moments of our lives. Care, therefore, does not in itself undermine our commitment to human equality as a goal. It does, however, require that we provide a much more complex account of what being equal means than the assumption we are automatically equal upon reaching majority. In other words, it is not care itself that produces inequality but the context in which care occurs. When it occurs in a context of radical and abstract individualism, care-receivers will by definition appear to be inferior. If we changed this context by recognizing the many and varied ways in which we are (have been, or are likely to be at some time) both givers *and* receivers of care, the relationship between care and equality can be recast. In short, recognizing human interdependence and conditions of some forms of human inequality provides a stronger grounding for the needs for democratic institutions.

Conclusion

IN THIS CHAPTER I have argued for the value of care as a political concept. Although there have been basic starting assumptions that have excluded care from political thought, I have tried to show that these assumptions rest upon other assumptions that have relegated care to realms in which human judgment was supposed not to obtain. Once we clarify a concept of care that is free from the constraints of its supposed context and define care as the serious and complex set of practices that it is, we immediately recognize that care is not private, not banal, and not indiscriminately charitable.

Obviously I have not here resolved all of the issues that might arise as we begin to think about care as a political concept, nor have I provided a fully developed framework for thinking about care as a political idea. What I have suggested, however, is that care will be a valuable political concept and will fit with a feminist rethinking of equality, the relationship of public and private life, and democratic institutions.

Notes

---

1. My claim here is not meant to be exclusive: I believe that there are many other concepts that would also have to be included into the realm of the political in order to construct a complete feminist political theory. Among concepts that come to mind are the body and sexuality. I do not mean to suggest that previous feminist theoretical work has been only a type of reformism. Revising basic concepts such as equality, justice, autonomy, and notions of violence and security will revolutionize current political theories. But the burden of including something that has previously been conceived as quintessentially apolitical is a different matter and the one I engage in here.

2. The framework of care versus justice is ostensibly derived from Carol Gilligan's identification of two voices in *In a Different Voice* (Gilligan 1982). Gilligan herself disputes the claim that care was ever to be understood as an apolitical voice (1994); she points to the fact that the discussion of abortion as the main moral example women faced as one piece of evidence of the intrinsically political quality of arguing for a different sensibility towards morality mainly propounded by women. Nevertheless, interpreters of "care" versus "justice" have largely described care as apolitical or prepolitical, in contrast to justice, a political concern (cf. Kohlberg 1984 and Puka 1990). For some interesting discussions of care and justice as distinct moral perspectives, see Sevenhuijsen (1993) and Manning (1992). Other scholarly accounts of the nature of care include Benner and Wrubel (1989), Blustein (1991), Foucault (1986), Hugman (1991), and Mayerhoff (1971).

3. Although his argument is framed in terms of moral rather than political theory, Puka's argument (1990) that care is inappropriate because it inherently constitutes a kind of narrow, privatized, personalistic pleading presents another account of why care cannot serve as a basis for political theory. For a response, see Tronto (1993). Among feminist thinkers who have shown how a concept of care can be used politically see Sevenhuijsen (1993) and Sarvasy (1992).

4. See also Stiehm (1983). Whether or not this is an accurate reading of Aristotle is not the question here; compare e.g., Arendt (1958), Schwarzenbach (1994), and Yack (1993).

5. One place where the validity of this point is probably especially true is in the Pietist Protestant tradition. See Schott (1988). See also Weber (1946). Weber's model for the charitable type of caring is not so much Augustine as the Lutheran Pietist tradition. On the origin of this tradition and for a feminist account of its influence, see Schott (1988). For a critique of Weber's masculinism see, among others, Bologh (1990), and Brown (1988). That Christianity does not lend itself to serving as a civic religion because of its other worldly charitable qualities is an argument found in Machiavelli (1979) and Rousseau (1968).

6. Aristotle paid attention to the flourishing state, as did many political thinkers who followed him, including Machiavelli (1979) and Montesquieu (1949). In *The Social Contract*, Rousseau (1968) mentions that one can gauge the health of a polity by whether its population is growing; population increase implies that the people are flourishing. But Rousseau is willing to pay little attention to how that flourishing might occur. Indeed, he seems in *Emile* (Rousseau 1974) to presume that it can happen only if women are required to continue to take care of men, children, and the home. Other political theorists (with the exception of Marx) have not made this point a focus of their work.

7. The most common way to think of care strategically has been as a gender difference. Throughout the history of nineteenth- and twentieth-century feminist thought, the image of women as caregivers, who deserve special treatment because of this role, has been a staple of feminist thought. I have argued elsewhere that there were and are serious limitations to this type of argument (Tronto 1987, 1993; see also Pollitt 1992). Most important, to request that one be given power on the basis of some special attribute (such as being more caring) leaves one at the mercy of those who are more powerful insofar as they either recognize or refuse to recognize the value of that special attribute. Despite the ease and simplicity of the claim, then, that because women are carers they should be given some political benefit, this argument is rarely successful.

There is also another serious problem with this argument: it rests on a claim that is not largely true, empirically. For although it is true that women are disproportionately left with caring roles in our society, it is also the case that others are also involved in caring, and not all women are equally involved in caring. Because caring work is relatively lowly valued in our society, those who do caring work are disproportionately women and men of the lower classes, and in the United States, people of color. For feminist theorists to act as if all caring was the same or grew out of the experiences of the women with whom they were familiar commits a grave error (cf. inter alia, hooks 1984, Collins 1990, Eugene 1989, Lykes 1989).

8. Elizabeth Spelman (1991) has suggested that the question "who cares for whom" is crucial to any adequate understanding of care.

9. Nancy Fraser (1989) makes a similar argument about needs, but she does so from the standpoint of discourse analysis. My suggestion that we need to rethink the nature of political life, not just the nature of discourse, is a more basic claim. But what do I mean by needs? I cannot obviously describe a full theory of human needs here; readers might consult Heller and Feher (1991) and Nussbaum (1992).

10. "Feminist society might be seen as having various relatively independent and distinct segments. . . . Certainly the levels of caring and trust appropriate for

the relations of all members of society with all others will be different from the levels appropriate for the members of a family with one another. But social relations in what can be thought of as society as a whole will not be characterized by indifference to the well-being of others, or an absence of trust, as they are in many nonfeminist conceptions. What kinds and amounts of caring and trust might characterize the relations of the most general kind in society should be decided on the basis of experience and practice with institutions that have overcome male dominance.

"From the point of view of the self-interested head of household, the individual's interest in his own family may be at odds with the wider political and public interest. And aspects of mothering in patriarchal society have contributed to parochialism and racism. But from a satisfactorily worked-out feminist and moral point of view, the picture of the particularistic family in conflict with the good of society is distorted. The postpatriarchal family can express universal emotions and can be guided by universally shared concerns. A content and healthy child eager to learn and to love elicits general approval" (Held 1993, 223–224). On this point, see also Waerness (1990).

11. My thanks to Nancy Hirschmann for suggestions that she made in this discussion.

12. See, e.g., Ronald Rogowski's (1974) rational choice construction of a society of diabetics in which the members of the society would be willing to surrender political power to those who controlled the manufacture and distribution of insulin.

References

Abel, Emily and Margaret Nelson. 1990. *Circles of Care: Work and Identity in Women's Lives*. Albany: State University of New York Press.

Abramovitz, Mimi. 1988. *Regulating the Lives of Women: Social Welfare Policy from Colonial Times to the Present*. Boston: South End Press.

Arendt, Hannah. 1958. *The Human Condition*. New York: Harcourt, Brace.

Aristotle. 1962. *The Politics*. Trans. T. A. Sinclair. Harmondsworth, England: Penguin.

Augustine. 1972. *Concerning the City of God Against the Pagans*. Trans. H. Bettenson. Harmondsworth, England: Penguin.

Benner, Patricia and Judith Wrubel. 1989. *The Primacy of Caring: Stress and Coping in Health and Illness*. Menlo Park, Calif.: Addison-Wesley.

Blustein, Jeffrey. 1991. *Care and Commitment: Taking the Personal Point of View*. Oxford: Oxford University Press.

Bologh, Roslyn W. 1990. *Love or Greatness: Max Weber and Masculine Thinking: A Feminist Inquiry*. Boston: Unwin-Hyman.

Brown, Wendy. 1988. *Manhood and Politics: A Feminist Reading in Political Theory*. Totowa, N.J.: Rowman and Littlefield.

Cannon, Katie G. 1988. *Black Womanist Ethics*. Atlanta: Scholar's Press.

Collins, Patricia Hill. 1990. *Black Feminist Thought: Knowledge, Consciousness, and the Politics of Empowerment*. Boston: Unwin-Hyman.

Diamond, Irene and Gloria Orenstein, eds. 1990. *Reweaving the World: The Emergence of Ecofeminism*. San Francisco: Sierra Club Books.

Dietz, Mary G. 1985. "Citizenship with a Feminist Face: The Problem with Maternal Thinking." *Political Theory* 13(1):19–37.

Elshtain, Jean Bethke. 1981. *Public Man, Private Woman: Women in Social and Political Thought*. Princeton, N.J.: Princeton University Press.

Eugene, Toinette M. 1989. "Sometimes I Feel Like a Motherless Child: The Call and Response for a Liberational Ethic of Care by Black Feminists." In *Who Cares? Theory, Research and Educational Implications of the Ethics of Care*. Ed. Mary Brabek. New York: Praeger.

Finch, Janet and Dulcie Groves. 1983. *A Labour of Love: Women, Work, and Caring*. London: Routledge and Kegan Paul.

Fisher, Berenice and Joan Tronto. 1990. "Toward a Feminist Theory of Caring." In *Circles of Care: Work and Identity in Women's Lives*. Ed. E. Abel and M. Nelson. Albany, N.Y.: SUNY Press.

Foucault, Michel. 1986. *The Care of the Self*. New York: Pantheon.

Fowlkes, Diane L. 1992. *White Political Women: Paths from Privilege to Empowerment*. Knoxville: University of Tennessee Press.

Frankfort, Harry G. 1988. *The Importance of What We Care About: Philosophical Essays*. Cambridge, England: Cambridge University Press.

Fraser, Nancy. 1989. *Unruly Practices: Power, Discourse, and Gender in Contemporary Social Theory*. Minneapolis: University of Minnesota Press.

Gilligan, Carol. 1982. *In a Different Voice: Psychological Theory and Women's Development*. Cambridge, Mass.: Harvard University Press.

Gilligan, Carol. 1994. Remarks at the Annual Meeting of the American Political Science Association. New York, N. Y..

Held, Virginia. 1993. *Feminist Morality: Transforming Culture, Society, and Politics*. Chicago: University of Chicago Press.

Heller, Agnes and F. Feher. 1991. *The Grandeur and Twilight of Radical Universalism*. New Brunswick: Transaction.

Hirschmann, Nancy J. 1992. *Rethinking Obligation: A Feminist Method for Political Theory*. Ithaca: Cornell University Press.

hooks, bell. 1984. *Feminist Theory: From Margin to Center*. Boston: South End Press.

Hugman, Richard. 1991. *Power in Caring Professions*. London: Macmillan.

Kohlberg, Lawrence. 1984. *The Psychology of Moral Development: The Nature and Validity of Moral Stages*. San Francisco: John Wiley.

Lasswell, Harold. 1936. *Politics: Who Gets What, When, and How*. New York: McGraw-Hill.

Lykes, M. Brinton. 1989. "The Caring Self: Social Experiences of Power and Powerlessness." In *Who Cares? Theory, Research, and Educational Implications of the Ethics of Care*. Ed. Mary Brabeck. New York: Praeger, 164–179.

Machiavelli, Niccolò. 1979. *The Portable Machiavelli.* Trans. Peter Bonadella and Mark Musa. New York: Viking Press.

Manning, Rita C. 1992. *Speaking from the Heart: A Feminist Perspective on Ethics.* Lanham, Md.: Rowman and Littlefield.

Mayerhoff, Milton. 1971. *On Caring.* New York: Harper and Row.

Montesquieu, Charles de Secondat, Baron. 1949. *The Spirit of the Laws.* Trans. Thomas Nugent. New York: Hafner.

Noddings, Nel. 1984. *Caring: A Feminine Approach to Ethics and Moral Education.* Berkeley: University of California Press.

Noddings, Nel. 1990. "A Response." Review Symposium. *Hypatia* 5(1):120–126.

Nussbaum, Martha C. 1992. "Human Functioning and Social Justice: In Defense of Aristotelian Essentialism." *Political Theory* 20(2):202–246.

Okin, Susan Moller. 1989. *Justice, Gender, and the Family.* New York: Basic.

Piven, Frances Fox and Richard Cloward. 1977. *Poor People's Movements.* New York: Pantheon.

Pollitt, Katha. 1992. "Are Women Morally Superior to Men?" *The Nation* 225(22):799–807.

Puka, Bill. 1990. "The Liberation of Caring: A Different Voice for Gilligan's 'Different Voice.'" *Hypatia* 5(1):58–82.

Rawls, John. 1972. *A Theory of Justice.* Cambridge, Mass.: Harvard University Press.

Rogowski, Ronald. 1974. *Rational Legitimacy.* Princeton, N.J.: Princeton University Press.

Rousseau, Jean Jacques. 1968. *The Social Contract.* Trans. M. Cranston. Harmondsworth, England: Penguin.

Rousseau, Jean Jacques. 1974. *Emile.* Trans. Barbara Foxley. New York: Dutton.

Ruddick, Sara. 1990a. *Maternal Thinking: Towards a Politics of Peace.* Boston: Beacon Press.

Ruddick, Sara. 1990b. "The Rationality of Care." In *Women, Militarism, and War: Essays in History, Politics, and Social Theory.* Ed. Jean B. Elshtain and Sheila Tobias. Savage, Md.: Rowman and Littlefield.

Sarvasy, Wendy. 1992. "Beyond the Difference Versus Equality Debate: Postsuffrage Feminism, Citizenship, and the Quest for a Feminist Welfare State." *Signs* 17(2):329–362.

Schott, Robin May. 1988. *Cognition and Eros: A Critique of the Kantian Paradigm.* Boston: Beacon Press.

Schwarzenbach, Sibyl. 1994. "On Civic Friendship." Manuscript.

Seery, John Evan. 1990. *Political Returns: Irony in Politics and Theory from Plato to the Antinuclear Movement.* Boulder, Colo.: Westview Press.

Sevenhuijsen, Selma. 1993. "Paradoxes of Gender: Ethical and Epistemological Perspectives on Care in Feminist Political Theory." *Acta Politica* 28(2):131–149

Spelman, Elizabeth V. 1988. *Inessential Woman: Problems of Exclusion in Feminist Thought.* Boston: Beacon Press.

Spelman, Elizabeth V. 1991. "The Virtue of Feeling and the Feeling of Virtue." In *Feminist Ethics.* Ed. Claudia Card. Lawrence: University of Kansas Press.

Stiehm, Judith Hicks. 1983. "Our Aristotelian Hangover." In *Discovering Reality*. Ed., Harding and M. B. Hinikka. Dordrecht, The Netherlands: D. Reidel.

Tronto, Joan C. 1987. "Beyond Gender Difference to a Theory of Care." *Signs* 12(4):644–663.

Tronto, Joan C. 1993. *Moral Boundaries: A Political Argument for an Ethic of Care.* New York: Routledge.

Ungerson, Clare. 1990. "The Language of Care: Crossing the Boundaries." In *Gender and Caring: Work and Welfare in Britain and Scandinavia*. Ed. C. Ungerson. London: Harvester, Wheatsheaf.

Waerness, Kari. 1990. "Informal and Formal Care in Old Age: What Is Wrong With the New Ideology in Scandinavia Today?" In *Gender and Caring: Work and Welfare in Britain and Scandinavia*. Ed. C. Ungerson. London: Harvester, Wheatsheaf.

Weber, Max. 1946. *From Max Weber: Essays in Sociology*. Ed. H. H. Gerth and C. Wright Mills. Oxford: Oxford University Press.

White, Steven K. 1991. *Political Theory and Postmodernism*. Cambridge, England: Cambridge University Press.

Yack, Bernard. 1993. *The Problems of a Political Animal: Community, Justice, and Conflict in Aristotelian Political Thought*. Berkeley: University of California Press.

8

Rethinking Obligation for Feminism

Nancy J. Hirschmann

What is obligation, and why do feminists need to rethink it?

In the modern West, an "obligation" is a limitation on behavior, a requirement for action or nonaction that the actor/nonactor has chosen or agreed to. As opposed to "duty"—which may be a requirement that exists "naturally" (Rawls 1971) or "positionally" (Simmons 1979) but is not explicitly chosen by the person who has the duty—it is central to Western understanding of obligations that they arise from our voluntary and free actions. The paradigm for obligations on the liberal model is the promise and contract. For instance, if I accept an academic position, I incur an obligation to teach my classes, advise students, attend committee meetings, and so forth. By contrast, if I say to you "Give me your wallet or I'll blow your head off," most of us (unless we are of the Hobbesian persuasion[1]) would not say you are *obligated* to give me your wallet, although you may have a good reason to do so. Liberalism holds that all obligations must be explicitly taken on by the individual. Promising is its paradigm.

"Political obligation," which is the basis for citizens' obedience to laws, is similarly based on this idea of individual agreement, at least in Western democracies, and is particularly founded on the social contract. It is generally held that political obligations exist by virtue of the fact that citizens consent to the authority of the government; we are all familiar with the phrase "government by consent of the governed." This "consent theory" comes more or less from the early social contract theorists, most popularly Hobbes, Locke, and Rousseau, but also such lesser-known figures as Paine and Godwin, who rejected divine right and patriarchal theories of obedience and legitimacy in favor of a new concept of political legitimacy that depended on the will of the governed, not the governors.

The early social contract theories varied considerably in their specific conceptions of human beings and of the political society they should inhabit and yet shared many basic characteristics such as an emphasis on individual action, the rejection of patriarchy and divine right as formal models of political society, and most importantly the attempt to define and execute a particular concept of freedom. Consent theory begins from the premises most commonly attributed to Hobbes and Locke that all "men" are naturally free and equal. Equality existed at least in the power people had to pursue their desires; and for Locke they further had an equal "right" to appropriate property. They were "free" in that they did not depend on the will of others; this nondependence was essential to a full humanity. Freedom was defined in terms of what Berlin (1971) was later to call "negative liberty"; that is, we are free to the extent that external barriers—barriers that exist outside the self—do not inhibit us from pursuing our desires.

This concept of freedom was radical: not only was it a great departure from the hierarchical conceptions of social life of the previous century but it was also extreme. Autonomy and freedom required a concept of "man" as an isolated entity; the only legitimate connections to others are those initiated by the individual or agreed to by her, of her own free choice. This "abstract individualism" involves the notion that we can abstract individuals from relationships, from social context, and even from qualities of humanness that some kinds of feminism have deemed vital, namely the capacity and need for connectedness and relationships.

In light of this extreme individualism, the reason for "consent" lay in theorists' recognition that some relationships are desirable in the daily course of pursuing our individual needs and interests. But since any relationship is highly likely to involve a curtailment of individual freedom—and hence part of one's essential humanity—by creating an obligation, such relationships can be tolerated only if they are entered into voluntarily. Everyone must choose their own relationships: in this way, the very condition that sacrifices humanity (being bound in obligation) becomes the instrument of its reassertion (free choice). This is reinforced by the notion that an individual's interests are being promoted through this curtailment; hence any relationship entered into voluntarily must be of some value to the partners in the relationship. As Hobbes says, "of the voluntary acts of every man, the object is some *Good to himselfe*" (Hobbes 1968, 192). Locke echoes this sentiment in observing that "no rational Creature can be supposed to change his condition with an intention to be worse" (Locke 1965, 398).

Yet such relationships of mutual agreement and gain are often not successfully achieved; that is, although they may be formed for mutual gain, they turn out to be antagonistic and hostile relations. For various reasons suggested by a number of theorists—insatiability of desire (Hobbes 1968), an inability to know the laws of nature or to reason fully (Locke 1990), the introduction of money (Locke 1965, 322–323), the lack of a common judge and known law (342–344), and the exaggeration of inequalities of wealth and strength brought about by the introduction of metallurgy and agriculture (Rousseau 1973, 83–90)—the state of nature always degenerates into a state of war, which Hobbes so famously characterized as "poore, nasty, brutish, and short" (Hobbes 1968, 185–186).

The only way to achieve the peace and order necessary for continued acquisition is to submit to an arbitrative authority, the Sovereign. The Sovereign—whether Hobbes's absolute monarch or Locke's representative parliament—creates an element of predictability by creating rules that make certain behavior punishable. It enforces the laws of nature, particularly by enforcing agreements between people and establishing rules of property. Even though average citizens are generally not involved in governing—with the possible exception of Rousseau, social contract theorists from Hobbes onward have rejected direct or participatory democracy—they are seen as the source of government, as the foundation for legitimacy. This new emphasis on humans' self-creative capacities leads to the notion that they are capable of creating all of their social relationships. Indeed, they *must* create all of their relationships if they are to preserve their human essence, their freedom. People's relation to the government is merely one of these relationships; hence no government is owed obedience unless citizens consent to its authority. Because of the radical and equal freedom of all, consent is seen to be the only way to create political obligations: it is a necessary condition. Furthermore, on this view, consent is also a sufficient condition for obligation; if we are to respect individuals' capacities for rational decisionmaking, then we must take individuals at their word when they consent.

Yet, this emphasis on natural freedom and equality, and the individual choice they entailed, was inherently problematic, for what was to guarantee that people *would* consent and thus end the terrible state of war? To address this concern, the social contract theorists almost uniformly relied on some version of rationality. Hobbes, in what I like to call a "rational fiat," argued that the state of war was so horrible that anyone who prefers not to enter the social contract does not know what she wants; if humans are machines seeking their perpetual motion, and if the end of all voluntary acts is some good to the self, then all people, by definition, want the social contract. Furthermore, they want to contract with an absolute sovereign because he can provide the greatest security for their lives.

Locke's infamous doctrine of tacit consent is methodologically equivalent; if you cannot see that the social contract is in your interest and thus become a "perfect member" by expressly consenting, your "tacit consent" will nevertheless be inferred from the fact that you live within the boundaries of a nation (regardless of barriers to emigration), that you use the roads and take advantage of other benefits the state provides in the daily course of living (even when such benefits cannot be avoided). Rousseau, to his credit, maintained that consent to the original contract had to be unanimous and explicit; but once formed, his doctrine of the "general will" similarly demanded consent by fiat from those who disagreed with legislative assessments, maintaining that doing so only forced citizens to recognize their "true" will and hence to be free.

Those of us sensitive to such doublespeak might have a little trouble with the idea that we fulfill political obligations, such as paying taxes to support nuclear weapons, because we have consented to them. We would be in good company. As far back as the eighteenth century, critics such as Hume (1953), Burke (1955), Hegel (1977), Bentham (1960), and the utilitarians have been scornful of consent theory.

Feminists have particular reason to be sensitive, since for ages women's silence, or even their express "no" has been taken to mean "yes." This is most obvious in regard to sex, but because of patriarchal rights of domination over women, it also applies to most if not all other aspects of women's lives as well. Throughout history women have been forced to "consent" to marriage, to motherhood, and to the activities, work, and roles that these have entailed for different classes and races of women.

Contemporary obligation theorists have claimed to champion this critique of consent theory's hypocrisy. Yet ironically, their own formulations of political obligation stress "even more emphatically than Locke that consent is the sole basis of legitimacy and obligation" (Smith 1985, 45). For instance, Tussman (1960), attempting to reconcile the centrality of consent to obligation in the face of the fact that many people do not even think about their consent, suggests that we "assume" that the majority of citizens give their consent and are like "political child brides," who let others protect and define their best interests. Pitkin (1965), through a creative reading of Locke, develops the notion of "hypothetical" consent: what perfectly free, rational beings would consent to determines what the average unfree, unequal person is obligated to. Flathman (1972) holds that critical reasoning will reveal to us that we have (or do not have) "good reasons" for respecting the authority of a government; although obligation is a "practice" and must operate within the confines of language (thus limiting what can count as a "good reason"), the final repository is individuals' ability to judge and decide for themselves, giving individuals the same "veto power" over their obligations for which he faults consent theory. Simmons (1979), although holding that no existing consent theory accounts for obligations, nevertheless holds that consent is the only possible ground for obligation, because it is the only way to preserve individual choice. Similarly, Pateman (1979), who incisively identifies the self-contradictory character of consent theory's liberal-democratic formulation, nevertheless argues for a more consistent consent theory that draws heavily on Rousseauist participatory democracy.[2]

Even theories overtly seeking alternatives to consent embody effectively the same fundamental assumptions of "natural" freedom and equality that make consent the only possible basis for obligation. For instance, Rawls's "fair play" principle depends on the active acceptance of benefits within a cooperative scheme. Although a context of justice is important, passive acceptance or nonavoidance of benefits does not generate obligations. This is juxtaposed to his concept of duty that is "natural" and not the product of choice; both duty and obligation involve "schemes" or ends that are just, but obligation, to be such, must be at base voluntary. However, within Rawls's structure, if one does not accept the benefits of a just scheme and hence has no obligation to it, one may still have a natural duty to it anyhow by virtue of its "justice"; if it is just, then one would have agreed to it in the original position. This fact calls into question the usefulness of Rawls's distinction between obligation and duty; for at least in the case of *political* obligation, my duties require me to do the exact same thing that I supposedly have no obligation to do, namely obey the law (Rawls 1964).

Thus consent theory, with all its contradictions, was not rejected but rather rewritten and recycled. Contemporary theories demonstrate a blind acceptance of voluntarism with its foundation of individual (negative) liberty as a prerequisite for obligation even when it does not make theoretical sense, and they reassert the importance of obedience to the state on a *voluntarist* basis even as they claim to reject consent theory. What this obscures is that even as they explicitly argued that governmental authority threatened human freedom and individualism, social contract and contemporary consent theorists alike implicitly accepted governmental authority as a "fact of human existence." Although ostensibly it is created by, depends on, and derives legitimacy from human choice, in fact humans have no choice: government must exist.

However, because individualism is *theoretically* more important than authority and order, authority must at least ostensibly *appear* to be based on the will of the people who will be subject to it. In this way, individuals' limitations on choice, via the establishment of government and law, is said to be an expression of choice, via consent. But this "voluntarism" is in reality camouflage for coercion; it is not genuine voluntarism. As a result, almost all of the voluntarist theories of obligation accomplish what Rousseau is singled out and excoriated for, namely forcing citizens to be free. Just as express consent became tacit consent, rational fiat, and the general will for original social contract theorists, for contemporary theorists it became implied consent, hypothetical consent, the assumed consent of the "political child-bride," or the recognition of "good" reasons.

But why is this a problem that feminists should particularly care about? I believe that a strictly voluntarist foundation for obligation betrays a masculinist bias that not only belies women's historical experience but perpetuates its exclusion from political theory and the public realm. The exaggerated emphasis on consent as the only legitimate way to establish relationships of obligation and the assumptions of innate human separateness on which it is based, reveal a masculinist conceptualization of the self, of "individuals," that runs contrary to women's historical experience and epistemology. Women's experiences have produced a "way of knowing" the world that gives priority to relationship and responsibility, that recognizes the ways in which we are deeply connected in each other's lives, and that takes relationship as a starting point for thinking about life rather than as the product of specific, conscious choice.

This is not to deny consent and choice as an important *part* of the basis for obligation; the consent tradition represents a vital historical move in theories of political allegiance in its initial rejection of patriarchal, divine right, and tradition-based authority. Social contract theorists recognized some previously obscured human qualities—namely the notion of will, the ability to act voluntarily, and the capacity for choice and self-creation—that indeed founded contemporary feminism and that many feminists are rightly reluctant to abandon. But it is one thing to conclude from these qualities that divine right and patriarchy are illegitimate; it is quite another to conclude that each separate and individual human being must decide for herself which obligations—political and otherwise—she will assume.

It is not consent per se, in all forms, contexts, and roles, that is problematic so much as it is the way in which consent theory totalized human experience by taking an historically specific, economically privileged white male as a universal standard for humanity. For such a totalization reduces obligation to a single source, namely consent, and thereby delegitimizes the historical reality of other sources of obligation. A feminist approach to obligation does not merely wish to replace consent with something else but rather to *decenter* consent, and its underpinning of atomistic freedom, to the end of recognizing other values, such as care and connectedness, which may be equal to freedom in their importance to human social life. A feminist theory of obligation is thus a plural theory of obligation: not in the sense that one source of obligation is as good as any other, but rather that every obligation has multiple sources. Consent may be appropriate to some contexts and some obligations, but not to others, and it rarely tells the whole story.

A Feminist Conception of Connection as Alternative Foundation

SEVERAL DIFFERENT STRAINS of recent feminist theory, ranging from psychoanalytic theory and moral psychology, to materialist feminism, ethics, and epistemology, all give rise to another concept of obligation that does not depend on explicit choice and takes care and responsibility as central elements of a moral schema that has existed at least as long as the social contract.

Object relations, a type of psychoanalytic thought, holds that because women, and not men, care for infants (from birth to 3 years), boys and girls will develop different understandings of themselves and of their relation to the world. This difference centers on self-other relations; in developing a sense of self through the social process of learning gender identity within the context of culturally created social relations of childrearing, boys tend to see themselves and the world in terms of radical separateness, girls in terms of connectedness and "empathy" (Chodorow 1978, Dinnerstein 1976).

Carol Gilligan (1982) has argued that this difference plays out in moral thinking, where she found that males tended to reason more in terms of individual rights and competing rules, although females conceive morality in terms of relationships and overlapping responsibilities. In the studies she and her colleagues (Gilligan et al. 1988) discussed, girls and women routinely sought to solve moral dilemmas through processes of communication and consensus and sought solutions that were "inclusive," whereas boys and men relied more on impartial adjudication to enforce a pre-existing hierarchy of rights.

Gilligan and Wiggins (1988) further identify "co-feeling" as an important aspect of this so-called feminine epistemology and ethics. Co-feeling involves the "ability to *participate* in another's feelings (in their terms)" (1988, 122). They juxtapose co-feeling to "sympathy," in which the self is the referent for assessing and measuring the other; the other is not directly considered as a self but is treated as object. Co-feeling thus involves greater concreteness, as well as greater contextuality, as any two people have different histories and other features that might cause them to feel quite differently in similar circumstances, in direct contrast to the assumptions of the rights model.

Co-feeling epistemologically echoes what Belenky et al. (1986) call "connected knowing," which involves an orientation towards relationship rather than rules, intersubjectivity rather than objectivity. "At the heart of [connected knowing] is the capacity for empathy. Since knowledge comes from experience, the only way they can hope to understand another person's ideas is to try to share the experience that has led the person to form the idea" (Belenky et al. 1986, 113). Empathy is described as "feeling with," as merging the self *with* the other, rather than the intrusiveness of imposing the self *on* the other. They contrast this to "separate knowing," the supposedly "masculine" model, which incorporates a concept of knowledge that is rule-governed and "objective." As an "adversarial form," separate knowing operates from premises of separation between knower and the known. It also displays a disjunction between knowing and feeling; objectivity is equated with dispassion, a process that excludes all private concerns and feelings, both one's own and those of one's adversary (1986, 122, 106, 109).

Patricia Hill Collins (1990) develops a similar "way of knowing" and ethic of care from African American experience. She particularly focuses on black women's style of mothering, which differs in significant ways from the patriarchal nuclear family model that underpins much of object relations theory. Collins holds that mothering in black communities is more communal, and that black women fill important roles as "community othermothers." At the heart of Collins's argument is the suggestion that the experiences of black female community othermothers provide a better model for a theory of care: indeed, she implicitly questions the ability of white women, as well as African American men, to embody such an ethic consistently because of their race and gender privilege.

Although black othermothering may provide the best model for care, however, the activities of mothering have been explored by white feminists such as Sara Ruddick (1989) as well, as the basis for a materialist analysis of care and connections, locating women's epistemological perspective in the work women do. The specifics of maternal practices in various cultures can be fairly widespread, but she nevertheless maintains that the kinds of material activities that shape mothers' lives produce an epistemological orientation called "maternal thinking," a major attribute of which involves attention to others' needs.

In spite of its essentialist tones, as one of the major "jobs" women have had throughout history, caretaking provides a materialist and historically specific basis for an ethic of care and an epistemology of connectedness. Other materialist feminists, such as Nancy Hartsock (1984), identify the more obviously caregiving aspects of childrearing as an important activity that shapes thinking (in fact she says that feminist object relations theory is itself "materialist" [238]), as well as such activities as cleaning and cooking. The material dimensions of providing care (as opposed to the emotional components of caring for or caring about) provide a significant ground for a feminist standpoint epistemology. They establish an important experiential basis for seeing the world in concrete and contextual ways that place relationship at the center of one's epistemological framework. Micaela diLeonardo (1984) makes a similar argument for a particular aspect of this work, which she calls "kinwork," referring to women's activities in sustaining family relationships and networks.

Thus, rather than promoting essentialism, I believe that all of these feminist theories, including object relations, are practice-oriented. The epistemological, moral, and psychological differences for which these theorists argue should be seen as the products of historically established experience rather than biology or nature. As Gilligan claims, care is characterized by theme, not necessarily by gender. Thus men have access to maternal thinking's conceptualization of the world by engaging in the practice, just as many women are likely to reject it for a variety of reasons and to have access to other modes of thought. Similarly, object relations theory holds that infant boys who are raised by fathers in shared parenting relationships should learn to see themselves as less separate and more connected and hence have greater access to empathy, just as infant girls should be able to develop more strongly individuated selves.

Yet, whereas the epistemology of connecteness and the ethic of care as located in women's experience are powerful feminist tools for rereading political theory, it is also clear that they have been the subject of considerable controversy within feminism. Although it is true that women have historically always cared for others, this role has often resulted in women's loss of voice and power. By giving up the self, by following the traditional feminine ethic of self-sacrifice, women have been oppressed. It is thus problematic to invoke care for a *feminist* theory, critics assert; what women need is to care *less*, not to valorize care.

For instance, Arlie Hochschild (1989) documents that women spend much more time on childcare and housework than men do. Part of this may stem from women "feeling" a greater responsibility due to cultural norms about "good" mothers and wives. Feminists cannot charge such women with "false consciousness." But we should not simply accept such feelings at face value. Rather, we need to see how men's nonparticipation perpetuates these feelings. When a baby needs changing, *someone* has to do it, and if cultural norms allow and even encourage men to opt out, women are left holding the diaper bag. Repeated often enough, this pattern sets up cultural norms and expectations—or reinforces ones that we are trying to change—that justify and perpetuate men's nonparticipation and put extra burdens on women who acknowledge or "feel" the responsibility that men deny.

Yet I believe that this critique is perfectly in line with most of the theorists drawn on above. Gilligan, for instance, suggests that the sacrifice of the self that has historically characterized women's caring does not help relationship but hurts it. Gender psychology does not maintain that women's self-sacrifice and loss of self is the ideal to be followed. Indeed, this extreme version of the "feminine" model is no less problematic than the hyperindividualism of the extreme "masculine" model. If women have been forced de facto to care so much because men have historically cared so little, then feminism must determine how to get men to care more.

Part of this task involves reconceptualizing the self as what Gilligan (1982) calls a "self-in-relationship" that falls between the two extreme models. This ideal recognizes that individuals cannot exist without relationship and community, and that we get our unique and individual traits and characteristics only through relationships. But at the same time, relationships cannot exist without selves, without individuals. Relationships require mutual and reciprocal participation, which in turn requires selfhood among participants.

Gilligan invokes the imagery of a web to indicate the ways in which we are all connected to each other: some directly, some indirectly and circuitously, but all constituting a network of interaction and interdependence. Thus, a relationship where one of the partners loses voice and becomes invisible is not a genuine relationship (Gilligan et al. 1990); becoming invisible means that there is a hole in the web, and the fabric of social relationships is compromised and jeopardized. If relationships really are important to women, she suggests, we have to learn to value ourselves as participants in them.

If one flat-out rejects these arguments for difference, of course, as some liberal feminists might, or if one takes such difference as evidence of natural inferiority, as some conservatives might, there is little room for further dialogue. However, even readers who view the above literatures with skepticism may be willing at least to consider their arguments hypothetically or perhaps symbolically. Although the historical evidence these theories draw on suggests that the different voice is a *woman's* voice, to leave it at that would be a reductive misrepresentation. The concepts and language offered by gender theory can be used effectively by political theory without embracing an essential view of gender.

Indeed, the aspects most useful in studying political theory are not to be found by taking these findings at face value. Rather, it is far more useful and accurate to take these as theories of *power*. As Joan Tronto suggests (Chap. 7, this volume), a care orientation is not specifically located in mothering activities and should not be limited to women. Care has historically been the responsibility of groups of people who are excluded from power (Hare-Mustin and Marecek 1990). "Women," both within specific racial and cultural boundaries and across them, have significantly constituted such a group. Women have historically been the ones to care for children and hence to have to think about the issues maternal thinking identifies. They have been responsible for the physical care of the home and the emotional care of other people, their daughters and sons have had to develop their gendered selves in relation to this fact, and these experiences combine to encourage women and girls to think in terms of connection, context, and relationship so that they can become the kinds of people who can engage in these kinds of activities.

Thus, although this mode of thinking is gender *related*, it is not gender *specific*; it is historically created and produced. And indeed, the concepts and categories offered by these theorists suggest a language and vocabulary of power that can transcend gender and that are very useful for political theory. After all, there have been and are men who have expressed the voice of care and connection, who have been just as marginalized as women. For instance, Martin Luther King (1969) talks about the "fabric of mutuality" and the centrality of community; he is importantly marginalized. Harding (1987) has discussed the "curious coincidence" of (white)

Western feminism and black (male) African world views; again, these latter views are marginalized as we in the West arrogantly dub them "third world." It is not merely coincidental that such marginalized men are frequently also members of other oppressed groups, particularly racial minorities, because the interconnections between gender and race are especially significant (Williams 1991; Crenshaw 1991).

Words like "feminine" and "masculine" can thus be viewed in part as abstractions that idealize and represent relationships of power; they are symbolizations of power relations. That these relations have one important source in gender is important but not exhaustive or exclusive. We should not forget that women have been historically important expressers of the voice of care. That voice has a history, and so does obligation, and indeed these two histories help constitute each other. It is not just coincidence that women have been for the most part powerless and expressed the voice of care. Indeed, the activities and obligations of the private sphere to which they have been assigned—childcare, nurturance, love—have required women to draw on and develop that voice. So we should not be surprised if women's experience highlights this voice for us. The crucial distinction between this position and essentialism, however, is that the theory does not *depend* on women, and women alone, expressing that voice. While rejecting the strict thesis that this is a "woman's voice," I would argue that there is a loose gender relationship, one that derives from history, material experience, psychology, and socialization. This grounding in women's experience is the whole point of calling it "feminist." Indeed, the word "feminist" not only recognizes the origin of this voice in women's experience but takes upon itself the task of transforming this devalued and ignored conception of reality into a conception that is valued and powerful, one that needs to be integrated with the skewed but dominant rights conception that pervades our public life and our epistemology.

This does not mean that rules, rights, and justice are "bad" while care and connection are "good." As gender psychology suggests, the extreme "masculine model," with its difficulty in connection and relationship, is really no more problematic than the extreme "feminine model" of loss of self. Furthermore, as Patricia Williams (1991) points out, *if* rules and rights are key to power, then feminists will not wish to abandon them entirely as means of empowerment. What is at issue once again is the *exclusive* focus on rights and rules as "the" voice of morality and the denigration of the voice of care as women's historical mode of orienation. The problem at the heart of political obligation is the epistemological absolutism of individual rights, freedom, choice, and consent. Feminism suggests that we need to consider what happens when we take connection and relationship as a starting point for thinking about politics, rather than a problem that politics needs to solve.

Care and Obligation

ALTHOUGH THESE THEORISTS vary in the particularities of an ethic of care and connection, and although they locate them differently in women's historical experiences, their work suggests that the exclusive conceptualization of obligation in voluntarist terms cannot explain or accommodate many aspects of social relations and bonds that women's experience in particular reveals. Women are actively excluded from the practice of liberal obligation by unfair and sexist implementation so that women are prevented from making choices, from participating in politics, or from consenting to the social contract.

But the problem does not end there. Liberal political theory defines obligation so as automatically to preclude women's experience from being adequately encompassed and accurately expressed. It is thus not merely a matter of "bringing women in" to liberal obligation theory; the only way women can be "brought in" is by abandoning their experience and adopting the public-private split, which separates their experience from "reality." Rather, women's experience suggests that the liberal definition of "obligation" needs to be broadened to include some nonconsensual aspects of life.

An example may illustrate the inadequacy of strictly consensual theories of obligation. Women have always been considered obligated to care for children, yet until recently have had little choice in the matter. Are such obligations completely invalid without consent? If so, then doesn't a woman have a right to abandon a baby whose gestation and care she did not consent to?

Legal authorities in most democracies, liberal or otherwise, would say no; but perhaps more significantly, many women who have had babies under such conditions might tend to agree. The obligation to care is not merely imposed by society on unwilling participants (which would clearly violate consent theory); it also is often recognized by women themselves—women who *also* recognize their lack of choice—suggesting something about human life and relationships that consent theory cannot comprehend. If a woman has a child against her preference but comes to love it, or is influenced by people she loves, she may recognize an obligation without fulfilling the necessary criteria for consent. She might refer to a different set of values in assessing her obligation; for example, love is an element in this scenario, for one does not necessarily choose to love, one can love "in spite of oneself," and be involved in all sorts of obligations as a result.

Consent theory tries to get around this apparent contradiction women's experience poses in several ways. First, it can refuse to recognize these as "obligations." It might indeed say that obligation doesn't even enter the picture. On the liberal model, obligations are always to do things that we would, all things considered, prefer not to do; the point of "obligation" is to provide a guarantee of performance, given the fickleness of human desire. But if a woman loves her child and chooses to care for it, then this is something she *wants* to do, and we don't need the notion of obligation to tie her to these activities. Or more accurately, obligation would enter the picture only if she at some later point no longer wanted to provide such care, in which case her previous voluntary provision would be cited as evidence of prior consent and hence of continued obligation.

Such an account is disingenuous, of course, because it abstracts the woman's choices and desires out of their context of women's relative choicelessness. Given the social requirements of marriage, sex, and reproduction, not to mention contemporary prohibitions on abortion and access to birth control, to speak of women's "choosing" to care for children is severely problematic by the standards of liberal individualism. It constructs women's "choice" much as Locke constructs the "tacit consent" of landless workers.

Even more commonly, however, liberalism tries to sidestep women altogether through the public-private split. That is, it takes all of those relationships that involve nonconsensual bonds—love, care, nurturance—and puts them in the private sphere, often under the label "natural duty of affection," and in fact assigns most of them to women. This leaves men free in the public sphere to declare that "obligations" are consented to, by definition. This is circular reasoning, and it has resulted in the recycling of consent theory rather than its resolution.

But if we take seriously the feminist notion of a moral reasoning that begins from premises of connection, responsibility, and response, an alternative formulation opens up. If relationship is the epistemological foundation, then connection is given, and obligation is a presumption of fact. That is, perhaps obligation must be considered from the standpoint of a "given" just as freedom is the given in consent theory. From this perspective, "recognition" of an obligation is not the same as "consent" to it. Recognition involves the admission of an obligation that *already* exists. Consent theory, in contrast, bases its claims to legitimacy on the notion that choice *creates* obligation. It is precisely this notion of creation that women's historical experience of relationships challenges.

Admittedly, the notion of "given" obligations is one that provokes uneasiness to our modernist sensibilities. In a century that has seen Stalin, Hitler, and Enver Hoxja, the notion of given obligation smacks of a totalitarianism that denies individual difference and that, indeed, will perpetuate women's subordination to reproduction, this time in the interests of the state rather than individual men.

I share such concerns. Within the liberal framework, such a construal borders on the nightmarish. Similarly, in drawing on women's historical obligations of care, I do not mean to put motherhood on a pedestal; babies have been abandoned and even killed by their mothers, and women have asserted the right to abortion in the name of self-interest. I am not saying that history dictates that women should or must raise children, either.

Rather, I am suggesting that the historical fact that many women have done so suggests the need for an alternate way to conceptualize obligation. Women's experiences tell us important things about *human* life, about parts of our collective existence that are ignored by political theory. The claim for given obligation must be seen in the context of a pluralist argument, namely the notion that obligations have multiple sources; the claim that they stem inevitably from relationship does not end the matter but only begins our inquiry. Again, it is epistemological and methodological, not just political. Its point is less to provide a new, complete formulation or definition than it is to reorient how we think about obligation and the role it plays in our daily and political lives, to introduce new kinds of questions.

So, for instance, in consent theory we seek to understand how separate individuals can develop and sustain connections and still be separate; how they can engage in relationships and still remain free. Thus, the central approach involves asking how obligations "arise," how they come into being. But if obligation is considered as given, then it does not really make sense to ask how it can "arise"; from a feminist standpoint, obligation would be a basic standard against which other things are measured, such as the freedom to act as one wishes. The central question thus shifts, to "How can I achieve some freedom and yet remain connected?"

In this shift, freedom—and along with it, consent—is not abandoned but *decentered*, its relationship to and place in obligation reconfigured. In consent theory, the assumption of freedom demands an explanation of any curtailment of that freedom such as obligations impose. From this feminist perspective, such an extreme demand can be questioned, because many desirable or necessary relations exist without such justification. Consent theory seeks to find areas and modes of connection that are safe, that can provide for needs without risking the loss of self. A theory that began with connection would try to determine how to carve out a space for the self without violating the imperative of care. It seeks a kind of freedom that keeps relationships intact. By placing obligation at the center, and making freedom something to be justified and explained, the importance of relationship to human life is brought out of the shadows of the sequestered private realm and into the public discourse of political theory.

This does not mean that freedom cannot *be* justified, that we cannot offer very good reasons for not fulfilling obligations; but justification must be offered. I have suggested elsewhere in this volume that it would be ludicrous, if not tragic, for feminists to claim that freedom, even in the liberal "negative" formulation of "freedom from," is not important to women. To the contrary, freedom is extremely important to women; but it is not the totem of human experience, nor is "freedom from" the only aspect of freedom that women and other historically disempowered groups need to draw on (Hirschmann,

Chap. 3, this volume). The adage of liberal freedom that my right to swing my fist ends where your nose begins sounds neutral enough until we realize just how big men's noses have become, constricting women's rights to swing their arms to pathetically small areas. Without a critical awareness that the context within which these arguments are articulated is one of liberation for the powerful and bondedness for the powerless, the notion of given obligation threatens to ensnare women more deeply in its grasp.

Indeed, the importance of freedom is ironically highlighted by its decentering. Rather than giving obligation the hegemonic priority that freedom has in liberalism, a feminist approach to obligation opens up our inquiry to see that the notions of individuality and freedom that underlie liberalism are rooted in contexts of relationships. It is because this context is at once implicitly depended on and yet explicitly ignored or denigrated that these notions can be manipulated and reconstructed to apply to economically privileged white males at the expense of white women, men and women of color, and the economically underprivileged of all races and genders. Placing obligation at the center of our discourse will thus restore freedom for more people by spreading obligations more fairly, rather than concentrating them in the powerless and establishing a dichotomy between the free and the obligated.

Thus the notion of given obligation should be treated as a methodological and epistemological proposition, urging us to focus on the questions we ask. If we take obligation as given, the issue becomes not *whether* an obligation exists—we do not try to determine whether a relationship has been created through consent—but *how* it is to be fulfilled. The question of "how" *presupposes* relationship, because it automatically requires conversation and negotiation between individuals in relationship. Taking connection as given, it tries to determine the relative spacing and placing of individuals within its constellation, and it does this through the participation of individuals who express desires and preferences but understand that those exist within a context of necessary relationships that require their participation.

The centrality of relationship, context, and partipation in turn all suggest the need for a participatory democratic framework within which the question of "how" and the content of obligations can be worked through. Participatory democracy provides a web or network into which our collective obligations fall, and it provides a mechanism for determining how to meet them. With its emphasis on negotiation, face-to-face interaction, talking and listening, participatory democracy provides an environment within which the relational elements of the care model can develop. Indeed, participatory democracy is the only political structure that itself attends to relationship through the processes of talking and listening. A participatory form of government allows for the full engagement of all citizens in political discourse. All citizens have the ability not only to make contributions but to have their contributions accepted and valued as well: they can speak, but they can also be heard. Including all in a full citizenship, one that is engaged in decisionmaking, agenda setting, discussion, and action, will encourage the development of humans' ability to think of concrete factors, of ends and outcomes, and not just of abstractions and processes. It provides the grounds and context for people to adopt an approach to moral and political issues that reflects the care, connection, and concreteness emphasized by feminist theorists.

Participatory democracy also reminds us that obligations often exist collectively. Taking obligation as given will not work if we maintain individualist assumptions. Consent theory entails seeing obligation as individually negotiated contracts between otherwise unconnected individuals. Even political obligation is seen as a series of discrete contracts that naturally unrelated individuals make with a government, which then serves as a conduit for citizens' relations with each other. Behind every individual agreement between citizens lies the prior contract each party has already made with government, a contract that makes subsequent agreements reliable because of the threat of sanction.

This individualist emphasis is not only misdescriptive of human relations; it is misdescriptive in a way that particularly impacts on women. For instance, in the example of pregnancy and childcare, individualism entails the assumption that the obligation is uniquely the woman's, and the burden is on her to justify nonfulfillment by proving nonconsent. In such a context, advocating given obligations seems to perpetuate masculine choice and feminine choicelessness. But that is less a problem with given obligation than with men's refusal to recognize it. Starting from an assumption of connection and obligation allows the claim that men must also care for children to enter public and political discourse. This could powerfully alter many political debates on policy regarding abortion, birth control, reproductive technology, and financial assistance to caretakers.[3]

Ironically, however, this suggests that shifting to the question "how" may not seem particularly radical; there is nothing in this requirement of negotiation that forces men or other powerful groups to participate. Indeed, the norms of patriarchy have historically ensured that women are the ones who are left with the responsibility of answering that question. This does not mean that the *question* is problematic, however, as much as our answer, and to deny that is to confuse philosophical foundations with practical implementation. The latter can be addressed through genuine democratic participation among equals. Methodologically, however, revealing this question of "how," and how liberalism obscures it behind the masculinist concern of "whether," makes it possible to identify the ways in which men shirk their given obligations on a daily basis by hiding behind the rhetoric of consent, forcing women to fill the breach.

It is thus very important to maintain the distinction between obligation and consent, for the liberal discourse that allies them ensures an inadequate vocabulary to describe women's experiences, their "choice," and their "obligations." Looking at obligation collectively can help maintain this distinction. If obligation is given, it is given for all, and the obligation is a shared responsibility. So if there was widespread recognition of the obligation of care, women would not have to fear that children will be left to die or worse if they themselves do not provide the necessary care. At the least, this shift in understanding would force social recognition that fathers have equal obligations.

In the process, by providing a broader network or web of relationships of obligated people, it would provide more space for those who are already overburdened. It would also offer validation for women who do not "feel" what the culture tells them they are supposed to feel (e.g., fulfilled by the activities of mothering, instead of angry and resentful) by helping to identify the ways in which such feelings are culturally constructed by a sexist society that lets men off the hook from their given obligations. Again, men's being more involved in nonconsensual bonds would increase women's freedom from them.

Rethinking Obligation: Epistemological Issues

IN ADVOCATING GIVEN obligation, of course, it is not the case that feminism would be suggesting anything radically new. Political theorists and philosophers such as Susan Okin (1989) and Robert Goodin (1985) have argued for the central place of vulnerability in theories of justice, suggesting that we are obligated to respond to such vulnerability. And of course Marx's dictum of "to each according to his need" provides a similar formula. More directly related, James Fishkin (1982) has argued for what he calls "general obligations" just as Rawls (1971) has asserted "natural duties."

The problem with such theories, however, a problem this feminist formulation shares, is determining where the boundaries of obligation lie. Particularly given the network or web imagery of connection that theorists like Gilligan invoke to describe women's conception of connectedness, do we have obligations to everyone and everything? If need and vulnerability provide a crucial genesis of obligation, it is also clear that these know few geographical, cultural, ethnic, or national boundaries. Yet, many in the West, regardless of our gender, might feel rather squeamish about this possibility. By locating obligation in relationship, and by seeing that relationship is all pervasive, it seems at best difficult to separate out obligation from deontology in general. Not only would this appear to make the task of political theory unwieldy, but obligation itself also threatens to overtake our lives.

That is the ostensible advantage of consent theory; it makes obligation fairly clear-cut. I know when I have consented and what I have consented to, so what my obligation is and how it came into being are fairly straightforward. "Obligation" is thus distinct from "ought." Yet this supposed clarity is a ruse. A feminist reading reveals that consent theory is in reality muddied by the political necessity of mechanisms like tacit consent, assumed consent, rational fiat and *forcer d'être libre*. Consent theory may *appear* a safe haven to retreat to in the face of such overwhelming questions concerning where our obligations end and how to enact them; but it really just sidesteps these important questions that, not so coincidentally, impact particularly harshly on the lives of women and children.

Feminist theory addresses such questions, but it may not be able to provide *prima facie* rules and procedures. That may be a primary reason to urge a "plural" approach to obligation, because as our focus moves from "whether" an obligation exists to "how" it is to be fulfilled we will need to consider a broad variety of factors.

And one of the first elements suggested by the question of "how" is the further question "how much?" That is, obligation must always be seen as a matter of degree. This may make the possibility of being obligated to "everything" more manageable, because we will not be obligated to all things to the same degree. The web imagery invoked by feminists suggests an appropriate conception of this idea; although some threads are connected directly to some others, and each thread is connected indirectly to all the others, some segments are quite far from others, and a complicated path must often be traced to get from one thread to another. There is no definitive, wall-like division of these aspects from each other, yet there is distance and distinction. Those more closely and directly connected have *prima facie* greater obligations; but these obligations stem beyond those direct connections in a weaker sense. Furthermore, specific threads can be broken without the entire web being compromised; if A and B break their direct connection, they still will have a less direct, more circuitous one. Obligation is thus not the all-or-nothing thing it is for consent theory.

Thus the criteria for evaluating "how much" must in turn invoke other elements, such as the character of connection. Some of these will seem strongly established, yet must be critically evaluated. For instance, parents are seen as particularly connected to their children. Taken uncritically, this could obligate women most heavily, since many cultures particularly emphasize the "special bond" between mothers and children. But if parenthood is a valid source of connection (leaving aside questions of whether, or at what point, a fetus is a person with whom one can have a relationship), then fathers must be seen as owing obligations of connection as strongly as mothers. If we burden one with special obligations of connection, we must burden the other.[4]

Furthermore, the "nature" of connection must be critically assessed from a feminist perspective. For instance, the reason that mothers are often seen as more intimately connected is commonly asserted to be biological. Yet, critical engagement of this belief will reveal that adoptive parents and parental figures can and often are much closer to children than biological parents. What makes the search for biological parents the topic of tabloid headlines is not biological compulsion but social privileging of such connection.

The question is not whether biological connections are "real," of course—at the least, medical and genetic history of biological origins are relevant—but how important they are. That depends on the social context that informs their emotional and psychological valuation; and that context is a patriarchal one. Hence, the genetic impulse that supposedly connects birth mothers is offered as a reason to ban abortion and discriminate against women in the workplace; but when such connection conflicts with the gender and class rights of a William Stern, they suddenly lose their validity and importance. We must look critically at the social context that defines connection; we cannot assume that one kind of connection is *prima facie* more binding than others, and we must apply the standards of connection equally between different parties, such as fathers and mothers.

A third factor determining "how" an obligation will be worked out, and the degree of obligation, involves available resources; just as need and vulnerability influence the determination of who obligations are owed to, so do those who are in a position to fulfill the obligation have a greater degree of obligation upon them. This is not simply a Marxian "from each according to ability" principle, of course; rather, it more complexly takes into account how those resources are currently being used, the other demands on those resources, and the other obligations the holder of the resource is already involved in. For instance, childcare often falls to women precisely because they do so much of it; it is their "expertise" that justifies men's passing on those obligations to women and that makes women often think it would be easier simply to care for the child than to teach their partners what to do. But that circularity again misdirects our attention; it may be precisely the fact that a mother is already performing over half the child care that requires a father to start fulfilling more of his shared obligations.

Further, we must consider not only what other obligations one is involved in, but why others *cannot* be so involved in any particular obligation. I suggested previously that nonfulfillment is something that requires justification, but that means that such justification is possible. So, for instance, raped Bosnian women can offer extremely compelling reasons for their opting out of the collective obligation to care for the children they have borne. Or a divorced father may be genuinely unable, for accepted, legitimate reasons—such as temporary disability from work—to pay child support for a given month; but he must demonstrate this to be the case against a fundamental assumption that he is obligated to pay such support. This contrasts to an individualist assumption, often made by many "deadbeat dads," that such explanations are never necessary, because obligations always depend on my choices; since most such fathers are ordered to pay support by courts, they can deny the legitimacy of the "obligation" because they did not consent.

And yet, a final element to consider *is* "consent," although its role and significance changes. Taking obligation as given does not negate the need for people to take responsibility for their voluntary acts; indeed, it emphasizes the importance of doing so, because it acknowledges the ways in which such acts take place in social contexts with profound and deep ramifications that may not have been anticipated by the actor, let alone "consented" to. Adults engaging voluntarily in heterosexual relations, for instance, may not intend a pregnancy, and it is disingenuous to say that they "consented" to it because they should know the statistical failure rates of the birth control methods they use. Nevertheless, an unintended pregnancy literally cannot be ignored, at least for women; it thus brings with it obligations on both partners to deal with it responsibly, whether that means abortion, adoption, or raising the child. Again, a feminist approach to obligation does not reject voluntarism outright but rather its reified and central place as the sole source of obligation.

This short list of possible issues to consider in addressing the question of "how" is meant to be suggestive, not exhaustive; the primary point, once again, is that no one single source can be pinpointed to identify the working out of obligation. Connection, voluntary action, need or vulnerability, resources available, as well as other obligations already existent will influence a determination of "how" an obligation is to be met.

It will be all too obvious that shifting our attention from "whether" I have an obligation to "how" we should fulfill our obligations will not make all questions of obligation cut and dried. But neither can one say that this shift, by not eliminating uncertainty, gets us no further than consent theory. The question of "how" to fulfill an obligation does not always have a determined and definitive answer; but it is a mistake to take that fact as a sufficient reason to conclude that we must leave the question of "whether" completely to the individual. Consent theory involves an all-or-nothing approach to morality and obligation, which denies at the outset the reality and necessity of the nonconsensual obligations with which women are historically familiar. Yet it is precisely the desire for the all-or-nothing approach that has given consent theory its hold, for it provides the (masculinized) individual with the illusion of total control over his life. Obligations exist only if one creates them, (political) connection can exist only by virtue of (social) contract. But many unplanned aspects of life exist beyond our control to create connection and obligation without our consent, a fact that reproduction makes most apparent but that is demonstrated by other examples as well. These examples, taken not solely but importantly from women's lives and history, compel our attention, as the contemporary demand for gender equality makes more and more apparent the fundamental ways in which the worlds of both politics and philosophy have been structured to exclude women.

On the one hand, this shift will help bring about the conditions necessary for true consent; through equalizing power, everyone is provided with fuller opportunities to choose their obligations. On the other hand, it can also help us open up our concept of obligation to allow for nonconsensual bonds without feeling threatened. Although consent is appropriate to many kinds of obligation, it is insufficient for many others and even irrelevant to still others. As part of a constellation of sources, choice, will, and voluntary action are located in a larger context of social relations, history, and material experience. Although liberal theory gives us some important values and concepts, such as a recognition of the individual as a social and political entity, it also distorts those concepts. A feminist theory of obligation based on relationship, care, and participatory community will not only clear our lenses of these distortions but will also redirect our vision to other values, social characteristics, and institutional constructions that liberal theory has ignored and denied or been unable to see.

Notes

1. Of course, I could try running away or disarming the thief, and in that sense I am not "obligated." But if there is no option but to die, then I am obligated *prudentially*; the only logical choice is to hand over my wallet. If I do that, Hobbes says, I have freely consented to do so; and free consent, in turn, entails obligation. This vicious circularity provides Hobbes's model for political obligation, where "running away" is never an option; the *only* option to the state of war is consenting to the sovereign, so of course I consent. And since such consent is (by definition) freely given, I am obligated to obey the sovereign. The analogy is not perfect, of course—once the robber's back is turned I have every "right" to pull out my own gun and get my (now "his") wallet back, whereas I can never change my mind vis-à-vis the social contract—but it clearly illustrates what I call below Hobbes's "rational fiat."

2. For other critiques of obligation, see Dunn (1980), Hirschmann (1992), chap. 2, and Walzer (1970).

3. Many will immediately argue that such "change" could work against women; if men have obligations to care for children, for instance, then it may seem they have rights to demand that women bear them. But I believe that such claims already misconstrue my arguments and do so in a context that already fails to embrace the idea that men's obligations really are given. The liberal idea that obligations automatically entail rights does not follow on this model, for that idea is premised on an assumption of natural freedom; rights are the quid pro quo for

bondedness, the way in which giving up freedom is simultaneously the expression of freedom. On the model envisioned here, men's greater obligation does not necessarily enhance their own freedom—and certainly does not do so at women's expense—but rather restores the balance between men and women and between freedom and obligation. Such an approach might allow unmarried men greater access to adoption and might help married men in custody battles but could never result in rights over women's bodies.

4. Indeed, given the unequal division of labor in pregnancy and parturition, this suggests that at birth, men should have an even greater obligation to children than women, since women have already contributed more to the shared fulfillment. Once again, this does not mean men would have concomitantly greater *privileges* than women (cf note 3). But as men took on more of their share of responsibilities, women would be better able to access *their* share of privileges.

References

Belenky, Mary Field, Blythe McVicker Clinchy, Nancy Rule Goldberge and Jill Mattuck Tarule. 1986. *Women's Ways of Knowing: The Development of Self, Voice, and Mind.* New York: Basic Books.

Bentham, Jeremy. 1960. *A Fragment on Government and an Introduction to the Principles of Morals and Legislation.* Ed. Wilfrid Harrison. Oxford: Basil Blackwell.

Berlin, Isaiah. 1971. *Four Essays on Liberty.* New York: Oxford University Press.

Burke, Edmund. 1955. *Reflections on the Revolution in France.* Ed. Thomas H. D. Mahoney. New York: Bobbs Merrill.

Chodorow, Nancy. 1978. *The Reproduction of Mothering: Psychoanalysis and the Sociology of Gender.* Berkeley: University of California Press.

Collins, Patricia Hill. 1990. *Black Feminist Thought: Knowledge, Consciousness, and the Politics of Empowerment.* Boston: Unwin-Hyman.

Crenshaw, Kimberle. 1991. "Mapping the Margins: Intersectionality, Identity Politics, and Violence Against Women of Color." *Stanford Law Review* 43:1241–1299.

DiLeonardo, Micaela. 1984. *The Varieties of Ethnic Experience: Kindship, Class, and Gender Among Californian Italian-Americans.* Ithaca, N.Y.: Cornell University Press.

Dinnerstein, Dorothy. 1976. *The Mermaid and the Minotaur: Sexual Arrangements and Human Malaise.* New York: Harper and Row.

Dunn, John. 1980. *Political Obligation in Its Historical Context.* Cambridge: Cambridge University Press.

Fishkin, James. 1982. *The Limits of Obligation.* New Haven, Conn.: Yale University Press.

Flathman, Richard E. 1972. *Political Obligation.* New York: Atheneum.

Gilligan, Carol. 1982. *In a Different Voice: Psychological Theory and Women's Development.* Cambridge, Mass.: Harvard University Press.

Gilligan, Carol, Nona P. Lyons and Trudy Hanmer, eds. 1990. *Making Connections: The Relational Worlds of Adolescent Girls at Emma Willard School*. Cambridge, Mass.: Harvard University Press.

Gilligan, Carol, Janie Victoria Ward, Jill McLean Taylor with Betty Bardige, eds. 1988. *Mapping the Moral Domain*. Cambridge, Mass.: Harvard University Press.

Gilligan, Carol and Grant Wiggins. 1988. "The Origins of Morality in Early Childhood Relationships." In *Mapping the Moral Domain*. Ed. Gilligan et al. Cambridge, Mass.: Harvard University Press.

Goodin, Robert E. 1985. *Protecting the Vulnerable: A Reanalysis of Our Social Responsibilities*. Chicago: University of Chicago Press.

Harding, Sandra. 1987. *The Science Question in Feminism*. Ithaca, N.Y.: Cornell University Press.

Hare-Mustin, Rachel and Jean Marecek. 1990. "Beyond Difference." In *Making a Difference: Psychology and the Construction of Gender*. Ed. R. Hare-Mustin and J. Marecek. New Haven, Conn.: Yale University Press.

Hartsock, Nancy. 1984. *Money, Sex, and Power: Toward a Feminist Historical Materialism*. Boston: Northeastern University Press.

Hegel, G. W. F. 1977. *The Phenomenology of Spirit*. Trans. A. V. Miller. New York: Oxford University Press.

Hirschmann, Nancy J. 1992. *Rethinking Obligation: A Feminist Method for Political Theory*. Ithaca, N.Y.: Cornell University Press.

Hobbes, Thomas. 1968. *Leviathan*. Ed. C. B. Macpherson. New York: Penguin Books.

Hochschild, Arlie with Anne Machung. 1989. *The Second Shift*. New York: Avon Books.

Hume, David. 1953. *Political Essays*. Ed. Charles W. Hendel. Indianapolis: Bobbs Merrill.

King, Martin Luther. 1969. "Letter from Birmingham City Jail." In *Civil Disobedience: Theory and Practice*. Ed. Hugo A. Bedau. New York: Pegasus.

Locke, John. 1965. *Two Treatises of Government*. Ed. Peter Laslett. New York: New American Library.

Locke, John. 1990. *Questions Concerning the Law of Nature*. Ed. Horwitz, Clay, and Clay. Ithaca, N.Y.: Cornell University Press.

Okin, Susan Moller. 1989. *Justice, Gender, and the Family*. New York: Basic Books.

Pateman, Carole. 1979. *The Problem of Political Obligation: A Critical Analysis of Liberal Theory*. New York: John Wiley and Sons.

Pitkin, Hanna. 1965. "Obligation and Consent: I." *The American Political Science Review* 59 (4):990–999.

Rawls, John. 1964. "Legal Obligation and the Duty of Fair Play." In *Law and Philosophy*. Ed. Sidney Hook. New York: New York University Press.

Rawls, John. 1971. *A Theory of Justice*. Cambridge, Mass.: Harvard University Press.

Rousseau, Jean-Jacques. 1973. *The Social Contract and Discourses*. Trans. G. D. H. Cole. London: J. M. Dent and Son.

Ruddick, Sara. 1989. *Maternal Thinking: Toward a Politics of Peace*. Boston: Beacon Press.

Simmons, A. John. 1979. *Moral Principles and Political Obligation.* Princeton, N.J.: Princeton University Press.

Smith, Rogers. 1985. *Liberalism in American Constitutional Law.* Cambridge, Mass.: Harvard University Press.

Tussman, Joseph. 1960. *Obligation and the Body Politic.* Oxford: Oxford University Press.

Walzer, Michael. 1970. *Obligations: Essays on Disobedience, War, and Citizenship.* Cambridge, Mass.: Harvard University Press.

Williams, Patricia. 1991. *The Alchemy of Race and Rights: Diary of a Law Professor.* Cambridge, Mass.: Harvard University Press.

9

Equalizing Privacy and Specifying Equality

Zillah Eisenstein

*I*n this brief chapter I simply wish to argue that truly democratic feminist theory must embrace women's differences and their similarities to others and among themselves. This requires a theoretical and political appreciation for both our privacy rights and the equality of needs (Eisenstein 1994, chap. 4, 6). In other words, we must individualize and particularize our notion of equality while socializing and democratizing our notion of privacy. Although this formulation oversimplifies my intent, it also clarifies my concern to democratize privacy via equality discourses.

Furthermore, because the right to privacy has always been racially coded—it has not granted the same protection to women of color that it has to white women—(white) feminists need to connect our thinking about privacy to the discourses of civil rights and the demand for racial and sexual equality.

My radical revisioning of privacy rights requires that equality of access must become part of the discourse of freedom of choice specified for female bodies. The right to privacy and the right to equality each greatly affects the meaning of the other. The privatization of state services attacks the essence of one's privacy if it affects one's ability to actually obtain one's choice. After all, the right to use contraceptives has little effect if they are not available or if one cannot afford to buy condoms or a diaphragm. Without a commitment to racial, sexual, and economic equality, privacy rights for women are reduced to a sham. They remain abstract rights for white, heterosexual men.

My vision of a radicalized right to privacy requires an affirmative and activist, yet noninterventionist, state. The state has to be willing to provide equal access to enable women's bodily integrity. Ensuring this integrity entails a notion of privacy that is underwritten by sexual and racial equality. Such equality is not part of the history of the constitutional right to privacy, which never included black slaves and has never been extended to homosexuals. Constitutional protection of the right to privacy has been granted to white women and women of color in the United States with significant restrictions; it is the exclusive right of those with the ability to utilize it.

Neoconservatives within the Reagan-Bush years embraced privacy in its negative sense: one must be protected from government; one is not entitled to anything from the government, such as a Medicaid-funded abortion. As the state became more privatized through the 1980s, society became less equal, and privacy rights became further encoded racially and sexually along economic lines. It is from this complex of multiple meanings that I want to retrieve a more egalitarian privacy for democratic theory.

Radicalizing Privacy and the Discourse of Rights

FOR ME, DEMOCRACY means individual freedom, which requires privacy of and for bodies as well as social, economic, political, sexual, racial, and gender equality. It does not mean rugged individualism as envisioned by Hobbes or Locke, or by J. S. Mill for that matter. Democracy involves a commitment to the individual, nevertheless—to an individual who has social connections and commitments but also autonomy. It also requires equality, but this conception of equality does not mean that everyone must be treated the same, but that everyone must be treated fairly while recognizing individual diversity. This construction of individuality and equality necessitates a recognition of individual differences.

Key to this vision of democracy are freedom for our uniqueness and equality for our similarity. We need freedom for individuals, and we need the various kinds of access that allow us to enjoy our freedom. For lack of a better or more precise language, we need a little bit of liberalism (the unrelenting focus on the individual) and a little bit of socialism (a commitment to equality between people).

Individual freedom and a right to privacy go hand in hand. Privacy as a concept connotes a preoccupation with the individual's right to be free: to be free from others' invasions, to be free from an interventionist state. It connotes the tremendously subversive and radical notion of the sovereignty of the individual and one's right to be left alone. Supposedly, we must be free to be different, be free to speak our minds, and be free from bodily harm. This radical vision of privacy has never been actualized in liberal democratic society, or even fully theorized. It is because of its radical dimensions that privacy has always been restricted and qualified by the interests of the state.

The radical side of privacy is not without its problems. Liberal theorists have always recognized this fact. Individuals cannot be completely free to do what they want, with no regard for the impact of their actions on others. Privacy, by definition, recognizes the tension between individual and collective needs. The boundaries between individuals and states are fragile, resulting in the troublesome tension between state neglect and state interventionism.

Other critiques of privacy are as varied as they are numerous. Because the concept of privacy focuses unabashedly on the individual, it makes both Marxists and neoconservatives uncomfortable, albeit for different reasons. Traditional Marxists reject the very idea of autonomous individuals. Rightists do, too, but from an utterly different viewpoint: that of religion. Neoconservatives attempt to restrict the construction of privacy as a constitutional right because there are no inherent restrictions to privacy. The very existence of restrictions on privacy speak to the subversive aspects of a nonrestricted understanding of it.

Many feminists and other progressives have argued that the right to privacy is an insufficient basis on which to establish the rights of women to control their own bodies or the rights of homosexuals to choose their own sexual expression. Some argue that privacy doctrine is misguided and flawed by definition, that its meaning and its continual restructuring will always rest with the state.

In contrast to this position, Elizabeth Fox-Genovese criticizes what she terms the absolutist individualism of feminism. She argues that feminists fail "to develop a notion of individual right as a product of collective life," that feminism reflects the "excesses of individualism" that deny the needs of society. The "right to choice," in her view, reflects a misguided notion of "women's absolute right to their own bodies" (Fox-Genovese 1991, 8, 241, 256–257).

Rosalind Petchesky has a much different approach. For her, the problem is not that feminist politics embraces privacy and the right to choice, but that feminists must insist on enlarging the right to privacy to include the social changes and public efforts that will make choice real for all women. Rather than rejecting "rights" theory, Petchesky asks that we extend its individualist moorings to a recognition of "social rights" (Petchesky 1990, xxi–xxvi). Such recognition will require a rethreading of privacy through an affirmative discourse that deprivatizes the state and assigns it responsibility for creating access to medical care, prenatal care, drug treatment programs, abortion, and other necessities.

All of these positions are unsatisfactory. An absent, privatized, yet interventionist, moralist state will not realize a feminist political equality. A radicalized notion of privacy requires a noninterventionist state in the realm of private choice and an activist one in creating and enabling the host of options from which one makes a choice. In more traditional language, we need freedom from the state in order to be free to choose, and we need equality that is open, even to the most vulnerable, in order to protect privacy.

I argue, cautiously, for a state that is affirmatively friendly to women and families (Hernes 1987). I do not mean to glorify or misrepresent the troublesome history of state invasion into the lives of women, especially poor women. But it is also necessary to recognize the problem of state privatization. It forms the backdrop for my discussion of public responsibility and state activism on behalf of women (Brown 1992).

My radical vision of privacy, defined as the individual's freedom to choose and the ability to get what one chooses, lands me squarely in the uncomfortable terrain of defending liberal rights discourse while critiquing it. Individuals need privacy from unwanted interference from the state, yet sometimes individuals need assistance from the state in order to get what they need; and in such cases, a noninterventionist state is insufficient. Privacy is *always* needed but is never enough (Petchesky 1990; Hurtado 1989).

I inscribe the liberal notion of privacy with an egalitarian text that does not assume sameness as a standard, but rather recognizes a radically pluralist individuality. Radical pluralism means that differences are not ordered hierarchically. They are not set up as oppositions. They are not tied up with, or reflective of, power relations (Eisenstein 1989). They merely reflect diversity.

The radical premise of privacy rights derives from their universal meaning in a society where discrimination exists. Because not all individuals are treated equally in the first place, privacy allows for a radical critique of its own violations. Liberal democratic discourse promises, rather than actually extends, the right of privacy to all. This is where the critique of liberalism begins. The promise of universality must be made real by extending privacy equally to all persons. But promises are not enough.

Privacy as a Contingent Right Granted by the State

THE IMPORTANCE OF understanding the intersection of privacy and equality is particularly clear in the case of abortion. The politics of privatization has deeply affected abortion rights. Privatization and moral absolutism have been in effect in this arena since the rulings in *Maher v. Roe* and *Harris v. McRae* declared state funding for abortion unconstitutional. These rulings directly affected poor women in need of public assistance. The *Webster v. Reproductive Health Service* and *Planned Parenthood v. Casey* decisions further privatized the state's role in abortion, affecting a much broader base of women. The restrictiveness of abortion law impacts any woman living in an anti-choice state. It affects any woman needing a late-term abortion. It affects teenagers needing parental consent.

The restrictions on privacy related to the procreative rights of women reflect a series of negotiations between state interests and individual women's rights. *Roe v. Wade* made quite clear the political construction of the right to privacy: the right is not absolute. A woman is not free "to terminate her pregnancy at whatever time, in whatever way, and for whatever reason she alone chooses." The Court found that "this right of privacy . . . is broad enough to encompass a woman's decision whether or not to terminate her pregnancy" (*Roe* 154–155) but that it does not constitute an unqualified right.

State interests define the contours of privacy. There is no "unlimited right to do with one's body as one pleases" (*Roe* 154–155). The zone of privacy extends to women's reproductive choices but remains restricted. The restrictions on women's reproductive choices are defined by a liberal democratic and patriarchal state. The "liberal" dimension of the state extends the rights of privacy to women as individuals. The "patriarchal" aspect of the state extends these rights to women as though they were men. Women's privacy is restrictive; it is not defined as a right to reproductive freedom.

The right to privacy, interpreted as a right to be left alone, first gained currency in 1890 with an article authored by Samuel Warren and Louis Brandeis (later to be appointed to the Supreme Court), entitled "The Right to Privacy" (Warren and Brandeis 1890, 784). Nevertheless, critics such as the unconfirmed Supreme Court nominee Robert Bork have argued that the right to privacy has been plucked out of thin air—that it is a new, undefined, unconstitutional right (Wulf 1991; Dworkin 1987a, 1987b).

Privacy rights are often set within the legal context of the due process clause of the Fourteenth Amendment, which says that no state shall "deprive any person of life, liberty, or property without due process of law; nor deny to any person within its jurisdiction the equal protection of the laws." The Fourth and Fifth Amendments are also used to justify the construction of privacy. Privacy was extended to childrearing in *Pierce v. Society of Sisters*, to procreation in *Skinner v. Oklahoma*, to the use of contraceptives in marital sexual intercourse in *Griswold v. Connecticut*, to the use of contraceptives in nonmarital sexual intercourse in *Eisenstadt v. Baird*, and to abortion in the first trimester in *Roe*.

Griswold established the notion that privacy was to be construed as a "peripheral right"; it made other, more specifically noted rights more secure. Using the Fifth Amendment's self-incrimination clause, the Court stated that a citizen could create "a zone of privacy which the government may not force him to surrender." In other words, although privacy may not be expressly stated, it is understood as "necessary in making the express guarantees fully meaningful." *Griswold* established, through the use of *Boyd v. United States*, that the individual is protected against "all governmental invasions 'of the sanctity of a man's home and the privacies of life.'" The use of contraceptives in marital relations lies within the "zone of privacy created by several fundamental constitutional guarantees," and any government regulation "invades the area of protected freedoms" (*Griswold*, 483–485; *Boyd*).

Justice Goldberg, in a concurring opinion, stated that although the Constitution does not name the right of privacy in marriage, "I cannot believe that it offers these fundamental rights no protection." He argued that marital privacy was on a par with other fundamental rights already specifically protected. He distinguished marital privacy from adultery or homosexuality, which are "sexual intimacies which the state forbids." It is specifically the intimacy of husband and wife that is not to be regulated (*Griswold*, 495, 499; *Poe v. Ullmann*, 553).

Justice Hugo Black, in his dissent, argued that there is no right to privacy per se; that instead there are "specific constitutional provisions which are designed in part to protect privacy at certain times and places with respect to certain activities" (*Griswold*, 479, 508). He rejects the comprehensive and broad right of privacy, which he argues can be too easily misconstrued. But the notion of marital privacy was upheld by the Court again in *Eisenstadt v. Baird*. Privacy was declared to be a "right of the individual, married or single, to be free from unwarranted governmental intrusion into matters so fundamentally affecting a person as the decision whether to rear or beget a child" (Einstadt, 453).

If *Griswold* established a right to privacy, *Bowers v. Hardwick* clarified its limitations: privacy is restricted to heterosexual sex inside marriage. *Bowers* makes clear that privacy is not a generalized construct without limits: that privacy is "given" by the state and can be either granted or not. In a 5-to-4 decision, the Court held that the Georgia statute criminalizing homosexual sodomy, even if consensual, was constitutional (Hyde 1988–1989, 57–63). The *Bowers* decision makes clear that there is no constitutional right of privacy for homosexuals. Privacy-based arguments do not support those who have no recognized right to privacy.

Justice White, writing for the Court in *Bowers*, stated that privacy applies to the realms of marriage, procreation, and (heterosexual) family relationships. Homosexual activity remains outside these spheres and therefore exists outside the scope of privacy doctrine (*Bowers*, 190–191). Justice Warren Burger, concurring in the decision, states that "there is no such thing as a fundamental right to commit homosexual sodomy" (*Bowers*, 196). Justice Harry Blackmun, in his dissent, stated that the question was not whether the federal Constitution conferred "a fundamental right to engage in homosexual sodomy," but rather whether it conferred the "most comprehensive of rights . . . namely, 'the right to be left alone.'" Blackmun criticizes the Court for refusing to recognize "the fundamental interest all individuals have in controlling the nature of their intimate associations with others" (*Bowers*, 205–208).

Privacy as a construct of the state has clear limits that can be added or taken away. The dilemma of privacy is that the state should not have the last word on who gets to have privacy, and yet the state must play a role in affirming its actual availability. In constitutional doctrine, the right to privacy is recognized in the realms of the bodily integrity and personal autonomy of heterosexuals (Bigge 1989, 261). Privacy also locates us within the "network of decisions relating to the conditions under which sex is permissible . . . the social institutions surrounding sexual relations, and the procreative consequences of sex" (Rubenfeld 1989, 744). Reproductive issues are at the heart of the right to privacy because they involve issues of bodily integrity that are deeply connected to our individual autonomy (Johnsen 1989, 179). Privacy demands that a woman have the right to choose the circumstances of her reproductive life.

The everyday discourse of privacy has come to have a much more radical meaning than its constitutional rendering ever intended. Rather than being envisioned as a partial and restricted right *granted* by the state, privacy is more often understood as an individual right that supersedes the interests of the state. This view underlies much of the popular support for abortion rights, however variable and confused this support may sometimes be. A majority of the American public are more ready to restrict state interference than to limit individual privacy. I do not mean to overstate the radicalism of popular notions of privacy, which can have a conservative side, as manifested in taxpayers' revolts and antiwelfare sentiments. Such notions can coexist with very contradictory discourses, such as the opinion that women who get abortions or delay pregnancy are selfish.

To the extent that the right to abortion has been constructed as a right to privacy, it operates in popular discourse as though it is fundamental to women's freedom of choice. So even though the right to abortion was initially constructed in and through a restrictive posture, the restrictions on it often appear as assaults on freedom of choice. This complex posture may in the end save *Roe*. But I do not want to make too much of the power of public discourse, particularly since the present Court seems so at ease with ignoring it. So let us stay for the moment with the restricted side of abortion doctrine.

Although *Roe* protects a woman from undue interference with her freedom to choose an abortion, it does not prevent a state from encouraging childbirth over abortion. One's right to choose an abortion does not translate into a constitutional obligation for the state to subsidize abortion (Petchesky 1990, chap. 3,4). After all, Congress has no constitutional responsibility to subsidize health care (*Harris v. McRae*, 315).

These limitations on the access to abortion greatly clarify the economic bias of privacy rights: women who can afford to pay for their own abortions have a right to their privacy; other women do not. The due process clause does not establish "entitlement."

This narrow and restrictive reading of abortion law was evidenced in *Webster, Rust v. Sullivan,* and *Planned Parenthood* (see Eisenstein 1994, chap. 4 for an in-depth discussion of these cases). Each of these decisions reiterated the idea that government has no affirmative role or responsibility in making abortion available. These rulings codify and institutionalize a privatized and nonegalitarian view of reproductive rights. A woman has a right to choose an abortion, but she has no right to actually obtain one.

These restrictions are not inherent to privacy in a conceptual sense, however. Rather, they are part of the political negotiations that have established the control of the state over women's bodies. There is no inherent reason why privacy cannot be an unlimited right in the realm of procreative choice; there are only political reasons. And these reasons—which are based in the privatization of public responsibilities by the state—extend beyond the abortion debate.

The Rehnquist Court has little interest in expanding the right of individual privacy any further than it has already been expanded. Some on the Court, for example, Justices Rehnquist and Scalia, seek to narrow and curtail its meaning further. The issue of privacy has come before the Court in many guises. Chief Justice Rehnquist, in *Deshaney v. Winnebago County Department of Social Services,* argues that the "due process clauses generally confer no affirmative right to governmental aid." The purpose of the clause is "to protect the people from the State, not to ensure that the State protects them from each other" (*Deshaney,* 196).

In this case, Joshua Deshaney, who lived with his father and was repeatedly beaten by him, was not removed from the home by the local social service agency, even though the agency was monitoring the situation. As a result of the beatings, the child suffers from permanent brain damage and is profoundly retarded. Joshua's mother sued. Rehnquist, writing for the Court, stated that there is no government responsibility to provide members of the general public with adequate protective services. To find otherwise would require an "expansive reading of the constitutional text" (*Deshaney,* 197). Privacy defines the rights of the individual to be free from the interference of the state. It does not define any responsibility of the state to the individual.

Democratizing Privacy, Particularizing Equality

THE ASSAULT ON women's reproductive rights has demanded that feminists both defend and push beyond the existing boundaries of a woman's privacy and her right to choose. Our new conceptions must encompass a notion of personal privacy, which is also grounded in women's collective and shared need for reproductive control of their bodies. Rosalind Petchesky eloquently advises that we must retrieve reproductive rights from the heavy baggage of liberal exclusivity with which they have been encumbered and ground ourselves in the actual political struggles of the civil rights and feminist movements. We must develop a definition of rights "that maintains a notion of women's moral and political agency both as individuals and as members of collectivities" (Petchesky 1990, 395).

Abortion is individual and collective: specific and universal at the same time. If one starts with reproductive rights, or the right to bodily privacy, at the core of one's theory, one establishes individual rights for women—which speaks of a social collectivity—rather than an individual, private right for a specific woman. The move is transformative of rights theory and of our understanding of privacy. Privacy then encompasses the issues of racial, sexual, and economic quality because it is not simply an individual concern.

It is especially important that once we move to the collective meaning of our individual status as women, we must push the boundaries of the racialized nature of patriarchal rights discourse. This next level of specificity—the specifying of equality—speaks to the diversity within the collectivity of women. By specifying the racialized meanings of female bodies, feminists can reimagine a rights discourse that could reinvent democracy. It will be a democracy inclusive of reproductive rights and accountable to women of color. To be accountable to women of color means to encourage diversity and variety. And a reproductive rights agenda will address the needs of all people for work, economic stability, sexual freedom, healthy bodies, prenatal care, and much more.

The National Black Women's Health Project and the National Institute for Women of Color criticize the feminist framing of abortion for not addressing the problems of access that many women of color face. These groups emphasize a reproductive rights agenda that includes not only greater access to abortion but also available health care, prenatal care, and economic justice. They locate abortion at the crux of a network of issues related to the economic inequity of racialized patriarchy. For example, the denial of access to abortion directly contributes to increased maternal mortality rates, which are nearly four times higher for black women than for white women in the United States. Moreover, abortion and family planning clinics funded by Title X provide the entry point for reproductive health care and minimal general health care for poor women. These clinics are the only places these women can get pap smears, mammograms, screening for sexually transmitted diseases, and so forth.

We must refocus the issue of abortion, and with it privacy, to the societal framing of how—and how "equally"—it is available. The lack of prenatal care is as problematic for some women as the lack of an abortion is for others. Teenage pregnancy and the poverty it writes into the lives of newborns is a problem of crisis proportions in the African American community. Contraceptive services, sex education, and AIDS prevention outreach are as important to any woman needing them as abortion is for others. For many black women, who are more at risk for breast and cervical cancer, hypertension, diabetes, lupus, and other problems, abortion appears as only one among many health needs. Recognizing the complexity of the health needs of women of color radicalizes abortion politics for all women. It pushes feminists beyond a notion of bodily privacy limited by middle-class white women's experience, extending it to encompass the experiences of working-class and poor white women, as well as those of Asian, Latina, and Korean women.

White women in the national abortion movement, along with women of color, need to rethink the differences of economic class and race to develop a more inclusive understanding regarding women's different levels of access to health care and abortion. They need to hold on to the universal framing of abortion rights—that any woman has a right to such choice—while recognizing that choices currently differ for women according to their racialized economic situation. The logical starting point for theory and politics is the individual (in her specificity) and her right to reproductive freedom (which is universal). We must connect the discourse of choice to the different meanings that life circumstance affords.

This means reinventing the liberal individualist language of privacy so that it challenges the inequalities of access women experience in accordance with their race, economic class, geographical location, age, and so on. Feminism needs to continually redefine the meaning of democratic rights to require equality of access via an affirmative and nonintervention-ist state.

Focusing on reproductive rights as a central facet of a feminist, antiracist, and progressive politics is different than limiting ourselves to an abortion politics limited to privacy doctrine. Reproductive rights enlarge the issue of abortion to related concerns: affordable and good health care; a decrease in infant mortality and teenage pregnancy, reproductive health, health services for infertility, and access to appropriate contraceptives (Rutherford 1992).

This view of abortion and privacy rights pushes beyond the identity politics of any one group of women by cutting through the racialized and economic class divisions that stunt pro-choice politics. It makes clear that identity is often multiple (Solomon 1992).

Issues of racism and sexism form a major part of the political landscape of the United States. The two issues sometimes require women of color to choose between and against themselves. African American feminist Judy Scales Trent terms this dilemma the "double jeopardy" of black women. They are a discrete group with multiple status as blacks and women (Trent 1989, 10, 12). African American feminist Kimberle Williams Crenshaw argues that the "intersectionality" of black women's lives is not recognized. They are said to be discriminated against in the same way as either black men or white women; there is no recognition that they are discriminated against as both (Crenshaw 1989, 140, 143). Or as Peggie Smith argues, black women experience "interactive discrimination" or "disproportionate and adverse specificity" (Smith 1991, 22, 31).

As part of feminist efforts to confront this, white feminists must make antiracist coalition work a priority. Reproductive rights is an agenda where there are definite possibilities. Why? Because reproductive rights, as a fundamental democratic right of all women, is located in an *in-between* space: between our rights and our access to them, between our reproductive specificity and our universal human claims, between an affirmative state and our bodily privacy. These issues cut across racialized economic lines.

The narrow focus on abortion (as disconnected from the need for jobs, good health care, and so on) reflects just how narrowed the defensive posture of feminism became during the rightist Reagan-Bush years. Women of color make clear that this narrowing must be reversed. There cannot be bodily privacy for all women without sexual and racial equality. The issues of access and privacy are interwoven. Their connection radicalizes the meaning of privacy for all women.

Democratic rights and equality need redefinition. Reproductive rights require reproductive freedom, and reproductive freedom requires equality of access to health care and abortion, as well as the freedom of individual choice. Put concisely: we need to democratize privacy and specify equality.

References

Bigge, Ellen. 1989. "The Fetal Rights Controversy: A Resurfacing of Sex Discrimination in the Guise of Fetal Protection." *University of Missouri–Kansas City Law Review* 57 (2):261–288.

Bowers v. Hardwick. 1986. 487 U.S. 186.

Boyd v. United States. 1886. 116 U.S. 616.

Brown, Wendy. 1992. "Finding the Man in the State." *Feminist Studies* 18 (1):7–34.

Crenshaw, Kimberle Williams. 1989. "Demarginalizing the Intersection of Race and Sex: A Black Feminist Critique of Antidiscrimination Doctrine, Feminist Theory, and Antiracist Politics." *University of Chicago Legal Forum* 2 (1989):139–167.

Deshaney v. Winnebago County Department of Social Services. 1989. 489 U.S. 189.

Dworkin, Ronald. 1987a. "The Bork Nomination." *New York Review of Books* 34(13):3–10.

Dworkin, Ronald. 1987b. "From Bork to Kennedy." *New York Review of Books* 34 (20):36–42.

Eisenstadt v. Baird. 1972. 405 U.S. 438.

Eisenstein, Zillah. 1989. *Female Body and the Law.* Berkeley: University of California Press.

Eisenstein, Zillah. 1994. *The Color of Gender.* Berkeley: University of California Press.

Fox-Genovese, Elizabeth. 1991. *Feminism Without Illusions: A Critique of Individualism.* Chapel Hill: University of North Carolina Press.

Griswold v. Connecticut. 1965. 381 U.S. 479.

Harris v. McRae. 1980. 448 U.S. 297.

Hernes, Helga Maria. 1987. *Welfare State and Woman Power.* New York: Oxford University Press/Norwegian University Press.

Hurtado, Aido. 1989. "Relating to Privilege: Seduction and Rejection in the Subordination of White Women and Women of Color." *Signs* 14 (4):833–855.

Hyde, Sue. 1989. "Sex and Politics: Challenging the Sodomy Laws." *Radical America* 22 (5):56–63.

Johnsen, Dawn. 1989. "From Driving to Drugs: Governmental Regulation of Pregnant Women's Lives After Webster." National Black Women's Health Project, 12347 Gordon Street SW, Atlanta, GA 30310; and National Institute for Women of Color, 1301 20th St. NW, Washington, DC 10036.

Maher v. Roe. 1977. 482 U.S. 464.

Petchesky, Rosalind Pollack. 1990. *Abortion and Women's Choice: The State, Sexuality, and Reproductive Freedom.* Revised. Boston: Northeastern University Press.

Pierce v. Society of Sisters. 1925. 168 U.S. 510.

Planned Parenthood of Southeastern Pennsylvania v. Casey. 1992. 112 S.Ct. 1791.

Poe v. Ullman. 1961. 367 U.S. 497.

Roe v. Wade. 1973. 410 U.S. 113.

Rubenfeld, Jed. 1989. "The Right of Privacy." *Harvard Law Review* 102 (4):737–807.

Rust v. Sullivan. 1991. 111 S. Ct. 1759.

Rutherford, Charlotte. 1992. "Reproductive Freedoms and African American Women." *Yale Journal of Law and Feminism* 4 (1):255–290.

Skinner v. Oklahoma. 1942. 316 U.S. 535.

Smith, Peggie R. 1991. "Separate Identities: Black Women, Work, and Title VII." *Harvard Women's Law Journal* 14 (Spring):21–75.

Solomon, Alisa. 1992. "Identity Crisis: Queer Politics in the Age of Possibilities." *Village Voice* 37 (June 30):27–33.

Trent, Judy Scales. 1989. "Black Women and the Constitution: Finding Our Place, Asserting Our Rights." *Harvard Civil Rights–Civil Liberties Law Review* 24 (1):9–44.

Warren, Samuel and Louis Brandeis. 1890. "The Right to Privacy." *Harvard Law Review* 4 (5):193–220.

Webster v. Reproductive Health Service. 1989. 492 U.S. 490.

Wulf, Melvin. 1991. "On the Origins of Privacy." *Nation* 252 (20):700–704.

10

Privacy at Home

The Twofold Problem

Anita L. Allen

For people who want privacy, there may be no place like home. Whether an ordinary row-house or an extraordinary houseboat, the residential dwelling is where American custom and law generally allow one the greatest freedom to look, speak, and behave as one pleases. Business and amusement outside the home call for a mode of conduct and appearance calculated to avoid unwanted attention and interference. In the workplace, punctuality, productivity, skill, and decorum are closely monitored by employers and co-workers. It is easy to covet the privacy of the superrich, the superannuated, those, typically women, who stay home to keep house or rear children. Yet, for women with families at home to care for, staying at home is not always a privacy blessing. Marriage, motherhood, housekeeping, dependence, and her own moral ideas of caretaking and belonging have made many a woman's homelife a privacy bane rather than boon.

The recurrent problem of privacy for women at home is twofold. First, women face the problem of overcoming inequitable social and economic patterns that substitute confinement to the private sphere for meaningful privacy. Second, women face the problem of enjoying and exploiting individual privacy without sacrificing worthy ideals of affiliation and benevolent caretaking to self-centeredness.

Feminists have pointed out that subordinate and caretaking roles at home have deprived women of the experience of meaningful privacy (Gilman 1898, Allen and Mack 1990). Although their lives have been centered in the nominal privacy of the family home, women have rarely had the opportunity to experience and take full advantage of privacy. Feminist critiques of women's privacy stress the undeniable: that the privacy of women secluded at home without powers of effective decisionmaking concerning sex, pregnancy, vocation, and lifestyle has been something of "an injury got up as a gift" (MacKinnon 1984, 52). Since the early nineteenth century, many American women, especially married middle-class women, have been relegated to the private household in economically dependent and legally subordinate positions (Klein 1984). Traditionally, men have served both as head of the household and as architects of social policy, doubly powerful arbiters of how women's time and personal resources at home could be expended.

Many American women are in the labor force, not at home. But many of these wage-earners, even professionals and businesswomen, go home to onerous caretaking and housekeeping roles inconsistent with meaningful opportunities for individual forms of privacy. There is still a privacy problem for women related to their roles within the private sphere,[1] even though *half* the female population now works outside the home. It is no wonder, then, that some feminists look upon the concept of privacy with skepticism and view the public-private distinction itself as entailing sexual injustice (Elshtain 1981, Okin 1977).

In recent decades, rights against governmental interference with effective decisionmaking in the areas of contraception and abortion, often described as "decisional privacy" rights, have increased women's ability to achieve and make use of beneficial degrees of privacy at home. Nonetheless, noted feminist legal scholar Catherine MacKinnon has rejected what she disparagingly labels "the idealogy of privacy," arguing that the personal privacy right espoused by liberal theorists and the U.S. Supreme Court in *Roe v. Wade* is only "a right of men 'to be let alone' to oppress women one at a time" (MacKinnon 1984, 53). The gist of MacKinnon's critique of privacy is that even though women officially have privacy and "free choice," men actually dominate their private lives, control sexual intercourse, and decide women's sexual and reproductive fates.

Critiques of privacy such as MacKinnon's go wrong at the point where the historic unequal treatment of women and the misuse of the private household to further women's domination is taken as grounds for rejecting either the condition of privacy itself or the long-overdue legal right to effective decisionmaking that can promote and protect that condition. Privacy, here broadly defined as the inaccessibility of persons, their mental states, or information about them to the senses and surveillance devices of others, does not pose an inherent threat to women. Sex, love, marriage and children no longer presume the total abrogation of the forms of privacy a woman might otherwise enjoy. On the contrary, women today are finally in a position to expect, experience, and exploit real privacy within the home and within heterosexual relationships. The women's movement, education, access to affordable birth control, liberalized divorced laws, and the larger role of women in politics, government, and the economy have expanded women's options and contributed to the erosion of oppressively nonegalitarian styles of home life. These advances have enhanced the capacity of American men and women, but especially for the first time women, to secure conditions of adequate and meaningful privacy at home paramount to moral personhood and responsible participation in families and larger segments of society. Instead of rejecting privacy as "male ideology" and subjugation, women can and ought to embrace opportunities for privacy and the exercise of reproductive liberty in their private lives.

All this implies, of course, that a degree of individual privacy is a good thing. Yet, privacy has moral opponents who view it as largely hostile to important moral, social, and political goals (Schoeman 1992). Like private property and individualism, privacy and the high value placed upon it have been denounced from the left as products of capitalism and its political ideology. Even some proponents of liberalism cast the condition of privacy and the value placed upon it as extreme tendencies within modern societies, major causes of social alienation and loneliness, and all-too-convenient "moral" excuses for moral and social irresponsibility. Most significant for our purposes is opposition to privacy grounded in the notion that privacy is inconsistent with the value most women are believed to rightly place on family, caring, intimacy, and community. Recent theorists suggest that women typically value concerned personal affiliation and intimacy over individual forms of privacy (Gilligan 1982).

The two strands of opposition to privacy directly related to women—that privacy is inconsistent with women's affiliative and caretaking ideals, and the rejection of privacy as a historic condition of subjugation through confinement to the home—warrant careful examination. Both strands point toward a feminist devaluation and de-emphasis of privacy. But this would be a mistake. Although there is a frank tension between privacy and concern for others, and although in the past women have been unfairly and wastefully confined to the domestic sphere under conditions of inequality, privacy and privacy at home are distinctly beneficial to women. Opportunities for meaningful privacy and privacy-related liberty are beneficial to women for reasons that include the familiar moral reasons for which feminists insist that equality is beneficial to women. Hence, far from advocating rejection of privacy as a condition and a concept, it is important that feminists suggest answers to the gender related privacy questions women repeatedly encounter in their private and in their public lives: How much privacy should we chose for ourselves? How much are we due?

The solution to the twofold privacy problem women face begins with promoting greater emphasis on opportunities for individual forms of privacy. Feminism does not require rejecting privacy. I start from the premise that despite the decline of the nuclear family household and privacy losses stemming from the use of confidential information and surveillance technology, the home remains, culturally and legally, the center of privacy in American life. Real privacy at home is possible for women to the extent that sexual privacy rights, innovative approaches to marriage, childcare, housekeeping, and their alternatives are tools women can use to secure the privacy home life can bring. Focusing on women's historic lack of privacy and the value of privacy for women is a way of exposing the myth that God, nature, morality, and the family require that women lead cloistered lives in the private sphere of the home but without meaningful and adequate individual forms of personal privacy.

Centers of Privacy

FOR MANY AMERICANS the home is the center for the experience and enjoyment of privacy. This is no mere platitude. Our homes are the place we most expect to be let alone in solitude or to deal selectively with others. Although the expression "home" can be used to denote a physical structure that serves as a residential dwelling-place, it has come to connote what home life can procure: being let alone, relaxation, candid expression, affection, sexual enjoyments, and familial ties.

Privacy at home can have deep significance for an individual's sense of well-being, dignity, and identity. It is a fact of life in our society that life at home is subject to consensual and nonconsensual quotidian losses through the actions of, to name a few, relatives, police, government, insurance investigators, peeping-toms, media, sales people, reformers, pollsters, plumbers, and neighbors. Yet, the customary expectation of privacy at home is reinforced by state and federal law. Unlike the United Nations Universal Declaration of Human Rights and the European Convention on Human Rights, the U.S. Constitution does not expressly provide for a right to privacy of the home.[2] Indeed, no express right to privacy of any sort is contained in the Constitution. Yet, the privacy of the home is protected by a number of constitutional provisions. The Third Amendment, which prohibits the quartering of soldiers in private homes in peacetime, reflects the idea as the home as a place in which citizens are entitled to enjoy undisturbed seclusion. Embodying James Otis's colonial-era sentiment that "a man's house is his castle," the Fourth Amendment guarantees individuals the right to be secure in their houses against unreasonable search and seizures. It has been held to protect individuals' "reasonable expectations of privacy," which extend to privacy in the paradigmatic sphere of privacy, the home (*Katz v. U.S.*). Relying on the Fourth and Fifth Amendments, the Supreme Court held late in the last century that the Constitution limits "invasions on the part of the government and its employees on the sanctity of a man's home and the privacies of life" (*Boyd v. U.S.*). Since then the court has held that Fourteenth Amendment liberty includes the right of the individual "to marry, establish a home, and bring up children" (*Meyer v. Nebraska*) and that obscenity prohibitions do not reach "the privacy of one's home" (*Stanley v. Georgia*). In the reproductive rights and sexual privacy cases of the past quarter-century, the Court has established that a constitutional right of privacy subsisting in the First, Third, Fourth, Fifth, Ninth, and Fourteenth Amendments protects consensual heterosexual intimacy in the home.[3]

Although home life does not deliver all the privacy a person may want, many homes reliably afford three forms of personal privacy. The first two domestic privacies are inaccessibility of the person in the senses of seclusion and anonymity. Anonymity is intended in the broad sense of limited attention paid rather than the narrower sense of undisclosed identity. The third is inaccessibility of personal information, especially the nondisclosure, through secrecy and confidentiality, of personal facts, opinions, or creative expression contained in documentary form. Homes serve as the repositories of cherished diaries, correspondence, photographs, audio and video recordings, and other mementoes and creative efforts intended for selected disclosure. These documents are deemed personal. Understood in relation to current societal norms, personal documents include those that relate closely to family problems, physical and mental health, sexual experiences, religious beliefs, finances, and performance in school.

Seclusion and anonymity, on the one hand, and inaccessibility of personal information, opinions, and expressions on the other, have a special relationship. Seclusion and anonymity of the physical person provide the opportunity for self-expression that makes its way into correspondence, diaries, and artistic efforts. It also provides the occasion for unembarrassed inspection of mementos and rumination about their significance.

Yet, it is plain that in the United States domestic privacy is a virtual commodity purchased by the middle class and the well-to-do. Privacy is bought and sold in the form of single family houses on privately owned land, townhouses, apartments, and recreational second homes in remote locations. The poor, whose "taste" for privacy might be equally keen, are compelled by economic necessity to accept smaller, thinner-walled, and more crowded accommodations. For New York City tenement dwellers earlier in this century, "privacy was a luxury too ridiculous to be considered" (Kennedy 1979, 97). This is true today in some urban communities where low-income individuals live in structures that do not shield co-inhabitants from one another and scarcely shield them from their neighbors.

The economically disadvantaged who rely on public assistance or live in public housing face additional obstacles to privacy (Pearldaughter and Schneider 1980). Privacy at home is diminished by the mandatory inspections of welfare caseworkers and housing authorities. Periodic and sometimes unannounced visits by agents of the state aim to detect and deter violations of the conditions of entitlement, of aesthetic standards, and of health and safety codes. Their effect is to compel the dependent poor to share privacy with strangers. Economic status can also affect the enforceability of privacy-related rights against trespass and to seclusion at home. The poor may find out of reach the legal aid and neighborhood police assistance needed to enforce the rights that protect and enhance domestic privacy.

Similarly unable to satisfy their taste for privacy are those in all social and economic strata whose homes are, for better or worse, public hospitals, nursing homes, and prisons. These institutions have purposes as different as punishment and health management. Yet, in each case the institutional way of life is artificially communal. Limited resources and cost containment measures usually mean not only sharing, but crowding. The institutional way of life is a life of unwanted intrusions by others, which affected individuals may be powerless to control. In hospitals and nursing homes, unwanted intrusions often have to be tolerated because of bona fide health-care objectives. In prisons, institutional security may require intimate body searches, cell searches, and surveillance.

Least able to satisfy a taste for privacy are the homeless. Urban "streetpeople" and "bag-ladies" sleep, eat, groom, commiserate, and so forth out of doors in places of public accommodation such as subways, train terminals, and building stairwells. A large percentage of the homeless are poor, unemployed, and ill. Many are cut off from their families, but among the homeless are families. They have no place to go, or no place worth going. Temporary shelters, public facilities, woods, fields, caves, or nightfall are poor substitutes for the more certain privacy of homes. It is conceivable, but barely, that among the homeless are a few robust men and women whose taste for domestic privacy is dwarfed for the freedom and anonymity of vagrancy.

Very small children are presumed to lack the self-consciousness that would mandate respect for their privacy. Indeed, parents may impose unwanted seclusion upon youngsters expressly to teach them that privacy ought to be respected. Once the desire for privacy develops in small children, their parents may justifiably deny them their desired levels of privacy on paternalistic grounds to assure discipline and safety. Teenagers living at home are typically allowed greater privacy than small children. But they may find their phone calls and visitors are monitored, their bedroom shared with younger siblings, and their diaries read. In a related vein, they may find that their sexual and reproductive preferences, their "decisional privacy," is effectively preempted.

Home management and supervision entail privacy losses. Consequently, parents may enjoy fewer private hours at home than their children. Tending to the needs of children requires spending substantial amounts of time in their presence and directly interacting with them. So too does the care of infirm adults. All other things being equal, caretakers enjoy less seclusion than noncaretakers or occasional caretakers. This observation relates importantly to any consideration of women's privacy at home. Women, whose lives at home as mothers, wives, and daughters often involve caretaking roles, have real problems finding opportunities for privacy.

Privacy in the Woman's Place

NOT ONLY IS the home recognized as the seat of the private sphere, but Americans commonly view privacy itself "as a set of rules against intrusion and surveillance focused on the household occupied by the nuclear family" (Roberts and Gregor 1971, 225). However, privacy must not be construed as synonymous with the norms of seclusion governing the separation of the nuclear family from the larger social world. This point is the starting place for understanding women's problem of privacy at home.

The problem of privacy for women at home is, in part, the problem of overcoming the tradition of inequality through confinement to the private sphere of home and family. In the name of sex equality, proponents of thoroughgoing sexual justice oppose privacy conceived as a man's castle and a women's place. In the name of genuine opportunities for personal privacy, they must also oppose this same flawed conception.

History reveals that women's roles in the private sphere have not entailed a plentitude of personal privacy. It is well documented that by the eighteenth century, Western women were economically and ideologically defined as people who cared for and supported others within the private sphere of home and family, rather than themselves being active in the world (Hall 1980). Yet, in early America the lives of both men and women centered around the home. For example, in early Puritan settlements women's tasks typically included childcare, housekeeping, and food preparation; their husbands' work as farmers, artisans, or shopkeepers kept them close by. Among the Puritan colonists the private sphere was not especially private by contemporary standards. Their religion and the exigencies of life in a foreign world rendered closeness and accountability an imperative.

In general, the homesteads of early American colonists offered a degree of seclusion for families and their servants. But the hardworking colonial lifestyle "left little room for privacy or non-conformity even among the free and affluent." Notable among those who were neither free nor affluent were women who earned passage to America as indentured servants or who were brought over as slaves. Sometimes expected to provide sexual services to their masters in addition to domestic and agricultural labor, these women enjoyed "neither privacy nor self-determination" (Kennedy 1979, 8). During the Revolutionary war women took over men's work at home, and some even fought alongside men in battle. Nonetheless, both the Constitution of the new American republic and the laws of the individual states accorded women an inferior legal status as private ancillaries of men rather than as public citizens.

As part of the nation's westward expansion, women—wives, missionaries, and fortune seekers—endured the hardships of the Oregon Trail. On their journeys and in their camps they shared mutually dependent lives

with fellow travelers, settling for very little privacy, even with respect to toi-
let functions and childbirth. Meanwhile, in the East and South, with the
coming of industrialism to the United States and the advent of wage labor,
the separation of men's work from the home became more marked. Men
increasingly went outside the home to work in industry; women remained
behind to labor in the home. Significant numbers of less affluent women
also became wage earners. Poor and working-class women worked in the
textile industry, the shoe and boot industry, and other industries deemed
suitable for women. New England "mill girls" left the relative seclusion of
their families to work in the textile industry. Mill girls commonly lived in
boarding houses operated by employers, where strict codes of conduct
were employed to keep feminine virtue intact. Poor and working-class
women in New York peddled wares from push carts and worked in gar-
ment and needle industry sweatshops. Or they found work as domestic servants as the affluent population multiplied with the growth of the
industrial economy. Live-in domestics could work hundred-hour weeks and
lacked both "independence and privacy." During the Civil War, women on
both sides "managed businesses, farms, and plantations while men fight,"
much as they had done during the Revolutionary War. Southern women
revived home industries to compensate for imported goods cut off by
northern sea blockades. Women made clothing and ammunition, taught,
nursed, worked in government printing offices, and trailed troops to cook,
do laundry, and provide sex. A few engaged in the extraordinary professions of teamster and steamboat captain (Kennedy 1979, 44, 102, 69).

Throughout the nineteenth century many women did stay at home.
Although women's share of the labor force increased from 7.4 percent to
17 percent between 1830 and 1890, a middle-class model of the family dic-
tated increasingly that the proper place for women was at home. Under
the familiar model it was the duty of a man to marry and to earn an
income for the support of himself, his wife, and their children. It was the
duty of a woman to marry and maintain a clean, cheerful, practical home
for her husband and the children she was expected to bear and rear.
Politics and commerce were public concerns and the concern of men,
whereas housekeeping, food preparation, childbearing and rearing, and
intimate relationships were private concerns and the concerns of women.
According to historian Barbara Weltzer, nineteenth-century middle-class
married American women were virtual hostages in their homes, held cap-
tive by pervasive middle- and upper-class ideals of "true womanhood" powerfully reflected in the popular women's literature of the day.

In the middle- and upper-income segments of the population, a clear
pattern emerged in the nineteenth century that continued through the late
1960s. Women worked, if they had to, but only until they married (although
during World War II many women worked outside the home temporarily in
defense industries). Working at all, even in secretarial posts in lush offices,

was seen by "middle-class moralizers [as] fundamentally incompatible with femininity" (Kennedy 1979, 94). Poor families subscribed to the ideal that women ought to remain in the home, in theory if not in practice. Women who had to earn wages often worked at home. They sewed, made artificial flowers, took in laundry, and cared for boarders.

In view of the seclusion made possible by life at home, women in traditional homemaking roles might be thought to have enjoyed a privacy boon. As Alan F. Westin has argued, "The developments associated with the rise of modern industrial societies—such as the nuclear family living in individual households, urbanization and the anonymity of urban life, mobility in work and residence, weakening of religious authority over individuals—all provide greater situations of physical and psychological privacy" (Westin 1967, 21). Yet, the amount of "physical and psychological" privacy a person possesses is not solely a function of increases in the number of hours spent in the nuclear family home, or increases in mobility, urban anonymity, and religious authority. The specific character of life within the nuclear family is more determinative of the available degree of meaningful privacy. Speaking of home-centered working-class urban women earlier in this century, Kennedy remarked that privacy played no significant role. For "living in crowded tenements, enduring pregnancies they could not prevent, struggling to find means to supplement factory wages . . . working-class women placed their first priority on survival" (Kennedy 1979, 96). Middle- and upper-income home-centered wives have not necessarily enjoyed situations of notable privacy either. Westin's theoretical account of the relationship between postindustrial opportunities for privacy may approximate a description of the consequences of industrial society for men. But as far as women are concerned, it is a misleading oversimplification.

Traditional home life in the United States appears to have fit the pattern observed in diverse cultures around the world. Women, in particular married women with children, "pay the social cost for whatever privacy men obtain in and through the nuclear family." An important social cost women have paid as guardians of the private sphere is inadequate personal privacy and the personal benefits that privacy entails. The lot of many women has been, to borrow Ruskin's words, self-denunciation rather than self-development (Moore 1984, 51–52). ⏴

To the extent that marriage is a love affair, it represents an obstacle to privacy that women in love will welcome. In the case of lovers, individual privacy must compete with shared privacy. Lovers relish being secluded and alone together; they share confidences and secrets; they share keepsakes of their relationship. Yet, shared privacy at home is a danger to women in love when it replaces individual privacy. Periods of separation from loved ones can promote traits of self-reliance and individuality that actually enrich relationships. The philosopher Montaigne eloquently bade his (male!) readers not to depend too much on their wives and on other external pleasures for happiness, but to find happiness in time spent alone in solitude in "a back shop all one's own" (Montaigne 1965, 174). Montaigne's point is that to build individuality and inner resources, it is important to be able to retreat periodically from others.

Maintaining a literal back shop of one's own is an expenditure most men—and especially most women—can ill afford. Writing of the importance of a place of one's own, feminist Charlotte Perkins Gilman contended that while the "progressive individualization of human beings requires a personal home, one room at least for each person . . . for the vast majority of the population no such provision is possible." Where money is not an obstacle to needed privacy, she continued, socio-sexual norms may be: "The man has his individual life, his personal expression and its rights, his office, studio, shop: the women and children live in the home—because they must" (Gilman 1898, 259).

Speaking of economic dependence, Barrington Moore observed that "even a strong yearning for privacy can evaporate in the face of an acute awareness of one's dependency on other human beings" (Moore 1984, 12). The same point could be made respecting the excessive emotional dependence sometimes associated with women in love. Emotional dependence can cause a woman to be unwilling to be separated from her lover or spouse; separations may provoke a high level of anxiety or loneliness that undermines her ability to benefit from time spent alone. Self-reliance can be an unattractive prospect for young women who, under the influence of infantilizing conventions for female behavior, are not prepared to strike out on their own, to utilize private time, or to value emotional independence. In such cases, the desire for privacy may be overcome by a felt need and desire for dependency.

The Value of Privacy for Women

THE PRECEDING DISCUSSION exposed the dimensions of half the twofold privacy problem faced by American women: the problem of overcoming the tradition of confinement to the private sphere of home, marriage, and caretaking roles as a substitute for and a barrier to genuine personal privacy. Liberal feminism presents one response to the problem by placing a high value on personal privacy and embracing the private sphere as occasions for privacy. Liberal feminism rejects forms of home life, sex role stereotypes, and sexual ties that foreclose privacy options for women. Although mindful of the ways in which traditional marriage, family life, and sex roles have resulted in inadequate privacy for women, liberal feminism in principle does not oppose marrying, mothering, and heterosexual relationships. Instead liberal feminism demands that those not be women's only options and that sex, marriage, and childrearing be, to take a phrase from Jean Bethke Elshtain, "reconstructed" consistent with sexual justice, through legal, economic and attitudinal changes. The liberal feminist looks with favor upon decisional privacy in the context of contraception and abortion, because she views it as a tool of female autonomy and privacy.

Catherine MacKinnon opposes the liberal feminist response to women's privacy problem. She rejects the "ideology" of the private because she assumes that it can be understood only in historical terms as referring to conditions of male hegemony and female inequality, conditions reinforced by the liberal democratic conceptions of political morality.

> It contradicts the liberal definition of the private to complain in public of inequality within it . . . . The democratic ideal of the private holds that, so long as the public does not interfere, autonomous individuals interact freely and equally. Conceptually, the privacy is hermetic. It *means* that which is inaccessible to unaccountable to, unconstricted by anything beyond itself . . . . It is personal, intimate, autonomous, particular, the original source and final outpost of the self, gender neutral. It is, in short, defined by everything that feminism reveals women have never been allowed to be or have, and everything that women have ever been equated with (MacKinnon 1984, 51).

To reject the private sphere for the reasons MacKinnon gives is to toss out the baby with the bath water. MacKinnon rightly condemned women's unequal control of sex and powerlessness to make decisions about matters most closely associated with their own bodies and self-development. She rightly judged that existing conditions of sexual inequality in the private sphere can undercut decisional privacy rights established by law on behalf of women. But these are not reasons to reject privacy, the private sphere, or the decisional privacy right of *Roe v. Wade* and *Planned Parenthood v. Casey*.

Decisional privacy rights have done more than supplement male authority over women. Many women still "second chair" men in sexual relationships, but *Roe* and access to birth control have helped to create new powers, new norms, and new expectations of self-determination among women. Decisional privacy must be recognized as one of the important remedies for the problem of sexual inequality and women's lack of meaningful privacy. Economic equality, by which I mean equal employment opportunity, equal pay, and greater recognition of the economic and social worth of the kinds of work women do, is another essential remedy. Political and governmental power are essential remedies as well. It is as mistaken to dismiss decisional privacy because it is impaired by residual male domination, as it would be to dismiss equal pay and comparable worth because their efficacy is impaired by residual male domination of private relations.

Male hegemony is not a reason to reject decisional privacy, and it is not a reason to reject the idea of privacy and the private sphere. Absent radical social reorganization, to reject the private sphere is virtually to reject the notion of reliable opportunities for seclusion, anonymity, and solitude. One of the great benefits of decisional privacy respecting birth control and abortion is that it enables women to enjoy important forms of privacy at home. Decisional privacy is a tool women can use to create and control the privacy available to themselves and those with whom they chose to share their private lives. So too are options about marriage, employment, and careers.

It is sometimes said that women do not want privacy but something better than privacy: opportunities for affiliation and caring. Seen as a woman's free choice in an age of options, the rejection of individual forms of privacy can be viewed as an acceptable postfeminist development. Seen as an inauthentic preference shaped by a tradition that relegated women to subservient care taking roles in the private sphere, the rejection of privacy must be viewed as unacceptable and an occasion for consciousness raising. In either case, a frank tension of special relevance to feminism exists between the idea of opportunities for personal privacy and the ideal of active participation in, and contribution to, families and communities.

This tension is the reason for the second of the twofold problem of privacy—that women value concerned affiliation above individual forms of privacy. Psychologist Jean Baker Miller has contended that women do not want autonomy as it is defined for men, but "are quite validly seeking a fuller not a lesser ability to encompass relationships with others, simultaneous with the fullest development of oneself." Women aspire to make themselves more and more accessible to others with whom intimacy is desirable, while achieving goals of self-satisfaction and fulfillment. According to Miller, women have seldom achieved both aspects of this goal. Their roles as subservient caretakers have robbed them of sufficient opportunity for self-development while also narrowing the range of their relationships:

> To concentrate on and take seriously one's own development is hard enough for all human beings. But, as it has been recently demonstrated in many areas, it has been even harder for women. Women are not encouraged to develop as far as they possibly can and experience the stimulation and the anguish, anxiety, and the pain the process entails. Instead, they are encouraged to avoid self-analysis and to concentrate on forming a relationship to one person (Miller 1976, 95).

Women's caretaking roles may serve to explain why they have seldom been able to experience and enjoy privacy or to develop and enjoy autonomy. Women's caretaking roles might help explain why some women appear not to value privacy as men define it.

Carol Gilligan's well-known studies suggest that attachment, rather than autonomy, and caring, rather than abstract principles of justice, dominate the moral sensibilities of women. According to Gilligan, men and boys tend to engage in a mode of moral reasoning and moral discourse that emphasizes rights and justice, construed as equal treatment, reciprocity, or fairness. Women and girls tend to engage in moral discourse that emphasizes relationships, responsibilities, and caring. For men, morality is primarily an injunction to respect the rights of life and self-fulfillment. For women it is an injunction to care. For men and boys, morality consists of making and applying abstract rules. For women and girls, morality consists of discerning needs and fulfilling them as contexts demand.

Gilligan's studies suggest that for women, being alone can signify danger rather than peace and solace. In one study, women projected violence most frequently in the only picture portraying a person alone, whereas the men most frequently saw violence in the only picture in which people touched.[4] Gilligan concluded that men and women apparently experience attachment and separation in different ways and that each sex perceives a danger that the other does not see—men in connection, women in separation.

This has particular ramifications for American women's freedom to choose in the areas of birth control and abortion; for "while society may affirm publicly the woman's right to choose for herself, the exercise of such choice brings her privately into conflict with conventions of femininity particularly the moral equation of goodness with self-sacrifice . . . it is . . . in their care and concern for others that women have judged themselves and been judged" (Gilligan 1982, 70).

If caring for others in lieu of exploring opportunities for personal privacy is what women want and believe they ought to want, the question remains whether that is what they in fact *should* want. The implication of Gilligan's work for privacy seems to be this: If we want to put an end to the psychological predisposition of women to care themselves into oblivion, and if we want to put an end to the belief that they have a duty to do so, then women's interest in privacy—restricted access and decisional privacy— must be strenuously protected by our culture and our laws. This conclusion is in line with Gilligan's own observation that changes in women's rights change women's moral judgements. They season feminine caring with respect for individual autonomy. Or, as she put it, women's rights season "mercy with justice." Women must be able to consider it morally permissible to care for themselves as well as others.

As a group, women have done too much caretaking at the expense of their own development as individuals. Intrafamilial caretaking duties have required that women forego solitude. The mother of a small child cannot blissfully shut herself out and allow herself to be ignorant of the child's needs. From the point of view of privacy, no matter how much women may enjoy them, motherhood and traditional marriage have a cost. As wives and daughters to men in business and the professions, women have assumed the onerous caretaking duties of social hostessing in addition to intrafamilial duties. Privacy can be a welcome, deserved sanctuary from affected social exchange in which one must observe conventions of politeness and attentiveness.

A degree of personal privacy is an important underpinning of a workable, humane family and community. It is also an important underpinning of female personhood. Self-development does not require that women pursue a selfish degree of privacy that precludes concern for others. Women need not abrogate responsibility to enjoy privacy. While Americans may overemphasize privacy to the detriment of shared intimacy and responsive beneficence, the existence of privacy customs, even in human societies that are models of cooperative interdependence, seems to indicate that there is no essential contradiction between privacy and affiliative ideals. The past two decades of increased independence for women have signaled that what is worthwhile in our society can survive without women being forced inhabitants of the private sphere who devote themselves exclusively to caring for others. Although for some women a private place and private time at home are desirable because they make additional productive work possible, private time is viewed by many others as leisure time. The lofty ideals that ground the argument for privacy are no less legitimate in view of the sobering reality that some women, like some men, will choose to devote a portion of their leisure activities that promote neither careers, health, intellect, good taste, nor human bonds.

Respecting others' privacy does not require that we should each approve how others spend their time. It requires only that we be tolerant (Richards 1980). The moral case for privacy does not presuppose relativism about moral good. Without a doubt, certain private conduct, such as sexual child abuse, is immoral and because of the patent harm involved should be halted. The moral case for privacy does not presuppose relativism about tastes or about what constitutes human flourishing. Rather, it is grounded in the belief that individuals should be permitted to live out their disparate nonconforming preferences. Control of how others' private time is spent is inimical to pluralism and individuality. Democratic liberalism thus dictates that it be largely left to individual choice whether the opportunities for privacy furnished by custom and law are used for good or bad, high-brow entertainments or low. As John Stuart Mill urged, only where the safety or well-being of others is directly at risk should private life be opened to public scrutiny.

This notion has particular significance for women. Domestic violence must be counted among practices that have served to deny women the solace and peace of mind they would otherwise enjoy in their private lives. Wife-beating and sexual violence in the home deprive a woman of a sense of her own worth and must undoubtedly "help to emphasize her dependence and make it more difficult to face life on her own" (Finkelhor and Gelles, 1983). Legal questions have been raised about the extent to which the state may justly and usefully interfere with domestic relations for the sake of deterring and punishing spousal violence. It is increasingly recognized that men and women should not be able to escape punishment for gravely injuring one another, solely by virtue of marriage or cohabitation. In 1986, a man convicted of assault and involuntary deviate sexual intercourse under Pennsylvania's Spousal Sexual Assault Statute appealed his conviction. He argued on appeal that the constitutional right to privacy inherent in marriage placed his cruelty toward his wife beyond the reach of the law. Fortunately, the court rejected his argument and upheld the constitutionality of the Spousal Sexual Assault Statute as "another step in the erosion of the common law notion of married woman as chattel (*Commonwealth v. Shoemaker*, 1986). The privacy of the home and marriage are not properly permitted to shield violence that deprives women of the capacity to utilize opportunities for privacy in the domestic sphere.

Conclusion

THERE ARE A number of distinct contexts in which women's desires for privacy can be thwarted. Privacy, in its paradigmatic sense, is restricted access. Restricted access in the senses of seclusion, solitude, and anonymity is the desire of women trapped at home with children, women about to give birth in a room filled with technicians, women who crave intimacy, women harassed by intruders in the streets, women hounded at work, and women strip-searched in prisons. Restricted access in the sense of confidentiality, secrecy, and reserve is the desire of women who reveal themselves in diaries, women who are victims of rape, women who want control over information about their reproductive choices, and women who seek to avoid prejudicial disclosures about marriage and sexuality in the employment setting.

Privacy is also decisional privacy. Privacy in this sense is really an aspect of liberty: freedom from coercive interference. Decisional privacy is the desire of women who want to be free to obtain contraception and medically safe abortions. It is the desire of women who want to decide who will be present when they give birth, and want to choose how to care for their disabled newborns and how to raise their children. It is also the desire of women who want to be left alone in their choice to enjoy casual sex or exchange sex for pay.

Feminist theorists have illustrated how the concept of privacy has been utilized in Western thought to devalue women's work and reject their claims to equality and self determination. The central criticisms I make of the private sphere—as constituted by home and family life—are that women have been confined to it and that it has not always been a context in which women can experience and make constructive use of opportunities for privacy. Given privacy's special value, there must be contexts in the lives of women in which they can reliably anticipate meaningful opportunities for personal privacy.

I take my argument for real privacy to be consistent with feminist objections to the private sphere that equate "the private" with conditions of female repression. My criticism, however, is only of a poor quality of life within the private sphere and not a rejection of the concept of a separate, private sphere. I leave open the question whether a normative distinction between the public and private spheres can ultimately be drawn, and if so, what principles ought to govern individual, group and governmental conduct respecting each.

Women have served well their traditional roles as guardians of the private sphere. The social experiences of the sexes in our society are sufficiently different that men and women may have contrasting attitudes about their own privacy. Many women enjoy and relish caretaking roles. Many readily embrace lifestyles that diminish individual privacy. It must not be concluded too hastily on this basis, however, that women are not keen on individual privacy. One can only speculate whether women in a condition of full equality would exhibit a stronger or weaker preference for privacy; whether, if free to do otherwise, most would pursue affiliative ideals even to the point of self-oblivion. But it is evident now that many caring women enjoy privacy and would relish more of it for their work and leisure.

Women in the United States must have significant opportunities for individual forms of personal privacy and private choice. These opportunities enhance traits associated with moral personhood. They make women more able to contribute up to the level of their capacities and participate as equals. The problem, however, is not simply acquiring the personal and decisional privacy women do not have; it is also the problem of getting rid of unwanted forms of privacy, such as outmoded conceptions of female modesty and chastity, or confinement in nuclear family homes as traditional caretakers. Thus while it might seem that the relationship of women to privacy is uneasy, even paradoxical, it is really no paradox at all, for the privacy given up is not the privacy sought.

How can policymakers and individual actors be more responsive to women's special privacy problem of possessing too much of the wrong kinds of privacy? We can start by seeking to understand the legal, economic, and social bases of meaningful privacy and private choice. At the same time, conditions by virtue of which women face so much unwanted, pernicious privacy must be eliminated. Finally, the internal uneasiness many women experience with increased privacy and independent decision making must be dispelled. The required changes cannot be expected to come about all at once. Fortunately, some of the most important changes have already occurred. Greater opportunities for privacy were opened up for women when they won basic reproductive liberty in the courtroom. Many women have been able to take advantage of their decisional privacy rights to abrogate motherhood or control family size, thereby creating private time and conditions of privacy at home. In addition, the women's movement, federal civil rights laws, the sexual revolution, and pervasive participation by women in government, business, and the arts have each helped to create new norms of female conduct. Women are no longer expected to make heterosexual chastity and modesty their special virtues. Women's privacy has already acquired new and better meanings.

Notes

1. I typically use "private sphere" to refer to home, to family life within the home, and to the kinds of intimate personal relationships and activities commonly associated with them. By "public sphere" I mean all other sites, conduct, experiences, relationships, organizations, and institutions. In the sense in which I use "public sphere," the term applies equally to what goes on behind closed doors between a nongovernmental employer and employee in a privately owned office building and to what goes on in the open air in the middle of a municipal roadway.

2. Article 12 of the Universal Declaration of Human Rights, adopted by the United Nations General Assembly in 1948, provides that "no one shall be subjected to arbitrary interference with his privacy, *family home* or correspondence, nor to attacks upon his honour and reputation. Everyone has the right to protection of the law against such interferences or attacks" (emphasis added). Article 8 of the European Convention on Human Rights adopts similar language. See Velu (1973).

3. Cases such as *Griswold v. Connecticut, Roe v. Wade,* and *Planned Parenthood v. Casey* can also been read to protect constitutionally the privacy of all sexual and reproductive intimacy in the home. Yet, the Supreme Court has upheld the constitutionality of state laws criminalizing sodomy between consenting adults at home (*Bowers v. Hardwick*).

4. There are noteworthy limitations to Gilligan's studies (Tronto 1987). One serious problem is that most moral philosophers would be uncomfortable with Gilligan's classification of rights, fairness, justice, reciprocity, and equality as belonging to an ethic of "justice." The concept of justice, which has roots in classical antiquity, predated the concept of individual rights by many centuries. The Aristotelian tradition equates justice with a happy, whole society wherein individuals possess appropriate virtues and exercise role-based, contextual responsibilities (MacIntyre 1981). Furthermore, caretaking concerns can be couched in rules and "right-respecting" language: we can say women *need* free choice in the area of reproductive concerns, or they have a *right* to it. But if this is so, we have to rethink the reliability of Gilligan's methodology: perhaps some of the men who used the "masculine voice" did so in spite of underlying "feminine" ethical concerns, just as women may have used the "feminine voice" in spite of underlying "masculine" conceptions and concerns.

References

Allen, Anita L. and Erin Mack. 1990. "How Privacy Got Its Gender." *Northern Illinois Law Review* 10 (3):441–478.

Bowers v. Hardwick. 1986. 106 S.Ct. 2841.

Boyd v. United States. 1885. 116 U.S. 616.

Commonwealth v. Shoemaker. 1986. 518 A.2d 591 (Pa. Super).

Elshtain, Jean Bethke. 1981. *Public Man, Private Woman: Women in Social and Political Thought.* Princeton, N.J.: Princeton University Press.

Finkelhor, David and Richard J. Gelles, eds. 1983. *The Dark Side of Families: Current Family Violence Research.* Beverly Hills: Sage Publications.

Gilligan, Carol. 1982. *In a Different Voice: Psychological Theory and Women's Development.* Cambridge, Mass.: Harvard University Press.

Gilman, Charlotte Perkins. 1898. *Women and Economics.* Boston: Small, Maynard.

Griswold v. Connecticut. 1965. 381 U.S. 479.

Hall, Catherine. 1980. "The History of the Housewife." In *The Politics of Housework.* Ed. Ellen Malos. New York: Schocken Books.

Katz v. U.S. 1967. 389 U.S. 347.

Kennedy, Susan Estabrook. 1979. *If All We Did Was to Weep at Home: A History of White Working-Class Women.* Bloomington: Indiana University Press.

Klein, Ethel. 1984. *Gender Politics.* Cambridge, Mass.: Harvard University Press.

MacIntyre, Alisdair. 1981. *After Virtue: A Study in Moral Theory.* South Bend, Ind.: University of Notre Dame Press.

MacKinnon, Catherine. 1984. "Roe v. Wade: A Study in Male Ideology." In *Abortion: Moral and Legal Perspectives.* Ed. Jay L. Garfield and Patricia Hennessey. Amherst: University of Massachusetts Press.

Meyer v. Nebraska. 1923. 262 U.S. 390, 399.

Miller, Jean Baker. 1976. *Toward a New Psychology of Women.* Boston: Beacon Press.

Montaigne, Michele de. 1965. "Of Solitude." In *The Complete Essays of Montaigne.* Trans. Donald M. Frame. Palo Alto, Calif.: Stanford University Press.

Moore, Barrington. 1984. *Privacy: Studies in Social and Cultural History.* Armonk, N.Y.: M. E. Sharpe.

Okin, Susan. 1977. "Philosopher Queens and Private Wives: Plato on Women and the Family." *Philosophy and Public Affairs* 6:345–369.

Pearldaughter, Andrea M. and Vivian Schneider. 1980. "Women and Welfare: The Cycle of Poverty." *Golden Gate University Law Review* 10:1043–1068.

Planned Parenthood of Southeastern Pennsylvania v. Casey. 1992. 112 S.Ct. 279.

Richards, David A. 1980. *Toleration and the Constitution.* New York: Oxford University Press.

Roberts, John M. and Thomas Gregor. 1971. "Privacy: A Cultural View." In *Privacy: Nomos XIII.* Ed. J. Roland Pennock and John W. Chapman. New York: Atherton Press.

Roe v. Wade. 1973. 410 U.S. 113.

Schoeman, Ferdinand. 1992. *Privacy and Social Freedom.* Cambridge: Cambridge University Press.

Stanley v. Georgia. 1969. 394 U.S. 557.

Tronto, Joan. 1987. "Beyond Gender Difference to a Theory of Care." *Signs: Journal of Women in Culture and Society* 12:644–663.

Velu, Jacques. 1973. "The European Convention on Human Rights and the Right to Respect to Private Life, the Home, and Communications." In *Privacy and Human Rights.* Ed. A. H. Robertson. Manchester: Manchester University Press.

Westin, Alan F. 1967. *Privacy and Freedom.* New York: Atheneum.

11

Privacy, Publicity, and Power

A Feminist Rethinking of the Public-Private Distinction

Martha A. Ackelsberg and Mary Lyndon Shanley

*T*he distinction between public and private has been a central feature of liberal political discourse since its inception. Both classic and contemporary texts of political philosophy have debated understandings of public and private as part of a discussion about the place of politics, economics, and domestic life in human society. Many contemporary feminist theorists have criticized the public-private distinction for categorizing women's activities and household life as "private," and in doing so simultaneously excluding women from such public activities as voting or holding public office, and shielding what happens in the home, including violence against women and children, from public scrutiny (Pateman 1988, 1989; Okin 1989; Elshtain 1974, 1981). At the same time, feminists have also worked hard to develop the notion that women have various rights to privacy, from the right to retain custody of their children to the right to choose a life partner to the right to reproductive freedom.

Privacy is not something natural, prepolitical, or extrapolitical, but a politically constructed and contested good. Calling some activity or sphere of action private can, depending on the circumstances, either reinforce the allocation of power, goods and benefits along lines of race, gender, class, and sexual orientation, or constitute a claim to political power and autonomy. Disputes over what is private and what is public therefore cannot be resolved simply by greater refinement and precision in the definition of these terms; part of the definitional resolution will involve a political settlement.

In this chapter we examine various disputes over what American law and society should regard as public, what as private and as a way of sharpening our perception and increasing our appreciation of the political judgments inherent in any particular use of these terms. The permeable and mutable nature of the boundary between public and private makes their meaning constantly subject to renegotiation and change. When the issue of where to draw the line between public and private arises in legal and public policy debates, the deployment and configuration of political, economic, and social power is invariably at stake.

The History of the Public-Private Distinction in Western Political Theory

"Public" and "private" have always been defined, and have taken on political meaning, in relationship to one another. Aristotle, for example, in defining the public (or political) arena as the realm where free and equal citizens engage in striving together toward the common good, distinguished it from the private domain, which, he argued, was characterized by relationships of inequality, dependence, and concern for meeting the necessities of life. Political philosophy, as he understood it, dealt with the public world of citizenship and equality; relations among unequals (e.g., between freemen and slaves, men and women, parents and children) were necessary conditions of politics, but not properly the concern of political analysis.

Early liberal theorists retained a distinction between public and private domains, but shifted their focus of attention in significant ways. In addition to addressing public and political roles and responsibilities, they attempted to define a zone of privacy as a way of delimiting the power of the state. Taking individual freedom as their point of departure, liberals focused on protecting individuals against the arbitrary exercise of power, a threat they perceived as emanating primarily from the state. Thus, both Hobbes and Locke argued that the only grounds for depriving a person of his freedom—the only way one becomes obliged to obey the orders of another—is his own consent (presumably for his own protection). From this perspective, the "public" came to be understood both as the socially constructed realm of power and domination *and* (following Aristotle) as the site for the exercise of political freedom; whereas the "private" was taken to be an unconstructed realm of "natural" freedom, free from relations of power and domination properly understood.[1] Along with this division went the assertion that politics had to do with relations *between relative equals* in the artificially constructed public realm and that insofar as relations of inequality appeared in the private realm, they were "natural" in origin, and therefore irrelevant to politics.

These definitions led later theorists to explore two sets of issues: (1) what constituted "public" and "private" and (2) where the line between them ought to be drawn. First, the primary concern of theorists with respect to the "private" domain seems to have been to set limits on state power. A claim to privacy was a claim to a realm where others had no right to intervene. Conversely, this assertion of a distinction between public and private reflected the assumption that relationships within the so-called private realm, relationships of voluntary (economic) exchange, of intimacy, and of domesticity, were not about power. Second, the "private" was taken to include everything that was not "political"—that is, economic relationships, friendship and voluntary associations, and domestic and familial relationships.

By the late nineteenth century, the development of industrial capitalism, and, in particular, of Marx's critiques of relationships under capitalism, had led even many non-Marxists to expand the notion of the "public" to include economic activity. Theorists began to recognize both that relations of power and domination were structured into the so-called free market and also that concentrations of economic power deeply affected political relationships. Marxists criticized liberals for limiting their analysis of power to the realm of "politics" and insisted that the public, the realm where the analysis of power is appropriate, had to be extended to include economic—and especially market—relationships. Although this perspective offered a powerful critique of the dominant liberal view, it still left largely intact the liberal assumption that the remaining private (and therefore "natural") sphere was not an important locus of constructed power relationships and was, therefore, largely irrelevant to "politics."[2]

Hannah Arendt worked with this construction of the boundaries of public and private but returned to a more Aristotelian emphasis on the public. Arguing that there are, in fact, three realms of activity characterizing the human condition—labor, work, and action—she stressed the importance of "action" (analogous to Aristotle's notion of the public-political) as the expression of human freedom and dignity, the realization of each individual's unique personality. "Labor," by contrast, corresponds to the cyclical biological processes of birth, growth, and decay. It is defined primarily by necessity and takes place largely in the family, the domain of private or household. The activity of such labor—though necessary for the perpetuation of life and the species—is repetitive, uncreative, and private, and hardly expressive of the full range of human possibility. "Work" is characterized by self-conscious "fabrication" and construction and may involve collective activity that realizes important creative aspects of human personality. Nevertheless, it is limited; it remains focused on those tasks necessary to maintain human life, tasks so bounded by necessity that they do not provide opportunities for the expression of individual freedom. For Arendt, then, the distinction between "public" and "private" takes on much more the connotation it had for Aristotle; the "private" domain may be necessary and important for human *existence*, but human freedom is fully realized only in the public arena, where, as Mary Dietz put it, "the revelation of individuality amidst collectivity takes place" (Dietz 1991, 236; see also Arendt 1965, 1968; Pitkin 1981). In this formulation, Arendt provides an important link between earlier liberals and more radical participatory democrats insofar as what she defines as "public," or the realm of "action," is also the realm of democratic politics. At the same time, her claim that the realm of necessity (and significantly of economic inequality) has no place in politics links her to a more conservative tradition.

What remains common to virtually all these formulations (despite their differences as to what is included within the "public" domain) is an understanding of the private as domestic and a fundamental distinction between that realm and everything else. Where economics fits in this schema remains, to some extent, in dispute; but a wide variety of theorists agree that the domestic, intimate, familial, and sexual relationships belong to the private. Further, these thinkers limit analyses of power, and especially of political power, to the public domain.

Two democratic theorists did examine relationships among household members and how these might influence public life, with quite different results. Jean-Jacques Rousseau argued that the domestic education of boys and girls would influence their understanding and performance of their roles as citizens. Although the discussion of the socialization of citizens in *The Social Contract* is apparently gender-neutral and focuses on institutions and practices that allow for the realization of the General Will, Rousseau's more specific treatment of (moral) education in *Emile* is sharply differentiated by sex. In that text, the education of boys focuses on the development of their autonomy and independence while that of girls emphasizes their dependence and the importance of molding their behavior to conform to social expectations. For Rousseau, such differentiation and gender inequality (in the context of an overall insistence on human equality) was justified on the ground that family stability depended on gender-differentiated roles and behavior, and family stability was essential to social stability. Hence difference and hierarchy between family members was, in Rousseau's eyes, not inevitable or natural (although it rested upon inherent differences between the sexes) but socially necessary (Weiss 1987, 1990; Okin 1979; Lange 1991).

John Stuart Mill, by contrast, argued that because the moral training for citizenship began in the home, and because women should be active in political life, the education of boys and girls should be identical (or at least very similar). Mill also fervently believed that relationships of male domination and female subordination in the household would foster habits of willfulness in men that would be antithetical to the respect for reciprocity essential to democratic political life. Mill's belief that sexual equality in the family was a prerequisite for a fully democratic political life was, however, an exception among Western democratic theorists. For most, the household and the polity appeared to be of different orders and were to be evaluated by quite different criteria (Mill 1970, Shanley 1991, Di Stefano 1991).

Feminist Challenges to the Public-Private Distinction

FEMINIST THEORY OFFERS a rich and multifaceted challenge to the traditional understanding that public and private domains are conceptually distinct and that activities are easily assigned exclusively to one or the other. Feminists have explored the ways the distinction obscures the exercise of power within the so-called private realm, masks the maleness of the public realm, and ignores the ways the public-private distinction itself is a social construction that reflects the exercise of power and the allocation of resources in *both* realms. The main focus of our discussion here concerns the way the social construction of private and public involves profoundly political struggles that affect not only our understanding of these terms, but the status of those who have different resources and authority both as private beings and as citizens.

The publication of essays like Jean Bethke Elshtain's "Moral Woman and Immoral Man" (1974) and Teresa Brennan's and Carole Pateman's "Mere Auxiliaries to the Commonwealth" (1979) focused attention on the ways the construction of the public-private distinction in Western liberal thought masked the maleness of actors in the public realm. Elshtain pointed out that since Aristotle, a public realm defined as the domain of power and domination had been counterposed to a private realm ruled by moral principle. She noted that Machiavelli and Weber, as well as Aristotle, associated the private sphere with women who, because of their identification with it and morality, were effectively deemed unfit for political life. This split between morality and politics, women and men, necessarily relegated women to the sidelines, and severely restricted both the content and conduct of politics by removing women's voices and concerns from political debates, and denied the relevance of "morality" to political life (see also Kraditor 1965, Degler 1965).

Brennan and Pateman, for their part, showed that the supposedly gender-neutral citizen of a liberal polity was, in the writings of both Hobbes and Locke, clearly a male head-of-household. That and later work of Pateman's made clear that structures of political participation, understandings of the meaning of "consent," and notions of what constituted the autonomy necessary for citizenship were all predicated on unstated assumptions about the availability of individual citizens to participate in political activity. These unstated assumptions included, most significantly, that the daily activities of the nurturance and sustenance of the male "citizen" and his family would be taken care of by someone else, either his wife or other women of his household. But the question of any political role for those women, or of the nature of their relationship to the man, was completely ignored. Familial or household relationships were relegated to the status of "nonpolitical" or private issues. Thus, while the categories of "public" and "private" were central to classical liberal theory, the theory itself was quite unconscious about the gendered nature of its categories. The much-vaunted public sphere of democracy and participation was, effectively, the exclusive domain of men (Pateman 1980, 1988, 1989, 118–140).

Other theorists explored the implications of this split between public and private for a more feminist vision of the social and political order. Michelle Rosaldo, a cultural anthropologist who attributed universal "sexual asymmetry" to the gendered differentiation of public and domestic spheres of activity in virtually every known society, found the roots of that differentiation in women's association with childbirth and childrearing. Everywhere, she argued, the biological fact of women's childbearing is elaborated into a complicated social system in which "men, in their institutionalized relations of kinship, politics, and so on, define the public order," and women "are their opposite" (Rosaldo 1974, 34; see also 22–35). As a result, "characteristic aspects of male and female roles in social, cultural, and economic systems can all be related to a universal, structural opposition between domestic and public domains of activity" (1974, 35). Key to overcoming the subordination of women, Rosaldo argued, is the abolition of this dichotomous distinction—an abolition to be achieved, not only by women engaging in the public world, but by men "taking on the responsibilities of the home" (1974, 42). Public and private would, then, continue to exist as somewhat separate domains characterized by different types of activity, but the boundaries between them would no longer be coincident with gender divisions.

More recent critics—including Rosaldo herself (1980)—have questioned whether the distinction between public and private can ever be separated from its gendered origins and point, as well, to the dynamics of power and domination at the core of *both* dichotomies. They argue that revealing the dichotomous gender construction of the public and private was very important but the spheres are neither distinct nor discrete; injustices in one affect relationships in the other as well. Catharine MacKinnon has argued (1989), for example, that all male-female relationships, whether intimate or not, exist in the context of social structures that reflect and encourage male sexual domination of women. Even if not all relationships are directly affected by such domination, power imbalances infuse multiple dimensions of the social world:

> Men's physiology defines most sports, their health needs largely define insurance coverage, their socially designed biographies define work-place expectations and successful career patterns, their perspectives and concerns define quality in scholarship, their experiences and obsessions define merit, their military service defines citizenship, their presence defines family, their inability to get along with others—their wars and rulership—defines history, their image defines god, and their genitals define sex . . . . For each of men's differences from women, what amounts to an affirmative action plan is in effect, otherwise known as the male-dominant structure and values of American society (1989, 224).

Most specifically, MacKinnon asserts that legal rules and the legal system, while ostensibly gender-neutral, inscribe and perpetuate the power of men over women in both the so-called public *and* private domains.

More generally, feminist critics have demonstrated, it is impossible to distinguish once and for all what is public and what is private. Both concepts are socially constructed and implicated in the other; and what each encompasses changes with time and place. "Privacy" implies a realm of freedom and intimacy, sheltered from the incursions of other individuals or of the state, and guided by love and reciprocity rather than justice or power; this boundary, however, is anything but firm or impermeable. As Susan Moller Okin has argued, "The domestic sphere is itself created by political decisions, and the very notion that the state can choose to intervene in family life makes no sense" (Okin 1989, 111, 129). The categories public and private are mutually interdependent and cannot be evaluated apart from one another; therefore, feminist analysis must address the ways power is exercised within each realm as well as in the distinction between them (see also Olsen 1983).

It is impossible, then, to distinguish clearly and permanently "public" from "private"; not only is the meaning of each understood in part by contrast to the other, but each category contains aspects of the other.[3] To offer just one example: the family, the quintessential domain of privacy, exists by virtue of laws that define who and what constitute a family (see *Moore v. City of East Cleveland; Village of Belle Terre v. Boraas*; Olsen 1983; and Ackelsberg 1989). Legal definitions of "family" are contested not only by those who demand that the state recognize the "privacy" due to their nontraditional families (e.g., protests against midnight searches by state welfare departments in the homes of welfare recipients; or claims for domestic partner benefits for gay and lesbian couples) but also by those who demand that the state *deny* familial privacy to those who abuse women and children within families.[4]

At this point we might well ask whether the feminist critique of the public-private distinction has so revealed the gender-based and permeable nature of the concepts of public and private that we should throw them out altogether. We think not. These analyses of the indeterminacy of public and private suggest that the meaning and application of these concepts are the locus of severe political struggle. Feminists in the United States have repeatedly battled to redraw the boundaries of public and private and to reveal the political uses to which the public-private distinction has been put. Rather than attempting to develop yet another set of criteria by which these determinations might be made more effectively, we suggest that such an attempt can never finally succeed. An examination of several moments of contention over privacy reveals that what is at stake is not (or is not solely) the correctness of a definition but a struggle over the configuration and distribution of power and resources.

Power, Political Struggle, and the Public-Private Distinction

WOMEN'S RESISTANCE HAS often expressed itself in struggles over the boundaries of private and public. In the United States, such efforts have included the antislavery movement, the antilynching campaigns of the late nineteenth and early twentieth centuries, recent efforts to stop sexual harassment and domestic violence, welfare mothers' rights movements, and the gay and lesbian rights movement, to name just a few. In each of these cases, a challenge to the accepted legal or social understanding of what was public and what was private also called into question conventional views of gender, race, class, and/or sexual orientation. Sometimes the struggle to define public and private involved asserting a right to privacy for people who had been denied it and the freedom it entails; at other times it meant piercing a curtain of privacy that kept oppressive relations from public view and judgment. Always the struggle over the construction of public and private has gone beyond disputed definitions to address the exercise of power.

Slavery: Privacy and the Denial of Privacy

Black women under slavery led the effort to analyze the construction of the role of the public-private dichotomy in maintaining a system of racial and sexual domination. Thus, Harriet Jacobs's narrative of slave life (1987) made clear how defining the plantation as the slave-master's private domain made possible his virtually limitless power over black women and men. In claiming slaves as their personal property, slave owners denied slaves themselves any privacy. The fact that the legal system provided no realm of privacy—including marriage and family—for human chattel was one of Jacobs's most strongly-felt indictments of slavery (Jacobs 1987; see also Burnham 1987). As Jacobs explained, "If slavery had been abolished I, also, could have married the man of my choice; I could have had a home shielded by the laws; . . . but all my prospects had been blighted by slavery" (1987, 54).

Jacobs's appeal to Northern women abolitionists focused not so much on the denial of civil rights to black slaves, but on the denial of a private realm, which Jacobs seemed to treat as a necessary foundation of citizenship. To be chattel, Jacobs argued, means to have no private life. Not only is the individual at the constant beck and call of the master, but, more fundamentally, slaves are denied the privacy necessary for establishing and maintaining family life, setting conditions for their own lives, or expressing any independent will. The argument here, about public and private, is two-fold: (1) the denial of privacy to slaves is a violation of human rights; (2) the denial of privacy to slaves, as well as masking white male power by treating its abuses as "private," is a deeply political issue, one that allocates power and resources in ways that go far beyond the specific issue at hand. It affects not only the possibility of slave marriage but any recognition that slaves may claim human rights.

Challenges to Lynching as Challenges to Privacy

At the turn of the century, in her analysis of lynching, Ida B. Wells carried this argument forward in exploring the centrality of social understandings of the "private" realm of sexuality and sexual relations to the maintenance of white power in both the public and private arenas. Wells attacked the myth that lynchings were mob reactions to the rape of white women by black men. She documented the fact that the majority of those lynched in the South between 1896 and 1900 were not even accused of rape but were killed in response to economic competition, self-assertion, or "insubordination" (Wells 1977, 32–34).

Wells argued that the (false) link between rape and lynching revealed how myths about black sexuality provided an essential underpinning for white domination over blacks in both sexual (i.e., private) and political (i.e., public) domains. The stereotype of black male sexual appetite made consensual sexual relations between white women and black men appear impossible; any such relationship would be considered rape; hence, it was a matter of public concern and a justification for lynching. Because the black community well knew that the vast majority of lynchings were not responses to rape, but rather to other forms of challenge to white hegemony (e.g., economic competition, "insubordination," and so forth), and because occasions for lynching were almost totally unpredictable, lynching served as an instrument of terror that stifled black self-assertion and initiative in all areas of life. Conversely, the legacy of white men's ready access to slave women and the stereotype of black women's promiscuity made it virtually impossible for a black woman to claim that any relations between herself and a white man were *not* consensual. Hence, such relations were always regarded as private, and rape prosecutions were virtually unknown. The intersection of these stereotypes of race and gender thus affected people in both their intimate and their civic relations. Wells's analysis exposed the ways the distinction between public and private constituted an exercise of power, both by constraining the terms of debate and by undermining the possibilities of resistance (Wells 1977, 1990; Ackelsberg and Shanley 1992).

Taken together, Jacobs's and Wells's analyses illuminate two dimensions of public and private: Jacobs emphasized the importance of privacy, seen as autonomy and the ability to set the terms of one's life course, as a necessary condition of citizenship, whereas Wells demonstrated how some claims to privacy mask the exercise of power. Both these dimensions are manifest in some contemporary social and political movements that show how the distinction continues to be contested.

Welfare Rights and the Claim to Privacy

Those who have been recipients of public assistance—both in the United States and in many other Western countries—have often had to struggle for the recognition of any zone of privacy free from public interference. Even before the days of "friendly visitors" (forerunners of contemporary social workers), those who have dispensed public charity seem to have treated poverty as a manifestation of social incompetence that justified intervention by those more favorably situated.[5] Barbara Nelson (1990) has demonstrated, for example, that, from its origins in Mothers' Aid, Aid to Families with Dependent Children carried with it elements of intervention and social control that were far more exacting than those of Workmen's Compensation, Social Security, or unemployment insurance. Programs were designed with the sense that poor people either had no need for, or no right to, the kind of privacy generally granted to "citizens" as a matter of course. By the mid-1960s, spurred on by the consciousness-raising of the Civil Rights movement, black women welfare recipients strenuously objected to the unannounced late-night searches for a "man in the house" (presumably designed to protect the state against fraudulent claims for support) perpetrated by welfare offices against their overwhelmingly female (and often black) clientele. In those cases, both class and race seemed to conspire to devalue the privacy of welfare recipients; and the demand to be free from such searches associated a right to privacy with basic citizenship rights (Piven and Cloward 1979, Amott 1990).

Although those searches were discontinued, the assumption that the internal relationships of families receiving welfare benefits are "fair game" for public scrutiny remains and continues to be a focus of resistance on the part of recipients. Thus, Daniel Patrick Moynihan's characterization of black female-headed families as manifesting a "tangle of pathologies" attempted to justify public policy intervention in the family and became the subject of numerous attacks and counter-claims.[6] In the contemporary period, attempts to use criminal law and/or welfare policy to regulate fertility (via the implantation of progesterone patches to prevent pregnancy) or control marriage and childbirth (via proposals to penalize women for bearing children and/or to reward them if they marry) indicate that the line between public and private may be drawn very differently when those affected by the proposed policy are poor and/or nonwhite. The situation of female welfare recipients seems to deny them a zone of privacy in a way reminiscent of Jacobs's complaint about slavery. In this case, however, class and/or economic dependency, rather than race or slave status, seem to have become a justification for regulating sexual and reproductive life.

Domestic Violence and the Call for Intervention

While many aspects of the welfare rights movement highlighted the ways the denial of privacy to poor families constituted an inappropriate exercise of power, activists in the battered women's movement have argued that the state has traditionally been all-too-ready to declare the home off limits to public investigation and intervention in the face of accusations of spousal or child abuse. Police are often reluctant to make an arrest when answering a call about a "domestic disturbance": they might try to quiet things down and urge the husband/abusive partner to "cool off" and curb his temper. Prosecuting cases of domestic violence is often a low priority in District Attorneys' offices. Courts are sometimes reluctant to issue orders of protection, on the grounds that doing so might mean splitting up a family. Probation offices are often slow to serve orders of protection (Schecter 1982, Jones 1994).

Activists in the battered women's movement point out, however, that state reluctance to intervene in the family "has often served to reinforce the power of its economically or physically more powerful members." Abuses of power directed against women and children within the family may become difficult if not impossible to discern because of reluctance to scrutinize family relationships too closely. Noting that "between 1.8 and 5.7 million women in the United States are beaten each year in their homes," Susan Okin argues that "the privacy of the home can be a dangerous place, especially for women and children" (1989, 128–129). If law and society label intervention to halt violence and prosecute abusive action as "interference" in family matters, family privacy becomes a cloak for what, in another context, the law would recognize as criminal assault.

We noted above that the state and other public welfare groups have often been more willing to intervene in poor families than in middle-class or wealthy ones. The pattern seems to hold true for cases of spousal and child abuse, as well as in welfare rights cases. Yet, as Linda Gordon has noted in her study of the history of domestic violence, poor and working-class women have often called upon "outside" institutions for protection for themselves or their children, despite the danger that those agencies might be as likely to remove a child from a home characterized by poverty as to prosecute an abusive father or husband (Gordon 1988, 1990). Apparently, no matter the extent of their subordination both in the home and in the political arena, women who claim a right to be free from abuse and intimidation in their homes are recognizing an important connection between citizenship rights and the public-private distinction. The harm done by domestic violence affects its victims not only as private individuals but as public persons or citizens as well, and failure to prosecute such offenses not only denies justice to that individual but also intimidates all victims of domestic violence.

Gay and Lesbian Rights, Publicity and Privacy

As did women in the welfare rights movement, advocates for gay and lesbian rights have struggled for a right to the privacy of their domestic arrangements. At the same time, like advocates for battered women and children, they highlight the ways existing laws obscure the privileging of heterosexual relations in the same way that familial privacy obscures male power. The gay and lesbian rights legal reform agenda is multifaceted, including civil rights legislation to prevent housing and job discrimination, repeal of antisodomy laws, legal recognition of same-sex domestic partnerships or marriage, elimination of prejudice against divorced parents who are gay or lesbian in child-custody determinations, elimination of prohibitions against gays and lesbians being foster or adoptive parents, and repeal of the ban on military service for gays and lesbians. Not all activists support all these goals with equal fervor, and a debate has developed over the question of the desirability of legal marriage for same-sex couples. But a variety of organizations, including the National Gay and Lesbian Task Force, Lambda Legal Defense Fund, and the National Center for Lesbian Rights have all pushed for equal civil status for lesbians and gay men.

Many of the arguments for lesbian and gay rights invoke the argument that consensual sexual activity between adults is a private matter that should be shielded from state scrutiny. Criminal statutes against same-sex activity, which take the form of antisodomy statutes, seem to deny gays and lesbians rights of privacy that the Supreme Court articulated in a number of decisions during the 1960s and 1970s that we discuss later; and the prohibition against same-sex marriage seems to contradict the Court's ruling in *Loving v. Virginia* that the choice of a marriage partner is "one of the 'basic civil rights of man.'"[7] The struggle to obtain legal recognition of a right to privacy in consensual sexual conduct is, therefore, central to the agenda of the gay and lesbian rights movement.

The development of the legal right of privacy began in 1965, and seemed to hold out the promise that same-sex couples would, before too long, be able to invoke that doctrine to shield their relationships (and themselves) from charges of criminal activity. The Court's first articulation of a constitutionally protected "right to privacy" was found in *Griswold v. Connecticut*. *Griswold* struck down a Connecticut statute that prohibited both the use of contraceptive devices and the act of counseling others to use such devices. The majority opinion, written by Justice Douglas, argued that marital sexual relations belong to "a zone of privacy created by several fundamental constitutional guarantees." Seven years later, in *Eisenstadt v. Baird*, the Court held that this right of privacy pertained to individuals as such, not only to married couples: "If the right to privacy means anything, it is the right of the *individual*, married or single, to be free from unwarranted governmental intrusion into matters so fundamentally affecting a person as the decision whether to bear or beget a child." These decisions invoked privacy to protect the freedom of nonprocreative sexual expression for consenting adults.

The Court also displayed concern to protect consensual intimate relationships in *Loving v. Virginia*, which struck down a Virginia statute prohibiting marriage between white persons and persons of different races. The Court declared that marriage is a basic civil right and "one of the vital personal rights essential to the orderly pursuit of happiness by free men." The choice of a marriage partner was a liberty protected by the Due Process Clause that the state could not abridge. The Court held that antimiscegenation laws violated the Equal Protection Clause as well as the Due Process Clause. Such laws affected not only the possibility of marital intimacy but the civil equality of blacks and whites as well; antimiscegenation laws were inevitably "an endorsement of White Supremacy."

In light of this twenty-year history of protection for consensual sexual activity between adults based both on the privacy of sexual and procreative behavior and on freedom of choice of marital partner, many advocates of gay and lesbian rights were stunned when, in 1986, the Supreme Court held that the right of privacy did not prohibit states from outlawing acts of sodomy between consenting adults (*Bowers v. Hardwick*). Certain sexual acts, undertaken in what would have seemed to be the privacy of a bedroom, were defined as appropriate for public regulation. Since the Georgia sodomy law applied equally to heterosexual and homosexual activity, in upholding the statute, the Court seemed to retreat from its decision in *Griswold* that sexual relations within marriage are private and properly protected from the scrutiny of the state. At the same time, the Court misread the statute as concerning only homosexual sodomy. In basing its decision on the lack of any tradition recognizing homosexual sodomy as a protected activity, the Court made clear that what was at stake was the power of the state to privilege heterosexual marriage and to outlaw non-heterosexual intimacy.

In denying privacy to same-sex couples, the Court failed to recognize the importance of Harriet Jacobs's insight, echoed in *Loving v. Virginia*, that the right freely to construct relationships of intimacy is not only an essential human right but also an important foundation of citizenship. More recent struggles over repealing the ban on military service for gays and lesbians insist that all people be able to assume the rights and responsibilities of citizenship, regardless of sexual orientation. Military regulations that exclude (open) gays and lesbians from service deny (closeted) gay and lesbian military personnel the full expression of their personhood at the same time that they restrict one expression of citizenship for those outside the armed services. In constructing gay and lesbian relations (as distinct from heterosexual relations) as matters of public, rather than private, concern, both the courts and the military simultaneously deny a right to privacy and justify public interventions that reinforce heterosexual privilege.

The Thomas Confirmation Hearings and the Confusions of Public and Private

These and other social movements over the course of the last century have highlighted the ways the public-private distinction both masks and reinforces exercises of power in society on the bases of race, gender, class, and sexuality. At times, claims to privacy assert the civic personhood of those denied privacy; at other times, those same claims protect the powerful from challenges to their domination.

Many of these complicated dynamics of power were strikingly revealed in the Senate hearings on the nomination of Clarence Thomas to the Supreme Court. Anita Hill's charges that Thomas had sexually harassed her when she worked for him at the EEOC constituted a claim that his "private" behavior was relevant to the public debate on his suitability for the Supreme Court.

The dynamics of the Thomas hearings were very complex, with Thomas himself being the object of racial stereotyping and hatred, and his supporters invoking damaging stereotypes of black women (Morrison 1992, Painter 1992). By accusing the Committee of engaging in a "high-tech lynching," Thomas raised the specter of racism and the legacy of white supremacy in an effort to shield his behavior from public scrutiny. In casting himself as the victim of a racially motivated, trumped up charge of sexual misconduct meant to scuttle his rise to power, Thomas saved his nomination but distorted the analogy between his own situation and that of victims of lynching. His use of the analogy obscured the fact that his accuser was not a white woman or her white male "defender," but a black woman; and she was not a person more powerful than he but his employee.

By its nature, sexual harassment, "the imposition of unwelcome sexual demands or the creation of sexually offensive environments," is usually not witnessed by others even when it takes place in the workplace. Harassment often involves "anxiety, depression, and loss of status and self-esteem" for the individual, although for women as a group, it serves "to perpetuate views of females as sexual objects, to intimidate them from entering non-traditional occupations, and to impair their educational and employment performance, all of which reinforce patterns of gender inequality" (Rhode 1989, 231–232). According legal recognition to the concept of sexual harassment meant that behavior that had previously been treated as "private," and dismissed as "dalliance," "flirtation," "game," or "petty slights suffered by the hypersensitive" was now seen to have public consequences (the words and phrases are from a variety of Court cases, cited in Rhode, 235). Like domestic abuse, sexual harassment constitutes an exercise of power that limits women's "private" (in this case workplace) participation and, relatedly, her ability to exercise her rights of citizenship.

In the context of the confirmation hearings, Thomas successfully portrayed Hill and the Senate Committee, rather than himself, as guilty of violations of privacy. He denied that the behavior Hill complained of had ever taken place and contended that all questions about, or allusions to, his sexual behavior constituted inappropriate intrusions into his private life. Thomas was largely successful in his efforts to privatize those issues through arguments that manipulated both race and class identity (Crenshaw 1992). Thus, his accusation that the charges against him appeared racially motivated effectively silenced the all-white Senate Committee. No one thought to point out that the analogy was deeply flawed: Lynch mobs had used trumped-up charges of rape of white women to kill black men and terrorize the black community; no lynching recorded by Ida B. Wells or uncovered by subsequent research was perpetrated by an accusation from a black woman (Fraser 1992). Thomas appropriated black racial identity for himself and made Hill's racial identity invisible, rendering her symbolically white.

A similar strategy confused issues of class identity. Thomas consistently painted himself as a hard-working black man, who had scraped his way up from the poverty of his share-cropping grandfather. These images both called upon and challenged dominant stereotypes of the "lazy black man." At the same time, he contrasted his own climb to the top with that of his "welfare mother sister," who didn't know what to do when the check was delayed. As a number of commentators have pointed out, however, Thomas's self-presentation denied the ways his climb to the top—portrayed by him as his personal, "private" triumph over adversity—was facilitated by the policy achievements of the civil rights movement and affirmative action programs (Higginbotham 1992). Further, and more significant, he painted an inaccurate picture of his sister, which played heavily on conventional racial stereotypes of "black welfare mothers" (Collins 1990, Fineman 1991, Lubiano 1992). Left out of the story was the fact that his sister had only recently joined the welfare rolls and had been forced to do so when she undertook to care for their aging aunt, a "private" responsibility that had fallen to her rather than to Thomas, apparently, because of gender. Further, the hearings consistently erased Anita Hill's own class background (which was as poor as Thomas's) and identified her with her white, middle-class supporters. That identification made it difficult for the Senators (or the television-viewing public) to recognize the exercise of economic power or domination that constitutes an important (although usually hidden) component of sexual harassment.

Conclusions

BOTH "PUBLIC" AND "private" are contested and highly political terms. Not only is the line of demarcation between public and private socially, juridically, and politically constructed, but determinations of what is private and public are significantly influenced by sex, race, class, and sexual orientation. Many of those who have addressed issues of privacy have (rightly) pointed out how relegating women to the private domain kept them out of the public world of paid labor and political participation. Others, including Harriet Jacobs, have recognized that the ability not to be consigned by others to the private sphere but to claim it for oneself is an important right of citizenship and a significant measure of political power.

Nevertheless, although this overview suggests the importance both of helping women to assume public roles and responsibilities and of providing protection for individual autonomy, it also makes clear that to think of either "public" or "private" as a fixed category is misguided. There is no typology or set of procedures that will allow us to draw a line between public and private that will be appropriate for all times and circumstances.

The multiple uses of the word "privacy" around matters of human reproduction and family life show how deeply implicated questions of power and resources are in this term. Many women claim the right to use birth control or obtain an abortion as a right to privacy. Such an assertion insists that individual women, not individual men or the state, make these fundamental decisions about their procreative activity. At the same time, supporters of women's decisional autonomy also acknowledge that other aspects of childbearing and childrearing should not be thought of as private or affecting only women. The state should recognize its obligation to provide children with adequate nutrition, medical care, and education, and individual men should take responsibility for their sexual activity and the rearing of their offspring. Both the demands for reproductive rights and for recognition of the profoundly social dimension of care for children involve contestations over what is private and what is public about family life. If the resolution of those struggles seems to come from greater refinement in our understanding of those terms, it is because that refinement will incorporate political decisions about the configuration of decision-making authority and the allocation of goods and services both within the household and in the larger society.

Both the history of the public-private distinction in Western political philosophy and the variety of policy debates examined here indicate that when the line between public and private becomes a matter for public debate, we should take it as a signal to scrutinze the configurations of power that have a stake in the issue under discussion. What constellation of power is manifest in the existing practices? Whose power is being challenged by the claim of a right to privacy? Or whose interest would be served if the demand for public "intervention" were met? Although we cannot definitively draw a definitional line between public and private for all circumstances and all times, we must be alert to the issues of power and influence at stake in any particular attempt to do so.

Notes

1. See Locke (1963, pars. 4–9, 54–63, 95–99) on different kinds of freedom; also Rousseau (1978, Bk I, ch. 2,6,8) on the distinction between "natural" freedom and "political" or "civic" freedom.

2. In some of their writings, Marx and Engels seemed to acknowledge that families, for example, were also affected by relations of domination and subordination; but, for the most part, they saw these relationships as consequences of capitalism and thought such private hierarchies would disappear under socialism or communism. See, especially, Engels (1962, 217–241). For some important contemporary feminist critiques see Landes (1989); Hartman (1976, 1981); and O'Brien (1983).

3. For a useful summary of feminist perspectives on the public-private split see Pateman (1989) and Kymlicka (1990), esp. 247–262.

4. On this latter point, see Gordon (1988, 1990).

5. For an historical overview, see Polanyi (1957); Gordon (1988); and Lefkowitz and Withorn (1990).

6. See, for example, Rainwater (1967); also Stack (1974). Some of Moynihan's concerns about the structure and internal workings of black welfare families were taken up in new form in Wilson (1988), whose assumptions about welfare recipients were criticized by Fineman (1991).

7. As of 1989, sodomy was a crime in 24 states (editors of the *Harvard Law Review* 9); and in 1996, Hawaii's attempt to extend legal recognition to same-sex marriages is still being challenged in the courts.

References

Ackelsberg, Martha. 1989. "Redefining Family: Models for the Jewish Future." In *Twice Blessed*. Ed. Christie Balka and Andy Rose. Boston: Beacon Press.

Ackelsberg, Martha and Mary Lyndon Shanley. 1992. "Gender, Resistance, and Citizenship: Women's Struggles with/in the State." Paper presented at the Social Science History Association, Chicago.

Amott, Teresa. 1990. "Black Women and AFDC: Making Entitlement out of Necessity." In *Women, the State, and Welfare*. Ed. Linda Gordon. Madison: University of Wisconsin.

Arendt, Hannah. 1965. *On Revolution*. New York: Viking.

Arendt, Hannah. 1968. *The Human Condition*. New York: Viking

Bowers v. Hardwick. 1986. 106 S. Ct. 2841.

Brennan, Teresa and Carole Pateman. 1979. "'Mere Auxiliaries to the Commonwealth': Women and the Origins of Liberalism." *Political Studies* 27 2:183–200.

Burnham, Margaret. 1987. "An Impossible Marriage: Slave Law and Family Law." *Law and Inequality* 5:187–225.

Collins, Patricia Hill. 1990. *Black Feminist Theory*. Cambridge, England: Unwin-Hyman.

Crenshaw, Kimberlé. 1992. "Whose Story Is It, Anyway? Feminist and Antiracist Appropriations of Anita Hill." In *Race-ing Justice, En-gendering Power*. Ed. Toni Morrison. New York: Pantheon.

Degler, Carl. 1965. "Revolution Without Ideology: The Changing Place of Women in America." In *The Woman in America*. Ed. Robert J. Lifton. Boston: Houghton Mifflin.

Dietz, Mary. 1991. "Hannah Arendt and Feminist Politics." In *Feminist Interpretations and Political Theory*. Ed. Mary Lyndon Shanley and Carole Pateman. University Park: Pennsylvania State University Press.

Di Stefano, Christine. 1991. *Configurations of Masculinity: A Feminist Perspective on Modern Political Theory*. Ithaca, N.Y.: Cornell University Press.

Editors of the *Harvard Law Review*. 1990. *Sexual Orientation and the Law*. Cambridge, Mass.: Harvard University Press.

Eisenstadt v. Baird. 1972. 405 U.S. 438.

Elshtain, Jean Bethke. 1974. "Moral Woman and Immoral Man: Reflections on the Public Private Split." *Politics and Society* 4:453–473.

Elshtain, Jean Bethke. 1981. *Public Man, Private Woman: Women in Social and Political Thought*. Princeton, N.J.: Princeton University Press.

Engels, Friedrich. 1962. "The Origins of the Family, Private Property, and the State." In *Marx, Engels: Selected Work,* vol.2. Moscow: Foreign Languages Publishing House.

Fineman, Martha. 1991. "Images of Mothers in Poverty Discourses." *Duke University Law Journal* 1991:274–295.

Fraser, Nancy. 1992. "Sex, Lies, and the Public Sphere: Some Reflections on the Confirmation of Clarence Thomas." *Critical Inquiry* 18 (Spring):595–612.

Gordon, Linda. 1988. *Heroes of Their Own Lives.* New York: Viking.

Gordon, Linda. 1990. "Family Violence, Feminism, and Social Control." In *Women, the State, and Welfare.* Ed. Linda Gordon. Madison: University of Wisconsin Press.

Griswold v. Connecticut. 1965. 381 U.S. 479.

Hartman, Heidi. 1976. "Capitalism, Patriarchy, and Job Segregation by Sex." In *Capitalist Patriarchy and the Case for Socialist Feminism.* Ed. Zillah Eisenstein. New York: Monthly Review Press.

Hartman, Heidi. 1981. "The Unhappy Marriage of Marxism and Feminism." In *Women and Revolution.* Ed. Lydia Sargent. Boston: South End Press.

Higginbotham, A. Leon, Jr. 1992. "An Open Letter to Justice Clarence Thomas from a Federal Judicial Colleague." In *Race-ing Justice, En-gendering Power.* Ed. Toni Morrison. New York: Pantheon

Jacobs, Harriet A. 1987. *Incidents in the life of a Slave Girl.* Cambridge: Harvard University Press.

Jones, Ann. 1994. *Next Time, She'll Be Dead: Battering and How to Stop It.* Boston: Beacon Press.

Kraditor, Aileen. 1965. *The Ideas of the Woman's Suffrage Movement.* New York: Columbia University Press.

Kymlicka, Will. 1990. *Contemporary Political Philosophy: An Introduction.* Oxford: Clarendon Press.

Lange, Lynda. 1991. "Rousseau and Modern Feminism." In *Feminist Interpretations and Political Theory.* Ed. Mary Lyndon Shanley and Carole Pateman. University Park: Pennsylvania State University Press.

Lefkowitz, Rochelle and Ann Withorn. 1990. *For Crying Out Loud: Women and Poverty in the United States.* New York: Pilgrim.

Locke, John. 1963. *Two Treatises of Government.* Ed. Peter Laslett. Cambridge: Cambridge University Press.

Loving v. Virginia. 1967. 388 U.S. 1.

Lubiano, Wahneema. 1992. "Black Ladies, Welfare Queens, and State Minstrels: Ideological War by Narrative Means." In *Race-ing Justice, En-gendering Power.* Ed. Toni Morrison. New York: Pantheon.

MacKinnon, Catharine. 1989. *Toward a Feminist Theory of the State.* Cambridge, Mass.: Harvard University Press.

Mill, John Stuart. 1970. *The Subjection of Women.* In John Stuart Mill and Harriet Taylor Mill, *Essays on Sex Equality.* Ed. Alice S. Rossi. Chicago: University of Chicago Press.

Moore v. City of Cleveland. 1977. 431 U.S. 494.

Morrison, Toni. 1992. "Introduction: Friday on the Potomac." In *Race-ing Justice, En-gendering Power*. Ed. Toni Morrison. New York: Pantheon.

Nelson, Barbara. 1990. "The Origins of the Two-Channel Welfare State: Workmen's Compensation and Mothers' Aid." In *Women, the State, and Welfare*. Ed. Linda Gordon. Madison: University of Wisconsin Press.

O'Brien, Mary. 1983. *The Politics of Reproduction*. Boston: Routledge and Kegan Paul.

Okin, Susan Moller. 1979. "Rousseau's Natural Woman." *Journal of Politics* 41:393–416.

Okin, Susan Moller. 1989. *Justice, Gender, and the Family*. New York: Basic Books.

Olsen, Frances. 1983. "The Family and the Market: A Study of Ideology and Legal Reform." *Harvard Law Review* 96 (7).

Painter, Nell Irvin. 1992. "Hill, Thomas, and the Use of Racial Stereotype." In *Race-ing Justice, En-gendering Power*. Ed. Toni Morrison. New York: Pantheon.

Pateman, Carole. 1980. "Women and Consent." *Political Theory* 8 (2):149–168.

Pateman, Carole. 1988. *The Sexual Contract*. Stanford, Calif.: Stanford University Press.

Pateman, Carole. 1989. "Feminist Critiques of the Public/Private Dichotomy." In *The Disorder of Women: Democracy, Feminism, and Political Theory*. Stanford, Calif.: Stanford University Press.

Pitkin, Hanna. 1981. "Justice: On Relating Private and Public." *Political Theory* 9 (3):327–352.

Piven, Frances Fox and Richard A. Cloward. 1979. *Poor People's Movements: How They Succeed, Why They Fail*. New York: Pantheon.

Polanyi, Karl. 1957. *The Great Transformation*. Boston: Beacon Press.

Rainwater, Lee. 1967. *The Moynihan Report and the Politics of Controversy*. Cambridge: MIT Press.

Rhode, Deborah. 1989. *Justice and Gender: Sex Discrimination and the Law*. Cambridge, Mass.: Harvard University Press.

Rosaldo, Michelle Zimbalist. 1974. "Woman, Culture and Society: A Theoretical Overview." In *Woman, Culture and Society*. Ed. Michelle Zimbalist Rosaldo and Louise Lamphere. Stanford, Calif.: Stanford University Press.

Rosaldo, Michelle Zimbalist. 1980. "The Use and Abuse of Anthropology." *Signs* 5 (3):389–417.

Rousseau, Jean-Jacques. 1978. *On the Social Contract, with the Geneva Manuscript and Political Economy*. Trans. Judith R. Masters and ed. Roger D. Masters. New York: St. Martin's Press.

Schechter, Susan. 1982. *Women and Male Violence: The Visions and Struggles of the Battered Women's Movement*. Boston: South End Press.

Shanley, Mary Lyndon. 1991. "Marital Slavery and Friendship: John Stuart Mill's *The Subjection of Women*." In *Feminist Interpretations and Political Theory*. Ed. Mary Lyndon Shanley and Carole Pateman. University Park: Pennsylvania State University Press.

Stack, Carol. 1974. *All Our Kin*. New York: Harper and Row.

Village of Belle Terre v. Boraas. 1974. 416 U.S. 1.

Weiss, Penny. 1987. "Rousseau, Antifeminism, and Woman's Nature." *Political Theory* 15 (February):81–98.

Weiss, Penny. 1990. "Sex, Freedom, and Equality in Rousseau's *Emile.*" *Polity* 22 (Summer): 603–625.

Wells, Ida B. 1977. "Lynching and the Excuse for It." *The Independent*, May 16. Reproduced in *Lynching and Rape: An Exchange of Views*, by Jane Addams and Ida B. Wells, edited and with an introduction by Bettina Aptheker. Occasional Paper no. 25. New York: American Institute for Marxist Studies.

Wells, Ida B. 1990. "Lynch Law in All Its Phases." In *Ida B. Wells-Barnett: An Exploratory Study of an American Black Woman, 1893–1930.* Ed. Mildred I. Thompson, vol. 15 of *Black Women in United States History.* Brooklyn, N.Y.: Carlson Publishing.

Wilson, William Julius. 1988. *The Truly Disadvantaged.* Chicago: University of Chicago Press.

12

All the Comforts of Home
The Genealogy of Community

Shane Phelan

Community has been an ideal of Western political thought at least since Christianity. In its related form of nationhood, it has been an intimate, everpresent part of the fabric of political theory. Whether in Plato's abstractly ordered republic, in the lives and writings of the Hebrews, in Augustine's City of God, in Marx's vision of Communist society, or in feminist models of political structure and process, the desire for mutual belonging and recognition has been central to politics and theory.

The last century has shown us the potential horrors of a politics conducted in the name of peoples, nations, or ideologically constructed communities, but the last half of that century has also witnessed a resurgence of the claims of communities and peoples. In forms as diverse as Sandinista Nicaragua, Lithuanian self-determination, lesbian and gay politics, the nationalisms of peoples of color in the United States, and contemporary conservatism, we see the continuing appeal of community as a vision of human relations that resists the advance of the modern state. This return leads us to ask whether it is possible to honor the desire for community or whether it belongs as a relic of an immature past, occasionally bursting forth but never to be fully let loose. We can and must, however, move beyond those alternatives, based on that vision and desire, to see whether there is another way to think community that is neither tragic nor totalitarian.

I will examine the identitarian and deconstructive presentations of community and argue that neither of these can do the job we need. Producing genealogies of community/ies may, however, enable us to locate (which is not to ground) political action without naturalizing or reifying the identities involved in that action.

Identitarian Community

WHAT DIFFERENTIATES COMMUNITY from other social interactions and structures? This may be the hardest part of theorizing about community/ies,
for there is tremendous ambiguity about the term. Sociologists have used
"community" to designate virtually any group of people on the basis of a
bewildering variety of characteristics: George Hillery has stated that the
only thing shared by sociological definitions is that "they all deal with people" (Hillery 1955, 117). Political theorists have used the term in a multitude of ways from the Stoic and Christian *communitas* to juridical notions
of "community standards." Thomas Bender defines community as "a network of social relations marked by mutuality and emotional bonds," by
"shared understandings and a sense of obligation," by "affective and emotional ties rather than by a perception of individual self-interest" (Bender
1978, 8). R. M. MacIver and Charles Page assert that "wherever members
of any group, small or large, live together in such a way that they share, not
this or that particular interest, but the basic conditions of a common life,
we call that group a community. The mark of a community is that one's life
may be lived wholly within it" (MacIver and Page 1962, 8–9). Anthony
Black argues that a community is "the unit upon which every human being
depends for his or her sense of who they are and where they stand in the
scheme of things" (Black 1988, 87). In these presentations community is
not a matter of shared goals or principles (except secondarily) so much as
one of shared lives.

In many of these definitions, a community is defined by the common
characteristics of the membership. Within community, these become
something more than characteristics; they stretch out to become identities.
Thus, when Michael Sandel says that communities help members to
become less "opaque" to themselves, he is referring to the ways in which
common understandings and practices create not only the knowledge that
comes from familiarity but the knowledge that comes from common identity (Sandel 1982, 172–173).

There are several versions of this sort of argument. In the fullest ascriptive presentation, our common identity is based upon a primordial bond, a
"natural" basis for community. For example, Judy Grahn's search for lesbian history ascribes an identity based on sexual practices and cultural
roles across times and cultures (Grahn 1985). Even many ascriptivists, however, recognize that the "natural" basis of community can only develop into
full community through social relations that foster a collective consciousness, a recognition of others as like ourselves. The crucial element is the
recognition of others as bound to us and like us. Self-reflection can then
aid us in knowing about others, and observation of others may tell us
important things about ourselves. Further, this identification requires that
we understand ourselves not simply as "like another" in certain discrete

ways but as sharing a common identity, a common membership within a concrete community.

We can also imagine and form nonascriptive communities that are nonetheless based in mutual identification or consciousness of kind. In this view, communities are voluntary associations of individuals. They are distinguished from family, geographical, or political units into which we are born in that we choose to enter and remain and can choose to leave without logical contradiction or legal consequences. Thus Julia Stanley says that a community is "composed of individuals who have many ideas and experiences of our lives that we share" (Stanley 1978, 6). She states that "one joins a community because she finds companionship, support, and commitment to common ideals within that community," and that this community is "internally defined by its members on the basis of shared experiences and common interpretations of events in the real world" (6–7). Here a community is fully voluntary: Stanley distinguishes a community from a subculture, which is based on external definitions of the identities of the members. A community, and the identity of its members, on the other hand, is consciously chosen and fashioned by those members. Here we see both a voluntarist conception of community and a use of that conception to distinguish stigmatized, externally imposed identities from valorized, self-fashioned ones. It is, in Gramscian terms, an attempt to wrest hegemony over the definitions of the members' lives from the dominant culture. The community is defined not simply by interaction or bonds or understandings but is also (at least implicitly) defined as autonomous from a "society" or "culture" that marginalizes a given group. In the community, it seems, one is always in the center.

In this case it appears that a community can never be ascriptive. If we choose our community, the identity we achieve or recognize there is not a pregiven datum. Things are not that simple, however. What is involved here is a process of rearticulation that reascribes us, as it were, not necessarily by challenging notions of primordial or "true" identity, but by relocating our identities. We may thus refer to "created communities," not in stark contrast to "natural" (ascriptive) ones, but along a continuum of relations between space and time on the one hand and consciousness on the other.

This voluntarist notion of community goes back at least to the early Christians, who distinguished their religious relationships among themselves from their political, kinship, economic, or gender relations. As Sheldon Wolin has explained, the Christian vision of community contained "ideals of solidarity and membership that were to leave a lasting imprint, and not always for good, on the Western tradition of political philosophy" (Wolin 1960, 97). The early Christian church arose in a period of empire, in which most people (and especially women) had no say in the major issues of political life. Increasing inequality and popular disempowerment left a ripe field for a religion that urged its adherents to focus on another world. This search for God's will, this focus on the next life, in fact bound Christians together on earth. The Christian community was one that denied the spiritual importance of temporal inequalities among its members, although it did not require their elimination. Through a sharp separation of physical from spiritual, Christianity could reject hierarchies and still coexist with them. The "community of believers" provided a counterweight to the alienation of imperial subjection and loss of public meaning. The community shared a common goal, common norms for behavior, and common values.

Although the church and its priests were acknowledged not to be perfect, the contrast between the "community" as a nonpolitical entity of common values and understandings and "society" or "polity" as a realm of limited bonds and veiled force has continued to dominate Western thought to this day. Today, the community is the other of the state: whereas the state, center of power and force, operates through regulation and bureaucracy, "community" is seen as the spiritually rich site of meaningful interaction and voluntary action.

There are several questions for us to ask of this double. We can easily undermine the presentation of community outlined above by pointing to the play of power within understandings, values, and norms. We can deconstruct the opposition between meaning and power, understanding and power. This is especially urgent for groups and individuals who are consciously aiming at greater diversity and openness in their theory and practice. This deconstruction has been done extensively and thoroughly by many feminists. Iris Young argues that traditional understandings of community as the alternative to the impersonal state "can reproduce a homogeneity that usually conflicts with the organization's stated commitment to diversity" (Young 1991, 235). She locates the problem in the model of community as "copresence of subjects" that mandates self-transparency and transparency to others. This vision of community rests on the same logic as that of identity as self-presencing, as a place of noncontradiction. This in turn assumes that the self is a unity, that it need not be accounted for. The consequences of such an assumption are a failure to inquire into the technologies of self that have gone to construct that self, its desires and aims, self-understandings, and explanations of conflict in terms of personal failures. Neither ascriptive nor voluntarist conceptions of community, therefore, do the work that feminist theory and politics require.

Community as Compearance

ONE OF THE virtues of the communitarian approach is its reminder that shared characteristics are not sufficient for community; "shared characteristics," in fact, only exist as such within a given community of understand-

ing. Without such understanding, there is no reference by which to characterize anything. Communities are not formed of or by individuals with pre-
existing "characteristics" unless they are sharing a characterization
borrowed from another community. Rather, the characteristics are created
over time as part of building a community.

Thus, we see that community is constitutive in an important sense.
Communitarians, however, have too often taken this to mean that the community preexists its members. If questioning stops here, we find a reified
"community" that constitutes individuals, without itself requiring constitution. Community does not preexist its members, but consists in "the singular
acts by which it is drawn out and communicated" (Nancy 1991a, 152). This
does not, however, mean that "we" perform "acts" that we thereby designate
as "community"; this would be a return to liberal positivism. Rather, it means
that communities do not exist outside of our common activities. We are still
constituted by community, but that does not give to community a prior, separate existence, for community is simultaneously constituted by us.

In *The Inoperative Community* (*La commonaute desoeuvree*) and later work,
Jean-Luc Nancy argues that community is a matter of "being-in-common,"
in which "being-with" is not a modifier or predicate of being but is the
ground of being itself. Thus, the way in which beings are is always already
in common; there is no such thing as being without community, being
without being-in-common. As Nancy puts it, "community is simply the real
position of existence" (1991a, 2). Humans do not arise in isolation, as the
communitarians remind us, but neither does "the community" exist
beyond the being-in-common of particular people. Community is not only
constitutive of us; community is performative, consisting only in the
process of being-in-common. There is no "community" beyond this,
although there are institutions, geographical locations, and populations.
These, the centers of communitarian thought, are more often the sites of
the denial of community in favor of identity, of the common, the same.

This usage of "community" seems to defy our common understandings
of the word. Generally, community appeals not just to that which is simply
"in common" but to "the common," the *same*. Community has been firmly
entrenched within the logic of the same that mandates self-identity and
unity among members. In such definitions, community becomes an
essence, a thing to be studied and acted upon and used. In Nancy's terms,
such essentializing amounts to "the closure of the political" (xxxviii), shut-
ting us off from the insecurity and instability of actually being-in-common
and wrapping us in common being, in sameness. Politics, the art of being-
in-common, is eliminated when we fix identities and locations in this way.
This helps us to see that our "common understandings" of community trap
us into antipolitical postures even as we try to valorize "differences."

While Nancy's description has something in common with the sociological descriptions of community/ies as sites of human interaction, there is a

crucial difference. Most of the sociological definitions assume a stability and autonomy to the self that Nancy's version lacks. If communities are seen as sites for interaction among preexisting persons, then the assumption is that the self is not substantially formed by its environment—the liberal fallacy. If they are treated as sites of constitution of selves, then the self is historically denser but not necessarily problematic: we can now say that "the community" shapes the individual, without questioning the identity of that community. In order for this to be satisfying, however, we must make the second error: assuming the stability and sufficiency of community. By "stability" I mean relative harmony and sufficient univocity that the person produced by the community will "have an identity" with herself. The "community" that constitutes us is unified and fixed enough to have an identity ("the community") with a clear history, values, and aims. It is this assumption that leads communitarians to see community as a source of strength, as "home," as the opposite of alienation. The self is reinforced by its community.

Nancy's presentation differs from these in its questioning of the root of community, being-in-common. Rather than being a source of support, Nancy's "being-in-common" is the locus of anxiety and vertigo that the Western philosophical tradition has fled from. Drawing on Heidegger's instruction about being, Nancy argues that being-in-common means not stability and identity but "*no longer having, in any form, in any empirical or ideal place, such a substantial identity, and sharing this* (narcissistic) '*lack of identity*'" (xxxviii; emphasis in original). Community is the arena in which we are forced to recognize the play of forces and desires that are human experience. Identitarian accounts and expectations of community are precisely the repression of this anxious reality.

A mundane example will serve here. Robert Nisbet states that the "archetype, both historically and symbolically" of community "is the family, and in almost every type of genuine community the nomenclature of family is prominent" (Nisbet 1966, 48). This has certainly been the case in feminism, as many writers have agreed (e.g., Martin and Mohanty 1986). Some have argued that this is a dangerous metaphor for community and I agree. But what is important here is the crucial question: how many of us experienced a family or home that was in fact what the rhetoric of community invokes as a model? Not only is "home" a bad metaphor for "community," it is a false model of home! Most homes are probably a perfect example of Nancy's description of community—as the primary site of being-in-common, they exemplify all the terrors and conflicts he describes. Although Nancy's discussion is more focused on the ontological than the everyday, this example points to the uses of deconstructive thinking about community. It is not sufficient to "wean ourselves," to give up the security of home; agency requires that we confront the myth of the secure home, the myth of the origin itself.

Nancy is not arguing that community is an unachievable ideal, as many have. He is not arguing that it is a lost mode of existence, a hostage of modernity or capitalism. Rather, he is arguing that it is a fact of everyday existence, but that it is suppressed in the search for "community"; because it does not look like the Greco-Christian model that fixes community as "the common," as identity of selves and interests, community is overlooked and denied. For Nancy, community is the ground of all possibility, but an unstable, shifting ground. Attempts to fix it are flights from community toward identity, flights from being-in-common to being common. The danger in this flight is precisely the "complacency that threatens any discourse of community," which is "to think that one is (re)presenting, by one's own communication, a co-humanity whose truth, however, is not a given and (re)presentable essence" (Nancy 1991b, 9).

The history of "lesbians" provides a useful example of this process. "Lesbian" is not an ontological category divorced from social reality but is an appearance of being that occurs only in certain place/times. There is no such thing as a lesbian without the category lesbian, and there is no such category outside of a human community. Lesbians "compear" (in Nancy's term, literally "appear together") only in and through community. This does not mean, however, that lesbian identity is simply solidified in community. Compearance does not mean mutual support for stable identity but continually threatens it. Compearance, Nancy states, "is of a more originary order than that of the bond" of one subject to another; "it consists in the appearance of the *between* as such" (Nancy 1991a, 29). Being-in-common means being with others, but this is the opposite of "being common." Being common is the continual denial of community in favor of oneness. Community in fact works to destabilize identity, as our being with others brings us face to face with multiplicity and differences. Thus, community is not a place of refuge, of sameness, but is its opposite.

The essentializing of community and the essentializing of identity and the subject are complementary. For example, the struggles among lesbians over race and class have produced a situation in which these characteristics are not only important, but vital; failure to address them and their effects is unacceptable. Too often, however, middle-class white women have participated in these struggles in ways that prevent us from fully addressing "others." We learn the words to use, the adjectives that I suspect for many are modifiers of the basic noun "lesbian." However, we are continuing to essentialize when we simply use these words—"Chicana," "working-class"—as though they refer to stable, homogeneous characteristics or identities. This sort of essentializing tells us that we already know about those with whom we are in common, because we know some labels and so (think we know) some characteristics. It enables us to retain the idea of community as a thing by compartmentalizing it, accounting for its various segments and spaces.

The modern subject, the unified, self-reflective, and autonomous originator of its actions and emotions, is a concept that makes being-in-common impossible to conceive. Even as we are drawn to community, the allure of the subject limits our ability to think beyond models of association or ascription. A full thinking of community requires that we move past the subject as origin or fixed point to a self that is a node of communications.

What is left if we give up that subject and its objects? We are left. We who live in the density of immanence but never wholly so. As compearance, we live our lives immediately, in the given, but never simply *as* the given. As a space for presencing, community is more of a continual possibility, and an urging toward possibility, than a reality. Invocations of community/ies are calls for spaces of presencing, but when those calls become criteria for membership they betray community.

Compearance as presencing together, community as compearance, is a "negative" concept (Hoagland 1988, 3). Following our example, we may say that "lesbian" has no positive content, no "meaning" by which we measure ourselves. Lesbian is a name given by heterosexuals to designate those who differ from them, and a criterion for designation. "We lesbians" may reverse that, saying that we can change the meaning of the word, but this is simply substitution. In either event, the naming of lesbians appears here to be an injustice. The naming of lesbians is the attempt to fix identity, to provide a determinate content by which we shall know ourselves and one another.

The rejection of fixed identity on the part of lesbians contributes to the destabilization of the idea of the "feminist community" as well. The "women's community," lesbian code for the lesbian community, has always been an inadequate way to express the plural alliances and affinities of lesbians, or of feminists of any sexuality. The reassuring unity prescribed by early feminist accounts of lesbian identity has increasingly given way to recognition of the diversity of lesbian lives. "The community" has become a "place that is unknown and risky, that is not only emotionally but conceptually other; a place of discourse from which speaking and thinking are at best tentative, uncertain, unguaranteed" (de Lauretis 1990, 138). This is always the fate of the ideal of community; it is due not to a failing of a conception, nor a political defect, but to the tension within community itself, which is, within being-in-common. As an ideal of harmony and wholeness, community can never satisfy its own demands. As the lived ground of human existence, community is never whole or harmonious, but it is precious nonetheless. We can best realize community in our lives not by willing it directly but by continuing to call it into existence, by compearing as our never-the-same selves.

Getting Specific About Community

ALTHOUGH THE STRONG communitarian position seems to lead too often toward direct entailments between personal identity and political position, the deconstructive view leaves too much room. The antidote to totalitarian thinking seems to be continual deconstruction of identities and ways of life. This is a crucial and unfinished project for a planet filled with resurgent nationalisms, but it is insufficient to address concrete political struggles. Without some fixing of identity, however provisional, common action will not occur. It is here that specificity becomes crucial. Getting specific can make the link between the recognition of the ontological insecurity of community and the daily solidity and reality of particular communities.

Communities may be nouns in the English language, but that does not make them things. Rather than abandon "community," I propose that feminists think of it as a process. In the process of community, personalities are created. Persons do not simply "join" communities; they *become* microcosms of their communities, and their communities change with their entrance. As Mary Follett puts it, "Our loyalty is neither to imaginary wholes nor to chosen wholes, but is an integral part of that activity which is at the same time creating me" (Follett 1912, 580–581). In her focus on process, Follett shares a certain awareness with Nancy of the becoming of community. She does not, however, use that awareness to abandon identity altogether. She is a communitarian but certainly no lover of static communities and traditions. Her focus on process impels us toward a vision of communities, as of individuals, as constantly becoming.

Using Follett's notion as a guide, let us return to the problem of community. I want to argue that "communities" engage in four major processes. These processes do not all constitute and occur in every community at every time, but if none of them are operative I would not say that there is a community.

First, a community provides a space of taken-for-grantedness, a space where we are supported. Lesbian community, for example, insulates lesbians from hostility to their sexuality. That community is the place or space (in a nongeographical sense) where it is "alright (or even better) to be a lesbian," where being a lesbian is simply not an issue. Thus, lesbian community/ies may enable a lesbian to stop reacting to heterosexual presumptions, anxieties, attacks, and imperatives and to envision and build a life she chooses.

Second, a community can be a beacon for those who would become members. This is not the same as insulation or protection. A community presents the possibility of being a member and thus presents the possibility of certain ways of being. Prior to the emergence of a mass feminist movement, those women we now might call feminists were either "neurotic," "independent," or "exceptional." In Betty Friedan's classic phrasing, the daily malaise of sexist oppression was "the problem that has no name." Feminist movements provide the opportunity for women and men who reject sexism to identify with others, even others they will never meet.

Communities also model behavior and help members and new entrants interpret their lives. This is a crucial function of any community, ascriptive as well as elective. Even "ascriptive" communities do not accept that anyone of a certain heritage is doing that heritage right—one may be called a "bad Jew," a "traitor to the race," and so forth. These statements rest on an implicit assumption that identity is known through group membership and that that membership carries unambiguous mandates for living one's life. This modeling process need not be rigid or narrow, although it often is; communities are also sites for the negotiation of membership standards.

Finally, communities may provide the base for or result of political mobilization. By "political mobilization" I mean the movement out of the community into the hegemonic cultural, legal, and political systems. The gay liberation movement was built on the communities that earlier activists had fostered, but lesbian feminist communities arose out of shared opposition to gay male and heterosexual feminist politics. Early 1970s lesbian-feminist groups were explicitly feminist and political (Echols 1989). These locations and their descendants operate/d as "free spaces," training centers for citizenship and activism that extend beyond the group itself to form alliances with other groups for common ends (Evans and Boyte 1992).

Clearly a given community can engage in some of these processes without doing the others. Just as important, the nature of a community will depend crucially upon which of these are seen as central to it. The aura around the word "community" leads us to certain expectations that rest on and reinforce the call of identity, of sameness, and it is this that needs disconnection. Nancy's deconstruction, however, is insufficiently politically oriented to serve as more than a philosophical reminder against identitarian hubris. We need an analysis that bears his points in mind while recognizing the political necessity of common construction and (limited) identity.

Although we cannot hope magically to eliminate the aura around community, we may be able to limit it by getting specific about the histories and our expectations of our communities. A genealogy of modern communities and identities can provide us with the denaturalization and the historical location that are simultaneously needed to rethink community. I will make this point by contrasting a genealogical, 'specific' approach to community with the two alternatives I have just outlined.

Against communitarianism, genealogy brings a recognition of the price of communal identities, traditions, and institutions. Often this may amount to nothing more than shifting perspective to see who is excluded within "their own" community. For example, Jewish women are and are not "Jews." As Cynthia Ozick relates,

> In the world at large, I call myself, and am called, a Jew. But when I sit among women in my traditional shul and the rabbi speaks the word "Jew," I can be sure that he is not referring to me.... When my rabbi says, "A Jew is called to the Torah," he never means me or any other living Jewish woman.... My own synagogue is the only place in the world where I am not named Jew (Ozick in Pogrebin 1991, 50).

Ozick calls attention to the very concrete, everyday way in which she is not included in "her" community, in the community in which Jewish men would surely locate her. This sort of exclusion occurs for many of us: women in male-dominated institutions, lesbians within the category "women," people of color among "nonracially defined" groups. Calling attention to the actual implicit requirements for membership is part of getting specific about who and what we are talking about.

Susan Okin has performed this task for the communitarian theorists who present a harmonious and ordered world. By pointing to the domination and exclusion in the traditions they celebrate, and by calling male communitarians to task for their failures to acknowledge these, she reveals their communities to be just that—*their* communities (Okin 1989).

This is a critique that is needed and that is familiar to all feminists and lesbians. In one way or another, we have been made acutely aware of our exclusions or silences. This critique is not enough, however. What is needed is a further examination of the exclusions and productions *within* the "central" population, of the production of the hegemonic selves celebrated by the communitarians. This has been the forte of deconstruction, the source of its disturbing power. All those who have been attached to the idea of stable, unitary identities as the basis of order or change have been distressed at the disruptive effects of such views.

A view that serves only to remind us of the provisionality of our identities is a step in the right direction away from identitarian politics, but in itself, it is only a step. Although the fixing of identity is a form of oppression, it is crucial that we examine the particular identities provided or imposed on us. Whereas rich white heterosexual men do indeed "suffer" from identity and its discontents, their suffering is rather drastically different from that of welfare mothers, people of color, gays and lesbians, or any other stigmatized and/or deprived groups. The virtue of specificity as a methodological imperative is the ability to demarcate various overlapping sites of struggle in a social space. Where the communitarians would cover struggle up or sanitize it, and the deconstructionists sometimes express unease with a politics that rests on identity (which is to say, virtually any group politics), the genealogist can and must recognize both the ultimate provisionality of identities and their daily solidity in relations of power.

Genealogy and Exclusion

WHITE MIDDLE-CLASS FEMINISTS' position as insiders on the outside while outsiders on the inside requires attention to the ways in which we, as insiders, build "our" communities. The process of becoming central is always a process built on a logic of opposition. Although some exclusion is the inevitable coproduct of doing community, the dynamics of exclusion make this a more complex and dangerous process than may appear at first. In justifying the exclusion of nonfeminists, we necessarily rely upon implicit or explicit ideas of what "those people" are like. This must be contrasted to what "we" are like if we are to be able to distinguish feminist contexts, subcultures, and communities from nonfeminist ones. Although we may be able to make a contrast that seems nonhierarchical, the contrast can only become meaningful for us, can only be relevant, if certain virtues or vices are associated with these practices. Thus a genealogy of feminist communities must first examine who feminists contrast themselves to in order to become feminists.

The construction of "a" feminist community has also excluded those who do not fit the implicit model of a feminist. Such models are imparted not only through words and pictures, through direct statements such as "feminists are/do such and such," but are also transmitted through the concrete daily practices of such a community. A community centered on a bookstore will not be a community that values illiterate women. A lesbian community that is monolithically aligned with feminism will feel alien to lesbians who either are not feminists or have no interest in feminism.

Constructions function through opposition and difference, and this will not change because "we" want to be inclusive. Feminists of all positionalities may strive for nonreactive constructions, those that begin in affirmation of self rather than denigration or expulsion of the other. This is not a goal to be fully achieved, however, but a limit to be approached. My purpose here is to suggest that rather than finding a way to entirely eliminate this dynamic, we must urge ourselves toward greater self-consciousness about the political and cultural contexts and effects of our constructions. Feminists (and nonfeminists as well) need to be willing to face the reality of exclusion if we are to engage in it responsibly. Denial that "we" exclude others (whichever "we" is in question at the time) serves not to convince those excluded that they are welcome but to prevent solidarity across differences and exclusions that might even be productive. It is to present ourselves as unreliable and irresponsible. Exclusions, to the extent they are needed, must be acknowledged and argued about.

Specificity and the Limits of Identity

GETTING SPECIFIC IS crucial for white middle-class feminists because, as we think our way through community and political allegiances, we face two temptations. On the one hand, it is tempting to forget that we are in fact central within our communities. This leads us to retain self-images as marginal, as powerless, as necessarily radical and democratic. On the other hand, we may celebrate our centrality within "feminist communities," replaying the motifs of harmony, of univocity, of free self-disclosure and transparency. Both of these are inducements to avoid the pain of liminality.

A more specific theory aids in resisting these temptations by bringing us face to face with the multiplicity of factors and forces that have made our lives. When I refuse to essentialize or naturalize womanhood, or lesbianism, when I say that these do not exist without their respective categories, I do not do so to deny that women in the past and present have lived their lives through these categories and experienced them as "natural." I mean to highlight that contemporary gender and sexual identities are inextricably bound up with the rise of sexology and other discourses that did not just liberate but created and targeted populations for policing. These discourses are not relics but still play a large part in most of our lives. This forces us to acknowledge that communities will never be simply a place of coming together as whole selves but will be the site of pain, confusion, and anxiety as well as love, acceptance, and security.

To an extent, this is being done. However, we have only begun this process, and there are many pitfalls ahead. The first is to imagine that we can solve this problem by pluralizing community—to refer to "communities" instead and have done with it. Thus we might have a "white lesbian community," a "Chicana lesbian community," a "disabled lesbian community," and so forth. This is useful in some cases, where there actually are communities of the sort being referred to. But this raises two problems.

First we have the problem of internal difference. No matter how many modifiers we attach to "community," we will not eliminate difference(s). The modifier approach enables us to shut down some conflict by making implicit exclusions explicit, but it does not deal with the basic problem. How do we decide which modifiers rate a "community" of their own and which are simply characteristics of individuals? This is not a question that can be resolved theoretically. This is a matter of politics, confrontation, and contestation. Further, this approach continues to rely on the logic of the same by implying that when we parse them down enough, we will find groups that are the same enough—common enough—that they will agree on how to live and what to do. This rests on the fallacy of identity—the belief that our actions and ideas are *simply* the product of social location, so that if we "specify" the location tightly enough we will be the same.

bell hooks addresses the defects of this position when she argues against feminism as an identity and in favor of feminism as a position that one advocates—a "movement to end sexist oppression" (hooks 1984, chap. 2). As an identity, feminism becomes a "lifestyle" that allows one to feel radical without doing anything—"withdrawing from the system" becomes as valuable as changing it. A focus on identity also forces people to polarize between "feminists" and "nonfeminists," whereas a political commitment is more flexible. This is the second problem with simple multiplication of communities: as a single strategy, this does not provide members of different communities with any reasons for common action. The usual situation, an external challenge to a shared characteristic, is not a reliable basis for common action because it is too easy to get disgusted with or tired of the "others" that one is "forced" to work with. Simply put, adjectives will not a political force make.

A specific theory of community, then, will acknowledge that communities are indeed locations for the production of meaning and value, that this is a worthwhile, even vital function in human life. However, this production is not simply the manifestation of what we have in common (this elusive "we") but must be the site of questioning who "we" are and what "we" are doing together. Rather than basing community on what we have in common, we can only come to community by negotiating about what we will have in common, what we will share, and how we will share it. Our language cannot be that of simple ascription, where we know who we are in advance, and it cannot be that of total voluntarism. We are thrown together, we lesbians, we feminists, we women, we humans; but we are not thrown randomly into a world without history.

Against strong deconstructionist views, genealogy insists on the reality of provisionally fixed identities and locations and mandates that we examine not just the differences between us but also the linkages. If we are to embark on political change, we need something between old-fashioned interest group liberalism and strong community. Genealogies of community help us adjudicate among and perform the functions of community.

Genealogy does not "insulate" us from hostility if by that we mean never having to be conscious of it. Feminist communities are not simply detachable from the social formations that surround them and in which we grow up and live much of our lives. Therefore, we cannot ask that "our" communities do so. They can, however, provide a space for critical distance from those larger formations. This distance, this "breathing room," is a crucial function of feminist community, but it is not to be bought at the price of grand theories of identity and truth.

As a visible space for the "presencing" of feminist values and processes, a community of feminists is responsible for refusing the bait of identity. Feminists should not be concerned to present "the" feminist position on any given issue but must open public discussions to the range of feminist perspectives and concerns. Thus, our visibility needs to be strongly detached from the temptation to present icons of feminism. Such a community will know its own history and will know where that history fades into obscurity. It will not be afraid of the truth of its history.

Rather than engaging simply in identity consolidation, a feminist community informed by its own specificity will welcome the specificity of each new member's mode of life. The role of interpretation must be separated from that of gatekeeping, or to put in differently, our feminisms must become more porous and plural. This requires a shift from logical discourse (someone is a feminist if and only if . . .) to narratives of feminist lives. How then does one know if a given person is a feminist? This paranoid question must give way to others—what does this person's feminism mean for her? What does her life have to teach us? This is a move from a logic of exclusion through demarcation to a logic of inclusion, enlarging both the community and the meaning of feminism. Lest anyone fear that this meaning will become too vague to be useful, we must remember that this process is occurring within a society with its own strong notions of what feminism is; it will police our borders for us. Rather, feminists must refuse the narrowing of possibilities that consistently occurs in political debate in the United States.

Finally, more specific theories will foster political mobilization. Genealogies of particular communities can show us exactly what forces are working to produce a community and to make the other three functions so necessary. They will lead us to the avenues of change in particular places. Although grand theories posit single causes and huge, monolithic forces, genealogies help us to see the cracks and breaks, the places to drill and chip and huff and puff. They show us particular "local" causes of situations and thus aim us toward their elimination or transformation.

Getting specific about community/ies means that we acknowledge both the appeal of the communitarian call to wholeness and the deconstructive challenge to such calls. More important, however, it moves at a tangent from this debate to address the historical and contemporary foundations of these process/entities we call "community" to address, not what needs to be done to really have community or how to live without it or with the recognition of its instability, but how we have and do construct the communities we live in, what discourses we are living within, their costs and hidden implications. Getting specific provides the link between identity politics and broadbased movements for change by bringing identities out of their isolation and into a world of multiple locations and discourses. This means moving beyond (though not dispensing with) community to alliances, from identity to justice.

References

Bender, Thomas. 1978. *Community and Social Change in America*. New Brunswick, N.J.: Rutgers University Press.

Black, Anthony. 1988. *State, Community, and Human Desire: A Group-Centred Account*. New York: St. Martin's.

de Lauretis, Teresa. 1990. "Eccentric Subjects: Feminist Theory and Historical Consciousness." *Feminist Studies* 16 (1):115–157.

Echols, Alice. 1989. *Daring to Be Bad: Radical Feminism in America 1967–1975*. Minneapolis: University of Minnesota Press.

Evans, Sara M. and Harry C. Boyte. 1992. *Free Spaces: The Sources of Democratic Change in America*, with a new introduction. Chicago: University of Chicago Press.

Follett, Mary P. 1912. "Community is a Process." *The Philosophical Review* 28 (6):576–588.

Grahn, Judy. 1985. *Another Mother Tongue: Gay Words, Gay Worlds*. Boston: Beacon.

Hillery, George. 1955. "Definitions of Community: Areas of Agreement." *Rural Sociology* 20:111–124.

Hoagland, Sarah Lucia. 1988. *Lesbian Ethics: Toward New Value*. Palo Alto, Calif.: Institute of Lesbian Studies.

hooks, bell. 1984. *Feminist Theory: From Margin to Center*. Boston: South End Press.

MacIver, R.M. and Charles Page. 1962. *Society*. New York: Macmillan.

Martin, Biddy and Chandra Talpade Mohanty. 1986. "Feminist Politics: What's Home Got to Do with It?" In *Feminist Studies/Critical Studies*. Ed. Teresa de Lauretis. Bloomington: Indiana University Press.

Nancy, Jean-Luc. 1991a. *The Inoperative Community*. Minneapolis: University of Minnesota Press.

Nancy, Jean-Luc. 1991b. "Of Being-in-Common." In *Community at Loose Ends*. Ed. Miami Theory Collective. Minneapolis: University of Minnesota Press.

Nisbet, Robert. 1966. *The Sociological Tradition*. New York: Basic Books.

Okin, Susan Moller. 1989. *Justice, Gender, and the Family*. New York: Basic Books.

Pogrebin, Letty Cottin. 1991. *Deborah, Golda, and Me: Being Female and Jewish in America*. New York: Crown.

Sandel, Michael. 1982. *Liberalism and the Limits of Justice*. Cambridge: Cambridge University Press.

Stanley, Julia. 1978. "Lesbian Relationships and the Vision of Community." *Feminary* 9 (1):4–9, 57–60.

Wolin, Sheldon. 1960. *Politics and Vision*. Boston: Little, Brown.

Young, Iris Marion. 1991. *Justice and the Politics of Difference*. Princeton, N.J.: Princeton University Press.

13

Reflections on Families in the Age of Murphy Brown

On Gender, Justice, and Sexuality

Iris Marion Young

*I*n May 1992, Murphy Brown gave birth cantankerously to a strapping baby born before millions of television viewers.[1] To the amazement and amusement of many of us, the next day Vice President Dan Quayle denounced Murphy Brown in a speech to the Commonwealth Club in San Francisco. She's gone too far when she has a baby with no father. An independent woman such as this is a dangerous role model.

It is no coincidence that Dan Quayle's speech came as America was rocketing from the experience of its greatest disorder since the 1960s: the uprising in Los Angeles. Normalcy was suspended, chaos reigned, fear and anger gripped our cities. The world was turned upside down: African American street gang members appeared on national television as authoritative news analysts.

Dan Quayle's castigation of Murphy Brown works as an appeal to the basis of all order, The Family. The Family means original unity and comfort, a presocial pastoral state of nature without encounter and conflict with strangers. It means an orderly hierarchy of father, mother, and children, where authority is clear and each knows his or her place and duties. Appeal to The Family evokes visceral feelings of comfort and security. As I will discuss below, The Family draws a clear boundary between legitimate and illegitimate, but like all boundaries it is arbitrary. Evocation of danger to or dissolution of The Family conjures up fears of identity loss, exposure, extreme vulnerability, what Quayle called "lawless social anarchy."

Whenever uttered in America today the decrying of single motherhood would have a racial subtext, but in the context of this our great disorder the text was not very sub. The root cause of the riots in Los Angeles is the break- down of the family in the ghetto. Black women irresponsibly, shamelessly have babies without fathers, they sponge off taxpayers and can't give the kids a decent life. Being only mothers, they cannot discipline their sons, who run loose on the streets with guns and torches. The Law of the Fathers is our only hope against being swallowed in the conflagration. "Children need love and discipline. They need mothers and fathers. A welfare check is not a husband. The state is not a father. . . . Bearing babies irresponsibly is simply wrong"(Zoglin 1992).

As apparently intended, Dan Quayle's speech launched a summer- long presidential campaign debate on "family values." What might have looked like solid ground for the status quo and conservatism turned out to be pretty muddy terrain. Although Republicans and Democrats quietly colluded in letting the issue of racism in the cities sink back into its nor- mal rumbling silence and tacitly agreed that single mothers are a social problem, polls bounced around about what good families are and the policies to support them. While Colorado voters approved of an antigay referendum, for the first time in American history a party's candidate for president explicitly supported some rights for gay men and lesbians (though not marriage). The same candidate was able to turn Republican opposition to family leave against them and to tie the issue of family values to economic recovery.

In the indomitable American way, the drama climaxed on television. There is a general rule in American journalism that the press is not sup- posed to report on events that are about to occur. But in the third week of September 1992 this cardinal rule was flagrantly broken, as media eyes focused on the still to come fall season premier of *Murphy Brown*. *Time* magazine featured Candice Bergen, who played the role of Murphy Brown, on its cover, sporting a "Murphy Brown for President" button. On the morning before the evening of the great season premier, no less a publica- tion than the *Wall Street Journal*—so staid and respectable that it never prints photographs, only artist rendered sketches—printed an editorial on "Murphy Brown's Baby." It too lambasted the fictional Murphy and resounded Quayle's alarm at poor single mothers. "Not many disagree now," they said, "that the best cure for childhood poverty is a live-in-dad."

The trope of The Family and its invocation as the signifier of order touches such deep chords in the American heart that for many years radicals have been in a rhetorical retreat from the brazen calls for the abolition of marriage and the pluralization of life styles that were typical of the late 1960s and 1970s, as well as typical of earlier Emma Goldman types of radicalism. Those of us who seek to undermine the oppressions of straight women, gay men and lesbians, and people of color of both sexes and sexual orientations, however, should do what we can to break the mystical hold of The Family on people's minds. As the terrain becomes more slippery, we may get a foothold for change; and we may also get mud in our eyes.

In this chapter I consider how issues of gender and sexuality should be analyzed as issues of justice. Applying some of my previous work on justice, I argue that the dominant distributive paradigm of justice is not well suited for conceptualizing many of the issues of justice most central for feminists, issues involving sexuality, reproduction, and family. Those few theorists of justice who do analyze issues of justice and family tend to presuppose the institution of marriage as given, and I will argue that their reliance on the distributive paradigm can account for this.

A feminist theory of justice should criticize the institution of marriage itself on the grounds that it draws an arbitrary line between legitimate and illegitimate relationships and accords special privileges to the former. Thus I consider what a conception of families should be that does not specifically privilege some relationships but rather extends the privileges, protections, and obligations currently restricted to married couples and their children to other kinds of relationships. Law, policy, and social practice should break the linkages that currently exist between heterosexual coupling, partnership, parenting, and property rights. The Family should be deconstructed into a series of rights and obligations.

Justice, Gender, and Sexuality

IN RECENT YEARS certain feminist philosophers such as Susan Okin (1989), Joan Tronto (1991, 1993), Marilyn Friedman (1987), and Sara Ruddick (1992) have questioned the assumption, held by many feminists, that justice should be opposed to care, or that concepts of justice cannot serve feminist moral theorizing about family, sexuality, and personal relations.[2] This development in feminist moral theory is overdue, in my opinion. As the primary political virtue, justice should be central to feminist moral theory and politics. As Susan Okin rightly and forcefully argues, moreover, the history of male theorizing about justice ignores male domination and male privilege as issues of justice, largely because they wrongly assume that family relations are prior to or outside of the realm of social relations to which issues of justice apply. The issues of sexual liberation, reproductive rights, sexual division of labor, equality in family relations, and so on, that are central to feminist politics must be understood as issues of justice. This implies, I suggest, a need to rethink the meaning of social justice beyond the distributive paradigm that dominates in contemporary Anglo-American philosophical approaches to justice.

In *Justice and the Politics of Difference* (Young 1990) I have defined and criticized this distributive paradigm. It assumes that all questions of justice are about the distribution of social benefits and burdens among individual and groups. These benefits and burdens may be tangibly measurable, such as income received or tax paid. But distributive theorists also speak of intangibles like power and self-respect as goods distributed among agents, a way of speaking about power and self-respect that I believe wrongly reifies relations and processes.

Due to the rejection of the concept of justice as relevant to the specific moral and political concerns of feminism, there are very few philosophers who have considered moral issues of gender as issues of justice. Most of the few who do analyze gender issues as issues of justice work within the distributive paradigm. James Sterba (1991, chap. 5), for example, restricts his understanding of issues of justice to the distributive questions of equal opportunity and welfare. He argues that a feminist conception of justice conceives human traits as evenly distributed across sexes and that this implies a transformation of the family in such a way that there would be no gender specific roles in it.

Susan Okin's is probably the best known and most thorough account of issues of gender and justice (Okin 1989). After criticizing important male theorists of justice, including Rawls, for ignoring issues of justice in the family, she modifies Rawls's theory of justice as fairness to apply to relations between men and women in the family. When radically applied, she argues, Rawls's principle of equal liberty and equal opportunity must imply an abolition of a gender division of tasks and status. Most particularly, the sexual division of labor that allocates primary responsibility for household labor and childrearing to women must be eliminated. Although such reforms require change in attitudes and behavior of most men and many women, they also imply specific and far reaching changes in both government and social policy—to support child care services, parental leave policies, and more flexible and family-sensitive public workplace policies.

In extending Rawls's conception to the family, Okin relies on a distributive paradigm of justice. The social injustice that women suffer consists in our having fewer benefits and more burdens in the general pattern of social distribution.

> Political power and office, hard work, money and commodities, security—
> Are any of these things evenly distributed between the sexes? In each case,
> the assignment of women to the functional role of actual or potential wife
> and mother, and primary parent, to basic or at least periodic dependence
> on a man, has a great deal to do with the fact the women, in general, ben-
> efit less from the benefits and are burdened more by the burdens in the
> distribution of social goods than are men (Okin 1989, 113–114).

There is no denying the claim that women suffer distributive injustice. Issues of distribution are important issues of justice, and this is as true for questions of gender justice as other kinds of questions. But it is a mistake to reduce all issues of justice to issues of distribution for two primary reasons. First, the distributive paradigm tends either to distort or ignore issues of justice not easily conceived of in distributive terms. Second, the distributive paradigm tends to presuppose institutional structures within which distributions take place as given, without bringing the justice of those institutional structures themselves into question.

The distributive paradigm conceives all issues of justice as packages of goods that are possessed by individuals. With this paradigm philosophers and political actors tend to focus on issues like the distribution of property, income, or jobs as the primary issues of social justice. When applied to feminist issues, this focus foregrounds issues of equal opportunity, the distribution of positions, tasks, economic and social resources between men and women, but ignores or obscures many issues of gender justice that are not so obviously distributive. Thus neither Sterba nor Okin, for example, include issues of sexuality and reproduction in their discussions of gender and justice; I believe this omission can be traced at least partly to their applying a distributive understanding of justice.

One can argue that what is most original about contemporary feminist politics is its raising the most private and personal realms of sexuality and reproduction as public issues of social justice. The systematic harms and inhibitions brought upon women as individuals and as a group by prostitution, pornography, rape, incest, and sexual harassment cannot obviously be conceived as distributive inequalities. These entail systematic issues of justice that are broadly speaking cultural: concerning the organization of sexual practices, the meanings attributed to them, and the representational and symbolic forms associated with sexuality.

Some of the injustices suffered by men and women who wish to form sexual partnerships with people of their own sex can perhaps be conceived in distributive terms. Conceiving injustice toward gay men and lesbians in terms of discrimination, that is, the denial of benefits on arbitrary grounds, uses a distributive concept. But many gay men and lesbians find this too narrow an understanding of their oppression. Violence, stereotyping, stigma, and similar oppressions are not well covered by a distributive paradigm; issues of justice and sexual orientation also turn on the cultural meanings of masculinity and femininity and, like the above issues of the sexual oppression of women, the representational and symbolic forms associated with sexuality.

Justice in procreative and parenting relations is equally ill conceived in distributive terms. Selma Sevenhuijsen argues that the attempt to apply Rawlsian principles of justice to child custody disputes yields absurd results. For cases where parents dispute about who will have primary custody over their children or about what rights the noncustodial parent will have, it is not at all clear what can be seen as distributed. Conceiving the children as objects to be distributed among parents surely does not respect those children. But it is also conceptually weird to think of rights as the subject of distribution. Justice in custody disputes instead concerns attention to the concrete relationships between parents and children, and the most appropriate way to create enforceable right to foster and facilitate the most beneficial set of intimate relations (Sevenhuijsen 1991).

Many other contexts of reproduction and parenting raise issues of justice not fruitfully conceptualized as involving the distribution of some kind of goods. Practices of contraception, abortion, surrogate pregnancy, in vitro fertilization, lesbian and gay parenting, and so on raise complex issues of justice and policy questions of how law and bureaucracy should morally conceive and structure relationships, a set of questions not assimilable into a distributive understanding of justice.

When philosophers or political actors try to raise issues of justice not obviously about the distribution of goods, they usually try to reconceive them in terms of costs and benefits distributed among social actors. Such reconceptualization, however, often distorts what is at stake in questions of justice when they are about decisionmaking power, the definition of social positions and their relations and obligations, or culture and life style.

The recent Supreme Court decision on abortion rights can illustrate this distorting effect. Many hailed *Planned Parenthood v. Casey*, which the Court decided in June 1992, as a great "compromise," because it managed to conceive the abortion issue in "more or less" terms. States may have an interest in making abortion more costly, whether in time, money, or emotional stress, but they are not permitted to raise those costs "unduly." Through this supposedly middle of the road mechanism the Court has allowed an issue of decisionmaking power and access to services to be complexly reconceived distributively as a large series of different rights. The decision will likely have greater impeding consequences on young, poor, and rural women, thus following and reinforcing existing distributive inequalities (cf. Young 1992).

The second and perhaps more important problem with the distributive paradigm of justice is that by focusing on the allocation of benefits and burdens within institutional structures, it obscures those institutional structures at the same time that the paradigm assumes them as given. Thus it fails to evaluate the justice of the institutions themselves that provide the conditions and practices that both produce the benefits and burdens and define the social positions among which they are allocated. For example, many contemporary discussions of social justice ask whether justice permits or requires taxing the rich in order to meet the basic needs of the poor. This distributive way of formulating issues of economic justice presumes without making explicit a social structure with divisions between rich and poor, never asking whether this structure itself is just.

Discussions of gender-justice that focus on the distribution of benefits and burdens between men and women frequently assume the institutions of marriage and normative heterosexuality as given, and within which distributions occur. Thus Okin, for example, writes as though the primary issue of gender-justice is the distribution of household and childrearing tasks, and the distribution of paid work, between a husband and wife (cf. Kymlicka 1991). It is certainly not Okin's intention to be heterosexist, and indeed in several passages she refers to gay and lesbian couples as important models of egalitarian relationships (Okin 1993). She certainly does not intend to suggest with Dan Quayle that married mothers are better than unmarried ones. My suggestion is that because she considers the distribution of labor and resources within the family as the primary issue of gender-justice, she tends to presuppose as given the dominant family norms, which privilege marriage without calling their justice explicitly into question.

To summarize, distribution is only a part, albeit an important part, of the social circumstances that feminist principles of justice should evaluate. Issues of justice also include decisionmaking power, the definition of social positions with their relations and obligations, and culture, which are not reducible to distribution. A broader conception of justice takes not fairness but liberation as its ultimate ideal. This broader conception says that social justice concerns the degree to which a society contains and supports the institutional conditions necessary for all its members to develop and exercise their capacities, express their experiences, and participate in determining their actions and the conditions of their actions. Injustice consists in oppression and domination, which often involve distributive inequality or deprivation, but also involve cultural and relational inhibitions and harms.

What's Wrong with Marriage?

IN *OF WOMAN BORN* Adrienne Rich (1977) distinguishes between the institution of motherhood as a structure that systematically oppresses women, on the one hand, and the practices, joys, loves, and pains of particular mothers in particular contexts, on the other. She condemns the institution of motherhood as oppressive and morally backward but urges that mothers and the practices of mothering are often good, useful, and not adequately supported.

Rich's concept of compulsory heterosexuality (Rich 1983) can point to a similar distinction between the institution of marriage, on the one hand, and particular relationships of love and commitment between particular men and women, on the other. In what follows I argue that the institution of marriage is fundamentally unjust and should be eliminated.

This argument does not condemn long-term relationships of sexual love and affective commitment between men and women; I myself happily and by choice live in such a relationship. Relationships such as mine, however, ought not to have the special privileges and legitimacy they currently have. As my argument proceeds, it will become clear that I believe that the elimination of the special privileges of marriage entails not removing the state from relationships but rather reconstituting the meaning of family and thereby extending the privileges that marriage now confers on some people to many other relationships.

But just what is marriage? Taking a cue from the "family values" debate, we can say that marriage is the keystone of The Family as defining order and legitimacy. The institution of modern marriage normatively links the regulation of sexuality, procreation, and property. Legally, marriage has always been male sexual rights over women, the private rights of a particular man over the sexual behavior of a particular woman. The institution of marriage is still the cornerstone of patriarchal power. Important feminist treatises have shown how practices like prostitution, pornography, rape, and sexual harassment are either part of or derived from this institution of marriage, and I will not repeat those arguments here (Pateman 1988). The important point for my argument is that marriage contains a notion of the sexual rights that men have over women, which rights men often appear to assume in other relationships.

Marriage is also an exclusive institution (Colker 1991) that enforces heterosexuality, inasmuch as it is defined as the legal union of a man and a woman, and necessarily one of each. An alleged justification of this exclusivity is sometimes that marriage is linked to procreation. Thus marriage defines The Family by defining parental rights and excluding others from parental relationships. Marriage, finally, is linked to property and economic stability. Historically, of course, a major function of marriage is the preservation or enlargement of property.

One might claim that the definition and linkages of marriage that I have just expressed no longer correspond to the social realities of advanced industrial Western societies. The truth in this objection motivates the argument of this paper and the urgency of a "family values" debate. But in sorting out the terms of this debate we should be clear on how the institution of marriage, as distinct perhaps from the practices of relationships, remains a significant regulator of social norms, that is, the establishment of respectability and legitimacy. This is so in the areas of sexuality, procreation, and property.

Many states in the United States still do not recognize marital rape as a crime. Even where rape in marriage is criminalizable, moreover, many juries refuse to recognize that forced sex in marriage, or even in relationships like marriage, is a legal wrong. These facts show that the definition of marriage as male sexual property rights over women is alive and well.

Although heterosexual sex outside of marriage has become much more common and accepted in the last twenty-five years, the Murphy Brown debate shows that marriage still generally regulates the norms of procreation. A child born out of wedlock may no longer be legally registered as a bastard, but dominant norms still treat such behavior as deviant or pathological. A woman can still lose her job or otherwise be punished for bearing a child on her own, and some courts will uphold such actions (*Chambers v. Omaha Girls Club*). Unmarried heterosexual couples who have been in a sexual and affectionate relationship, more often than not, decide to get married when they desire to have children. Although there are positive legal reasons for making such a decision, involving protections for the children and for the parents in relation to the children in case the relationship dissolves, for most the entrance to legal marriage also carries an aura of settledness and respectability.

Although marriage is a formal alliance of property today only for the few in Western societies, entering marriage and setting up a family entails major consumption activities for those who can afford them. Marriage continues to be associated with property in the form of a privately owned home, along with large and expensive consumer items to go with it (cf. Singer 1992, 78–79).

The institution of marriage retains the major social function of conferring legitimacy on people and relationships. Thus marriage, as the keystone of The Family, stands for order itself because it draws a boundary. It creates an unambiguous line between the licit and the illicit. It reproduces this order by granting privileges to those who fall on one side of the line and by stigmatizing those who fall on the other side.

Even today the privileges of marriage are many, and we should not need reminding. Marriage entails privileges of property and income—privileges of ownership and inheritance, insurance benefit, credit access, specific tax privileges, social security benefits, survivors' benefits for spouses of veterans, and immigration privileges (Minow 1991a). Marriage usually confers rights in relation to children, although the privileges of biological parentage sometimes snarl up this benefit. Married people have a privileged access to reproductive technologies, both to aid and curtail reproduction. They are the preferred clients of adoption services. Marriage gives people the privilege of gaining access to, taking care of, and signing consent forms for their spouses housed in bureaucratic institutions like hospitals, treatment centers, rest homes, or prisons.

The other side of the privileges of marriage is its oppressions. The institution of marriage privileges heterosexual couples and oppresses homosexual couples, and this certainly is one of its major functions (Mohr 1988). Few gay men or lesbians have chosen to challenge legally the restriction of marriage to heterosexual couples. Every court that has heard such cases, however, has rejected the challenges. Frequently the courts give no reasons for excluding homosexuals from the rights and privileges of marriage other than asserting that marriage is *by definition* a union of one man and one woman (Buchanan 1985; Schwarzchild 1988–1989; Minow 1991b). The Hawaii decision may be a turning point because it asks for good reasons for excluding homosexuals from marriage, and it is not likely that the lower court will find reasons that satisfy the decision.

In the age of Murphy Brown it is important to observe, however, that lesbian and gay households are by no means the only families that suffer stigma and disadvantage by being excluded from the privileges of marriage. In 1989 nearly twenty-five percent of all children in the United States and more than half of all African American children lived with one parent. The large majority of these parents are women. Single mother households have been increasing rapidly, both as a result of increased divorce, decreased remarriage after divorce, and a steady rate of birth without marriage. From a statistical point of view, then, families headed by women have become normal.

Neither social policy, social attitudes, nor social theory treats female headed households as legitimate, however. The woman who voluntarily or involuntarily lives with children alone must not only contend with employers and public bureaucracies that assume parents have the assistance of coparents, but they also face serious stigma. Both never married and divorced mothers commonly face employment, credit, and housing discrimination.

Even among those who call themselves liberals, moreover, public policy discussion usually treats single motherhood as an aberration and social pathology. Liberals and conservatives in policy discussion often share the judgment that the best cure for the poverty, stress, and discrimination that many single mothers face consists in getting or keeping them married. Thus William Julius Wilson's otherwise progressive social democratic program for addressing the problems of poor people argues for a jobs policy targeted at men so that they can marry poor single mothers and support their children (Wilson 1986). Because nearly one-quarter of single parent families live in poverty, William Galston argues that child oriented family policy must favor marriage. Thus he calls for legal changes that would make divorce more difficult (Galston 1991, 284–288; Young 1995).

Rates of out of wedlock births and divorce rates may well be a sign that some men and women are taking their family commitments less seriously than they should, especially their commitments to children, preferring to indulge their own desires. But rise in single motherhood also signals the refusal by many women to tolerate the infidelity, subservience, and battering that too many wives put up with in the past. It appears that increasing proportions of never married or divorced mothers prefer not to be married, moreover, even though they must deal with low wages, welfare bureaucracies, difficulties of parenting alone, and stigma (Arendell 1986).

Surely it is a gross infringement on liberty to send mothers the message that they should get and stay married, whether they like it or not, or face poverty, discrimination, stigma, and even, in some cases, punishment.

The institution of marriage, finally, tends to oppress unmarried people who wish to set up a household or otherwise be thought of as family. Friends or relatives who wish to set up a common household are often forbidden or discouraged from doing so by zoning laws or housing construction presuming and enforcing a small nuclear family. Efforts at deinstitutionalization and independent living for people with developmental or emotional disabilities have often been stymied by this prejudice about who is a proper family. Four mildly retarded men may have formed bonds of mutual caretaking and companionship in a common household, but zoning rules against "group homes" may impede their living together (Macedo 1991, 64–65). Recent amendments to the Fair Housing Act are beginning to serve as the basis for challenging such obstacles.

Rights of personal access and tax privileges are often not extended to grandparents, brothers and sisters, cousins, or nonkin household members who share resources and care for one another. This fact makes marriage and the nuclear family unjust to racial and ethnic groups where extended family caretaking is the norm (Vega 1990).

I conclude that the institution of marriage is irreparably unjust. Its original and current meaning is to solidify male power in relation to women and to draw an arbitrary line around legitimate relationships. Its historical function has been to use women as a means of forging alliances among men and perpetuating their "line." Today when those functions are diminished, but hardly absent, marriage's injustice consists primarily in its discriminatory granting of privileges. Marriage privileges specific ways of living and variously inhibits, stigmatizes, and penalizes other ways of living. A basic principle of liberal justice is that societal norms should regulate the rights and obligations of exchanges, relationships, and institutional structures, without privileging some particular ways of life. The institution of marriage violates this principle, with oppressive and disadvantaging consequences for many people. If we are not to privilege particular relationships or ways of life, then what it means to be a family must be redefined and pluralized (Minow 1991b).

Legal Reform and Cultural Revolution in Families

ANY PROJECT OF defining runs the risk of simultaneous over and under inclusion—of ruling out some aspects of social reality one means to include or including some one means to exclude. This is especially so in defining family, where we wish to broaden the concept beyond that of heterosexual coupling through legal marriage but not make it so broad that any and all relationships become familial. Mindful of these problems, in redefining family we should aim at a rough and ready characterization of attributes, some but not all of which should be present to call a relationship family.

In this spirit, I define family as follows: people who live together and/or share resources necessary to the means of life and comfort; who are committed to taking care of one another's physical and emotional needs to the best of their ability; who conceive themselves in a relatively long term, if not permanent, relationship; and who recognize themselves as a family. Family are the ones who care for you when you are sick and for whom you care when they are sick. Family members are mutually obliged to remember one another's birthdays, the ones on whom we dump our troubles. Family entails commitment and obligation as well as comfort; family members make claims on one another that they do not make on others. I am obliged to consider the lives of my family members when considering a career move, but I am not obliged to consider the lives of others.

I cannot imagine a society without families in this sense. Children best flourish in families in this sense, a relatively small group of committed intimates that help them develop a sense of self. Many adults choose not to live in families so defined, for at least part of their lives; they choose to live alone or in more loosely defined collectives. But at other times of their lives most adults want families for the same reason that children need them; they help provide a rooted sense of self and mutual concrete caring.

The Family as defined through the institution of marriage normatively links a series of relationships that can and should be deconstructed. The Family in that conception implies a two-parent, heterosexual couple living with their genetic biological children and sharing resources. A reconceptualization of family must break this series of implications. I shall argue that most of the rights, privileges, and obligations that in current law fall to married couples and biological parents should be disconnected and extended to other kinds of relationships in legally generalized forms. Before taking up that argument, however, let me consider briefly some other approaches to legal reform in family relationships. These include getting the law out of relationships, encouraging private contracts for relationships, and a functional approach to family law.

Some people conclude from arguments like those I have made that justice requires not privileging any ways of living, and law and state policy should be removed entirely from defining and regulating family relations. I used to conclude this myself. If families are private and personal, and the state and law are general, public and quintessentially impersonal, then simple logic seems to dictate that the two should have nothing to do with each other. Although there are reasons to demand that state institutions be far less intrusive than they currently are in some families, particularly poor families, today the removal of all legal definition, relation, and adjudication of family relationships would not serve justice for several reasons.

The law must thus define and be prepared to help adjudicate the ambiguities, issues, and conflicts that may arise among family members or former family members. The most important of such claims and obligations concern children. The state and law must provide protections for children in cases where particular adults do not protect them or have disputes about their relationships to children. Legal regulation of families is also necessary to protect adults who are vulnerable within families, either because of choices they have made that render them economically dependent, or because they are old, ill, or disabled. As I will discuss later, even in the absence of conflict or neglect, families often need various kinds of state support and recognition to promote the flourishing of their members. As Martha Minow argues, even when the state draws a boundary between itself and families, it functions to regulate both sides of the boundary. Withdrawing state regulation will not promote the freedom of families; instead we need legal norms that are able to conceptualize rights in a way that attends to and responds to the context of particular relationships (Minow 1990, 268–283).

Some people suggest that the best way to guarantee such particularity is by encouraging people to draw up private contracts delimiting the precise terms of their relationship as they define it. Although I think that individuals should be able to make contractual agreements about what they consider private affairs if they choose, and to a large degree people have this ability today, a private contractual approach to family law reform has several problems, both practical and philosophical.

The ability to draw up the terms of a private contract about intimate relations presupposes class privilege. Many people cannot afford the services of a lawyer for such purposes; many people do not understand enough about legal language and possibilities to know what they would want to put into a contract. Private contracts spelling out particular terms of intimate relations, moreover, can only work for adults; relations between adults and children must be regulated by other means.

Perhaps even more important, intimate relationships are too open-ended and multifaceted to come under contractual agreements. People who live together, commit themselves to care for one another, and raise children together have a more complex, many-sided, and unpredictable relationship than do those who enter a business contract, for example. In many situations it is impossible to predict what their life situation, resources, feelings, and relationship with children will be in ten years. This unpredictability and changeability partly accounts for why courts sometimes invalidate private contracts concerning intimate relations.

This point leads to a philosophical objection: that the framework of contract thinking is simply inappropriate, even immoral, when applied to intimate relations. Where contract conceptualizes relations as a product of explicit and voluntary agreement, family relations are often not chosen.

Even where a relation was chosen at one time, aspects of vulnerability, dependency and commitment often develop in families that are not explicitly chosen. The framework of contracted relations, moreover, is possible only against the background of more fundamental kinds of social bonds, of which families are an important kind (cf. Pateman 1984).

A third approach discussed in family law as an alternative to the existing legal biases that privilege family relations incorporating marriage is the functional approach. Relations that function as familial in people's lives may often emerge or develop that do not fit the normal rules of family but still ought to be recognized in order to do justice to individuals in situations of dispute or need. Thus courts and other state agencies should be able to operate according to general criteria of such functions to determine particular family rights and obligations. As with family contracts, I think there should be room in legal and policy reasoning for such a functional notion of the family. But a functional approach to family cannot substitute for formal rules delimiting familial rights and obligations, as well as formal means of declaring family membership. Relying solely on a functional understanding of family would be costly and possibly intrusive, since every case that came before courts or bureaucracies would have to involve an investigation into the actual nature of a particular intimate relation. It would also leave potential disputants too much at the mercy of a particular official's interpretation of the meaning of family functions.

Reform in family law, as I conceive it, would specify general rules and standards of family relationships but at the same time deconstruct the legal obligations and privileges currently associated with marriage. The chain of implications must be broken that starts with heterosexual rights of sexual intercourse, to connect this with joint property, shared resources, and the right to expect support, and also connects sexual rights with exclusive rights and exclusive obligations regarding children. Issues, of sexual rights, property and resources, procreation and parenting, that is, should be more disconnected.

As I discussed earlier, the institution of marriage still contains the assumption that a man has sexual rights over a woman. As Foucault argues, a major meaning of the modern family is the regulation of sexuality and the definition of sexual rights (Foucault 1981). But sexuality is indeed an area where state and law should keep out. The idea of sexual rights should become incoherent. No one—that is, whatever kind of relations they have with another person—ever at any time should be in a position where they do not have a right to say no to sex. Although sexual love can be an important element in some family relationships, legal rules and standards about families should assume nothing about sex and certainly should not require any demonstration of sexual intimacy. Sex is neither a necessary nor a sufficient condition for families.

The legal and cultural abolition of the idea of sexual rights, and the formal disconnection of sex from family, would truly be a revolutionary change. The patriarchal idea that men have sexual rights over women with whom they are intimate continues to bias the justice system against the victims of acquaintance rape 'or even against victims of sexual harassment. The assumption remains strong, moreover, that a family implies that some member of the household has regular sex with another member of the household. Promotion of gay male or lesbian households as families, for example, often does little to challenge this assumption of sex as a necessary condition for family, even though it is not uncommon for the domestic partner of a gay man or lesbian to be a different person from his or her current lover or lovers. The assumption that sex is an essential attribute of families disqualifies as families household forms that many people live as families, such as single parent families. The assumption that familial relations are or ought to be sexual, moreover, may discourage the formation, development, or recognition of some kinds of families that some people need or want, as in my example earlier of the mentally disabled men. Finally, although I have no evidence to support it, I have a hunch that the patriarchal assumption of sexual rights in families is a source of child sexual abuse.[3]

The concept of domestic partnership has been a creative proposal for addressing the exclusion of gay men and lesbians from the benefits of marriage, and some cities and private companies have adopted the concept to a limited degree. As a method of deconstructing marriage, I would propose that a concept like domestic partnership be universalized. By a simple process of legal registration, any adults should be able to register as domestic partners. I do not even see a reason that only two adults should be allowed to register together as partners; although because of state or employer benefits that partnership would confer, I think it might be reasonable to declare a limit to the number of persons who can register as domestic partners to one another.

Domestic partnership, in the universalized and enlarged form that I conceive it to be, would carry all the current rights and obligations of marriage having to do with property, support, resources, and access to one another in institutionalized settings—rights of joint ownership, inheritance, to be carried on medical and life insurance policies, immigration rights, rights to visit partners housed in hospitals or prisons, rights to be consulted in treatment options and to sign consent forms, rights to claim continued resource support at the time of partnership dissolution. Domestic partnership, however, would imply nothing about sex. Although heterosexual lovers and homosexual lovers might wish to enter domestic partner relations, so also might sisters or unrelated persons wishing to establish a long-term shared household but who are not sexually involved.

Family law should of course be especially directed at the purposes of nurturing and protecting children. Reproductive and parental rights are currently attached to marriage, and this link too should be deconstructed. All adults, whatever their personal life circumstances, should have equal access to reproductive technologies. Adoption services should not be allowed to discriminate against categories of persons. At the time of the birth of a child, certain people will declare themselves parents of that child, or the child will be given up for adoption. Usually the biological mother of the child will be one of these persons, but the mere fact of her giving birth ought not to make her a parent. Similarly, although I am inclined to agree that something should be done to make men more accountable for the procreative consequences of their sexual activity, the mere fact of being the genetic father of a child should not automatically give a person rights and obligations in relation to that child (cf. Shanley 1993). For one thing, this can force a mother to have continued contact with a man she no longer wishes to know. Contrary to currently dominant legal norms, it should be possible for the declared parents of a child to be of any sex (Polikoff 1990).

The law should also not assume, as it currently does, that a child can have only two parents. The controversies about the rights of birth mothers who have contracted to bear a child for another couple have raised, in a new and unique way, the question of whether more than two people can have parental rights and obligations in relation to a child. Increased divorce and remarriage have also necessitated raising this question. No legal forms can prevent the hurt and confusion that divorce produces for many children. If a child forms a domestic relationship with a new adult that enters her household, however, who wishes to take on the commitment to parenting her, that adult should be legally able to become her parent without her having to give up a legal relation with a parent she already has.

But what is this legal relation of parent? Although the legal status of parent entails certain rights which courts may decide vary with circumstances—control over health care, religious education, custody or visitation rights for parents who do not have primary custody rights, and so on—I conceive that parenthood primarily involves responsibilities. To declare oneself a parent is to promise to support a child to the best of one's ability, both materially and emotionally, until the child reaches adulthood. Thus although I reject the idea that genetic fathers should be forced to support the children of their issue, fathers or mothers who have taken on the commitment of parenting by declaring themselves parents can be made to pay even if they divorce the other parent(s) and leave the household. The idea of "child first" divorce policies is sensible in this respect. Courts should make child support awards to a large degree by calculating what the child needs to have a decent life. More vigorous enforcement of postdivorce child support responsibilities than currently exists, such as attaching paychecks, is consistent with a more universal and just family policy.

If courts consistently ruled for child support awards that put the needs of children first, however, they might sometimes unfairly burden parents who have left a household, most often men, who would because of these constraints be unable to form or enter new families or make other life choices. For this and other reasons, the welfare of children should be deconstructed from marriage in a final sense: we should not assume that a married couple is solely responsible for the welfare of their biological children. If children are the future of a society, then all the adult members of a society have some responsibility to support all the children. Although declared parents would have primary responsibility for the material and emotional support of children, many if not all parents require extensive social supports in carrying out those duties, and nonparents should contribute significantly to such supports.

A just policy of family pluralism would consist not in the state's remaining neutral among family forms, treating them all according to the same rules no matter what their attributes, but rather would positively differentiate among some kinds of families for the sake of providing them with the support that will make them flourish equally with others. In principle all families need social supports to flourish and be appreciated, but some more than others. I will conclude by briefly discussing such social support issues for two categories of families: families of people with disabilities and single-parent families.

Even with the passage of the Americans with Disabilities Act, our society has very far to go before it appreciates people with disabilities. Parents of people with disabilities often need a great deal of financial and social support for their families to flourish; although some such financial and social support is available to such parents today, too often parents feel they must fight for every dime, struggle with service providers over the nature of services, and they feel that the level of support they receive is inadequate. As I have already mentioned, adults with disabilities ought to be able to form families of their own, outside their parents' homes and outside institutionalized settings, if they wish. But they often need financial and social supports in their family settings that others do not require. Empowering people with disabilities to form families includes their being able to parent. Perhaps not all people with disabilities are able to raise children, and many do not wish to try. Many people with disabilities can successfully parent, however, with sufficient financial and social support.

I write this paragraph nearly two years after Murphy Brown gave birth. Major magazines such as *The Atlantic* continue sounding the alarm about single mothers (Whitehead 1993). Children of single mothers are more likely to be poor than other children. The children of single parents, however, often have an earlier sense of independence and more companionate relations with their parents than do other children. Parenting alone, on the other hand, is harder than parenting with a partner or partners, which can lead to lack of time and other stresses that make the children's lives less peaceful and stable than they might be if there were more than one adult in the home.

A just and liberal society would have abortion and contraception programs and access of a sort that would aim to ensure that every child a woman bears is a wanted child. If we had such policies in the United States today, there would probably be far fewer single mothers. But there would still be many, either because women choose to bear children on their own or because parents would continue to separate.

Social justice requires that single parent families be valued and appreciated, and that they be given the social support they need to flourish. Among such social support policies are pay equity schemes to equalize women's wages with men's, expanded welfare support, and vastly expanded child care subsidies, including child care services to enable teenage mothers to continue with school. The United States could also emulate some European countries in developing "mother's houses," where single mothers live in private apartments but also have opportunities for shared cooking and child minding (Hayden 1984, 137–138).

I have argued that a distributive paradigm of social justice tends to bias the thinking of those who think about gender justice away from issues of sexuality and reproduction. Because dominant approaches to justice consider how benefits and burdens should be distributed within institutions, moreover, theorists of justice and family usually assume the institution of marriage as given. Feminists must question the justice of the institution of marriage itself. Declaring marriage unjust then requires a feminist theory of justice to conceptualize legal frameworks for family relations that deconstruct the series of relations currently joined in the legal framework of marriage and family. Family justice, finally, implies social policies that appreciate plural family forms and provide social support for families, especially for those families with special needs.

Notes

1. Thanks to David Alexander, Ruth Colker, Christine Di Stefano, Stephen Macedo, Martha Minow, Deborah Rhode, and Molly Shanley for comments on an earlier version of this chapter. Thanks to Carrie Smarto for research assistance.

2. Carol Gilligan first opposed the norm of justice to more particularist feminist moral concerns that she called care (Gilligan 1982). Many feminist theorists followed her in assuming that justice is a value of public bureaucratic life inappropriate to more relationally oriented contexts of action. But in recent years there have been important challenges to this opposition between justice and care.

3. See Foucault, (1981, 109): "In a society such as ours, where the family is the most active site of sexuality, and where it is doubtless the exigence of the latter which maintain and prolong its existence, incest—for different reasons alto-

gether and in a completely different way—occupies a central place; it is constantly being solicited and refused; it is an object of obsession and attraction, a dreadful secret and an indispensable pivot. It is manifested as a thing that is strictly forbidden in the family insofar as the latter functions as a deployment of alliance; but it is also a thing that is continuously demanded in order for the family to be a hotbed of constant sexual incitement".

References

Arendell, Terry. 1986. *Mothers and Divorce: Legal, Economic, and Social Dilemmas.* Berkeley: University of California Press.

Buchanan, G. Sidney. "Same-Sex Marriage: The Linchpin Issue." 1985. *University of Dayton Law Review* 10.

Chambers v. Omaha Girls Club. 1987. 834 F. 2nd 697 (8th cir.).

Colker, Ruth. 1991. "Marriage." *Yale Journal of Law and Feminism* 3 (Spring):312–326.

Foucault, Michel. 1981. *History of Sexuality, Vol. 1, An Introduction.* New York: Vintage Books.

Friedman, Marilyn. 1987. "Beyond Caring: The De-Moralization of Gender." In *Science, Morality, and Feminist Theory.* Ed. Marsha Hanen and Kai Nielsen. Calgary: University of Calgary Press.

Galston, William. 1991. *Liberal Purposes.* New York: Cambridge University Press.

Gilligan, Carol. 1982. *In a Different Voice.* Cambridge, Mass.: Harvard University Press.

Hayden, Delores. 1984. *Redesigning the American Dream.* New York: W. W. Norton.

Kymlicka, Will. 1991. "Rethinking the Family." *Philosophy and Public Affairs* 20:77–97.

Macedo, Stephen. 1991. *The New Right v. the Constitution.* Washington, D.C.: CATO Institute.

Minow, Martha. 1990. *Making All the Difference: Inclusions, Exclusion, and American Law.* Ithaca, N.Y.: Cornell University Press.

Minow, Martha. 1991a. "Redefining Families: Who's In and Who's Out?" *University of Colorado Law Review* 62:269–25.

Minow, Martha. 1991b. "Free Exercise of Families." *University of Illinois Law Review* 1991 (4):940.

Mohr, Richard. 1988. "Policy, Ritual, Purity: Mandatory AIDS Testing." In *Gays/Justice.* New York: Columbia University Press.

Okin, Susan. 1989. *Justice, Gender, and the Family.* New York: Basic Books.

Okin, Susan. 1993. "Sexual Orientation and Gender: Dichotomizing Difference." Presented at a conference on Democracy and Difference sponsored by the Conference for the Study of Political Thought.

Pateman, Carole. 1984. "The Shame of the Marriage Contract." In *Women's Views of The Political World of Men.* Ed. Judith H. Stiehm. New York: Transnational Publishers.

Pateman, Carole. 1988. *The Sexual Contract.* Palo Alto, Calif.: Stanford University Press.

Planned Parenthood of Southeastern Pennsylvania v. Casey. 1992. 112 S. Ct. 2791.

Polikoff, Nancy D. 1990. "This Child Does Have Two Mothers: Redefining Parenthood to Meet the Needs of Children in Lesbian-Mother and Other Noncontractual Families." *Georgetown Law Journal* 78 (February): 459–575.

Rich, Adrienne. 1977. *Of Woman Born.* New York: W. W. Norton.

Rich, Adrienne. 1983. "Compulsory Heterosexuality and Lesbian Existence." In *Powers of Desire: The Politics of Sexuality.* Ed. Ann Snitow, Christine Stansell, and Sharon Thompson. New York: Monthly Review Press.

Ruddick, Sara. 1992. "Justice in Families." Address to the American Philosophical Association, Eastern Division, December.

Schwarzchild, Hannah. 1988-1989. "Same-Sex Marriage and Constitutional Privacy: Moral Threat and Legal Anomaly." *Berkeley Women's Law Journal* 4:94–127.

Sevenhuijsen, Selma. 1991. "Justice, Moral Reasoning, and the Politics of Child Custody." In *Equality, Politics, and Gender.* Ed. Elizabeth Meehan and Selma Sevenhuijsen. London: Sage Publications.

Shanley, Mary L. 1993. "Fathers' Rights, Mothers' Wrongs?: Reflections on Unwed Fathers' Rights, Patriarchy, and Sex Equality." Presented at the Conference on Feminist Ethics and Social Policy. University of Pittsburgh.

Singer, Linda. 1992. *Erotic Welfare.* New York: Routledge.

Sterba, James. 1991. *How to Make People Just.* Totowa, N.J.: Rowman and Littlefield.

Tronto, Joan. 1991. "Gender, Care, and Justice in Feminist Political Theory." Working papers of the Anna Maria Van Shuurman Centrum of the University of Utrecht.

Tronto, Joan. 1993. *Moral Boundaries: A Political Argument of an Ethic of Care.* New York: Routledge.

Vega, William A. 1990. "Hispanic Families in the 1980's: A Decade of Research." *Journal of Marriage and Family* 52 (4):1015–1024.

Whitehead, Barbara Defoe. 1993. "Dan Quayle Was Right." *The Atlantic* 271 (April):47–84.

Wilson, William Julius. 1986. *The Truly Disadvantaged.* Chicago: University of Chicago Press.

Young, Iris Marion. 1990. *Justice and the Politics of Difference.* Princeton, N.J.: Princeton University Press.

Young, Iris Marion. 1992. "The Supreme Court and Abortion." *Dissent* (Fall).

Young, Iris Marion. 1995. "Mothers, Citizenship, and Independence: A Critique of Pure Family Values." *Ethics: A Journal of Moral, Political, and Legal Philosophy.*

Zoglin, Richard. 1992. "Sitcom Politics." *Time* Magazine 140 (12):44–47.

About the Book

In this important book, thirteen leading feminist political theorists provide reconstructions of central concepts in traditional Western political theory. Feminist
scholars have been redrawing the landscape of political theory for over twenty-five
years, but these essays aim to do more than offer feminist critiques of existing theories. Rather, they provide feminist visions of how political concepts can be reconstructed.

   Some of these papers are completely new; others are extensions or reformulations of ongoing work. All seek to answer the question: If feminists maintain that
existing theories are problematic and exclusive in terms of gender, race, sexuality,
and class, what kinds of theories should we put in their place? As such, this volume
constitutes essential reading not only for feminist thinkers but also for traditional
philosophers and political theorists, for whom this question presents a vital
methodological, intellectual, and political challenge.

About the Editors and Contributors

Martha A. Ackelsberg is Professor of Government and Women's Studies at Smith College, where she teaches courses in urban politics, feminist theory, political theory, and political participation. In addition to *Free Women of Spain: Anarchism and the Struggle for the Emancipation of Women* (1991), she has published numerous articles on Spanish anarchism, women's activism, democratic theory, and the politics of families. She is currently engaged in work on gender and citizenship.

Anita L. Allen has been a Professor of Law at Georgetown University Law Center since 1987. Her teaching and scholarship relate to the ethics and law of privacy, reproductive rights and responsibility, tort law, legal philosophy, and professional ethics. Additional interests include race relations policy, and law and literature. She has published many articles, as well as two books: *Uneasy Access: Privacy for Women in a Free Society* (1988) and (with co-authors) *Cases and Materials on Privacy Law* (1992).

Christine Di Stefano is Associate Professor of Political Science at the University of Washington, Seattle. She is the author of *Configurations of Masculinity: A Feminist Perspective on Modern Political Theory* (1991) and has published several articles on feminist political theory. She is currently at work on a book-length study of autonomy and an edited anthology of feminist critical engagements with Karl Marx.

Zillah Eisenstein is Professor and Chair of the Department of Politics, Ithaca College, Ithaca, N.Y. She has written several books of feminist theory, including most recently *The Female Body and the Law* (1988), *The Color of Gender* (1994), and *Hatreds: Sexualized and Racialized Conflicts in the 21st Century* (1996). She has participated in feminist activity since 1970 and is active in the reproductive rights movement.

Nancy C.M. Hartsock teaches political theory at the University of Washington, Seattle. She is the author of *Money, Sex, and Power: Toward a Feminist Historical Materialism* (1983 and 1984) and *The Feminist Standpoint Revisited: Essays on Politics, Power, and Epistemology* (Westview, forthcoming). She has been a critic of poststructuralist thought and is working on a book tentatively titled *Postmodernism and Political Change*.

Nancy J. Hirschmann is Associate Professor of Government and teaches political and feminist theory at Cornell University. She is the author of *Rethinking Obligation: A Feminist Method for Political Theory* (1992) and several articles on feminist political theory. She is currently writing a book examining the concept of freedom through the perspective of women's lived experiences such as domestic violence and veiling.

Kathleen B. Jones is the Associate Dean of the College of Arts and Letters at San Diego State University and Professor of Women's Studies. She is the author of *Compassionate Authority: Democracy and the Representation of Women* (1993), co-editor, with Anna Jonasdottir, of *The Political Interests of Gender* (1988), and co-editor, along with Cathy Cohen and Joan Tronto, of the forthcoming anthology of essays on women and U.S. politics *Women Question Politics*.

Jane Mansbridge is the Jane W. Long Professor of the Arts and Sciences in the Department of Political Science at Northwestern University and a Faculty Fellow at Northwestern's Center for Urban Affairs and Policy Research. She is the editor of *Beyond Self-Interest* (1990) and author of *Beyond Adversary Democracy* (1990), *Why We Lost the ERA* (1986), and articles in feminist and democratic theory. Her current work, based on interviews with working-class white and black U.S. women, explores the effects of feminism, as a social movement, on nonactivists and vice versa.

Shane Phelan teaches political theory at the University of New Mexico. She is the author of *Getting Specific: Postmodern Lesbian Politics* (1994) and *Identity Politics: Lesbian Feminism and the Limits of Community* (1989) as well as several articles on feminist and political theory. She is also the editor of *Playing with Fire: Queer Politics, Queer Theories* and co-editor of *We Are Everywhere: An Historical Sourcebook in Gay and Lesbian Politics*, both published by Routledge.

Mary Lyndon (Molly) Shanley is Professor of Political Science on the Margaret Stiles Halleck Chair at Vassar College. She is author of *Feminism, Marriage, and the Law in Victorian England, 1850–1895* (1989) and editor, with Carole Pateman, of *Feminist Interpretations and Political Theory* (1991). She is currently editing, with Uma Narayan, *Reconstructing Political Theory: Feminist Perspectives* (forthcoming), an anthology of essays reinterpreting concepts important to Western political theory, and she is writing a book on ethical issues in contemporary family law.

Joan C. Tronto is Professor of Political Science at Hunter College and the Graduate Center, City University of New York and Coordinator of the Women's Studies Program at Hunter College. She has published many essays on the ethic of care and a book, *Moral Boundaries: A Political Argument for an Ethic of Care* (1993). Her current work involves applying the care ethic to democratic politics in liberal democratic states.

Iris Marion Young is Professor of Public and International Affairs at the University of Pittsburgh, with affiliated appointments in Philosophy and Political Science. She is author of *Justice and the Politics of Difference* (1990) and *Throwing Like a Girl and Other Essays in Feminist Philosophy and Social Theory* (1990). She is currently working on a study on communication and democratic theory.

Index

DATE DUE

GAYLORD			PRINTED IN U.S.A.